TH
EXPLOR

THE INN EXPLORER'S GUIDE

FRANK BOTTOMLEY

Illustrated by Paul R. Bottomley

Kaye & Ward: London

Published in Great Britain by
Kaye & Ward Ltd
The Windmill Press, Kingswood, Tadworth, Surrey

ISBN 0 7182 1800 0

Printed and bound in Great Britain by
Biddles Ltd, Guildford and King's Lynn

To my colleagues
Sid Cross and Marlene Godfrey
with thanks for their interest
and help

INTRODUCTION

It may seem rash to add to the vast literature on English inns but, on the other hand, it would seem perverse to omit the subject in a series concerned with exploring England's historic heritage. The main practical difficulty is the size of the subject – it is estimated that there are some 17,000 pubs in the country and any listing is bound to leave out someone's favourite or cherished personal discovery.

What this book endeavours to do is to provide background information in the *Glossary*, as has been done in others in the series: to explain what may be found and why it exists. Sometimes this has involved broadening treatment to extend outside the pub itself but it is hoped that the information there propounded may lead to a greater appreciation and understanding of the changing yet traditional English pub. Inn signs are an important part of the story and there are many books confined to this topic alone, yet it could hardly be omitted. A solution has been attempted by including many articles on particular names/signs within the glossary as well as general articles on types of names and names in general.

The *Gazetteer* lists pubs alphabetically by name of town or village. The large numbers have compelled a restriction to England and an attempt to reduce this by picking out pubs which have additional interest: architectural, historic, literary, social or some particular idiosyncracy. These have been supplemented by others which are good examples of their type. Besides a brief description each entry gives a map reference.

FURTHER READING

There is a vast bibliography on pubs and their lore: for a particular small example see s.v. *Literature* in Glossary. Of the general books one might instance: D. Batchelor, *The English Inn* (Batsford, 1963); W. Gaunt, *Old Inns of England* (1958); A.E. Richardson, *Old Inns of England* (1948); M. Jackson, *The English Pub* (1976); H.A. Monkton, *History of the English Public House* (1968). Particular areas have their recorders, often sponsored by brewers or local history societies, with such titles as 'Old Inns of . . .' or 'Inns of Character in . . .'.

Of particular topics, one might recommend for

Games and Sports:

R. Boston, *Beer and Skittles* (1976)
M. Brander, *Life and Sport of the Inn* (1973)
T. Finn, *Watney Book of Pub Games* (1967)
J. Wentworth Day, *Watney Book of Inns of Sport* (1949)

Law:
Lord Askwith, *British Taverns, their History and Laws* (1928)
J. N. Martin (reviser), James Paterson's *Licensing Acts* (1972 etc.)
Victorian:
M. Girouard, *Victorian Pubs* (1975)
R.W. Matz, *Dickensian Inns and Taverns* (1922)
B. Spiller, *Victorian Public Houses* (1976)
Furnishings:
Inn Crafts and Furnishings (Whitbread, 1951)
B. Davis, *Traditional English Pub* (1981)
Carlisle Nationalisation:
J. Hunt, *City Under the Influence* (1971)
Anecdotal:
K. Fidler, *Stories of Old Inns* (1973)
R. Keverne and H. Innes, *Tales of Old Inns* (1939)
R. Watson, *A Scrapbook of Inns* (1949)
Inn Signs:
E.R. Delderfield, *Inns and their Signs* (1975) and several other books on same subject
Worth searching out are the older and rare books such as:
R.V. French, *Nineteen Centuries of Drink in England* (1862)
C.G. Harper, *Historic and Picturesque Inns of Old England*
Old Inns of England (2 vols.)
and for the wider explorer there is always *The World Guide to Beer* (1977) ed. M. Jackson.

GLOSSARY

ACCOMMODATION
In the sense of 'lodging' is the business of the inn (q.v.) as distinct from the tavern or alehouse. Places charging for accommodation are to keep records of their guests, particularly if they are aliens. An innkeeper may not select his guests nor may he refuse to supply a traveller with food and lodging without reasonable excuse and he is responsible for the safety of the guest's goods and person within reasonable limits.

ADMIRALS
A seafaring nation has honoured its naval heroes by pub names and signs, including Codrington (1770–1851) and Harvey (1758–1830) both commanders at Trafalgar; Hardy, Nelson's flag-captain at the same engagement; Duncan (1731–1804), victor at Camperdown; Hawke (1705–81) who was also a reformer; Keppel (1725–86), a colleague of Anson; Viscount Exmouth (1757–1833) and Paul Jones (1747–92), a former privateer.

ADVERTISING
A pub or inn needs to advertise its nature in order to fulfil its function and to avoid embarrassment to others. This necessity was met from the beginning by a distinctive sign (q.v.) which merely advertised its existence. Later, pubs and inns advertised verbally – drawing attention to the liquor or accommodation they could offer in the most general terms. Finally, they advertised their owner, usually a brewer whose products were the staple. In most pub advertising now, the name of the brewer is the featured element, often more prominent than the sign or name of the house. One suspects that, with a discerning public, this last stage might be counter-productive and act more as a warning than as an invitation.

Adam & Eve

AGRICULTURE
The great leap forward necessary for civilisation, requiring stability, industry, co-operation with nature, and delayed satisfaction. The invention of alcoholic beverages seems synchronous with agriculture. The great ones, product of grape and corn, certainly depended on agriculture and they were a natural concomitant of its festivals, particularly harvest. The close association between pub and country work and play is amply indicated in inn names and signs including *Barley Mow, Man & Scythe, Man & Flail, Sheaf & Sickle, Haycock, Harvest Home, Jolly Farmer, Jolly Thresher, Harrow, Harvest Moon, Farmer's Boy*. Animal husbandry has also left its mark (see *Bull, Cow*, etc.) including sheep-rearing (*Shepherd & Crook, Shepherd's Boy*). *Wheatsheaf* may indicate a baker rather than a farmer but there is no doubt about the universal significance of the *Plough* indicated by the inscription on the demolished inn at Filey:

Barley Mow

He who by the Plough would thrive
Himself must either hold or drive

AIRCRAFT
Inn names reflect contemporary industry and record new inventions. The inn names referring to aircraft include Air Balloon, Buccaneer, Comet, Canopus, Flying Lancaster, Jet & Whittle, Propellor, Walrus, Wayfarer, Wellington. Some of these will doutless cause confusion and misinterpretation in future years as has happened to former inn names and signs.

ALE
see also *Beer*

Ale and beer were originally synonymous, the former mainly used by the Danish east and the latter by the Saxon west. Ale was home-brewed in alehouse, inn, tavern, private and religious houses with immensely varied results. Some of these differences were intentional as in the distinction between strong ale and small ale. At its best, medieval ale was a strong, clear, sweet-tasting brew.

Bitter beer became popular gradually following the introduction of hops (q.v.) in C15 but was opposed by the conservatives until the beginning of C17 and the word 'beer' which had gone out of use after the Norman Conquest became increasingly used to distinguish it.

The distinction between ale and beer had become marked by end of C15 with different brewers and even separate measures (the beer containers having greater capacity). When the competition had settled the brewers of both combined to form the United Brewers' Company in 1556 (London).

Barley, base of real ale

ALE BENCH
Remains a characteristic feature of old country inns – a seat in front of the house where the thirsty passer-by might rest and be refreshed, probably in the company of awaiting locals. It is an institution as old as Beowulf and like many ancient traditions attracted the iconoclastic fury of the C16 Reformers. One of the Homilies ordered to be read in the new Church in 1547 alludes inimically to those 'which upon the ale benches delight to set forth certain questions (hostile to the new religion)'.

ALEBERRY
A once popular drink made by boiling ale with spice and sugar and adding sops of bread.

ALE CONNOR
An examiner or inspector of ale (Med. to C18). His duties were eventually taken over by the gauger. He was appointed by the local authority to oversee the quality and to test the measures.

> A nose he had that gan show,
> What liquor beloved I trow,
> For he had before long seven years
> Been of the town the ale-conner.
>
> (Anon c.1380)

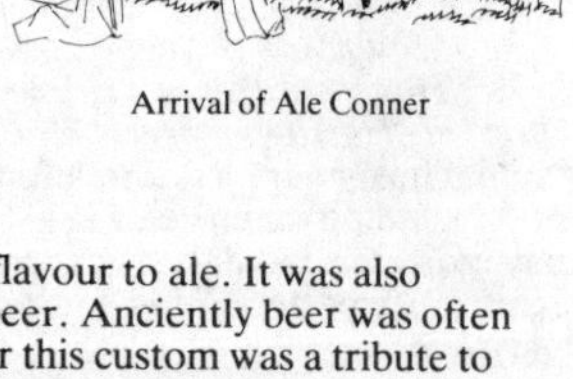

Arrival of Ale Conner

ALECOST
Ground ivy, once used to give aromatic and bitter flavour to ale. It was also believed to speed the maturing process of ale and beer. Anciently beer was often left only 12 hours to clear and one wonders whether this custom was a tribute to such processes and additions or evidence that our ancestors were content with unmatured ale.

ALE DAGGER
Small side-arm used in alehouse brawls up to C19. Christopher Marlowe was killed in such an incident.

ALE DRAPER
A fanciful C16 term for an alehouse keeper. It persisted in the parish registers of Whitby within C18.

ALE KNIGHT
A C16/17 expression, equivalent to the less vigorous 'lounge lizard' of C20. A votary of the tippling-house, a follower of Bacchus, a peace-time soldier whose object was the conquest of sobriety, finding fame not 'in the cannon's mouth' but in his reputation for consumption of ale.

C17 Toper – Ale Knight

ALE RENT
Ale was such a valued and esteemed commodity in Middle Ages that, particularly in the Anglo-Saxon period, rents were commonly paid in it. Peterborough Abbey e.g. let lands on condition, among others, that the lessee delivered yearly two tuns of pure ale and two tuns of Welsh ale.

ALES
Communal festivities centred round the consumption of ale. Besides Church Ales (q.v.) and Scot Ales there were Brides Ales, 'Weddyn Ales', Midsummer Ales, Lamb Ales, Tithe Ales, etc. Bede Ales were a development of medieval works of mercy (cf. Bede House) – drinking parties to raise money for a member of the community who had fallen on hard times.

ALE STAKE (POLE)
One of the earliest, if not the earliest indication of the availability of ale for public sale. It was a long pole attached to the front of the house or standing in the road before the door. Usually it was thrust through a sheaf of barley, later embellished with a garland or wreath of evergreen and indicated a fresh brew requiring the services of an ale conner to assess it. The additions to the stake could include a bush, a bunch of ivy or even a wisp of straw (in Scotland). By C15 the bush, often box, had developed into a very large and distinctive advertising garland which, it was said, was not required by a good wine. Later developments brought the addition of an effigy, carved and painted, supported in a hoop suspended from the end of the stake (origin of 'cock-a-hoop'?).

ALE STOND (STAND)
The medieval equivalent of the modern bar.

ALE TASTER see also *Ale Conner*
A kind of standards inspector first recorded in the City of London (1377). Elsewhere he was a manor or vestry appointee and his duties included proclamation of permitted prices, sampling of ale offered for sale and approving standards of different grades. When brewers or brewsters wished him to call they erected an ale stake (q.v.).

ALE WARMER
Cone-shaped utensil which the explorer may occasionally discover among a bar's bric-a-brac. It was usually made of copper and placed in the embers of the hearth and used as a method of warming winter drink.

Ale Stond

ALLIED BREWERIES LTD
One of the 'Big Seven' national breweries based in London and said to be the largest drinks company in Europe whose interests include some 8,000 pubs in England and Wales. Founded 1961 through merger of Ind Coope, Tetley Walker and Ansells. Also controls Harveys (wine and sherries), Showerings (Babycham), Britvic (fruit juices) and Coates, Gaymers and Whiteways (ciders). Besides pubs, it owns two Dutch breweries and a chain of nearly 50 hotels. Has ale breweries at Burton, Birmingham (2), Leeds, Warrington, Romford and lager breweries at Wrexham, Alloa. Its products include draught bitter and dark mild, a wild range of bottles, cans and kegs among which are Double Diamond, Triple A Strong Ale and Skol lager.

ALLS, THE THREE etc.
The original medieval form of this interesting name and sign seems to have represented a monk (I pray for all'), a knight ('I fight for all') and a villein ('I work for all'). It is an interesting sidelight on this functionalist view of society that the historian Froissart (c.1335–1404) thought that warriors strove to win glory, common people talk about their glorious deeds and the clergy write down their feats of arms.

Later, king was added ('I rule over all') and the other figures were updated: monk being replaced by post-Reformation parson and villein by agricultural labourer. In some versions the labourer is replaced by John Bull who 'pays for all' and examples of five or six 'Alls' exist, usually including the Devil or Death ('I take all').

Occurrence e.g. at Ovington, Northumberland.

AMALGAMATIONS
When two inns were amalgamated, either for convenience or to end competition, the signs of both were often combined in the new name. This fact explains some curious associations in pub names of the '– and –' variety but ignorance of this origin has sometimes gives rise to fanciful explanation e.g. *King's Head and Eight Bells*, Chelsea.

ANCHOR
Originally a religious sign (cf. Heb.viii, 19), symbol of the theological virtue of Hope. Hence 'We anchor in Hope' said to be first words of Pilgrim Fathers when *Mayflower* reached N. America, commemorated in sign at Welling, Kent. Later the sign naturally became associated with sailor's taverns (origin of game of Crown and Anchor?). There is the ancient *Hope and Anchor* at Hope Cove, Kingsbridge, Devon. Anchors are often 'blue' and there is an *Anchor Bleu* at Bosham, Sussex.

Anchor

ANECDOTES
Many inn names and signs took their origin from a specific event in the history of the house or its neighbourhood. It is often worth enquiring of the origin of a peculiar name though the explanation is not necessarily true! Some examples with alleged explanations are:

Dog, Over, Glos. Murderous robbers were traced by pub's dog and inn, formerly *Talbot*, was renamed (1754) in its honour.

Donkey and Buskins, Layer-de-la-Haye, Essex. Drunken farmer used his own leggings to protect his donkey from thorns.

Drum & Monkey, Stamford Lincs. Travelling showman who used the pub.

Drunken Duck, Hawkshead, Lancs. Result of its consumption of grain soaked from a leaking ale-barrel.

Eagle & Child. C14 legend of Stanleys who found a child in an eagle's nest and adopted this device as their crest.

Eagle and Child

Lover's Leap, Stony Middleton, Derby. Suicidal girl saved by her crinoline acting as parachute.

Moonraker. Wiltshire smugglers caught raking a pool for concealed brandy explained their activity by saying that they were creaming the cheese (moon reflected in water).

Rattlebone commemorates Anglo-Saxon warrior who 'bandaged' with a tile a dreadful abdominal wound inflicted by Danish foes.

Tommy Ducks. An incompetent signwriter who left himself insuffícent space for the name of the landlord (Tommy Duckworth).

Travelling Hen, Ponts Hill, Heref & Worcs. Fowl which hitched 'lifts' on lorries calling at inn.

Who'd Have Thought It – several explanations, including expression of surprise when former landlord was granted a licence.

Widow's Son, Bow, London, said to commemorate domestic tragedy of only son who went to sea and never returned.

ANGEL see also *Religious Names*

A popular inn name, dating from the Middle Ages. More properly it should be Archangel, perhaps Gabriel but more likely Michael who was patron of knights and of military orders such as Templars and Hospitallers who were great providers of inns for pilgrims and travellers. The *Angel* of Grantham is certainly St Michael and the sign at Wetherby is a recognisable attempt at depicting this archangel. The gold noble, first minted in 1465 and current until C17 was called an 'angel' because it had a representation of St Michael on obverse (cf. sign at Birch, Essex). There is a unique *Angel's Reply* at Hitchin, Hertfordshire, and *Angel & Crown*, Highbury, London, may represent amalgamation (q.v.) or perhaps originate in a sign depicting Coronation of B.V.M.

Angel

ANIMALS see also *Cat, Dog, etc.*

Antelope is recorded in Lincoln in 1634 and over 60 animal varieties still occur on inn signs including *Beaver, Bleeding Wolf* (Scholar Green, Cheshire), *Camel's Head, Caribou* (Glasson, Lancs), *Coney* (old name for rabbit, at West Wickham, Kent), *Elephant* (with and without its Castle), a *Little Elephant* at Knaresborough, *Giraffe, Gnu* (Stedham, Sussex), *Kangaroo, Kicking Cuddy* (donkey), *Mole, Panther, Polecat*.

ANTI-FEMINISM see also *Women*

The cheating ale-wife, brewster or woman keeping an ale-house was a common theme in medieval carving and literature. She typifies the sin of Fraud, figures in the Chester Plays and appears on a misericord at Ludlow being carried off to Hell wearing a peaked head-dress and still clutching her false measure. There are occasional remnants of male chauvinism in inn signs of which perhaps the best known is the Quiet or *Silent Woman*, usually represented without a head. There is also the *Shrew Beshrewed* (Hersden, Kent).

Anti-Feminism

ANTIQUITY
The most ancient drinks in this country seem to have been metheglin or mead, made from wild honey; cider from the crab apple; and ale.

ARCH
The yard of an old inn is usually entered through a large arch, normally capable of being closed by heavy doors. This arch may well have features of interest: the name of the inn carved in or above its voussoirs, signs of its being heightened to admit the big coaches of the C18 or it might still retain the hooks in its underside from which game and joints once hung in a cooling and fresh breeze. The original inn kitchens usually were positioned just inside the archway, more often than not on the right.

ARCHITECTURE
Pub architecture as a distinct genre is a creation of the late C19. Before this time the architecture of a public house was that of a private house of the same period, size and geographical locality. Peculiar pub architecture is capitalistic and mercantile: the reason for its development was to increase the profit of owners and brewers (when these were not the same). Its exterior was an advertisement and its interior a sales promotion area. It was aimed at the insecure working class in much the same way that a good deal of contemporary merchandising is aimed at exploiting the insecure teenager.

Nineteenth-century pubs were the antithesis of the clubs for which the rising middle-classes had abandoned them. Inside them 'it was all glare, glitter and rattle; and barmaids as fat and vulgar as the lamps that hung outside, answered back across the bar' (Girouard, p. 92). The outside, whatever the architectural 'style', was invariably flamboyant and undoubtedly a pub, proclaiming the fact from the moment it came in view.

Modern developments have included brave efforts to continue tradition in a contemporary style, honest attempts to recover the typical atmosphere (q.v.) of old pubs and wild 'gimmicks'. Perhaps the classic work on pub interiors is *Inside the Pub:* M.A.C. Gorham & M. Dunnett (London 1950). See also *Traditional English Pub:* B. Davis (London 1981). More technical is *Planning and Equipment of Public Houses*: F.W.B. Yorke (London 1949). Interesting articles may be found, *inter alia*, in *Architectural Review* of October 1949, June 1950, December 1958, February 1976.

ARISTOCRACY see also *Marquis, Monarch, People*
Much concerned with the post-Reformation development of inns and hotels and earlier their accommodation had provided many inn signs (see Heraldry). Many of them had their names or titles transferred to inns, usually as some form of tribute. Examples include: *Duchess of Kent, Duchess of Sutherland, Duke of Clarence, Duke of Cumberland* alias *Duke William* better known as the Butcher Cumberland of the Jacobite Suppression after 1745, Duke of Marlborough, *Wellington* (1769–1852), alias *Hero of Waterloo, Iron Duke, Dook* (Falmouth), *Old Duke*. It is difficult to identify which particular *Duke of York* inn names refer to – probably Frederick, C19 Field Marshal. The *Empress of Russia* seems to be the tyrannical Catherine the Great.

A wide variety of *Lords* includes *Clyde* (of Indian Mutiny), *Cornwallis, Eliot*, antagonist of Charles I. *Lord Louis* of Mountbatten, uncle of Duke of Edinburgh, *Lord Truro* commemorates the lawyer who defended Queen Caroline.

Of princes, the *Prince of Wales* is the most common but there is also *Prince Leopold*, a son of Queen Victoria, *Prince of Orange* (1626–50), *Prince Regent* or 'Prinny' who became George IV.

ARMS see also *Trade*

The . . . Arms is a very frequent name for an inn or public house. Its origin is medieval and probably originated in armigerous guests displaying the signs of their presence over or about their lodging. Its use is also common when an inn adopts as a sign the arms of the landlord e.g. *Devonshire Arms*. But there are less obvious sources (see Heraldry) as, for instance, *'Saye and Sele'* (name of title) and *Sheaf of Arrows* (badge of Cecils).

Arms

Some are open to misinterpretation: they may be badge of county rather than count and e.g. *Bruce Arms*, West Tanfield, W. Yorks has sign referring to Robert Bruce when it should bear arms of Brus, local landlords who have fine cenotaph in church.

Cayley Arms, Bromton and the renamed *Osbaldestone Arms*, Allerston commemorate Sir George Cayley (1799–1853) who, though lacking a suitable engine, is claimed as the first inventor of the aeroplane.

ASSEMBLY ROOMS see also *Long Room*

An C18 addition to the inn's amenities, sometimes built within, sometimes an adjunct and sometimes entirely separate. It was for upper or upper-middle class assemblies, most frequently balls or 'routs' but was also used when convenient for other large meetings, political or social. These rooms, a suite centered round a large hall, were located on an upper floor and were usually ornately decorated and equipped with a musicians' gallery. A few survive but rarely with anything of their former splendour. Examples at Beverley, Southwell, Knutsford, etc.

ASSIGNMENTS

One of the most underestimated uses of the inn or tavern is its function as a meeting place, especially where the time is inexact and the first to arrive may sit in shelter, well-warmed and provided with a fortifying drink. There is no need to give examples of this function which is so common as to pass almost unnoticed in descriptions of the purpose of pubs but it is perhaps worth mentioning that the first meeting of Boswell and Johnson was arranged to take place at the *Mitre* in London's Fleet Street.

ASSOCIATIONS

A particular attraction and interest of pubs derives from their literary and personal associations. Other examples will be given elsewhere but here we will mention that Sir Thomas Laurence, portraitist, grew up in *Bear*, Devizes, Wilts., that *Gun*, Deptford Reach, London was a meeting place of Nelson and Lady Hamilton and that *Rothley Court*, Leicestershire, has associations with the historian Macaulay and Wilberforce who abolished slavery. *Swan*, Coleshill, Warwicks., is mentioned by Addison (1711) as is *George*, Keswick by Hugh Walpole while *Peldon Rose*, near Colchester, Essex, figures in Baring-Gould's novel *Mehala*.

ATMOSPHERE

An indefinable but essential quality of the good pub. The thoughtful explorer might seek to analyse it and to define a scale along which it could be measured. It is related to such factors as welcome, conversation and character while the latter seems to be a function of inanimate furniture and animate clientele. It can derive to some extent from decoration (or its lack), to the presence of typical pub games and amusements and it might be assisted by location, and possession of such amenities as a garden, provision of snacks and meals. A subtle and frequently

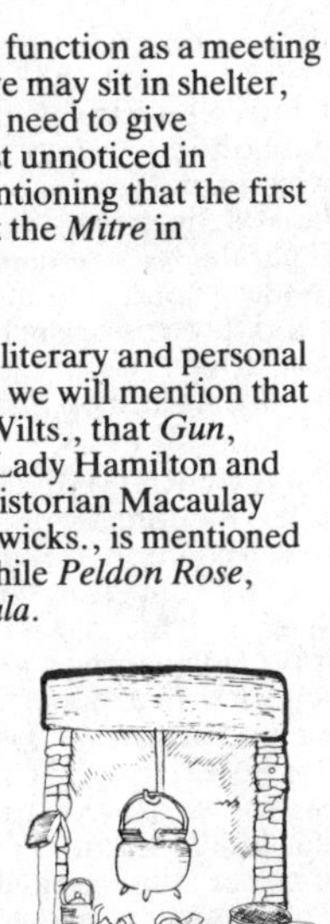
Open Fire – always important part of atmosphere

underestimated source of atmosphere is the way in which the internal space in public use is divided, not only horizontally but also vertically.

Atmosphere can be destroyed or aborted before birth by sham decoration, gimmicks, exclusiveness or the dominance of one particular type of customer. A particular enemy is dominating 'canned music', particularly of juke boxes, These may produce an atmosphere suitable for such 'feelies' as a disco but they are death to the 'talkies' which are a prime purpose of pubs.

BALL
Quite often occurs in inn signs. Modern names may associate it with Bat (see Sports) but its older form is probably of heraldic derivation, roundes as in e.g. the Cornish coat of arms. When coloured the ball is usually *Golden* but *Blue Ball* (possibly witches' or clairvoyants') also occurs. There is the inevitable *Old Ball* and this has sometimes been given a cricket association.

BALLADS see also *Folk Lore*
Many have been written on the subject of ale, particularly in C16–17. The Roxburghe Collection among Hareleian Manuscripts comprises a noteworthy group which includes the famous 'Sir John Barley-Corne'. Others include 'Mr Mault he is a Gentleman', 'Submit, Bunch of Grapes', 'The Merry Hostess', 'The Praise of Yorkshire Ale', 'A Health to All Goodfellows' and 'The High and Mighty Commendation of a Pot of Good Ale'.

Ballads in general have also been a source of inn names, particularly from the Robin hood sage but lesser-known ones have contributed e.g. *Miller of Mansfield*, Goring, Oxon.

BAR
In the modern sense of a counter over which drinks could be purchased is a surprisingly modern furnishing. Until comparatively recently, drinks in all parts of a public house were brought to the customer's place by waiters, potboys or other servants or, in the smaller houses, by the host himself. The C19 bar was a separate, self-contained room, approximating to the reception desk or office in a modern hotel. The introduction of the 'spirit store' (q.v.) type of counter into the bar of taverns began to transfer the traditional image of a (public) house into a shop where there were 'customers' rather than 'guests'. The exterior was also affected producing a 'shop front' with conspicuous advertising of favoured 'brands'.

Engraved Glass – 1914 for Bar Door

BAR FURNISHING
A bar is defined as a counter at which drinks are sold or a licensed room containing such a counter. A licensed room not containing a counter is usually referred to by another name (see Lounge, Saloon, Snug, etc.). Back Bar Fitting (Back Fitting, Sideboard Fitting) is the furniture at the back of the servery behind the bar counter. It provides storage and display for bottled beer, wines, spirits, glass and other sundries. In a modern house it may have refrigerated shelving, usually has its own integral lighting and is an important decorative and advertising feature.
Bar Sundries are the small items, excluding fittings and furnishings, such as till, crown-cap owners, cocktail shakers, etc.
Bar Walk (Apron). The area of floor along the front of the bar, subject to considerable wear and tear and therefore often finished in a hard material even where carpets are generally omnipresent.
Pot Shelf. A special receptacle, often fixed above or on the bar counter, to provide ready access to drinking vessels, especially glasses, and sometimes made into a featured element of the internal decor.

Counter. The essential element may be polished hardwood, sometimes copper or zinc-covered. Its front is commonly panelled but in modern pubs it may be brick, stone or flashily decorated with buttoned leather, ceramic tiles, etc. Traditionally, there is a brass rail along its lower face for the greater comfort of the occupants of bar stools. Its surface also supports the beer engines (q.v.) though in earlier days these were sometimes fitted against a neighbouring wall. The bar counter often incorporates a wicket, i.e. a door with a flap above giving access to the drinking area from the servery. Cold shelving may be incorporated in the back bar fitting below the level of the bar top and more rarely beneath the bar itself. Fittings generally include optics (q.v.) and may include rare survivals such as stillion, snob-screens or spirit urns (q.v.).

Ancient Bar Stool

BARLEY WINE
Strongest form of beer, matured over many months.

BARS see also *Private, Public, Saloon,* etc.
Traditional pubs tended to have three bars, variously named but generally equivalent to Public, Private and Saloon. These corresponded to social level but perhaps more importantly to function. The increasingly class-conscious C19 saw a proliferation of sub-divisions based on class through the whole range only extended from working to lower-middle class.

The current tendency, sometimes ostensibly in the interests of pseudo-democracy but fundamentally for economic (i.e. profit) motives, is to destroy walls to create the one-bar pub which economises on service and increases drinking space and therefore profit on sales.

Public bars are generally more basic and drinks tend to be less expensive but they also have additional facilities such as provision for traditional pub games (q.v.). Private bars are for regulars and close groups and their main business is reminiscence, praising the past and criticising the present. Saloons have almost all become lounges with something of the atmosphere of a drawing-room party but any difference of style, which should induce differences of mood and perhaps encourage or tolerate differences of dress is to be welcomed.

If we have to have single-bar pubs, can we at least expect them to be divided into distinguishable areas?

BASS CHARRINGTON
One of the 'Big Six' and the largest brewing business in Europe. It possesses over 20,000 outlets and strong representation in wines and spirits together with Canada Dry soft drinks. Founded 1967 by merger of Charringtons United with Bass, Mitchell and Butler – themselves the product of a series of previous mergers. Their products include Bass and Worthington draught and a range of bottles and cans which include naturally conditioned White Label, Bass Export, No. 1 Barley Wine and Carling Black Label lager.

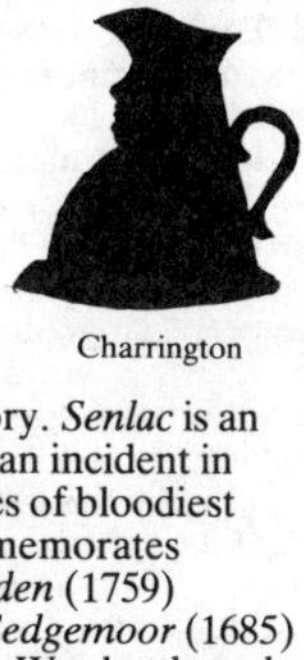
Charrington

BATTLES AND SIEGES
The significance of some names requires a little knowledge of history. *Senlac* is an alternative for Hastings and *Swordsman*, Stamford Bridge, recalls an incident in another great battle of 1066. *Crooked Billet*, Towton, has memories of bloodiest battle (1461) in Wars of Roses while *Standard* Northallerton, commemorates defeat of Scots by English under their sacred banners in 1138. *Minden* (1759) belongs to Seven Years War and Moodkee to Sikh War (1845/6). *Sedgemoor* (1685) saw defeat of rebellion v. James II. *Arroyo* (1811) was a Peninsular War battle and *Alma, Balaclava, Inkerman, Odessa, Sebastapol* belong to Crimean War (1854–56). *Vigo* (1702), *Two Ships* (1807) commemorate naval engagements.

BEDFORDSHIRE
The brewery at Biggleswade is a subsidiary of Greene King (see Suffolk). The independent brewery at Bedford belongs to Charles Wells with about 270 tied houses scattered through S. Midlands. It produces two draught beers, an above average keg and the range of bottled beers includes Fargo Ale and Old Bedford Ale.

BEER see also *Ale*
Beer with hops was introduced from Holland at beginning of C15 and opposed by traditionalists as both new-fangled and foreign, e.g.

Hop – essential ingredient of beer

> Beer is made of malte, of hoppes and water; it is the naturall drynke for a Dutche man and now of late dayes it is much used in England to the detryment of many Englyshe people; specyally it killeth them that be troubled with the colyke and the stone and the strangulation; for the drynke is a cold drynke; yet it doeth make a man fat, and doth inflate the bely, as it doth appere by the Dutchmen's faces and belyes. If the bere be well served and be fyned and not new it doth qualify heat of the lyver. (Andrew Boorde: *Dyetary of Health*, 1542)

Even a century later, opposition was still being strongly expressed:

Skimming Mash

> Now to write of Beere, I shall not need to wet my pen much with the naming of it, it being a drink which Antiquitie was an Alien or a meere stranger to, and as it hath scarcely any name, so it hath no habitation, for the places of houses where it is sold doth still retain the name of an Alehouse . . . Beere is but an Upstart or Alien in respect of Ale. (John Taylor: *Drink and Welcome*, c. 1645)

The word beer also included within its connotation fermented drinks from a variety of herbs and plants: neetle, parsnip, spruce, tar, treacle, ginger. Some of these are still produced domestically and should not be despised. 'Small beer' was weak beer and hence figuratively meant a thing of no consequence.
bombard: a large can or vessel for holding beer.
chiller: funnel-shaped pot, made of tin, to take chill off beer over fire.
cooler: large, shallow vat for cooling beer.
corn: grain used for brewing.
engine: suction pump, worked by hand, which raises beer from cellar to servery.
faucet: machine for injecting air to make beer foam.
float: hydrometer for measuring density of beer-wash.
fountain: see engine.
garden: enclosure attached to pub or inn for outdoor drinking. No necessary implication of flowers, shrubs, etc.
heading: a mixture intended to revive flat beer.
horse: the power of a traditional brewer's dray.
house: not licensed for wine or spirits.
machine: see engine.
money: originally an allowance of cash to servants instead of traditional provision in kind.

pot: generally a pewter vessel, holding a quart or pint, probably originally made of wood in form of miniature barrel.
pump: see electric, pull.
tray: one fitted with upright ends and central division to carry two rows of beer pots.
vinegar: made from beer (cf. malt vinegar) as distinct from wine vinegar.

BELLARMINE see also *Toby Jug*
Small jugs of glazed earthenware, first made in Germany in C15 and used in next century as containers for imported Holland Gin (which was introduced to England at this time). As a piece of Protestant propaganda these jugs were formed into a caricature of the venerable Cardinal Bellarmine, a major Catholic apologist of the period. They are sometimes known as 'Greybeards'. *Artichoke*, Orpington, preserves some original examples discovered during alterations to the house in the present century.

BERKSHIRE
In Abingdon is the brewery of Morland's f.1711 and now with some 240 tied houses in Berks. and S. Oxon. with overflow into Hants and Surrey. There is also a flourishing free trade in their products which include three draught beers and a range of bottled including Monarch.

BILLIARD ROOM see also *Games*
A provision in larger town pubs in later C19 and usually known as Billiard Saloon. Developments since World War II have sadly brought the extinction of the billard room as brewers thought of more profitable use for the space.
Rare examples survived into 1970s but now seem to have entirely disappeared.

BEAR
One of the commonest animals to appear as sign or name. The popularity stems from several causes: heraldic, particularly in the case of the *Bear and Ragged Staff* which was the Warwick crest. Performing bears were also popular elements in fairs and side-shows. Above all, there was the barbarous sport of bear-baiting. *Bear's Head* and *Bear's Paw* occur as do *Old Bear, New Bear, Conquered Bear* and *Two Bears*. They occur in the usual colours: Black, Brown and White (the latter has been said to refer to one of Drake's ships) and there is a rare *Red Bear* at Sherburn-in-Elmet.

Bear & Billet

BELL
An extremely popular element among pub names and signs, probably due to the ecclesiastical origin of inns and many pubs. It occurs in various numbers: single, four, five, eight and twelve. *Ring o' Bells* is said to refer to the practice of hand-bell ringing but it may refer to a 'set' of tower bells. The operators are referred to in *Six Ringers*, Felmersham, Beds. and *Clanger*, Houndsditch, London, seems to refer to a fire-bell. The rare *Bell and Hare*, Tottenham, where the sign shows a hare leaping over bell, book and candle (instruments of exorcism) is said to allude to witchcraft and the belief that witches could transform themselves into hares.

Ring o'Bells

BILLET
As inn name/sign, it is usually *Crooked*. Its origin is sometimes explained as referring to the small log from which inn signs were sometimes made but it is much more likely to be heraldic. It occurs as a synonym for staff in *Bear and Billet*.

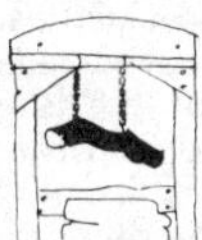

Billet

BIRD see also *Eagle, Falconry*
It is claimed that there are between 1,200 and 1,300 pub signs featuring birds, representing more than 60 varieties and including some extinct ones like *Bustard*. The popularity of *Swan* may be related to its association with the Vintners Company and *Three Cranes* was once of quite frequent occurrence. *Raven* is said to derive from part of arms of Mary I and *Owl* occurs a number of times including *Wise Owl* and *Blinking Owl*. The mythical *Phoenix* was a religious symbol and *Dotterel* is a rare species of plover. The common *Bird in Hand* is explained as derived from falconry or as proverbial while the origin of *Magpie and Stump* is complicated by the fact that 'magpie' could mean either ½d or ½ pint and 'stump' can equal 'pay up'. Magpies were also considered to be 'lucky' birds and this has been offered as an explanation for their occurrence in inn names. There is a *Gaping Goose* (e.g. Garforth, W. Yorks) and the *Turkey*, Keighley, brews its own beer.

BISHOP
i. A drink, popular in C18, variously compounded but its chief ingredients included wine, oranges or lemons and sugar. It was thus a sort of British Sangria. The word was also used of mulled and spiced port.

ii. Rare inn sign but examples include Bishop Blaise, patron saint of woolcombers (Richmond, N. Yorks), *Bishop Lacey*, famous bishop of Exeter (1370–1455), There is also St *Stephen Langton* who became Archbishop of Canterbury in 1205 and, above all, St *Thomas à Becket* who held the same office and was martyred in 1107. A very popular name in Middle Ages but obliterated, along with his shrine, as opponent of the very Erastianism which Henry VIII so notoriously exemplified. At least one survivor in SE London.

BLACK
As an epithet in inn names is applied to *Boy* (see Servants), *Cap* (often the sign depicting witch on broomstick), *Friar*, i.e. Dominican a religious order f. beginning C13 and quickly established in England (1221). *Black Lion* is heraldic (see Lion), *Black Prince* (1330–76) was the popular eldest son of Edward III. *Black Venus* is, disappointingly, a Devonshire local expression for a black sheep. *Blackamoor* is a sign introduced by Crusades (q.v.).

BLUE
Occurs in a wide range of contexts. *Blue Ball* is said to be the crystal ball of the fortune-teller. *Blue Boar* is the heraldic badge used by the Tudor supporting Earls of Oxford. *Blue Bowl* was a kind of Bristol Ware used for the making of punch. *Blue Boy* is probably named after Gainsborough's famous picture through the postilions of George IV wore a blue livery. *Blue Lias* is a north country limestone, transported by canal, alongside which this name occurs. *Blue Vinney* is a blue-veined cheese made in Dorset.

BOAR
The wild boar was a doughty denizen of the countryside and provided a worthy adversary for its courageous hunters. A boar's head was the centre-piece of Christmas feasting with a carol in its honour and this is probably the cause of the popularity of *Boar's Head* as an inn sign. The *White Boar* was a badge of the House of York and used by Richard III while the Blue belonged to the de Veres who were to support the usurper Henry Tudor. It is said that many *White Boars* were painted blue after the battle of Bosworth in 1485 as a prudent sop to the new regime.

Boar

BOARD AND LODGING
The composite phrase is said to originate from the 'board' (trestle table) on which inn food was served and the lodging of rushes on the floor which was offered to poorer folk in a medieval hospice. For an alternative explanation, see below.

Board

BOARD INNS
Hostelries offering quick food and inexpensive lodgings which developed in C19. In 1823 Scarborough e.g. had 11 Board Inns. Their name was taken from the board on which cold meats were kept to provide an ever-ready meal. This is also said to be the origin of the expression 'board and lodging' but cf. supra.

BOATS see also *Ships*
Inns are obviously closely related to any form of Transport (q.v.) and Boats have given their name to many an inn or public house. Perhaps the most common occurrence is *Ferry Boat* since the inn-keeper often doubled as ferryman. The narrow boats of the canals (q.v.) also brought much trade to existing public houses as well as providing a need which had to be filled. There are even cases of boats being themselves public houses.

BOOT
Boot or Shoe is the most common article of apparel occurring in inn signs. It is said that cobblers had a reputation for thirst and that a boot was associated with St Crispin their patron saint. In Bedfordshire, Buckinghamshire and Huntingdonshire, the *Boot* is associated with John Schorne, a native of Monks Risborough who became parish priest of North Marston in the Middle Ages. He was popularly regarded as a saint and occurs with recognised ones on the rood screen at Suffield, Norfolk. *Boot* is also associated with Lord Wellington who gave his name to a fashion in footwear and in St Albans *Wellington* and *Boot* occupy opposite sides of the same street. *Boot and Shoe* occur in combination e.g. Greystoke, Cumbria, where this sign is said to commemorate an inn-keeper who also plied the trade of cobbler.

BOOZE
As a verb occurs in quite respectable authors in C17 and is found as early as 1634. It is used as a noun meaning draught or drink.

BOOZER
More definitely a slang term coined to describe the grand Victorian street-corner pub – a metropolitan type originating from the gin habit. It was concerned more with profit on the part of its owners and oblivion on the part of its users than with the social and recreative functions of the traditional alehouse which survived as a country type.

BOTTLES
Bottle-making was a recognised trade by 1373 in England but such bottles were made from leather and used to transport liquor from cask to table or on longer journeys. Glass bottles (squat, coarse and clumsy) came into use in C17. Bottled beer keeps longer and in C18 when improvements were made in the shape of the bottles (usually wine) so that they could be laid down in the cellar. There is a *Wall Bottle* at Knottingley W. Yorks.

Bottle

BOWLING GREEN
Many large inns provide a bowling green as part of their amenities and some houses even acquired the name *Bowling Green*. Very few of these ancient greens survive in use (one is allegedly haunted) but their shape and/or location may sometimes be discerned transformed into a beer garden or even a car park. Some modern houses have restored this association.

For some 70 years the Crown Green Bowling Championship has been decided on the green of the *Waterloo* hotel, Blackpool which, in consequence, has given its name to the event.

BRANDY see also *Spirits*
In later C17 French brandy was cheap and increasingly popular in this country since the tax on ale and beer had increased their price. The increase in spirit consumption not only affected drinking habits but also the national economy as farmers were unable to sell their barley. In 1673 a petition was presented to Parliament seeking to ban the import of brandy, rum, tea and coffee. It included the following words:

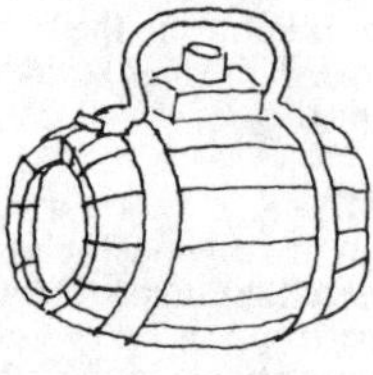
Small Brandy Barrel

> Before Brandy, which has now become common and is sold in every little alehouse, came to England in such quantities as it now doth, we drank good strong beer and ale, and all laborious people (which are far the greater part of the kingdom) their bodies requiring after hard labour some strong drink to refresh them, did therefore every morning and evening use to drink a pot of ale or a flagon of strong beer, which greatly helped the promotion of our own grains and did them no great prejudice; it hindreth not their work, nor did it take away their senses, nor cost them much money . . .

BREWERIES see also under *Counties* for Independents
The beer scene has, until lately, been dominated by the conglomerates known as 'the Big Six' who own more than half the pubs in the country. The 'Big Six' are the following: Allied Breweries, Bass Charrington, Courage, Scottish and Newcastle, Watney Mann & Truman, Whitbread. See entries under each name.

BREWING
Long regarded as essentially a woman's task as is indicated in such words as brewster and alewife. The only exception seems to have been in male religious houses whose ale was markedly superior to the domestic product and which was famed throughout Europe in the Middle Ages. Nearly all inns produced their own ale until C18. Examples of their equipment survive e.g. in Shibden Hall Museum, Halifax which was removed from *White Bear* as recently as 1953. Whatever the size of the operation, whether domestic or factory, the process of brewing involves six main operations: Milling, Mashing, Boiling of the former mash, now 'wort', Cooling, Fermentation, Racking.

Representation of C17 Ale Wife

Brewing has left some traces in inn signs including *Brewers Arms, Two Brewers, Malt Shovel*(s), *Three Tuns* and *Beehive* which reminds us that sugar is a comparatively recent ingredient and that ale and mead were once sweetened with honey.

BRIC-À-BRAC see also *Collections*
Collections are unified whereas bric-à-brac is heterogeneous and only held together by the fact that it is one room. Pub bric-à-brac tends to be copper or brass and often includes agricultural or sea-faring material, perhaps with horse furniture as the most common source. Obviously countryside material is very appropriate to a rural pub as in marine material to a seaside house. Curios are also self-justifying as is material relating to inns and taverns: old accounts, rules of the house, bills of fare, advertisements of past functions and other ephemera. The decorative use of former bar or brew-house utensils is equally suitable.

BRITANNIA TABLE
An almost universal item of Victorian pub furniture, thoughtlessly expelled by modernisers and now frequently being replaced in reproduction form. It is a three-legged table with circular top and usually has a decorative medallion on each leg which often, though not always, is a representation of Britannia.

Late Victorian Britannia Table

BRITISH BEER
Though beer is by far the most widely distributed alcoholic drink in the world (see M. Jackson: *World Guide to Beer*, London 1977), British beer is unique. England, Ireland, Scotland and Wales are the only countries where the principal beers are brewed by top-fermentation. Consequently, their flavours can only be fully appreciated at cellar temperature and chilling is destructive of their richly varied and sophisticated palate.

BRITISH ISLES
In drinking, as in most things, Scotland has its own traditions: its brewing is peculiar to itself and Traquair House is exemplary. Above all, it is distinguished by its devotion to whisky and its magnificent variety of single malts. Inevitably, Ireland is again different on both sides of its border but for once these differences are sometimes for the better.

The smaller islands should not be forgotten, particularly the Isle of Man and the Channel Islands which are self-governing and not part of the United Kingdom. The former has a historic Purity Law while the Channel Islands not only produces excellent and interesting beers but sells them at lower prices and over more convenient hours.

BROWN ALE
The bottled form of mild ale (q.v.), sometimes known as 'Home Brewed'. The well-known 'Newcastle Brown' is better described as a strong dark ale rather than placed in the category of a normal brown ale.

BUCK
Its wide distribution as an element in a pub's name is an indication both of the former extent of deer forests and the popularity of hunting among the upper classes though venison frequently appeared on tables lower down the social scale. There are *Buck's Head, Buck's Horns, Running Buck* and *Golden Buck*. More imaginative are *Buck in the Park* and *Buck in the Vine* and there are combinations such as *Buck & Bell, Buck & Dog* and *Buck & Hawthorn*.

BUILDING MATERIALS
A pub of any antiquity invariably uses local materials for its building and the results of this practice are an important element in the variety which is one of the most pleasant attributes of the English inn. It also helps the pub to 'belong', to be part of the natural landscape and not an eyesore or obvious intrusion.

BULL

Bull

One of the commonest pub names and its frequency has been explained as due to three causes: a religious origin from 'bulla' a collegiate or ecclesiastical seal; bull-baiting; its significance in animal husbandry. The inn-sign bull is most commonly Black but may be Blue, Golden, Grey, Pied, Red, Spotted or White (*White Bull*, Gisburn, Yorks. commemorates famous herd of white cattle which occupied Gisburn Park to C19). They can be in Spectacles, in th' Thorn, Chained or Flying, Great or Little and they occur in many combinations: *Bull & Butcher*, and with *Gate, Horseshoe, Oak, Royal, Stirrup, Swan, Wharf. Bull & Mouth* is said to commemorate a minor naval victory over the French at Boulogne Mouth in the reign of Henry VIII while *Bull & Gate* may refer to the subsequent treaty signed at the gate of Boulogne.

BUSH
One of the earliest tavern signs and originally Roman whence the saying that 'a good wine needs no bush' (i.e. advertising). The sign was transferred to alehouses in England (see Ale Stake). Because this sign was general and not very distinctive it was often combined with another sign as in the case of the famous old *Bull & Bush*. Eventually the Bush element was often dropped altogether. The curious may like to note that *Bush* at Garforth, W. Yorks. has a neighbouring *Bird in Hand*.

BUSH HOUSE
A name given to a temporary tavern or beer shop set up to meet the increased consumption which occurred on Fair Days. The institution was abolished in C19 and its present-day equivalent is the market-day extension or the seasonal licence granted to some houses in seaside resorts, etc.

BUTT see also *Vessels*
A large cask which could contain 126 gallons of wine or 108 gallons of beer, also known as pipe. *Half Butt*, Great Horkesley, Essex, seems to be uniquely so named. There is a *Butt & Oyster* at Pinmill, Suffolk and a rare *Porter Butt* in York Place, Bath.

BUTTERED ALE
A beverage, formerly popular, composed of sugar, cinammon, butter and ale brewed without hops.

CAMBRIDGESHIRE
North Brink Brewery at Wisbech belongs to Elgood's who have some 60 tied houses radiating from the town. They produce mild and bitter draughts, an above average keg and the bottled range includes Old English. St Neots has Paine's brewery with 24 tied houses in vicinity together with a little free trade. They produce two draught and a range of bottled beers.

CAMRA
The Campaign for Real Ale, a unique consumers' association concerned with the production of traditional beer and its availability. It disseminates information in the annual Good Beer Guide and other occasional publications. It has been an effective pressure group: increasing awareness, probably saving real ale from disappearing altogether, and pushing for more informative labelling, and criticising the near monopoly of the 'Big Six'. It has still a long way to go: minimum malt content, chemical additives, restricted choice for consumers, and deserves more support.

CANAL PUBS
The house at the canalside, often named *Boat, Navigation, Barge, Ship* or *Anchor*, represented far more to the narrow-boat operators than a source of liquid refreshment. It was an information centre where news of the outside world could be picked up, messages left for other members of the boating fraternity and communications received from them. Canal pubs were trading centres; not only for direct purchase but also parcels offices where items could be left or picked up. They were also social centres, not only providing relaxation from the heavy work of operating narrow boats but places where meetings (including courtship and marriage) could be arranged and carried out. For their modern use see Nicholson's *Real Ale Guide to the Waterways*.

CANALS
The burst of canal-making in C18 and early C19 brought social mobility and new needs, some of which were met by new waterside pubs or the development of old ones. These prospered in the early days of the Industrial Revolution until inland waterway traffic declined due to the competition and sometimes deliberate policy of the railways. It is good to know that this great asset is being now appreciated and that canals are being restored if only for mainly recreational purposes. Many inn or pub names reflect the development of canals: *Bridgewater* commemorates not only a famous canal but the 'Father of Canals'; *Grand Trunk* refers to the Leeds–Liverpool, opened 1816; *Paddington Packet* recalls a barge service of the *Grand Union* which has also given its name to a number of pubs; *Tunnel House*, near Coates, Gloucestershire was originally built as a hostel for the builders of the canal tunnel. The most common derived name is *Navigation*, the technical name for artificial waterways. *Navigator* was the term for the canal excavator, later shortened to 'navvie'. There are also *Barge Horse, Boat and Horses, Row Barge, Anchor, Barge* and even a *Romping Donkey*. *Ship*, Acaster Malbis still shows hole pierced to provide bargees with drink without their needing to stop the horses.

CANNED MUSIC
Live music was a common accompaniment to social drinking from the earliest times but mechanical music arrived in C19 with introduction of musical automata. These were clockwork musical boxes brought into play by the insertion of a penny. The king of these devices combined a musical box with an elaborate clock. The most popular tunes were 'gaily melancholic' but their greatest attribute was that they were subdued unlike the raucous Juke Box which has replaced them and is an aggressive enemy to the chief social function of pubs – conversation.

Some modern pubs have 'piped' music produced from an endless magnetic tape. The choice represents the publican's taste rather than the whimsy of juvenile customers and there is one in the North of England which appropriately plays Mozartian divertimenti.

CARAMEL
Burnt sugar used for adding colour to beer.

CARLISLE
The location of many munition factories in this area in World War I and the loss of armament production through drunkenness among workers led not only to the general provisions of the Defence of the Realm Act ('DORA') but to a unique experiment wherby the breweries and pubs in the neighbourhood of Carlisle were taken over into State control. The scheme was dismantled in 1974 with differing judgements to its effects. The former State brewery was acquired by Theakstons, the excellent Yorkshire independent brewery, in order to cope with the increasing demand for their traditional beer.

Old Peculiar (Theakstons)

CARRIERS
Like coaches transporting people, the goods-carrying trade was closely associated with inns, though (generally speaking) with different ones. Inn-keepers were used as agents for storage of goods to be collected or delivered and sometimes provided a local delivery service in the neighbourhood of their house. Many inn signs recall this function including *Carter's Rest, Jolly Waggoners, Old Wagon, Van & Horses*.

CASE IS ALTERED
There are many 'explanations' of this intriguing name of which a number include the element of soldiers returning from the Peninsular War early in C19 and setting up as pub-keepers on their gratuities. Their Spanish memories allegedly produced this name as a corruption of either 'casa alta' (the high house) or 'casa del saltar' (dance hall). A different approach offers a legal explanation involving an alteratior to a lawsuit: this is the meaning implied by the sign at Eastcote. Akin to this is the alleged remark of a new landlord taking over from a predecessor who had been bankrupted. Finally there is the suggestion that it is a corruption of 'Casey's altar' with a supporting anecdote. One's only response to this is 'Rubbish'!

CASTLE
Is a popular inn name and provides a good opportunity for sign painters. Its origin may be heraldic, related to a local landmark, or derive from the memory of a vanished fortress. *Ypres Castle*, Rye is named from the medieval Ypres tower beneath which it stands. *Star Castle*, St Mary's, Scilly, is unique in that it is actually a late C16 castle, the last stronghold of the Royalists in the Civil War and with subsequent associations with Charles II.

Windsor Castle

CAT
Frequently occurs in inn names but it is not necessarily the domestic feline. There were medieval ships called 'cats' and Scottish border raiders were allegedly called 'cats' (among other things). *Cat and Bagpipes*, East Hardsley, Yorks. probably has this reference. Other combinations include *Cat and Cabbage*, a playful allusion to the tiger and cabbage rose badge of the former Yorkshire and Lancashire Regiment; the *Cat and Cracker*, from the catalytic cracker at an oil refinery; the unexplained *Cat & Mustard Pot* at Shipton Moyne, Wilts. *Cat's Whisker*, Childwal Merseyside may refer to the essential element in an old crystal set but the phrase has since come to mean something extraordinarily good. There are *Laughing, Squinting, Mad, Rampant* and *Romping Cats* as well as a *Tabby Cat, Burmese Cat* and a *Ginger Tom*. Cats can also be found 'in t' well' and 'in t' window'.

The puzzling *Cat and Fiddle* remains enigmatic. The subject occurs on a Normar carving in the church at Adel, Yorks. and appears on medieval misericords in Hereford cathedral, Wells cathedral and in Beverley Minster. A possible explanation is that it is a pun or rebus on 'Caterina Fidelis' i.e. St Catherine of Alexandria, a very popular saint in the Middle Ages and one of 'Ten Holy Helpers'. She died c. A.D. 310 and her well disseminated legend included the story of her being broken on the wheel and this may explain origin of '*Cat in t' window*'.

CATTLE see also *Bull*
The Cow makes many appearances in inn names; there are numerous *Brown Cows* occasional *Spotted* ones and a *Shorthorn* occurs at Appleton Wiske, Yorks. A number of famous cattle have received at least local commemoration: *Ketton Ox*, Yarm; *Durham Ox*, Crayke (which once belonged to Durham abbey); *Castle Howard Ox*, York; *Blackwell Ox*, Carlton in Cleveland; *Wensleydale Heifer*, West Witton; *Airedale Heifer*, Mirfield; *Craven Heifer*, frequently in W. Yorks.

CELLAR

There is an almost inevitable association between the word 'cellar' and the word 'drink' and the expression 'He keeps a good cellar' can be a tribute both to the quantity and quality of the referent's store. We are reminded of the song: 'Simon the Cellarer' and the care that has gone into cellarage from monastic times to the diminishing present. The skills of resting, broaching and maintaining proper temperature were once critical to the inn-keeper's craft as well as the necessary careful corellation of supply and demand.

'Simon the Cellarer'

CHANGED NAME

It is possibly a minority only of ancient pubs which have preserved their original name. Changes stem from a variety of causes of which political and religious conformity are perhaps the chief: *Pope's Head* changed into *King's Head, White Boar* into *Blue Boar*, etc. Amalgamations (q.v.) is another reason to which we might add the preferences or prejudices of a new landlord. Some names are changed in an attempt to upgrade the social status of a pub or to diminish bad associations. Others commemorate a recent incident in the pub's history or a desire to keep in mind a national hero or event. Some recent changes are an attempt to give a (spurious) individuality to an outlet for mass-produced drinks or hopefully to attract the curious. Examples and causes of changed name are an interesting field of enquiry for the explorer.

CHANNEL ISLANDS

The States of Jersey have substantial holdings in the Ann Street Brewery at St Helier and their dividends go to local charities. The Extra Special Bitter is claimed to be the strongest keg beer in U.K. and Mary Ann Special is a strong bottled Pale Ale. Its 50 tied houses include the oldest pub in Jersey: *Forester's Arms*, Beaumont but most houses are free and Mary Ann beers are available throughout the island.

Guernsey Brewery Company of St Peter Port, has 40–50 tied houses but most business is free trade which extends to other Channel Islands. It produces a draught mild, keg bitter and range of bottled beers.

There are also Randalls of St Helier with some 30 tied houses plus substantial free trade which produces two kegs and three bottled beers. R.W. Randall of St Peter Port has 17 tied houses but most trade is free. It produces draught mild, a keg bitter of high gravity and three bottled beers.

CHARITIES

Medieval 'works of mercy' and later charities which followed this tradition frequently provided for the free distribution of ale to poor persons, farm labourers and schoolboys. The drink was usually accompanied by some form of food: bread, mince pies, cake, meat.

CHASER

A short drink followed by a long or contrariwise. The usual combination is beer and whisky, but remember:

Beer after whisky
Makes you feel frisky,
But whisky after beer
Makes you feel queer.

CHEESE see also *Food*
In view of the contemporary popularity of the dubious Ploughman's Lunch as a bar snack it is perhaps surprising that the association of cheese and pub is less obvious in inn names. I have only found the occurrence of the famous *Cheshire Cheese* and the less well-known names of *Blue Vinney* and *Double Gloucester*.

CHEQUERS
A frequent inn name in England with some 300 occurrences (there is also one in shattered Pompeii). The sign is probably derived from the ancient counting board, used for reckoning and money-changing, which is the origin of the word Exchequer. Also trade mark of Wilson's Brewery.

Arms with Chequers Board

CHESHIRE
Marston, Thomson & Evershed are at Burton and have some 800 widely dispersed tied houses and even more extensive free trade. They produce three draught beers, two keg, wide bottled range including Owd Roger and sweet stout. Everard's (see Leicestershire) working brewery is at Burton.

Warrington also has two breweries: Forshaws, with over 300 tied houses in Lancashire, Cheshire, Staffordshire and N. Wales, making two draughts and a bottled range including Top Hat and Buckle Dark Ale; Greenhall Whitley (who own further breweries in St Helens and Wem, Salop.), with nearly 1,500 tied houses widely spread over West Midlands and produce three draughts, two kegs and range of bottles including Five Star and Old Chester.

George & Dragon
Wilmslow, Cheshire

CHURCH ALE
Parishoners subscribed a quantity of barley, according to their ability, to church-wardens or parish officers who therewith brewed strong ale. This was sold back to the parishioners during the celebration of a church festival (Christmas, Easter, Whitsunday or Patronal Festival), and the substantial profits went to the church fund, poor or fabric. The Reformers naturally found them 'superstitious, sources of gluttony and drunkenness and a variety of other evils'. However, they managed to survive and were called 'Christian Ales' in early C17 until the Puritans finally succeeded in abolishing them during the Commonwealth. Besides Church Ales, Brides Ales and Scot Ales there were Bid (Bede) Ales, Give Ales, Cuckoo Ales, Help Ales, Tithe Ales, Leet Ales, Lamb Ales, Midsummer Ales, Weddyn Ales. Some of these are obviously variant names for the same thing. There were also Mary Ales in honour of B.V.M. where the proceeds went to the adornment of the Lady Chapel or Lady Altar.

CIDER
The traditional West Country beverage, what Chesterton called 'the apple-wine of Hereford' but the real thing is getting rarer in pubs and there are few restricted cider houses left. There is still a true draught cider available, made by Farmers, there is also a keg cider made from fermented concentrated apple-juice. Bulmers own a large number of pubs in the West Country which they operate as free houses apart from a cider monopoly. Blackthorn is a recommended bottled form, Scrumpy is great if you can take both the sharp taste and the alcoholic content but remember:

Beer on cider is a good rider
Cider on beer makes you queer.

Hereford has a museum of Cider with reconstructed farm ciderhouse, working cooper's shops, etc.

CLEVELAND
Camerons own the Lion Brewery in Hartlepool and some 700 tied houses mainly in the county, in Durham and in Yorkshire. Draught beers include Strongarm and they also produce kegs and a variety of bottled beers.

CLOCK see also *Parliament*
A legible clock is a very important piece of bar furniture because of Permitted Hours (q.v.). It allows the customer to monitor drinking time and facilitates the landlord's task in complying with this particular (and peculiar) aspect of the law.

CLOSING TIME see *Permitted Hours*

CLUB ROOM
Upper rooms of inns were often used for local social and administrative purpose including the accommodation of local courts. In C18 such rooms often developed into characteristic Assembly Rooms (q.v.) but in humbler houses they continued to provide a meeting-place for local groups, including benevolent and friendly societies. They provided a home for debating societies, discussion groups and the nascent Trade Unions.

In C19 a popular alternative use was as a Music Room where the sentimental singer, the mimic and impersonator, the black-faced minstrel, the ventriloquist or the step-dancer could find a stage and an audience. From this use, the Concert Room and later the Music Hall developed.

COACH
Coaching brought a new purpose and life to inns on major routes and the coaching era has been seen as the inn's 'finest hour'. It is only to be expected that this activity has left a very considerable mark on inn names and signs and even the old Falcon coach itself which once ran to Holsworthy, Devon was found a dignified and appropriate resting-place outside *Falcon*, Bude, Cornwall. The commonest associated name is *Coach & Horses* with alternatives of *Coach and Four* and *Coach and Eight*. The pub of this name in Newcastle has provided a variation in its sign which shows a rowing eight with their coach. The coach's own names have been transferred to inns on their former route, e.g. *Dairy Maid, Eclipse, Gloster Flying Machine, Red Rover, Royal Blenheim, Royal Mail, Quicksilver Mail*. The 'Fly' and the 'Bull' on the London–Portsmouth route produced the hybrid *Flying Bull*, Rake Hants. There is a *Coaching House* at Chudleigh, Devon and other names from the era include *Postboy, Posthorn* (see also *Roads*).

Coach and Four

COCK
Delderfield attributes this common sign to Greek mythology and a symbol of sunrise. It is much more likely to be derived from Petrine associations (like the weather-cock), the 'sport' of cock-fighting (q.v.) as in *Fighting Cocks* or the obvious prominence of this bird in a predominantly rural country. In any case, a cock is not always what it seems. Three Cocks near Glasbury, Radnors. is said to refer to the 'cock horses' kept at the inn to help waggons up the hill. The cock horse led and

Cock & Hen

assisted the trace horse and is the origin of the children's game and reference in nursery rhyme. *Cock & Bottle* was a sign formerly indicating that the house provided both draught and bottled ale, the 'cock' being the tap used to draw ale from the barrel. The expression 'cock-a-hoop' has been derived from the practice of withdrawing the cock from the barrel and laying it on the hoop (or top) so that drink had to be consumed as fast and the resulting free flow.

COCKTAIL see also *Mixtures*
Originally a slang term for a hybrid or mixed drink, whether shaken or stirred. Like chewing-gum and coca-cola, it is an American invention becoming 'smart' in this country in the 1920s when fashionable hotels introduced 'cocktail bars' for its purveyance. The base is usually spiritous to which varied colouring and flavouring liquids are added. It produced a variety of derivative articles varying from shakers through sticks to parties.

COFFEE ROOM
In response to the competition of the new coffee houses in C18, the larger inns put aside one of their own rooms, generally placed for convenience just off the entrance hall, for the consumption of this beverage, comfortably furnished, and usually supplied with newspapers in the hope of attracting back the clientele of the club-like coffee house.

COLLECTIONS see also *Bric-à-Brac*
The personal collections of licensees have a number of functions: they express individuality, improve the look of a place and help to give the impression of being in someone's house. As well as being often interesting in themselves, they provide a talking point and improve social interaction. These curiosities and mementoes, the result of individual interest and effort should be distinguished from 'thematic' treatment of bars which is often no more than a Brewer's decorator's gimmick.

COLLIERS' PUB
There seems to be a characteristic miners' pub to be found particularly in the colliery villages of South Yorkshire and County Durham. Such seem to be very large houses with numerous rooms, including a big music or concert room. The bars are long and noisily filled. The main drink is beer which is consumed in large quantities. These pubs provide important social centres particularly for such hobbies as gardening, pigeons and whippets. Most of these establishments seem to have been built in the earlier part of the present century and are now often in direct competition with the flourishing clubs. Names do not necessarily indicate the clientele, often being derived from locality but older (and usually smaller) examples may be called *Miners' Arms*. *Colliers' Arms*, Elland, W. Yorks. is a canal-side pub.

COMMERCIAL
The advent of the commercial traveller produced a new clientele for inns. He arrived rather earlier than some might think for when *George*, Southwark was rebuilt after disastrous fire of 1676 its attics were fitted out inexpensively to accommodate commercial travellers (then persons of inferior social status) by providing rooms in the attics separated only by thin wooden partitions and entered by simply constructed, but lockable, doors. Later inns were to specialise in this traffic and many still bear the legend 'Family and Commercial'. They were extremely popular at the turn of C19/20 but the type tended to disappear later because it lacked 'glamour'.

COMMUNICATIONS

Waggon

The development of inns is connected with the extension of settlement on the one hand and the increase of movement on the other. The first inns were provided on pilgrim routes and on the main lines of communication and they tended to establish themselves at points where there would be delay or concentration of travellers: tops of passes, half-way points, river-crossings, ports and later at toll-houses and railway stations. The inn at *Senton Bridge* in desolate Wasdale was the nucleus of the subsequent village. A *Passage House* often occurs at a canal or river crossing, e.g. Hackney, Devon. *Stepping Stones*, Westhumble, Surrey was on a pilgrim route. The C17 Turnpike Trusts aimed at improving roads and gaining reimbursement through tolls have left their memorial in *Turnpike* and *Tollgate*. Ports have many *Anchors* and other names and there is a *Port Royal* at Exeter. Canals (q.v.) have left their mark, particularly in the *Duke of Bridgewater* and there is a *Big Lock* on the Chester Canal dating from 1772. Stage coaches have left many traces and so have the railways. More sophisticated and up to date is *Early Bird*, Nottingham which carries the name of one of the first communication satellites. Finally we should not forget the numerous examples of *Bridge, Ferry, Ferry Boat*.

COMPETITIONS see also *Barmaid*

The 'fun and games' of inns have long included simple competitions, often associated with prizes or wagers and varying from 'girning' to guessing the number of coins in a bottle on the bar. The first world beer-drinking contest took place in 1968 at Bilton, Humberside – a village which does not possess an inn. It was a badly supported event, producing only eight competitors and the winner drank seventeen pints of bitter in 60 minutes and then collapsed. There was also a 'yard of ale' competition which was won in 14 seconds. The 'fastest pint' award was won in 3.2 seconds.

CONDITIONING

either (a) artificially brewing – filtered and pasteurised before putting into kegs.
(b) naturally in cask.

CONDUCT

Advice and warning about behaviour in inns and taverns was often expressed in verse, e.g.

He that doath upon the table sit
A pot of porter shall for-fe-it.
All you that bring tobacco here
Must pay for pipes as well as beer;
And you that stand before the fire,
I pray sit down by good desire;
That other folks as well as you,
May see the fire and feel it too.
Since man to man is so unjust,
I cannot tell what man to trust;
My liquor's good, 'tis no man's sorrow,
Pay to-day. I'll trust to-morrow.

An inn at Sittingbourne, Kent used to have the following lines glazed and framed above the door:

Call frequently,
Drink moderately,
Pay honourably,
Be good company,
Part friendly,
Go home quietly.

COPPER
Vessel used in brewing where the wort is boiled for 1–2 hours together with carefully selected hops and a proportion of sugar to produce the desired flavour. It halts all enzyme activity and helps to control the strength of the finished beer.

CORNWALL
The St Austell brewery has some 130 tied houses concentrated in south-west of Duchy and produces two draught beers, an unpasteurised keg and an interesting bottled range which includes Prince's Ale, one of the strongest beers brewed.

CORPORATIONS
A characteristic social phenomenon of the Middle Ages which extended to guilds, colleges and companies. They were designed not only to protect the common interest but also to maintain standards, set just price and do works of charity. The (Ale) Brewers Company was incorporated in 1437 while the Beer Brewers Guild was officially formed in 1493. They were united in a single Brewers' Company in 1536. The Mystery of Hostelers came into existence in 1446 and changed its name to the Innholders' Company in 1473.

Full Arms of
Innholders Company

CORRUPTIONS
Some difficult inn names have provoked some very fanciful interpretations, a tendency parodied by G.K. Chesterton in first chapter of his *Flying Inn* e.g. 'The Saracen's Head' from 'The Saracen is ahead' and the 'Green Dragon' from 'The agreeing dragoman'. One suspects that the generally accepted explanation of the *Goat and Compasses* as a corruption of 'The Lord encompasseth us' is of this order. Similarly, *Bag o' Nails* is given as a perversion of 'Bacchanalia' and *Cock and Pye* from 'By God and the Pyx' cf. Chaucerian oath 'by Cockes bones'. *Dog and Bacon*, Horsham, is said to be a version of 'Dorking Beacon' which can be seen sometimes from the inn's windows. *Cuttle*, Rugby is said to be a compound of 'cut' meaning canal and 'well' and *Dumb Flea*, Meldreth, Cambs. from 'Dumfries' while *Merry Mouth* is from Murimuth, a local landowner. *Frightened Horse* is probably a transmogrification of the 'freighted horse' of the packman while *Bleeding Horse* is said to be a misunderstanding of an ancient sign of a horses head with the 'spots' that heraldically depict ermine. *Moses Gate*, Bolton, Lancs. was originally Mossgate meaning a road to a moorland bog. *Mitre*, Tonbridge Kent is said to have originally been Charles the Martyr while the *Rabbits*, Stapleford Tawney, Essex are said to originate in the 'rebates' of joinery. Finally, *Wig and Fidgett* is a corruption of something like 'whicken-fitchet', Old English for 'white polecat'!

Elephant & Castle
(Corruption of
Infanta of Castile?)

COUNTY
As an inn name, it seems to have proliferated in C18–19 and was related to increasing ease of travel and wider social opportunities for the gentry. The name is more usually attached to an hotel rather than to an inn though some of its possessors are not very prepossessing.

COURAGE LTD.
One of the 'Big Six' based in London but with operating breweries at Horseley, Reading, Bristol, Plymouth (2), Tadcaster, Barnsley and Newark. It has a canning plant at Alton, Hants. and controls some 7,000 pubs, hotel groups, wine, spirit and soft drink interests together with cider and a share in Harp larger. The entire enterprise is owned by Imperial Tobacco. Its draughts include Best Bitter, and Director's Bitter; there are kegs and cans and a wide range of bottled beers which include Bulldog Pale Ale, Magnet Old, Barley Wine and Russian Imperial Stout (one of the strongest beers brewed and conditioned in bottle for two years).

COURT HOUSE
Inns were frequently used as local centres for the dispensation of justice and for a variety of court meets including ecclesiastical sessions. Examples include *Speech House*, Forest of Dean; *Tally Ho*, Littlehampton, Devon; *Red Lion*, Kingham, Kent; *Church House*, Torver nr. Coniston Water; *Hundred House*, nr. Great Witley, Heref. & Worcs.; *Coach and Horses*, Buckland Brewer, Devon.

COW see also *Cattle*
A very common pub name and the beast can be *Red, Dun* or *Spotted* as well as *Brown*. There is even a *Blue Cow* at Kesteven, Lincs. The Dun Cow has particular associations ith North-East because the fugitive monks from Lindisfarne, seeking a safe resting-place for their most treasured possession, the body of St Cuthbert, were told to build a permanent shrine for it when they saw a Dun Cow. There is a *Dun Cow* with a very rare stone sign at Bishop Middleham, Durham. There is a rare *Crazy Cow*, many a *Cow and Calf* as well as a *Spotted Calf* and a *Fatted Calf*. *Cow and Snufflers* occurs and there are many heifers, particularly with regional adjectives such as Craven or Wensleydale.

CRIMINALS
Have left many memorials in pub names including *Busby Stoop*, near Thirsk; *Cunnard's Grave*, near Shepton Mallet, Som.; *Jacobs Post, Sixteen String Jack, Twin Foxes*, Stevenage, Herts. In this group we should perhaps include *Corsair*, Birkenhead; *Jack Horner* the notorious non-royal profiteer from the monastic dissolution, *Rake*, Littleborough, Lancs. and the *Poacher's Pocket*, Walderslade, Kent.

CROSS
Since the Cross is the Christian symbol *par excellence*, it might well be expected to occur as or on inn signs. Its origin is usually ecclesiastical or heraldic, sometimes both. Its colour is usually white or red but it can be other colours – blue and golden for instance. On an inn sign it may refer to a former or existing wayside cross dating from the Middle Ages or a market cross but quite frequently it refers to a crossroads. The Maltese Cross became the badge of the Knights Hospitaller (Order of St John of Jerusalem) and some inns with this sign may have originated as hospices of the Order e.g. St John's, Cornwall.

Besides the Cross, things could be crossed: *Cross* or *Crossed Keys* is frequent. It is the symbol of St Peter and indicates a former ecclesiastical connection. There is also *Cross* or *Crossed Hands*, a symbol of unity and friendship which probably originated in C17, and *Cross Pipes*.

CROWN
Over 1,000 houses with this name or sign which is a compliment to the royal house and an assertion of loyalty. In some cases it may be a substitute for Mitre or Tiara. Some inns took this name because they stood on Crown lands which were stolen from the Church at Dissolution of Monasteries or a later period in the Reformation. They thus assert a new situation and a possessive commitment to it e.g. Minchinhampton, Glos. which belonged to French nuns until suppression of alien priories in C14.
Crown & Cushion – the crown is ceremonially carried on a red velvet or silk cushion.
Crown & Mitre – an assertion of loyalty to state and church or to the State Church. A very popular name in early modern times.
Crown & Stirrup – a reference to royally empowered use of 'stirrup' by verderers to measure hunting dogs to ensure that they complied with Forest Laws.
Crown & Old Treaty refers to the attempted treaty between Crown and Parliamentarians in 1645.
Crown can also refer to a coin worth five shillings. Half crowns survived until 1969 – sign at Hereford.

CRUSADES
Created many new inns, particularly under the auspices of the Crusading Orders. Some of these hostels survived as inns after the Reformation e.g. *Angel*, Grantham. Those of the Crusaders who returned had many tales to tell and doubtless many of them concerned a *Saracen's Head*. Variations of this sign include *Turk's Head, Blackmoor*, etc. The *Trip to Jerusalem* gave its name to one of the oldest inns in the country, at Nottingham, and other associated signs include *Crusader*, Garforth and probably *Gentil Knight*, Canterbury and *White Knight*, Crawley.

George and Dragon

CURIOSITIES
i. Of signs:
Bladebone, Buckleberry Common, Berks. named from large prehistoric bone discovered in vicinity.
Bridgewater Squib commemorates explosive celebration of 5th November in town.
Crocodile, Dane Hill, Sussex – not the reptile but 'tongs' used by smugglers to retrieve contraband sunk in shallow water.
Daylight, Kent, Sussex celebrates the passing of the first Daylight Saving Act in 1916.

The curious *Railway*, Penarth

Dog in the Doublet, Crowland, Lincs.
Letter B, Whittlesey, Cambs. Licences for unnamed inns are distinguished by letters of the alphabet. In this case the 'B' never got a name. Sign puns on 'let 'er be'.
Long Arm & Short Arm, Lemsford, Herts. refers to adjoining roads.
Mother Huff Cap, nickname for ale-wide. 'Huff cap' is the froth on ale/beer.

ii. Of inns:
Beer sold by the Pound – there are a number which claim this peculiarity.
Beehive, Grantham has a 'live' sign.
Running Pump, Carnforth, Lancs. has a working pump built into its frontage.
Pack of Cards – resembles a pack of cards.
Dovecot, Billericay resembles one of and bars on different levels continue whimsy with such names as 'Seed Box'.

CUMBRIA
Old Brewery, Caldergate, Carlisle was taken over by State in 1916 and became centre of State Management Scheme with about 170 tied houses in a radius of about 20 miles. Scheme was wound up in 1974 and, in spite of accusations of monopoly, unbiased opinion agreed that it offered better range than brewer's tied houses.

Jennings Brewery, Cockermouth has about 80 tied houses in west of county and more extensive free trade. Produces two draughts, a good keg and range of bottled beers including Export.

Workington Brewery f.1792 has over 100 tied houses in Cumbria and a free trade extending to SW. Scotland. Produces two draughts, a strong keg, and a bottled range including Export and a stout.

Hartleys have been brewing in Ulverston since 1754 and have some 30 houses in N. Lancashire and Lake District as well as supplying clubs and linking with major breweries. Their draught beers include XB and their houses sell draught Guiness, Whitbread bottled and sometimes Tankard.

CYCLISTS
Invention of cycle gave a new impetus to travel, especially among the less wealthy. Small country inns saw in touring cyclists a possible compensation for the loss of coaching trade to railways and provided inexpensive accommodation and meals. By 1937 the Cyclists' Touring Club had 4,000 inns carrying their signs which still survives fixed to the outside wall of some houses (e.g. *Bell*, Bethersden, Kent).

DARTS
The commonest pub game, sometimes called Arrows ('arrers') developing rapidly between the wars, perhaps due to the Leeds decision of 1908 that it was legal in pubs since it was a game of skill and not chance. Unfortunately, its runaway success has not only ousted many older and localised games but also variants of darts itself (Yorkshire Board, Five Board, Lancashire Board, Log End) are disappearing as the games becomes national, international and even a TV spectacular.

DATING
The date of a pub's building (or reconstruction) may be marked on the structure. Common locations are over the doorway (often on lintel), on the façade, or on gable end. Less obvious indications are in the form of the coat of arms if the house is named *The . . . Arms*. In large or elaborate buildings architectural detail will give a rough date if we remember that styles took time to travel and pub builders were usually very traditional. Most houses are simple, built by local workmen and designed by local builders, thus it is often difficult, without other evidence, to decide on structural grounds whether a pub is C17, C18 or even C19. Oral 'evidence' is not too reliable and tends to be at least a century too early.

It is important when discussing a pub's date to distinguish between date of present building, its date as licensed premises and the date of the first pub on that particular site.

DECORATION see also *Bric-à-Brac, Collections, Fitting*
C19 was heyday of pub architecture and saw a great deal of sculptural decoration including three dimensional representation of the pub name. The bar with its panelled front, containing arches and elaborate back-fitting (q.v.) provided great opportunities for the pub joiner or cabinet-maker. Light fittings and mirrors are also important decorative features (see Glass) and opportunities were also provided by the china handles of the beer engines and the china barrels to contain spirits. Unfortunately much of this portable material has now vanished into private collections.

The Tons, Barnstaple, Devon

DEER see also *Buck*
The medieval delight in 'the running of the deer' has left its mark in pub names including *Deer Leap, Red Deer*.

DEROGATORY see also *Corruption, Humorous*
Besides the contempt of familiarity, there is also affectionate derogation and this is found in local names for inns whose official name is more respectable. *Black Swan* generally becomes 'Mucky Duck' and an inn in Gloucester changed its official name to '*Dirty Duck*'; *Red Lion* can become 'Scarlet Cat'. This process can be assisted by incompetent sign writing or imperfect sign painting so that *Swan and Sugar Loaf* becomes 'Duck & Acid Drop', *Tiger and Rose* Becomes 'Cat and Cabbage'.

DESCRIPTIVE
Many pub names are simply descriptive of the building and/or its appurtenances. So we get *Big Kitchen, Big Window, Chimney Corner, Thatched House*, etc. If the notion is extended we get *Pin Cushion*, Wyberton, Lincs. *Lumbertubs* from refuse carts using adjoining fields as a dump and *Stone & Faggot* for an C18 alehouse attached to a bakery which used stones heated by faggots. *Farmhouse* unexpectedly occurs in Landown Road, Bath. Other 'houses' include *Stone House, Garden House,* rare *Spotted House*, while Pontefract has *Beastfair Vaults*.

DICKENS
Charles Dickens has become, in the last century, a sort of secular patron saint of English pubs which are avid in their search for relics or associations. The connection is not without good grounds.

There are certainly 50 and perhaps nearer 100 inns mentioned by Dickens or used by him as literary background and there are not a few which claim to have accommodated him while actually writing. Unfortunately, too many have succumbed to time, destruction and improvement. Examples are indicated in the Gazetteer, here we will merely mention *Great White Horse*, Ipswich, *David Copperfield*, Rochester.

DISSOLUTION OF MONASTERIES (1536–1540)
The destruction of the religious houses took with it not only their inns and hospices but also their breweries which had been the biggest in the country. Some managed to continue their business under different auspices and in a different building. The centrality of Burton in brewing was established by the Benedictine abbey f.1004 making appropriate use of the excellent water and Joules brewery in Stone, founded by monks in the twelfth century, survived right up to 1974 when it was killed off by Henry VIII's spiritual descendant, Bass Charrington. (Boston, op. cit. p. 27).

DISTILLERS COMPANY
Founded in reign of Charles I in 1638 with the main purpose (apart from profit) of regulating material and methods of distilling in the interests of public health. Its privileges were withdrawn in early C18 to encourage home distilling as an attack on French Brandy (which had produced smuggling and decline of corn sales). This move produced the disastrous era of cheap gin, satirised by Hogarth and provoking the beginnings of the Temperance Movement.

Arms of Distillers Company

DISTILLING see also *Spirits*
A method by which spiritous liquor can be produced from almost any vegetable raw material. Its chief instrument is

the still which raises alcoholic content by evaporation. Unfortunately, a variety of highly dangerous alcohols can arise from this process and the royal physicians of Charles I and his queen drew the King's attention to the fact resulting in the formation of the Distillers Company (see above).

DIVISIONS
Generally speaking, the provision of drinks to the public is and has been confined to the ground floor of public houses except in the case of some larger establishments. Until last decade of C19 the tendency was to increase the number of divisions or 'bars' in the drinking area, so that in a large city put there could be as many as 15 compartments some of which were aptly described as 'boxes'. From 1860s this process reversed so that bars gradually became larger and fewer until the 1950s when the drinking area had become a single room with a central bar.

DOGS see also *Animals*
Have long been a factor in English life and were a valuable export in Roman times so it is no surprise that they feature in pub signs and names. As a group, hounds are naturally popular: *Badger Hounds, Foxhounds, Greyhound* as well as *Horse & Hound*. The most common breed is *Talbot*, a hunting dog, popular in Middle Ages and later with packmen, now defunct. It was also heraldic and was used as badge by Earls of Shrewsbury. *Talbot*, Hartlebury got a very favourable mention in 1784. Other 'breeds' include *Dog Tray, Basset House, Brighton Suff, Chocolate Poodle, Claro Beagle, Jack Russell, Pointer. Bulldog*, Oxford refers to university policeman.

Talbot

Dogs can be *Black, Old* or *Spotted* (Talbot?) and occur in many combinations: with Bacon, Crook, Duck, Fox, Gun, Hedgehog, Pheasant, Pot, Snipe, Partridge. Also occurring: *Shepherd & Dog, Talbot and Falcon, Two Dogs* and there is a *Dog House* at Frilford, Berks.

DOGGEREL see also *Inscriptions*
A good deal of doggerel formerly accompanied inn advertising and was frequently attached to the sign. The following examples may stimulate the explorer to begin his own collection.

John Uff
Sells good ale and that's enough;
A mistake here,
Sells foreign spirits as well as beer.

My name, like my ale, is Good,
Walk in and taste my own home-brewed.
For all that know John Good can tell
That, like my sign, it bears the *Bell*.

To roadsters who enter a welcome he snorts
While they fill up his *quarters* and empty his quarts
(attached to sign of *White Horse*)

The Dick, being lame, rode holding the pummel,
Not having the wit to get hold of the rein;
But the jade did so snort at the sight of a Cromwell
That poor Dick and his kindred turn'd *footman* again.
(attached to sign of *Tumble Down Dick* referring to Richard, Oliver's destined successor and showing popular attitude to 'Protector' as distinct from that of Whig historians)

When this comical stick grew in the wood,
Our ale was fresh and very good;
Step in and taste, O do make haste,
For if you don't, 'twill surely waste.

(attached to sign of *Crooked Billet*)

To Gentlemen and Yeomen good,
Come in and drink with Robin hood.
If Robin Hood be not at home,
Come in and drink with Little John.

(*Robin Hood & Little John*)

Rome not from pole to pole, but step in here.
Where naught excels the shaving but the beer.

(combined barber-shop and ale-house)

His liquor's good, his pot is just,
The landlord's poor and cannot trust;
For he has trusted to his sorrow,
So pay to-day; he'll trust tomorrow.

Long have I travelled far and near
On purpose to find out good beer,
And, at last, I've found it here.

Although the engine's smoke is black,
If you walk in, I've ale like sack.

(early industrial tavern)

Under these trees, in sunny weather,
Just try a cup of ale, however;
And if in tempest or in storm,
A couple then to make you warm;
But when the day is very cold,
Then taste a mug a twelve month old.

(rural inn)

DOMINOES
Probably Chinese in origin and introduced into England by French prisoners of war in C18. There are usually 28 pieces ranging from double blank to double six. In some places the sets may contain more and are numbered to double nine and even higher.

Ideally, dominoes is a quiet game for the old, played in a concentrated silence interrupted only by the swirl of mixing, the slap of a well-played tile or the knock of frustration.

Dominoes

DONKEY
This maligned beast of burden has been recorded in a number of inn names which include *Kicking Donkey*, *Roaring Donkey*, *Romping Donkey* and the inexplicable *Donkey and Bacon*.

DORSET
J.A. Devenish have a brewery at Weymouth (and another at Redruth, Cornwall). Their tied houses number over 400 mainly in Cornwall, Devon and Dorset and there is an extensive free trade. Devenish's produce three draughts (including Wessex PA) two kegs (they also supply Whitbread's Tankard) and an interesting bottled range which includes Wessex Pale Ale and Crabber's Nip.

Eldrith Pope brews in Dorchester and has, besides an extensive free trade, some 200 tied houses in Dorset with outliers in Hants, and Somerset. They make four draught beers (including Special IPA and XXXX), three kegs and a wide bottled range which includes the famous Hardy Ale, allegedly one of the strongest beers in the world.

Hall & Woodhouse of Blandford Forum own some 250 tied houses in Dorset, Hants, and parts of Somerset and Wiltshire. Free trade extends along west of South Coast. They produce three draught beers, three kegs and a range of cans and bottles including Badger XXXX and Stingo Barley Wine.

Palmers of Bridport have 60–70 tied houses, mainly in Bridport. They produce two draughts and a bottled range which includes Tally Ho.

DRAGON

Originally heraldic. The Welsh fought under the banner of the Red Dragon while the Northern English preferred a White. The *Dragon's Head* occurs in inn signs as does *Green Dragon, Red Dragon*. I know of no White Dragon nor of a Black Dragon though the latter figured in the arms of Edward IV and other prominent persons.

Green Dragon, Dronfield, Derbys

DRAMA

see also *Literary, Theatre*

Since early drama was often staged in inn-yards (q.v.) it is no surprise to find inn names with dramatic associations which include many *Shakespeares*, an *Encore* ('Same again') at Stratford and commemorations of authors and actors: *Garrick, Talma, Gilbert & Sullivan* while *Paul Pry* is the proverbial figure who originated as the hero of John Poole's comedy of 1825.

DRINKS, ANCIENT AND MODERN

The names and ingredients of drinks could be an area of exploration in itself but even the most general and introductory guide to inns and their associations can hardly pass without mentioning some of our forefathers' favourite tipples and their imaginative names. A variety of beer cups were produced during C18–19 with such names as Clamber-clown, Cock Ale, Hugmatee, Humpty Dumpty, Knock-me-down. Most recipes are lost but we know that Cock Ale was fortified with a boiled and jellied cock to which were added dates, mace, nutmeg and raisins, and that its production involved a second fermentation. Many of these compounds were included among the home-produced offerings of contemporary inns which, in country districts, might also add such domestic products as Elderberry Beer, Cowslip Ale, Blackberry Ale, Apricot Ale and China Ale which was flavoured with China root, coriander seed, etc. One of the most remarkable concoctions was Egg Ale whose basic recipe required 12 gallons of ale, gravy from eight pounds of beef, 12 eggs, a pound of raisins, oranges and spices, two quarts of Malaga sack with sugar added after a three weeks' maturation.

The compound drinks of the upper classes significantly had such names as Bishop, Cardinal, Lawn Sleeves and Pope. Malmsey was a commonly drunk wine as was sack (sherry) and Canary Sack which was probably a fortified wine from Tenerife. Ancient beverages included Bragget, Bragot or Bragawd which was ale-based but with a variety of possible additions which could include cinammon, cloves, galingale, ginger, honey, mace, nutmeg and pepper. Idromellum and metheglin were based on honey. Hippocras was a medicinal drink, flavoured with ambergris, brandy, cloves, ginger, grains of paradis, musk and pepper! Posset was a general name for a mixture or 'cup', sack posset based on sherry was known in C16 and 'posset ale' was a general name for ale compounds with medicinal properties. Hum is mentioned in C16/17 – its obscure ingredients may have included spirits and it was certainly a 'mixed' drink of considerable potency. Flip was popular a century later and consisted of spiced ale with added spirits (gin or rum). Without these it was sometimes known as Egg Hot (since the ale was boiled) and without ale but with spirits it was called Sailor's Flip.

Ale Cups are too numerous to mention individually but they included such drinks as Brown Betty, Tewahdiddle, Copus Cup and Hungerford Park. Among the Cold Cups were Parting Cup and Cold Tankards (such compositions often included borage as does the contemporary Pimms No. 1).

DRINKING-UP TIME

The licensing laws allow a period of ten minutes immediately following the end of a period of permitted hours (q.v.) for the consumption of liquor already ordered. If the liquor was supplied for consumption as ancillary to a meal provided by the premises this time is extended to half an hour.

DRUNK

This human state seems to have tapped a special vein of verbal inventiveness and the compilation of a list of synonyms is an interesting task. It might include: being kicked by the brewer's horse, bevvied, blotto, bottled, flutered, half-cut, high, inebriated, jarred, jugged, kaylied, legless, mortal, paralytic, pickled, pissed, plastered, ponked, sloshed, smashed, steamboats, steaming, squiffy, stewed, stotious, stonkered, stoned, tanked, tiddly, tight, tired and emotional (hangover produces fragility), under the influence, well away, zonked.

Aggressive Tosspot
(from C17 woodcut)

The condition is due to one over the eight, being in liquor, having a few, having enough, getting a few inside, having the drink taken, being full as an egg, having a drop too much and can produce the state of being the worse for liquor or even being blind drunk. Roget's Thesaurus has an interesting collection of euphemisms and synonyms. The situation has always attracted the creative word-maker and there are some splendid C17 and earlier expressions as well as the products of Cockney rhyming slang which include: elephant's trunk, Brahms and Liszt, solo whist and Isle of Wight. 'The ale passion' was a C17 expression for the headache brought on by drinking.

DRUNKENNESS

Was punished under the later Tudors by the 'Drunkward's Cloak' – a public parade clothed in a barrel with top and bottom knocked out and with holes pierced for the offender's arms. Under Stuarts it could be met by six hours in the stocks. Notice that these punishments were only for the lower classes whose offences were public. The upper classes who administered the law could get drunk in private. The real problems which laws against drunkenness have generally ignored in their concern with effect rather than cause have included the state of water, the absence of alternative beverages, competitive drinking, ideas of machismo and social convention and the general condition of life and society.

The Puritans objected to drunkenness on religious grounds and were extremely hostile to alehouses, etc. in spite of the fact that Cromwell's mother was a brewster and that he himself reduced the tax on whisky in Scotland and unwittingly laid the foundations of the port trade which was to flourish in C18–19. The Restoration led to inevitable reaction and people drank heavily 'on principle' and later, in spite of the obviously evil effects of cheap gin, there was a reluctance to interfere with personal freedom and heavy drinking was the rule rather than the exception well into C19.

DUCK

Dog and Duck reminds us of the barbarous sport of duck-baiting in which a pinioned duck was set upon by dogs. On a pleasanter note there is a *Drunken Duck* at Hawkshead, Lancs. and a *Whistling Duck* at Banwell, Somerset. For *Mucky*

Duck see s.v. Derogatory and for *Tommy Ducks* s.v. Corruptions. Perhaps this is the place to mention the whimsical 'Duck or Grouse' notice affixed to the low beams of some improved pubs.

DUKE see *Aristocracy*

EAGLE
In inn signs is usually the heraldic imperial *Spread Eagle*. The *Eagle and Child*, alias 'bairn and babbie' is the badge of the Earls of Derby. There is a *Mountain Eagle* at Queensbury, W. Yorks.

Spread Eagle

ECCLESIASTICAL see also *Religious Houses*
A sign with ecclesiastical reference may indicate that the inn was formerly ecclesiastical property so that *Mitre* could indicate former possession of bishop or mitred abbot. Many names are a reminder of a former religious house in the vicinity e.g. *Abbey* at Byland, Kirkstall and Guisborough (though the latter was actually an Austin priory). *Priory*, Hull recalls the austere Carthusian house brutally suppressed in 1539. *York Minster*, Soho once belonged to diocese of York. *Parson and Clerk*, Streetly, Staffs. recalls an C18 feud between these two servants of the Established church.

Many ancient hostelries originated in church provision for pilgrims and wayfarers, e.g. *George and Pilgrim*, Glastonbury; *Angel*, Grantham; *New Inn*, Gloucester; *Red Lion*, Colchester; predecessor of *Falstaff*, Canterbury; *George*, Norton St Philip, and as we are reminded by *Shaven Crown* at Shipton-under-Wychwood, Glos.

Their parish councils still own *Royal Oak*, Meavey, Devon and *Plough*, Horbling, Lincs.

EIGHTEENTH CENTURY
In some ways the apogee of inn development and of liquor consumption. The former was partly the result of an approximate tripling of population from C17 producing trade boom and increased travelling. Private trading spread from markets to inns whose owners quickly developed facilities to attract customers from the old fashioned markets, e.g. *New Inn*, Exeter. Almost any town with a market established from 1700 or earlier is likely to have a number of inns which were built at this period, e.g. Newcastle under Lyne still possesses *Bull's Head* and *Wine Vaults*. Developments in sleeping and eating accommodation were linked to the expanding coaching trade: the provision of quick meals during the half-hour timed stop, sometimes in a specially reserved and prepared dining room and improved lodging for overnight guests. Bedrooms of this period often had their own four-poster and mahogany furniture including a mirror, a washing-table and a wig-stand. Rooms were still named rather than numbered and were identified as Moon, Star, Crescent, Paragon, etc.

C18 Inn Kitchen Servant

Inns themselves were a source of wealth and produced a series of grand establishments of which *Dukes Head*, King's Lynn is one of the earliest examples. About 1700 the magnificent baroque façade was added to the inn of 1685. Other examples are the splendid *Red Lion*, Blandford (c.1732), the *George*, Northampton which, according to Defoe, cost more than £2,000 and 'looked more like a palace than an inn', and *Bull*, Stamford which a contemporary said 'would pass in England for a palace'. A modern historian (P. Borsay) remarks: 'The city potentates of the Italian Renaissance were to find their parallel among the great urban inn-keepers' (History, Feb. 1982, p. 4).

The period also saw a climax of heavy drinking: beer and spirits among the lower, and wine, particularly port, among the upper classes. Between 1710 and 1750 the duty on beer (unlike spirits) remained constant at 5s. a barrel and brewers, aided by the scientific spirit of the time, improved their beer in taste, appearance and strength to meet the competition from spirits. It is the period of porter and of customers mixing the three basic beers to produce 'three threads'. It is also the period of gin (q.v.). Among the upper classes a moderate drinker consumed two bottles of port during and after dinner and was known as a 'two bottle man' but there were also three and four bottle and even six bottle men.

ELECTRIC PUMPS
The pump is rarely visible but its presence is indicated by a counter mounting containing a glass cylinder or sphere which holds half a pint and refills after each half pint is dispensed. Some of these systems include special taps which can control the amount of head (q.v.) in accordance with local preference.

ELEPHANT
Pub signs include *Elephant's Head, Elephant's Nest* (Tavistock, Devon) and *Elephant and Hind* (Dover, Kent). The commonest occurrence is in form *Elephant and Castle* said to be related to the fact that this was the crest of the Cutler's Company. Another explanation offered is that it is a corruption of Infanta of Castile but there seem to be older and deeper significations since the elephant and castle occurs in church decoration, particularly in misericords (e.g. St George's Chapel, Windsor (twice); Carlisle Cathedral; Exeter Cathedral; Gloucester Cathedral; Cartmel Priory; St Helens, Garstang; Manchester Cathedral; St Katharine's, Stepney; Beverley Minster; St Mary's, Beverley).

Elephant & Castle
(Infanta of Castile)

ELIZABETHAN INNS
The number of inns at which Queen Elizabeth is alleged to have slept is legendary but there are a number of hostelries surviving from this period. Many of them lie along the main roads from London, particularly on the way to Ipswich but they are often disguised behind later frontages. Some show their age more obviously and perhaps mention should be made of the magnificent *Feathers*, Ludlow; the *Falcon* and *Bear & Billet*, Chester; *Peacock*, Rowsley; *Reindeer*, Banbury; *Rose and Crown*, Sudbury; *Red Lion*, Colchester; *Ostrich*, Colnbrook.

ENTERTAINMENT see also *Games, Theatre*
It is not for nothing that the architecture of a pub door bears a licence strip with the words 'licensed for music, singing and dancing'. This modern permission is hedged about by many legal restrictions and complications but the use belongs to an old tradition. Present-day large pubs in towns are often the home of a variety of entertainment: resident jazz groups are not unknown, pop groups are less rare and discos are comparatively common attached 'amenities'. Some entertainment continues the music hall tradition while some is nearer the American club with strip-tease, drag, go-go and topless barmaids.

Dobbers

Entertainment extends well beyond musical forms. There was an experiment of 'Poetry in Pubs' which did not seem to 'take off' and several pubs provide a 'salon' for the exhibition of local (and other) artists. Pub company to many is entertainment enough, perhaps with traditional games in another room.

'ENTIRE'
A predecessor of porter which, in turn evolved into stout (q.v.). It is said to have been invented in Shoreditch in early C18 and became so popular by C19 that it not only held pride of place east of the City but was obtainable in most parts of England. Its popularity declined through C19 and porter itself vanished in the early part of C20.

ENTRANCE
The entrance to a pub is worthy of some attention. It may be grandiose; up a flight of steps and through a pillared portico, or it may be surreptitious; an almost unnoticeable doorway in a side alley.

There are various architectural and decorative means of drawing attention to the entrance and they are worth exploring:

Entrance

> Emphasis can be given by means of contrasting colour, tone or texture, by projecting canopies or structural hoods or at night by careful application of tones, colours and arrangements of light. One may be reluctant to walk into total gloom, but if at the end of a short tunnel of darkness a gleam of warm-coloured light can be seen, the man who feels that he could do with a pint will find the invitation irresistible. (B. Davis, op. cit. 87).

ESSEX
Halstead has the brewery of Cooks but they have no tied houses and only supply free trade and domestic customers, and retail shops in Ipswich and North-east Essex. Their Best Bitter can be supplied in pins to private customers at a few days' notice. Range of bottled beers include a dryish stout.

Ridley's have a brewery in Chelmsford and over 60 tied houses in the country. Their products include two draught beers, a keg and range of bottled beers including Old Bob and Bishop Ale.

ETIQUETTE see also *Round*
It is customary to give some sort of greeting before ordering one's first drink. If friends or acquaintances have preceded you they may offer to buy this for you. If you try to reverse this process, the correct riposte is 'I'm in the chair'. Having acquired a drink it is deemed churlish to let it reach your lips, however avid, without a murmured toast (q.v.) to the buyer, the barman or the air.

EXCISE DUTY see also *Smuggling, Tax*
When excise duty was imposed on beer in 1849, it was set at 7s. 9d. a standard barrel. The current duty on a bottle of whisky is in the neighbourhood of £5 a bottle.

FACILITIES
The good pub has always offered more than drink. In C18 a market town inn could offer improved stabling, storage and warehousing, news rooms with local and London papers, sale-rooms, banking facilities, common rooms, post office amenities, etc. A contemporary list might include live and/or recorded music, pub games, children's room, garden, car park, accommodation, room for meetings or functions, meals and/or snacks.

Early Facilities

FALCONRY
Many inn names are derived from this medieval sport of which the commonest is *Bird in Hand*. *Falcon*, Micklegate, York, has a carved eagle on an upper floor as well as the one on the sign.

FAMILY ARMS see also *County*
e.g. Anglesea, Ashlea, Ashburton, Berkeley, Bottomley, Clarendon, Clifton, Devonshire, Dundas, etc. These arms usually belong to the local landowner or former landlord and owner of the inn (see *Manorial Inn*). Such signs can offer a fine opportunity for heraldic painting. Many of these names are not original and were changed in C18/19 to give more apparent status to houses with traditional and common names. Shortly afterwards a democratic reaction led to an outburst of naming inns in terms of Trade Arms, e.g. Bakers' Arms, Carpenters' Arms, Chandlers' Arms, etc. (see *Trade Signs*).

FEATHERS
As a name must arise from bad sign painting! It is really a debased version of the 'fleur de lys', the lilies of France which have been used as a badge by the king's eldest son, the Prince of Wales, since C14. It occurs in forms of *Plume of Feathers, Prince of Wales' Feathers* as well as *Feathers* simply but I have not come across its occurrence as *Lily*.

FEUDAL SIGNS
When a medieval nobleman was in residence, his banner or shield of arms was displayed on the building. This practice also applied when he stayed overnight at the inn and this temporary patronage was sometimes perpetuated in the inn sign. Such displays also indicated loyalties and/or spheres of influence. Besides formal armorial bearings the aristocracy also made use of badges or cognizances which were often borne by their followers.
Red Lion is associated with John of Gaunt, Earl of Lancaster; *White Lion* with Edward IV; *White Hart* with Richard II, while *White Swan* was badge of Edward of Lancaster, slain at Tewkesbury (1471). There is also the *Bear and Ragged Staff* of Warwick, the *Star* of Oxford, the *Lion* of Norfolk, the *Sun* of York. The Welsh had a banner with *Red Dragon*, while the Anglo-Saxons preferred a *White Dragon*. Earlier the Saxons seem to have fought under the *White Horse* which later was adopted as a badge by the Hanoverians. The *Spread Eagle* originated with Charlemagne and was brought to England in C19 to commemorate an Austrian princeling.

Red Lion, Broadclyst, Devon

FIFTEENTH CENTURY
A city tavern of this period is described as 'a many-gabled building with numerous rooms, furnished with stools and benches and decorated with rich carving' while a contemporary country tavern is pictured thus: 'The proportions are diminutive, the timber almost extravagent in its scantling, the fireplace in the tap-room seems large enough to accommodate a crowd, while the woodwork of the high-backed settles, no less than the surface of the roughly plastered walls, indicate a finish by contact, unnoticed and unintentional.' (cited B. Davis, op. cit. p. 8).

FIRST AND LAST
A popular name for a pub on the fringe of a town which makes it the first on approach and the last on leaving (cf. *World's End*).

FISH
A popular inn sign and name, not only because of its association with the sport of angling but because of its earlier significance as a symbol of Christ and the use of *Three Fishes* as a symbol of the Holy Trinity. On misericords (e.g. Exeter Cathedral) a fish represents the Christian soul while a whale is

Fish

associated with the Resurrection. Specific fish occur as the eel-like *Lamprey* much esteemed as a medieval delicacy. There is a *Silver Oyster* at Colchester and a *Butt & Oyster* at Pin Mill, Suffolk. *Whale* (if we count it as a fish) occurs, as does *Shrimp*, Morcambe and there is a *Turtle*, Sandwich and a *Flying Fish*, Denton, Sussex. *Fisherman's Rest* is not uncommon and so is *Anglers* but *Fisherman's Hut* is rare – one in Leeds near site of former fish market.

FITTINGS

The interior decoration has always been an important sales factor in commercial public houses. Flamboyant, luxurious or curious fittings to attract customers appear along with the increasing hold of large breweries or spirit merchants. An architectural encyclopedia of 1833 commented:

> We may observe here that the fitting up of public-house bars in London forms almost a distinct trade and the expense insurred in this way by the owners of public houses is almost incredible, everyone vying with his neighbour in convenient arrangement, general display, rich carving, brass work, finely veined mahogany, and ornamental painting. The carving of one ornament alone . . . cost £100. Three public houses, or rather gin-shops, have lately been fitted up . . . at an expense, for the bar alone, of upwards of £2,000 each.

It was the Victorian era which saw interior decoration of the public house definitely and deliberately moving away from the model of the private house and the characteristic fittings of the newly flamboyant pub were mirrors, coloured glass, massive brasswork, flashy furniture in leather or plush (usually buttoned), encaustic tiles, bulbous ornate lamps, heavy wrought-iron grilles and screens.

The aim seems to have been to produce a flashy effect, combining glitter and opulence, especially manifested in the use and treatment of glass which was gilded, enamelled, embossed and cut.

FLEECE see also *Wool*

Source of national wealth in the Middle Ages, hence the Chancellor's Woolsack. The monasteries invented large-scale sheep farming and profited hugely from their industry and enterprise. The sign of *Fleece* is naturally common in sheep and woollen areas, particularly Yorkshire and the Cotswolds. *Golden Fleece* as well as symbolising the value of wool was the badge of a knightly order founded in 1430 by the Duke of Burgundy.

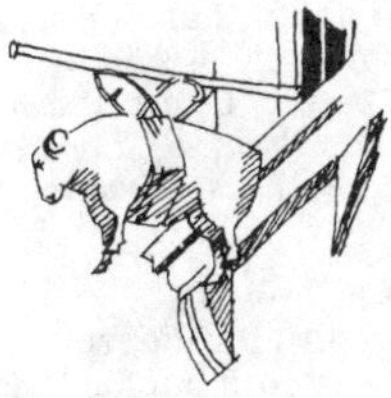

Fleece

FLOOR SURFACES

An underestimated source of pub character and atmosphere. There is an increasing tendency for floors to be covered in linoleum, plastic material or industrial carpeting. Older establishments may have the benefit of York stone flags which will ensure at least as long as the building above them. Rarer floor materials include Staffordshire bricks while red quarry tiles are quite popular in country pubs. Unfortunately concrete is not unknown. Edwardians were fond of coloured tiles on the floor as elsewhere and mosaics are sometimes found. Timber floors seem to be fast disappearing, at least from sight. Rubber had a vogue in 1930s and was followed by vinyl.

Rose & Crown

FLOWERS see also *Hand*

It is perhaps surprising that a country with such a love of gardening has so infrequently used flowers as inn signs. There is, of course, the *Rose*, red for Lancashire and white for Yorkshire.

Rose & Crown is said to symbolise the end of the Wars of the Roses by a Welsh crown which united both roses. In which case the rose should be the Tudor Rose. *Rose & Portcullis* was a Tudor badge, *Rose of Denmark* commemorates wife of our first Scottish king. *Rose Revived* celebrates the Restoration of 1660 after the Puritan years of the Commonwealth.

There is a rare *Woodbine* in Epping Forest and a *Pot of Flowers* at Stowmarket, Suffolk.

FOLK CUSTOM AND LORE see also *Gods, Mythology*
The public house's close involvement in all aspects of local life and thought has left a wide range of signs concerned with traditional ideas, local legend and folk custom. There is the *Cuckoo Bush*, Gotham, Notts.; *Hurlers*, Haworth, Yorks. and *Cheese Rollers*, Shurdington, Glos. The *Hobby Horse* turns up along with the *Morris Dancers* and the popular *Maypole*. Rarer is *Whiffler*, Norwich, an active participant in May Day revels, Morris dances and traditional processions. The more recent *Pearly Queen* has her memorial and so has *Tom Thumb*, the dwarf hero of a nursery tale popular since C16. See also *Green Man*.

FOOD see also *Cheese*
Not unnaturally, food frequently occurs in inn names and it has been suggested that its use as a sign was an indication to dine as well as sup. There is a *Round of Beef*, Cradley Heath, W. Mid., *Haunch of Venison* is not infrequent nor *Shoulder of Mutton* which is dubiously explained as indicating that the inn-keeper was also a butcher. There is also the unique *Shoulder of Mutton & Cucumbers* which gained fame from the delicate cucumber sauce that accompanied its mutton. *Sirloin*, Hoghton, Lancs. is near the house where the famous 'knighting' is said to have happened. Vegetables include *Bunch of Carrots* and *Round of Grass*, the 30 shoots which comprise a bundle of asparagus. There is *Plum Pudding, Land of Cakes* (referring to Burns's poem *Peregrinations*) and finally *Twist* (bread roll) *& Cheese*.

Pub Food
(from C18 woodcut)

FOOT-RAIL
Support for the feet, either in the form of a step or a rail. Sometimes the foot-rail is of cast iron but the best material is, as often, the traditional one – a gleaming brass tube supported at a carefully calculated height which makes a useful and decorative item blending well into any surroundings.

FOUNTAIN
Once a very popular name but now quite rare. It not only had associations with refreshment and the water of life but also with Our Lady. There are also rare bar fittings called beer or spirit fountains which provide an unusual form of dispense now less uncommon in Scotland than England.

FOX
Hundreds of signs refer to this animal with and without Hounds but *'Intrepid Fox'* commemorates Charles James Fox (1749–1806), politician. There is a *Snooty Fox* at Tetbury, Glos., and *Fox's Brush*, Grantham, Lincs. Apart from *Fox & Hounds*, combinations include *Fox & Burrow, Fox & Cubs, Fox & Duck, Fox & Elm, Fox & Goose, Fox & Grapes, Fox & Pheasant, Fox & Rabbit* with the variant *Fox & Coney*. *The Fox*, near Munden, Herts. was altered to *Fox with his teeth drawn* when the pub lost its seven-day licence.

The popularity of this name is not only an indication of the place of the fox in rural life, including its hunting but has other ingredients of a moral nature including Aesop's Fables and the medieval Reynard saga and animal satires which is also reflected in ecclesiastical carving including misericords (e.g. Christchurch Priory, Hants.; St Michael's, Mere, Wilts.; Chichester Cathedral (with goose) cf. Ely Cathedral; Chester Cathedral (with duck); St Mary's, Faversham (with grapes), etc.).

FREE HOUSE

Licensed house which is not owned by a brewery and whose landlord is therefore completely free to serve beers (and other liquor) of its own choice and from any legitimate source. Such establishments normally display prominently the words 'Free House' and are generally recommended because usually they offer a better and wider choice to the drinker.

FURNITURE

Traditional pub furniture is handsome, strong and 'domestic' in the sense that it parallels the sort of furniture found in contemporary private accommodation. The oldest survival is the settle (q.v.) with which may be associated benches, stools, tables and chairs (particularly variants of what used to be called 'Grandfather's chair'). Such items are usually simple but attractive in design and made of wood.

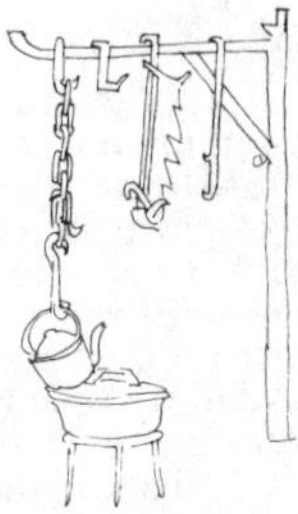

Old Fireplace Furniture

This basic furniture, like most things, became more elaborate in the Victorian period and buttoned plush benches appeared, often divided by screens of greater or less elaboration. They were also fond of cast iron and used it in the structure of pubs as well as in its furnishing and decoration. A particularly characteristic item was the Britannia table (q.v.) and a rectangular table with iron legs and stretchers called the Lion table. Some of their tops were marble. They introduced into the Saloon or Smoke Room a padded bench similar to that with which they equipped station waiting-rooms. An Edwardian variation of this was the cunningly carved 'tram bench' largely made of moulded plywood and pierced with decorative holes.

The public bar would remain basic and probably retain the 'kitchen table', a reminder of the origins of this room. All the above articles would be strong, workmanlike, durable, apposite to their purpose and each as Davis, op. cit. remarks 'with a perfection of its own'. Clocks began to be prominent and outside the public bar were often elaborate ornaments decorating the mantelshelf of a fireplace that was itself ornate.

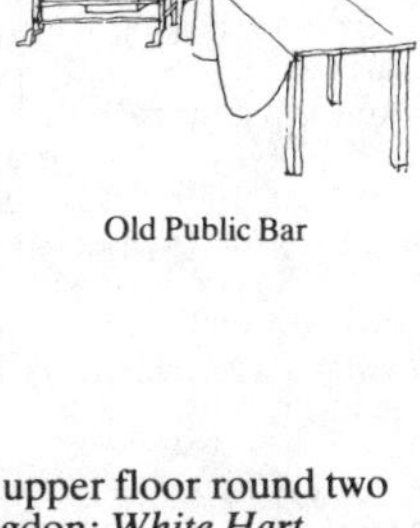

Old Public Bar

Subsequent developments may be categorised either as gimmickry or bourgeoise-domestic and show an increasing emphasis on soft furnishings which, in the licenced area, are often the choice of the tenant and paid for by him.

GALLERIES

Most ancient inns of any size once had open galleries on the upper floor round two or three sides of the interior courtyard (e.g. *George*, Huntingdon; *White Hart*, Chipping Norton). These galleries, as in other medieval buildings, provided an access passage to the rooms giving on to them. Increasing demand for comfort led to these galleries being later enclosed together with the stair that led to them from the ground. A surprising number of inn galleries survive in this modified form and are readily identifiable to the explorer.

GALLOWS (or Beam) SIGNS
Inn signs became increasingly elaborate and extended in C17–18 as inns vied with each other for publicity and custom. The gallows is a beam, often elaborately decorated, which extends from one side of the road to the other and from which the sign was hung. They became such a traffic hazard that they were severely limited by law in 1797 and few survive this and later enactments and demands for improvements. Remaining examples include *Four Swans*, Waltham Cross, Herts., a very fine example which cannot be removed without a special Act of Parliament; *Fox & Hounds*, Barley, Herts.; *Green Man and Black's Head*, Ashbourne, Derbys.; *Magpie*, Stonham, Suffolk; *Old Cock*, Halifax has a short beam which merely crosses a lane; *Olde Starre*, York is dated 1733; *Swan*, Stroud, Glos.

GAMES see also *Sports*
Pub games seem to be as old as pubs. These extended from such barbarous activities as bull-baiting, cock-fighting and duck-baiting to the gentler activities of bowling and the aristocratic sport of falconry (q.v.). Pubs provided, in or near the premises, pits not only for cock-fighting but also for ratting competitions which became very popular in C19. Many inns have been connected with the origin and development of a variety of games and sports. Billiards and Snooker were once very much pub games but they have been partly replaced by Pool, an American importation, which requires less room and is self-financing. The smaller and different Bar Billiards also survives together with rarer games such as Devil among the Tailors, Nine Man's Morris, Toad in the Hole and Ringing the Bull (or Stag). Card games include Euchre and Cribbage (the only card game allowed by the Gaming Act (1968) to be played in pubs for small stakes).

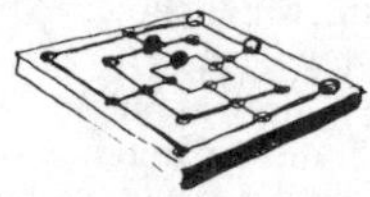

Nine Men's Morris
(ancient pub game)

Cock Fight

Skittles and Bowls (q.v.) still survive but under pressure as do bat and trap, knur and spell, conkers, marbles, quoits and tiddly-winks. Recent introductions vary from beer-mat flipping through table football and pin-tables to electronic video-games. Petanque or Boules has also been seen in the occasional pub car-park. There are also such madnesses as Spoof and dwile-flunking on which see Boston, op. cit. p. 157.

Ringing the Bull
(ancient pub game)

The present classic and dominant pub games are darts, dominoes and shove ha'penny (q.v.). On pub games in general, the curious may wish to consult: A.R. Taylor's *Pleasure at the Pub* (1976).

Skittles

Games have left some mark on signs and names but they are probably not responsible for *Chequers* (q.v.). There is however a *Pack of Cards*, and *Noughts and Crosses* and it is possible that both *Broad Face* and *Merry Mouth* are derived from 'girning'.

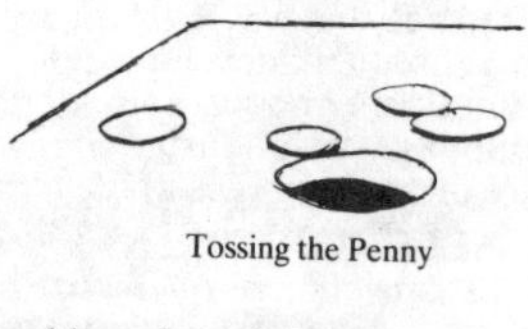

Tossing the Penny

GARDEN
Most old inns had large kitchen gardens where they could produce their own vegetables, etc. and traces of these can often be discerned behind the inn-yard. Pehaps the English climate or the commercial demands of drink-merchandising have not allowed the full potentiality of modern pub gardens to develop but there are some notable and pleasant examples. Rare London examples include *Three Tuns*, Fetter Lane; *Pine*, Chelsea; *Lamb*, Gray's Inn Road.

GATE
Inn with this name often marks the site of a Toll Gate on a Turnpike. Besides the simple *Gate*, there can be *White Gate, Crooked Gate, Gate hangs well* and the self-closing *Clap Gate*. This sign is often accompanied by an inscription (q.v.) e.g. *Gate*, Dewsbury has:

This gate hangs high and hinders none.
Refresh yourself and travel on.

GENERALS
The English have honoured a surprising number of generals in pub names. They include *Buller*, a V.C. who distinguished himself in Boer War, *Haig* who was C.-in-C. during World War I, *Allenby* another World War I general, *Elliot*, defender of Gibralter (1779–83), *Grant* who became USA president, *Havelock* of Indian Mutiny fame, *Rawdon* a Commonwealth leader who helped Restoration, *Tartleton* who distinguished himself during American War of Independence, *Wade* 'pacifier' of Highlands after '45, *Wolfe* who died at capture of Quebec in 1759. The Waterloo campaign produced *Blucher* and *Von Alten* and even *Napoleon* though inns with this name are usually balanced by a neighbour called *Wellington*.

GEOGRAPHY
Pubs are regularly geographical 'markers'. Sometimes they were the first building in a locality and gave their name to the township that subsequently gathered round them e.g. *Indian Queen*, Fraddon, Cornwall; *Holmbush*, nr. St Austell. The explorer may care to collect pubs that are indicated by name on standard maps.

Licensed houses seem to vie for a geographical distinction such as the most southerly e.g. *Polbream Hotel*, Lizard or most westerly e.g. *Land's End Hotel* (mainland) otherwise *Star Castle*, St Mary's, Scilly Isles. There are lots of claims to be the lowest pub geographically and many in Cornwall are just above the high-water mark e.g. *Mermaid*, Porth; *Rashleigh*, Polkerris; *Tolcarn*, Newlyn; *Porpoise*, Porthtowan. For highest see separate entry.

GEORGE
One of the most popular pub names, originating in Middle Ages as an abbreviation for St George and the Dragon. St George, about whom little is known for certain, was adopted as the patron saint of England as a result of the Crusades (q.v.) and his cult is associated with the foundation of the prestigious knightly Order of the Garter in 1344. Later the name may refer to one of the intruded German kings from Hanover.

George & Dragon, Exeter

GHOSTS
There is a *Phantom Coach*, Coventry, but on this subject see s.v. Hauntings.

GIANTS
Besides legendary giants some pub names commemorate historical persons of great stature e.g. *Childe of Hale* (John Middleton b.1578); *Daniel Lambert*, Leicester (b.1770 and died 1809 at *Waggon & Horses*, Huntingdon). The Cornish giant, Antony Payne, was born at *Tree*, Stratton in 1610.

GIN
Gin, an abbreviation of Genever from the city where it was first made, began to be imported from Holland through the Dutch connection (William of Orange) in later C17. When home-made beer was being taxed to pay for William's oppressive

invasion of Ireland, cheap gin flooded London, causing acute social problems which are partly indicated by the contemporary advertisement: 'Drunk for 1d, dead drunk for 2d, straw free'. At the peak of this situation, Hogarth engraved his famous Gin Lane with its companion Beer Street, showing the misery produced by the spirit in contrast to the robust contentment of the traditional beer-drinker.

Legislation was at first ineffective but by latter part of century the consumption of spirit had been reduced to a quarter of its peak at over eight million gallons a year!

There was new surge of gin consumption when in 1825 the duty on spirits was reduced from 11s. 8¼d. a gallon to 7s. and consumption doubled.

This is the era of the Gin-Palace (q.v.) and the time when gin earned its deserved soubriquet of 'Mother's Ruin' though, in fact, it ruined entire families.

GIN PALACES

Gin Palaces originated in the 1830s in an attempt to attract back the working-class spirit trade which the distillers had lost as a result of Wellington's Beer Act of 1830. The buildings themselves were designed to attract trade through their flamboyant style and luxurious furnishings.

With the passage of time and some modification to their function, surviving examples of this genre have become interesting specimens of interior decor and milestones in pub history. R. Boston e.g. commends Harringay for its surviving gin-palaces and singles out for admiration *Beaconsfield, Queens* and *Salisbury*. Other London examples include *Red Lion*, off St James Square; *Bunch of Grapes*, Brompton Road; *Salisbury*, St Martin's Lane; *Viaduct*, Newgate Street; *Princess Louise*, High Holborn. Outside the capital the following are very good examples of the type: *Crown & Kettle,* Oldham Street, Manchester; *Barton Arms*, Aston, Birmingham; *Waterloo*, Smethwick; *Vines*, Lime Street, and *Philharmonic*, Hope Street, Liverpool.

GLASS

Decorative glass is particularly a feature of Victorian and Edwardian pubs and good examples are worth searching for (many in gin-palaces, see above). There are a variety of forms of which the following are the chief: acid-etched: where the pattern is etched with acid on the reverse side; brilliant-cut: where stars, etc. are cut into the glass with a wheel and then polished; enamelled: clear glass coloured by a thin veneer of tinted glass blown on one side only. Also known as 'flashed glass'. Glass can also be embossed, leaded with coloured inserts producing a pattern or picture, and mirrored. The last is the most frequent treatment, often with advertisements superimposed upon the mirror.

Robey Pub Glass

GLASSES

Beer is generally served in pint, or occasionally, in half-pint glasses. In North 'a glass' = ½ pint. These should be officially stamped as containing the legal measure and some have an engraved line a little distance from the top to allow for the head. Drinking glasses with handles are called 'pots'. Large tulip-shaped glasses are called 'schooners', straight-sided glasses are 'tall hats'. In the more genteel pubs, ladies are served their half-pint in a stemmed glass. Similar glasses are used for strong beers and often for bottled beers. Occasionally pint pots survive but they are technically illegal. Service from pewter mugs is now extremely rare but there are pubs, usually in rural areas, where regulars provide and retain their own. Pewter

Pint Glass

mugs with glass bottoms were allegedly in demand by criminals, such as highwaymen, so that they could not be taken by surprise when up-ending their drink.

GLOBE
Tends to be C18–19 name for an inn which enjoyed or hoped to enjoy cosmopolitan patronage. In this sense 'globe' is equivalent to 'world'.

Globe, Theatre Street, Warwick

GLOUCESTERSHIRE
Stow-on-the-Wold contains Arkell's brewery, a small concern with only 17 tied houses in the surrounding countryside. It produces three good draught beers including SBA. These are also provided in bottle. It also has the small family brewery of Donningtons where ancillary power for some processes is still derived from a water-mill.

GOAT & COMPASSES
This name is normally explained as a corruption of 'The Lord encompasseth us', a Puritan motto during the Commonwealth period. It is certain that no inn would be given this name but a deliberate corruption by enemies of the Puritans is a possibility though there is no supportive evidence. *Goat in Boots* also occurs and as this animal is generally associated with the devil, corruption is a possibility. It has recently been pointed out that a Wine Coopers' Company in C17 Cologne bore arms impaling compasses, axe and dray with goats as supporters. England had a long and flourishing trade involving the import of Rhenish wine and there may be a connection here.

GODS
Quite a number of pubs bear the name of Graeco-Roman gods e.g. *Apollo, Mars, Neptune*. This seems likely to have been a C18 or later fashion. Surprisingly, Bacchus very rarely appears explicitly though *Bag o'Nails* is allegedly a corruption of Bacchanals and he is the 'boy' in *Boy & Barrel*.

GOOSE
Generally only seems to occur as prey in the association *Fox and Goose*, though there is a *Gaping Goose*, Garforth, W. Yorks.

GRAVITY   see also *Strong Ale*
Common British beers are of a markedly lower gravity than many elsewhere in Europe. The strongest regular draught beer has a gravity of 1,054.5 and 5.7 per cent alcohol by volume but the average brew is a mere 1,036 and 3.5 per cent alcohol. Since this is average, others must be less, including many local lagers.

Though there is no necessary connection between gravity and strength, a rough general guide for normally fermented beers may be obtained by ignoring the first two and placing the decimal point between the last two figures, thus OG 1,037 becomes 3.7 or an alcoholic strength of 3.7 per cent by volume.

Gravity after fermentation will clearly be different from OG and a strong ale may end up with a lower gravity than another ale though its OG was higher.

GREATER MANCHESTER
At Manchester is Boddington's brewery with 280 tied houses, mainly in Lancashire but with outliers in neighbouring counties and free trade. It produces three draught beers and a selection of bottled including Strong Ale. There is also Hydes with

about 50 tied houses, mainly in city but extending to North Wales and with considerable free trade. It makes three draughts, two kegs and a bottled range including two strong ales and a stout. Holt's is in Cheetham with some 80 tied houses mainly in suburbs. It produces two draughts and a range of bottled including Six X. At nearby Middleton Junction is Lees with some 200 tied houses and club trade. It produces three draught beers (including an above average bitter), three kegs and bottled range including Export (only sold in Wales) and Strong Ale.

There is also the Oldham Brewery, with about 100 tied houses mainly in town and its neighbourhood, and free trade, producing two draughts, three keg and bottled beers which include Old Tom.

GREEN MAN

Green Man or *Jack i'the Green*, a popular medieval image representing the spirit of fertility, the rejuvenating power of nature. He was also a character in May Day revels, frequently depicted in church carving – capitals and misericords. On inn signs this figure may be depicted inaccurately as a forester, verderer or even as Robin Hood.

Green Man

GREYHOUND

Said to have originated in a Tudor badge worn by King's Messengers until late C18 but iconographically it is much older than this and a greyhound with every rib showing, gnawing a bone, occurs on a misericord in Christchurch priory, Hants. This early image may refer to the sport of coursing and one suspects that this is the origin of its use as inn sign.

GUINNESS see also *Temperature*

Guinness is *the* bitter stout. This success must be largely attributed to brilliant advertising which began with Dickens's illustrator Phiz and has since included such famous names as H.M. Bateman and Rex Whistler. Guinness Extra Stout is probably available in every British pub: an unpasturised beer, conditioned in the bottle and with a gravity of between 1,042 and 1,045 being brewed towards the heavier end of this range in winter.

Draught Guiness is a slightly different brew, very creamy and with a gravity of about 1,040. It is pasteurised for the British market and dispensed by the company's own restrained pressure system. All Guinness is made from roasted malts, together with some roasted, unmalted barley which provides the dark colour and full body which accompanies the characteristic well-hopped taste. The froth (q.v.) is an important element and the total drink has received the support of the medical profession.

HALFWAY HOUSE

Inns with this name are usually found on the main lines of communication between two towns. They are, in fact, about half way and they obviously invite the traveller to pause and rest having reached this stage.

HAND

As an inn sign hand never appears simply but in such forms as *Bird in Hand* (hawking), *Four in Hand* (coaching), *Cross Hands, Friend at Hand* (Friendly Societies?), *Hand & Heart* and *Hand & Flower* for which I know no satisfying explanation. There is *Hand & Racquet*, Whitcombe Street, London W1 and *Hand & Shear*, Cloth Fair, London.

HAMPSHIRE
At Portsmouth is Gale's brewery with nearly 90 tied houses, some of them serving country wines. Also free trade. Products: five draught beers including HSB and XXXXX, a keg (perhaps above average) and a good bottled range which includes Prize Old Ale.

HARE & HOUNDS
A popular sign with a number of variations derived from the country sport of hare coursing. There is a *Bell and Hare, Hare & Greyhound* and even a *Hare's Nest*.

HARK TO . . .
Some hounds had a distinctive cry and their recognisable baying could be a useful directive in the hunting field. This is a popular inn name in North Country and each commemorates a famous local hound though locals may give an imaginative variant explanation. *Hark to Bounty*, Slaidburn; *Hark to Mopsey*, Normanton; *Hark to Rover*, Kirkstall.

HART & HIND see also *Buck, Deer*
A reminder that the country was mainly forest until modern times and that from the Norman Conquest, deer hunting was the preferred royal sport and savagely protected by law. Among the related names are *Golden Hart, Hart's Head, Hart's Horns, Red Hart, White Hart, Bald Hind, Hind's Head.* There is a very rare *Bald-faced Stag* at Buckhirst Hill, Essex.

White Hart, Henfield, Sussex

HAUNTINGS
There is a tendency among the romantic to expect a tale of haunting to be attached to an old building and some inns are very old buildings. A recent book by M. Alexander: *Haunted Inns* (1973) tells stories attached to *Royal Castle*, Barmouth; *Garrick's Head*, Bath; *Crown*, Bildeston; *Swan*, Brentwood; *Holman Clavel*, Blagdon; *Lord Crewe Arms*, Blanchland; *King's Head*, Craft Green, Kent; *Chough's Head*, Chard; *Black Horse*, Cirencester; *White Hart*, Caldmore Green; *Caxton Gibbet*, Caxton; *Ostrich*, Colnbrook; *Wheatshead*, Daventry; *Headless Woman*, Dudden; *Fleece*, Elland; *Royal Oak*, East Lavant; *Hop Bag*, Farnham; *Angel*, Guildford; *St Anne's Castle*, Great Leighs; *Little Abbey*, Great Missenden; *King & Queen*, Highworth; *Ferryboat*, Holywell; *Spaniards*, Hampstead; *Plough*, Holford; *Old Ferry*, Horning; *Langstone Arms*, Kingham; *Duke's Head*, King's Lynn; *Bull*, Long Melford; *Grenadier*, London; *King's Arms*, London; *Angel*, Lyme Regis; *Royal Oak*, Langstone; *Acton Arms*, Morville; *Grotto*, Marsden; *Ship*, Mousehole; *Trip to Jerusalem*, Nottingham; *Talbot*, Oundle; *Black Horse*, Pluckley; *Feathers*, Pocklington; *Dolphin*, Penzance; *Crown*, Poole; *Crown*, Pishill; *Blue Posts*, Portsmouth; *King's Arms*, Rotherfield; *Wellington*, Riding Mill, (Saltergate); *Falcon*, Saltergate; *Three Mariners*, Scarborough; *Bell*, Stilton; *Old Silent*, Stanbury; *Sun*, Saxilby; *Lion*, St Ives; *Bird Cage*, Thame; *George*, Wallingford; *George & Dragon*, West Wycombe; *Red Lion*, Wingham; *Rear*, Woodstock; *Old Inn*, Widecombe; *Weston Manor*, Weston-on-the Green; *Eclipse*, Winchester.

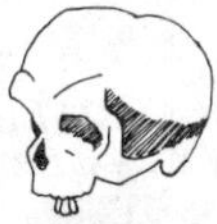
Skull

One suspects that some of these stories are 'scraping the barrel' and that having a ghost is a useful commercial gimmick yet the above list even is not complete and enquiries limited in time and space can add *Busby Stoop*, near Thirsk; *Green Tree*, Hatfield Woodhouse; *Manor House*, West Bromwich; *Cock and Bottle*, York while in another pub in the same city Roman soldiers march through its cellars. West Yorkshire houses claiming a ghost include *Royal*, Armley, Leeds; *Wyke Non-political Club*, Bradford; *Sutton*, near Cleckheaton; *Fleece*, Elland; *Sun*, Haworth; *Blue Bell*, Soyland; *Royal Low Moor*, Bradford. Across the Pennines, alleged hauntings include *Smallwater Jack's*, Burnley; *New Inn*, Foulridge; *Bridge*, Hapton; *Black Bull*, Huncoat; *Shakespeare*, Manchester; *Ring o' Bells*, Middleton; *Radcliffe Arms*, Oldham; *Rake*, near Rochdale; *Railway*, Waterfoot.

HAWKING see also *Falconry*
A popular sport among the gentry in the Middle Ages with a strict hierarchy relating type of bird to social rank. *Hawk & Hound* is perhaps the most frequent name and *Hawk & Buckle* – the boucle was the swivel to which a hawk was attached while being 'weathered'.

HEADS
On inn signs and in pub names seem to be of three main types:

King's Head,
Wellesbourne, Warks.

i. Mark of loyalty or affection as in *King's Head, Duke's Head*, etc. There is the particular case of the disappearance of *Pope's Head* after the Reformation, possibly also *Cardinal's Head*. In this category comes *Queen's Head* which may depict consort rather than sovereign. There is the special case of *King Charles' Head*, removed by the Parliamentarians, and its relation to the incompatability between pubs and Commonwealth.
ii. Trophies, particularly of the chase. These would include *Boar's Head, Hind's Head* and perhaps *Saracen's Head* (sometimes, by derivation, such 'heads' become heraldic and appear on signs in this secondary form).
iii. A small group of 'fashionable' heads, e.g. *Blackamoor's Heads* may be related to C18 fashion of black servants though this too might belong to the 'trophy' category.

HEALTH DRINKING see also *Etiquette*
This was certainly the custom at Roman 'commissationes' and at Saxon 'wassails' (q.v.) and the Christian Danes are recorded as toasting the dead, Christ, and St Michael the Archangel. A C17 observer of the English records that 'to drink at table without drinking to the health of someone in especial would be considered drinking on the sly, and an act of incivility'. Up to C18 this benevolent drinking involved sharing the same tankard, pot, etc. Present-day decadence has reduced the custom, except at formal banquets, to brief and single exchanges between pairs or groups and loner's salutation to the landlord with perhaps the offer of 'Have one on me'.

HERALDRY

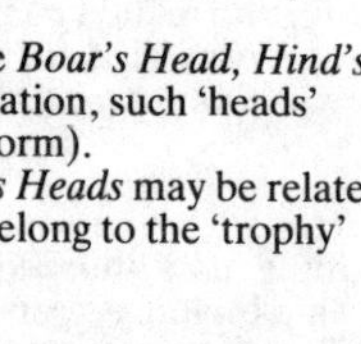
Original Arms
of Brewers Society
Quartering Arms
of St Thomas
(removed at Reformation)

Perhaps the most frequent single source of inn signs and names. Besides shields of arms, it includes badges such as *White Rose, Pelham Buckle, Stafford Knot, Three Legs of Man*. The surcoat bearing heraldic devices gave its name to the inn at which the Canterbury pilgrims congregated and there is still a *Tabard* in Hereford. Besides shield, crest and badge, inn signs have also made use of supporters e.g. *Griffin* and particularly the *Lion* and *Unicorn* (supporters of England and Scotland respectively) and their combination in *Lion & Unicorn* commemorates the Act of Union between the two kingdoms. It should be noted, however, that these beasts singly have other connotations and their use as signs may be derived from religious symbolism. Inns bearing the same '. . . Arms' offer a great opportunity for sign painters and explorers should cherish such examples as *Stansfield Arms*, Rawdon, W. Yorks.

HERO see also *Military, Sailors, Soldiers*
English heroes, whether national, folk, or mythical, have received their tribute in inn signs and names. *Hero, tout court*, seems to refer to Nelson who as *Nelson, Lord Nelson*, has had hundreds of inns named after him. This frequency may reflect not only national homage but the personal homage of discharged sailors investing their prize money in a pub. *Hero of Aliwal* is Sir Harry Smith, a campaigner on Peninsular War, etc. while *Hero of Switzerland* refers to the mythical William Tell. *Mafeking Hero* is Baden Powell who defended town against Boers (1900) and later formed Boy Scouts. A number of VCs are also commemorated in inn names e.g. Leefe Robinson who shot down the first Zeppelin in 1916.

HERTFORDSHIRE
Rayments of Buntingford is a small country brewery which both produces independently and supplies beers to Greene King. It has some 30 tied houses in the area with substantial free trade. Its three draught beers include BBA biter and there are kegs and a range of bottles. Rayment houses also stock Greene King bottled beers.

Greene King, Biggleswade, Beds.

McMullens of Hertford have about 200 tied houses within about 30 miles radius of county town with an extensive free trade extending to London and Watford. They produce three draught beers (one of which is available in plastic containers for home consumption), a keg, and a range of bottled including Olde Time Ale.

HIDING PLACES see also *Smugglers*
Secret concealment in inns for both persons and things seem to have developed from C16 to C19. Some hidy-holes were for priests seeking to avoid death at the hands of the Anglican authorities, some were to hide less worthy refugees from the clutches of the law; thieves, murderers, highwaymen, smugglers, etc. Besides secreting persons, inns also provided ingenious secret storage for contraband spirits, tobacco, silks, spices, etc. Many of these date from C18 and some survive. A priest's hole is claimed at *Whateley*, Banbury while *Blackboys*, Uckfield is said to have one secret chamber off the well shaft in the kitchen and another in the roof so well concealed that it hasn't yet been discovered!

HIGHEST
The highest pub in England is *Tan Hill* at 1,732 ft i.e. *c*.533 m above sea level between Reith and Brough. It is 3½ miles from a telephone and five miles from the nearest village. Other loftily sited inns include *Cat & Fiddle*, nr. Buxton at 1,690 ft or about 520 m; *Traveller's Rest* on summit of Kirkstone Pass, is at 1,500 ft or *c*.462 m; *Warren* on Dartmoor at 1,450 ft or *c*.446 m. Yorkshire has more inns (40+) above 1,000 ft than any other county and her second highest is *Withens* at 1,390 ft, *c*.428 m above Wainstalls, Halifax.

HIGHWAYMEN see also *People, Criminals*
Were the scourge of the coaching era and have many associations with inns. *Highwayman*, Skelmersdale New Town, Lancashire commemorates one John Lyon who planned his robberies at the nearby *Legs of Man* which allegedly possessed a secret passage. The last highwayman to be hanged in England was executed at Lancaster in 1815. *Dick Turpin* is remembered at East Finchley, London and is said to have frequented *Ram Jam*, Stretham, Cambs. and *Turpin's Cave*, Epping, Essex. He is said to have been born at *Crown*, Hampstead, Essex and was captured at *Green Dragon*, Welton, Humb. A pub has recently been given his name at Woodthorpe, nr. York. John Nevison, alias 'Swift Nick', made much use of *Three*

Houses, nr. Wakefield. It was he, and not Turpin, who made the desperate ride to York to establish an alibi. Nevison was arrested at *Three Houses* and hanged at York in 1680s.

HISTORIC INNS
Inns in general are so embedded in social history that it is somewhat invidious to single out any one but the following short list includes some of the most famous: *Star*, Alfriston; *New Inn*, Gloucester; *George & Pilgrim*, Glastonbury; *Angel & Royal*, Grantham; *Ostrich*, Colnbrook; *George*, Stamford; *Bat & Ball*, Hambledon; *Great White Horse*, Ipswich; *Royal George*, Knutsford; *Prospect of Whitby, Town of Ramsgate*, Wapping; *Lion*, Shrewsbury; *Pheasant*, Winterslow; *George & Dragon*, Yarm; *King's Head*, Monmouth; *Queen's Arms*, Charmouth; *Mermaid*, Rye; *Sun*, Hitchin.

HISTORY
Much national history is encapsulated in inns and their names, from the mists of legend to modern times, from Dark-Age kings to modern times when e.g. *Escape*, Mapledon Place, London honours the hundreds of servicemen who escaped from PoW camps during World War II. Names commemorate battles and campaigns, political and military leaders, social reforms and constitutional changes. Humbler folk history tends to be unrecorded in books and an inn may remind us of its obscurity by an enigmatic sign or a chance discovery during alterations such as the two skeletons unearthed in the *White Horse*, Chilham. (There was an earlier similar discovery during excavation of a tavern associated with the Roman fort at Housesteads). Other elements may survive in a legend or folk-tale such as that attached to *Hobbs Boat*, Lympsham, Somerset.

It was at the (demolished) *Bear* in Cambridge that Cromwell first plotted rebellion against his king; at *Angel*, Grantham, Richard III signed the death-warrant of Buckingham; Louis Philippe of France began his exile at *Bridge*, Newhaven and, in a minor vein, Elizabeth I is said to have boxed a page boy's ears at *King's Head*, Chigwell.

HOLE IN THE WALL
The origin of this name is obscure but it may be because the house or its predecessor was in or near a delapidation in an old town wall or had been inserted in the thickness of such a fortification. More fanciful is a dubious connection with Ezekiel viii, 7–10. Some pubs broke a hole in their own wall to make a hatch for quick service or to obviate the need for passers-by stopping. This seems to have been quite common in pubs on canal banks.

HOME BREWED
For over a millenium brewing at home was normal whether for consumption within a large household such as an abbey and its dependents or a great secular house. Brewing for sale also took place where the beer was sold and the distinction between brewer and ale-house keeper did not become marked until C15. By mid C16, wholesale brewing had become an established industry, a development which was probably accelerated by the destruction of the monastic brewhouses and the dispersal of their staff and the spread of the Protestant ethic which encouraged work and discouraged reception of charity.

HOME BREW HOUSES
Capitalistic mergers and closures, the encouragement of mass production with associated profits and the abolition of competition had, by 1973, reduced the number of licensed houses selling beer made on the premises to a minute remnant of five: *All*

Home Brewhouse Vat

Nations, Madeley, Salop.; *Blue Anchor*, Helston, Cornwall; *Old Swan*, Netherton, Staffs. whose products were also available at *White Swan*, Dudley; *Three Tuns*, Bishops Castle, Salop. and *Traquair House*, Inverleithen (though this house is in Scotland it has developed a number of outlets including *Cock & Rabbit*, Lee, Bucks.).

It is good to record that those brave five seem to represent an all-time low and the practice is returning, doubtless not unconnected with the activities of CAMRA (q.v.) whose 1980 guide adds *Fighting Cocks*, Corby Glen, Lincs.; *Fox & Hounds*, Stottesdon, Salop.; *Goose Eye*, Laycock, nr. Keighley; *Norfolk House*, Bristol; *Miners' Arms*, Priddy, Somerset; *New Fermor Arms*, Rufford, Lancs.; *Old House at Home*, Chidham, Sussex; *John Thompson Inn*, Ingleby, Derbyshire.

HORN

In inn signs, may derive from heraldry, from the hunting horn or the coach horn but rarely from the orchestral instrument. *Horns*, Nursling, Hants., gained its name from the warning sounds given by heavy drays which changed their horses at the inn after the ascent of the hill on which it stands.

Horn

HORSE see also *Dray, Racehorse*

A wide variety of horses have given their names to inns including the *Hobby Horse* of the morris dancers and its variant the *Wooden Horse*. The origin of name *Flying Horse* (e.g. Nottingham, Pontefract) is obscure. It has been connected with Pegasus, with a carousel and also with a kind of hobby horse mounted on a swing from which its rider tried to detach a ring from a quintain. There was a *Sea Horse* in York until it was renamed *Shire Horse* in honour of Sam Smith's reintroduction of dray-horses. *Suffolk Punch* and *Yorkshire Grey* also occur. *Pack Horse* is frequent along old packways and *Sumter Horse* was an earlier name for a baggage or pack-horse, while the *Pit Pony* is not forgotten. Horses occur in many conditions: Bleeding, Frightened, Rampant, Rocking, Running and Trotting and in many colours including Red and even Blue but it is surprising that *Brown Horse* is rare. There are said to be only four in the country e.g. Coley, nr. Halifax. Even rarer is *Aratan* (? Arabian) *Horse*, Aberford, Yorks. Racehorses (q.v.) frequently occur under their individual names. Horses occur in many combinations: the expected *Horse & Groom, Horse & Jockey, Horse & Hounds, Horse & Farrier, Horse & Trumpet* and the unexpected *Horse & Tiger* (Rotherham, Yorks.). *Horse & Chains* reminds us of the additional horses with spiked shoes which were linked to heavy waggons to give extra power uphill. *Horse & Crook* may be misleading as the latter word is the wooden pannier fitted to side of pack-horses. *Swingle Tree* is the crossbar to which draught horses are attached. *Nag's Head* is very common (see s.v. Humour) and even more frequent is *White Horse* (q.v.) as is *Bay Horse*. *Cleveland Bay*, (Redcar) was a Yorkshire horse bred for light carriage work.

Black Horse

HORSE RACING see also *Racehorse*

The 'sport of kings' has left its mark on pubs and not only in names such as *Winning Post, Gimcrack, Chase, St Leger Tavern*, Doncaster. *Red Lion* in same town has a plaque in dining-room commemorating the institution there of the St Leger Stakes in 1778.

HOST HOUSE

Old (C16/17) name for an inn.

HUMBERSIDE
Hull Brewery is now owned by Northern Foods. It has 200 tied houses largely concentrated in city and extensive free trade. It makes three draughts, two kegs, canned and bottles range including Double Anchor.

HUMOUR
Plays its part in pub signs and names usually in the form of weak puns as in *Cats* portrayed as 'good lickers', Woodham Walter, Essex. Both *Silent Woman* and *Honest Lawyer* are usually depicted without heads. *Labour in Vain* generally shows a black boy being scrubbed. There is evidence of male chauvinism not only in *Silent Woman, Quiet Woman* and *Headless Woman* but in *Nag's Head* as a muzzled woman and *Shrew Beshrewed* in a ducking stool. Some are a little more subtle as *Snig's* (eel's) *Foot*, Ormskirk and *Jolly Taxpayer*, Copnor, Hants. *Bull & Horns* nr. Gravesend has a bull in a china shop on its sign and there is a *Bull in Spectacles* near Lichfield. *Old House at Home* shows a very comfortable pig in its sty with which can be compared the sign of *Wild Boar*, Congleton. Many continue the medieval tradition of a 'rebus' or pictorial pun: *Howlett Hall*, East Denton, Northumberland has an owlet while *Monkseaton Arms*, Whitley Bay has a monk sitting on cannon balls; *Wych Way*, Brockhurst, Hants., has three witches; *Oystermouth*, Swansea, has a caricatured oyster with a big mouth; *Double Barrel* associates shot-gun and two beer barrels; *Maiden Over*, nr. Newbury shows a girl leaping over cricket stumps while *Copper*, Tower Bridge Road, London SE1 plays with a policeman and a washing boiler.

Nag, Little Bollington, Cheshire

There are many punning names of the kind: *Listen Inn, Same Yet, Nogg Inn*, and *Poppe Inn* of which no more needs to be said.

A similar sort of humour can afflict the interior of some pubs with notices such as 'Duck or Grouse', whimsical names for bars, or more commonly for the male and female lavatories. There can be faintly amusing placards behind the bar about the landlord's character, requests for credit (a very old complaint), and others about drinking often with vaguely sexual allusions and there may be displays of 'Old Rules of Inn', etc.

HUNTING
Country inns have been and often still are closely associated with country pursuits, especially hunting. There are many reminders of this in inn names: fox-hunting (see Fox), hare-coursing (see Hare and Hounds), badger hunting and stag hunting e.g. *Stag Hunters*, Brendon, Somerset; *Stag Hunt*, Ponsanooth, Cornwall; *Stag & Huntsman*, Hambledon, Hants., *Pride of the Forest*, Bristol. Particular hunts or packs are occasionally commemorated and there is the simple *Dog & Gun*.

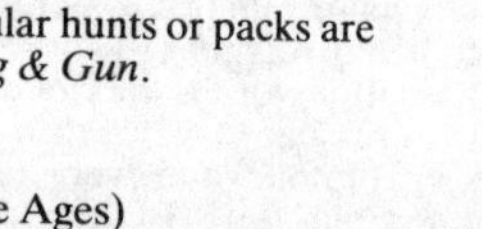

Hunter's Lodge, Axminster, Devon

IDENTIFICATION
The stages by which a pub was 'marked' seem to be:
1. A common sign – stake, bush or wreath (early Middle Ages)
2. Name of the house derived from particular sign (later Middle Ages to C18)
3. Name of landlord (C18–19)
4. Name of brewer (late C19 to C20)

The comparative prominence of these elements is interesting and in modern times it tends to be the name of the brewery to which the pub is tied which is featured while the landlord's name has been reduced to a small notice affixed to the door lintel. (Contrast this with landlords who have given their name to the pub, e.g. *Dick Hudson's*.) This change also represents development from a service provided by a house and a host to a commercial transaction via a retail outlet where sales depend more on extrinsic advertising than intrinsic quality.

ILLEGALITIES
Hush Shop – house which sold spirits illicitly.
Jigger – an illegal distillery.
Kiddley-wink – West country term for illicit alehouse.
Shebeen – Scottish/Irish term for house where beer or spirits were illicitly sold, brewed or distilled.

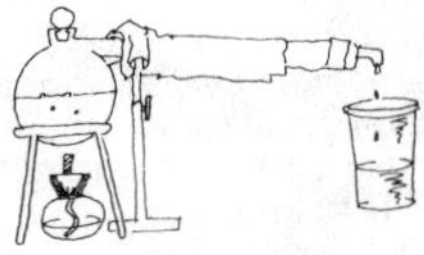
Small Still

IMPROVED PUBLIC HOUSES
A quasi-technical term related to the movement beginning after World War I to improve the public house's image in the minds of the general public. The movement often lacked feeling for tradition or aesthetic sense and a brewery's own description of the meaning of an Improved Public House went as follows:

> . . . the pulling down and large-scale reconstruction of antiquated houses; the building of new houses on more ambitious lines, with larger rooms and lounges in place of narrow and congested bars. It meant the re-equipment of public houses with modern furniture and schemes of decoration, and the introduction of the most up-to-date methods of lighting and ventilation. It meant the addition of assembly halls, games rooms, and children's rooms. The new local was altogether a larger, cleaner and brighter establishment with good architecture without and good decorative taste within. (cited B. Davis: op. cit. p. 11).

Some of the most disastrous effects of this 'improvement' policy are identified in *Inside the Pub* by M. Gorham and H.McG. Dunnett (Architectural Press 1950) and this work had some influence in improving subsequent design.

INBUILT PUB
Architectural term for a licensed house which is part of or integral with some larger building such as an office block.

INDEPENDENT BREWERIES see also *Home Brewed*
Traditional breweries which have not been absorbed by the 'Big Six' (q.v.) include: Boddington of Manchester, Darley of Doncaster, Border of Wrexham, Brakespear of Henley, Fullers of London, Lorimer of Edinburgh, MacLay of Aloa, North Country of Hull, Ruddle of Oakham, Sam Smith of Tadcaster, Shepherd Neame of Faversham, Theakston of Masham, Timothy Taylor of Keighley, Thwaites of Blackburn, Ward of Sheffield, Young of London. For a full list see final section of CAMRA's *Good Beer Guide*.

INN
Originally meant a chamber or set of chambers as in 'inns of court' but soon narrowed to lodging and board for wayfaring men and acquired this definition in common law: 'A place instituted for passengers and wayfaring men', 'a house where a traveller is furnished with everything he has occasion for, while on his way', 'a house, the owner of which holds out that he will receive all travellers who are willing to pay a price adequate to the sort of accommodation required, and who come in a situation in which they are fit to be received'.

C18 Highland Inn

The first recorded inns in this country were built by the Romans at the side of its first real roads which they also had constructed. When the Romans left and their roads decayed at least some of their inns seem to have survived as Dark-Age kings made laws for their better ordering.

Travelling on ecclesiastical or devotional business brought more wayfarers and so, from the beginning of England, the Church was much involved with inns. After the Reformation, with the almost total destruction of church provision, it seems that the out-houses of the landed nobility (who had often acquired church property) became inns and when they abandoned their town houses to settle on their great estates they often left behind a steward to entertain guests. Sometimes a purpose-built building was erected and the steward supplanted by an inn-keeper. The manor sign or coat of arms of the landlord often became attached to the new inn.

Inns have many alternative names which do not necessarily affect their legal status but may indicate a change of emphasis. They include host house, hotel, tavern, public house, victualling house, road house, coffee house, coaching house.

INN KEEPERS

Shield of Arms Innholders Company

In Middle Ages they were usually called hostellers and distinguished from harbergeors. The latter were wealthy citizens whose houses were large enough to accommodate paying guests and were usually required to be freemen of the city in which they offered lodging. The inn-keepers' responsibilities were greater and as long ago as the reign of the Confessor it had been enacted that if a man remained for a third night at an inn he became 'a third-night-awn-hinde' i.e. he acquired the legal status of a member of the house's 'familia' and his host, as head of the household was answerable if he committed any offence. The general principle of the inn-keeper's responsibility for his guests continued as he is still responsible, as far as reasonable, for the health and safety of his guests and for the preservation of their persons and possessions.

Traditionally inn-keepers seem to have acquired a kind of corporate 'persona' – the jolly host, bent on the entertainment, well-being and service of his guests. In C18, the traveller Carl Philip Moritz wrote:

> I shall avail myself of this opportunity to observe that the English inn-keepers are in general great ale-drinkers; and for this reason most of them are gross and corpulent: in particular they are plump and rosy in their faces I once heard it said of one of them the extravasated claret in his phiz, might well remind one, as Falstaff says of Bardolf, of hell-fire.

Bank of England, Ancoats, Lancashire, is a testimony to a former landlord who was described as safe as this venerable institution.

INSCRIPTIONS

The buildings themselves and most frequently the signs sometimes carry interesting inscriptions of which the following are examples:

> By Hammer and Hand all arts do stand.
>
> (Former *Hammer & Hand*, Hutton-le-Hole, N. Yorks.)

The former *Chequers* on old drove road above Osmotherley, N. Yorks. had on its sign:

> Be not in haste, Step in and taste. Ale tomorrow for nothing.

while the lost *Lion & Lamb*, Sheffield, had:

> If the Lion showd kill the Lamb,
> We'll kill the Lion if we can:
> But if the Lamb showd kill the Lion,
> We'll kill the Lamb to make a pye on.

The signboard of *Traveller's Rest*, Slaley, Northumberland still bears the following:

> When you go by and thirsty be,
> The fault's on you and not on me;
> Fixed here I stand and hinder none,
> Refresh, pay, and travel on.

The sign of *Mortal Man*, Troutbeck has:

> Thou Mortal Man that liv'st by bread alone,
> What is it that makes thy nose so red?

Noteworthy is the sedate inscription on lintel of upper floor fireplace in C18 extension to C16 *George & Dragon*, Apperley Bridge, W. Yorks.

> Not for the purpose of making a show but for necessary uses, Samuel Hemingway and Mary his wife enlarged this house
> AD 1704. These things are cherishing: victuals, drink, warmth, shelter which if thow possess, remember gratefully to give thanks to God.

Other examples at *Silent Woman*, nr. Dorchester; *Robin Hood & Little John*, Castleton, N. Yorks., *Robin Hood*, Cragg Vale, nr. Hebden Bridge, W. Yorks., *Mother Shipton*, Knaresborough, W. Yorks. Hogarth's *Man with a Load of Mischief*, painted for an old alehouse in Oxford Street, London had an inscribed couplet:

> A monkey, a magpie and a wife,
> Is the true emblem of strife.

INSECTS

Are rare except for *Bee, Beehive* (frequent) and unique *Beeswing*, Kettering, Northants – a reminder of time when honey was only sweetener. There is also a *Scorpion* and a *Cobweb* and Harlow New Town has a plethora of pubs bearing the names of moths and butterflies.

INVENTIONS

Have left interesting commemorations in inn signs and names: *Air Balloon* which may commemorate Montgolfier's first ascent (1783) or the near contemporary air race at Versailles or the use of this invention during the siege of Paris (1871). *Atmospheric Railway* commemorates Brunel's failed experiement in propulsion by air pressure (1836). The *'Impulsoria'* on sign at Yatton, Somerset, was a Heath Robinsonish device to replace locomotive. The first prefabrication is remembered in *Crystal Palace* and *Glass House*, a pit life-saver in *Davey Lamp* and inventors in *Jet & Whittle, John Baird* and *John Snow*. The inventor Marconi stayed at *Old Inn*, Mullion, Cornwall, while erecting his transmitter at Poldhu.

ISLE OF MAN

Has two independent breweries. One is at Castletown with about 40 tied houses which produces draught mild and bitter and a range of bottled beers. It also produces Jubilee Stout for Bass Charrington and distributes Carling lager. Okell's Falcon brewery is at Douglas and has about 80 tied houses on the island. It produces two draught beers and a range of bottles including Falcon No. 1.

The drinker in Man gains two advantages: lower beer duty and the benefit of the island's 1874 Pure Beer Act.

Okells Falcon

ISLE OF WIGHT

Burt's are at Ventnor with about 12 tied houses and flourishing free trade. Their draughts include a best bitter called VPA and there is a bottled range.

JOLLY see *Drunk*
The hard-drinking C18 identified the stages of drunkenness as jocose, bellicose, and comatose: 'Jolly' represents the first and most pleasant stage of this process. The adjective is frequent in inn names and is applied, among others, to Colliers, Cricketers, Fenmen, Fishermen, Millers, Pindars, Sailors and Watermen. When Millers are not Jolly, they seem to be Dusty.

Jolly Sailor
(Belhaven Brewery)

JUBILEE
Pubs with this name were usually named or renamed in honour of Queen Victoria's diamond jubilee (1897) or the fiftieth anniversary of her accession (1887).

JUG & BOTTLE
A common name for the off-licence or out-sales department of a pub. It usually had a small bar or hatch and a separate entrance from the street. The customer brought his own container to carry home draught beer.

Ancient Beer Jug

KEEPING BEER (Cellarage)
Real beer has to stand up to 48 hours in conditions of the right temperature before being tapped. This is to allow the sediment contained in traditional beer time to settle. Once tapped, this beer only keeps for a matter of two or three days. Keg beer (q.v.) is popular because it does not require this care, is easier to tap and produces less waste because of its keeping properties.

KEG
A form of draught beer which has been chilled, filtered, pasteurised, carbonated and put into pressurised containers. The commonest keg beers are Allied's Double Diamond, Bass Charrington's Worthington E, Scottish & Newcastle's Tavern, Watney's Red and Whitbread's Tankard. There seems little to choose between them.

KENT
Faversham has the brewery of Shepheard Neame with some 200 tied houses, largely in East Kent, with an extensive free trade. It produces five draught beers including Old English Stock Ale, two kegs and a range of bottled beers including the (occasional) Christmas Ale.

Six Bells,
Hollingbourne, Kent
(Medieval Inn)

KIDDLEY WINKS
Popular name for West Country beer houses (often those licensed under Wellington's 1830 Act) which sold spirits, often smuggled gin or brandy, on the side to regulars who indicated their complicity by a knowing wink.

KINGS see also *George, Royal Oak*
Inn names commemorate a range of English kings from King Coel (Cl?) to the present century. There are hundreds of *George's* though perhaps most of these refer to the saint rather than to a king, otherwise the most popular choices seem to be Henry VIII, (Elizabeth I), Charles I and Charles II.

Edward I

The Prince Regent, later George IV, is popular e.g. *Prinny's* in his favourite Brighton. *Ethelbert* is rare, *Richard I* appears as *Coeur de Lion* and *King Canute*, Canvey Island is a renaming of *Red Cow* after disastrous floods of 1953. Rarer monarchs include *King of Bohemia, King of Denmark*, commemorating his visit in 1606, and *King of Prussia* (Frederick II) – many of these had their names changed in the xenophobia of 1914–18. *William IV* is popular, often occuring simply as *King William. Edward VII* is named several times and his son *George V* also occurs.

KING'S ARMS
Very popular name. Some may reflect this changed allegiance of the Reformation, replacing signs which might be taken by the King's agents to show 'Popish affinities'. A new sign at Ockley, Surrey shows Nell Gwynne in 'the king's arms'.

KING'S HEAD
Possibly the commonest pub name in England. Before the Reformation many of these were *Pope's Head* until Henry VIII banished the Pope, along with the religious life (see Dissolution), from his empire. The king represented on the sign is most often Henry VIII though Shotley Bridge, Durham has Henry on one side and Charles I on the other.

Kings Head

KITCHEN
The large kitchen belonging to old inns was often separte from the main building and located in courtyard by side of entrance archway. Some of these kitchens survive with remains of the spits used for open-fire roasting. There may also be all or part of the roasting jack, the machine which turned the spit, though sometimes these have been removed as curios to adorn the public rooms.

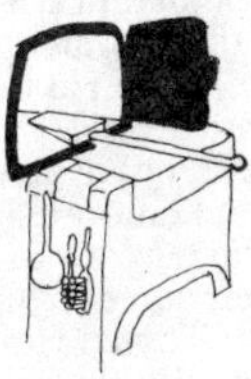

Old Bread Oven

LADIES ONLY see also *Women*
Bars with this restriction seem to have been introduced in the later C19. They provided an opportunity for respectable women to have an alcoholic drink in a public house without any implications of sexual licence. Rooms with this limitation were generally very small and temperance workers thought that these little secluded compartments were one of the causes of an increase in drunkenness among women in the 1890s.

LAGER
From the German word for 'store' since these beers were matured for periods up to a year. The main types of lager are: Pilsner, Dortmund, and Munich. The process was introduced into England when the Wrexham brewery was set up in 1882 (this now brews Skol). Allsops began to brew this light ale at the beginning of C20 and other brewers followed in 1920s and 1930s. Lager has a lower gravity than ordinary beer with an alcohol content of 3 per cent or less by volume. It is cheaper to make and can be sold at a higher price so the brewers win three ways!

LAMB & FLAG
Religious emblem – the Agnus Dei representing Christ's atoning death with the flag of His triumphant resurrection. It was popular with both Templars and Hospitallers who provided many hostels. It was later part of the arms of the House of Braganza and crest of Merchant Taylors.

LANCASHIRE

The county town has Mitchells with nearly 50 tied houses in locality with further club trade. They produce three draughts, two kegs and three bottled beers including City Shield Stout. Yate & Jackson have over 40 tied houses and supply two draught and two bottled beers. Blackburn has two large breweries: Matthew Brown with over 600 tied houses, mainly in Lancashire and Cumberland, selling their two draughts, two kegs and a variety of bottled beer; Thwaites with some 380 houses mainly in NW and wider free trade, who produce three draughts, two kegs and range of bottled beers which include Old Dan Nips.

Burtonwood Brewery, Warrington

LANDLORD

Title most likely derives from the fact that after Dissolution of Monasteries in 1536, the religious hospices which had formed bulk of inn provisions fell into hands of secular landowner or lord of manor and when they disappeared they were often replaced (sometimes on same site) by public houses owned by the landlord.

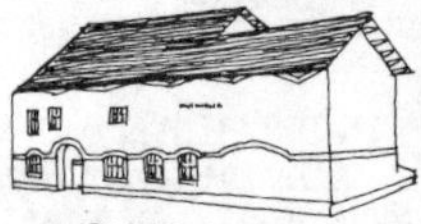

C16/17, Angel, Denton, Manchester

A plaque at *Moorcock*, NW. Yorks. indicated that the Perfect Landlord should possess the 'Dignity of an archbishop, Geniality of George Robey, Hope of a Company Promoter, Smile of a Film Star, Elastic Conscience of an MP, Voice of a sergeant-major and Skin of a Rhinoceros'. A codicil added that if he can say 'Time, Gentlemen, Please!' in a voice that combines Firmness, Regret, Condolence, Hope for the Future, Thankfulness for Past Favours, together with a suggestion that 'This Hurts Me Far More Than It Hurts You', then he will be well on the way to fulfilling the requirements of this office.

Sometimes, a famous host, brewer or brewster, has left a memorial in the name of their former pub e.g. *Mother Redcap, Dick Hudson, Just Peter* (formerly Railway), Holme on Spalding Moor (Yorks, Humbs.) is named for a former landlady nicknamed 'Peter', and above the old Huddersfield-Manchester road on the Pennine moors was *Nont* (Aunt) *Sarah's*. Other former landlords are commemorated in *Hales Bar*, Harrogate; *Lewins*, Halifax; *Whitelocks*, Leeds, and a current one in *'Arold's Free House*, Wakefield. Others, while not bequeathing their name to the house are sometimes remembered in literature or oral tradition, e.g. Samuel House, friend and partisan of James Fox and once landlord of *Intrepid Fox*, Wardour Street, London.

LARGEST

There are a number of claimants for the dubious honour of being the country's largest pub. A front runner appears to be *Downham Tavern*, Bromley, designed 1930 to serve a new housing estate. This monstrosity has two bars, one 45 feet, the other 60 feet long which allegedly allow it to serve over 1,000 customers at a time. It is probably exceeded by *Swan*, Yardley, Birmingham with its eight large bars.

LAYING DOWN

Any real beer benefits from a little 'ageing' and in old accounts we read of bright March beer and mellow old October. Some bottled beer, like Courage's Imperial is actually recommended to be kept a considerable time before opening.

LEGEND see also *Folk Lore, Myth*

A number of inns remind us of old tales: *Lady Godiva, Tom Thumb, Lincoln Imp, Eagle & Child, Robin Hood.* Many apparently inexplicable names may be debris of a lost legend just as many legends have not left a mark. Wiltshire people are known as *Moonrakers* but I know of no inn that commemorates the 'yellow bellies' of Lincolnshire or even the 'tykes' of Yorkshire.

Eagle & Child, Alderley Edge, Cheshire (Medieval Inn)

LEGISLATION see also *Licensee*

1215 Magna Carta laid down that there should be standard measures for wine and ale.

1266/7 Assize of Bread and Ale. From this date the civic authority in each area publicly announced the legal price of bread and ale, based on current prices of corn and malt.

1495 Licensing Statute gave JPs power to supervise and suppress local ale sellers.

1529 Legislation suppressed ecclesiastical brewing, a shadow of coming Reformation.

1552 JPs were given additional powers to license as well as suppress sale of liquor – powers which they have retained to the present day.

1553 Taverns limited to one in every town with the following exceptions: Bristol (6), Cambridge (4), Canterbury (4), Chester (4), Colchester (3), Exeter (4), Gloucester (4), Hereford (3), Hull (4), Ipswich (3), Lincoln (3), London (40), Newcastle on Tyne (4), Norwich (4), Oxford (3), Salisbury (3), Shrewsbury (3), Southampton (3), Westminster (3), Winchester (3), Worcester (3), York (9).

1590 An extra tavern was granted to Brightlingsea, Bristol, Colchester, Coventry, Exeter, Greenwich, Harwich, Hull, Ipswich, Lowestoft, Norwich, Sandwich, Southampton, Worcester.

1729 Brewster Sessions, at which retailers were licensed by JPs, instituted. These continue to function.

1736 Second Gin Act. A further attempt to reduce gin sale and consequent social disorder. Retailers now had to acquire a licence (costing £50) and pay £1 duty on every gallon of gin. Licences were restricted to victuallers. Problems persisted but gradually overcome by variety of other legislation.

1828 Ale House Act consolidated previous legislation and redefined controlling role of JPs.

1830 Beer House Act permitted householder, assessed to Poor Rate, to retail beer from his own house on payment of two guineas. Purpose was to discourage sale of spirits by making beer cheaper and more accessible.

1869 Act undid effects of above by returning all beer-houses to control of JPs.

1872 Legislation reduced permitted hours (q.v.) of opening, increased fines for drunkenness and licensing offences and appointed inspectors from new police force.

1915 Defence of Realm Act (DORA) imposed savage limits on permitted hours in order to increase munition production. Base of present opening times.

Licensing laws, like other legislation, have accelerated by a kind of geometrical progression in modern times and the current edition of Paterson's Licensing Laws, the accepted handbook on the subject, extends to nearly 2,500 pages!

LEICESTERSHIRE

Everards in Leicester is only a distribution centre, its operating brewery is at Burton. The firm has some 130 tied houses concentrated in the city with free trade in the area. It supplies three draught beers, including Tiger, a keg and variety of bottled. Hoskins is unique with one tied house in Market Bosworth but off-licence next to brewery dispenses two draught beers. Also produces kegs and cans and bottled range. Operation concentrated on home sales and local free trade.

G. Ruddle & Co. has its brewery at Langham which has 44 tied houses, largely in a 15-mile radius and a more extended free trade which includes supplying canned beer to Sainsbury's. It is among the few breweries which declares OG on products which include three draughts (counting County and occassional Barley Wine), five container beers with a good keg, and an interesting bottled range.

LICENCE STRIP
Narrow strip, often of metal or plastic, usually affixed to the lintel above main door of licensed premises, giving the name of the licensee and the extent of his licence e.g. Ale and Porter; Beer, Wine and Spirits; on or off premises; with or without Music and/or Dancing. The licensee is usually tenant or manager but he is not necessarily either and may not even be on the premises.

LICENSING
Licensing Sessions have sometimes been described as 'unlicensing sessions'. Licences have to be renewed annually and the assumption is that a regular application will go through unless the licensee has not behaved during the previous year. Some licenses die a natural death, others are refused on grounds of bad conduct.

LICENSING HOURS see *Permitted Hours*

LICENSING LAWS see also *Law*
The Common Law of England does not affect the keeping of inns, taverns, or ale-houses apart from the general requirement that they shall not constitute a nuisance. Statutory control began after the Reformation when Act of 1552 introduced licensing system and brought common ale-houses (tippling houses) under the vigilance of the Justices of the Peace. The ostensible purpose was to suppress the vice of drunkenness (among the lower classes) but there were also political and religious motives.

The system developed with time and was extended by the requirement that the granting of a magistrate's certificate was a necessary precondition for the allocation of an Excise license – the sole authority for selling intoxicating liquor. This control by lay magistrates is substantially complete apart from the rare exceptions provided by Parliamentary privilege, the freedom of the City of London Vintners' Company, the University of Cambridge and canteens belonging to the Army and Navy.

Contemporary legislation is mainly under the Licensing Act of 1953 and the Custom and Excise Act of 1952.

LINCOLNSHIRE
At Skegness is Batemans with about 140 tied houses in the area and some free trade. It produces three good draught beers usually contained in wooden casks and dispensed without pressure. Melbourns of Stamford no longer brews but its 30 or so tied houses frequently dispense Sam Smith's bitter.

Bull, Horncastle, Lincs.

LION
One of the most popular inn signs and has been a heraldic device from early times. It occurs in various colours of which *Red Lion* (q.v.) is most frequent, but there are *Black Lion, Blue Lion, Brown Lion, Golden Lion, Green Lion, Yellow Lion*. There can be more than one: *Three Lions, Five Lions*. The lion rampant is the device of Scotland while the 'Lions of England' are properly leopards. The *Lion & Unicorn* supporters of arms of United Kingdom is commonest combination but there are others e.g. *Lion and Pheasant*.

LITERATURE
There has been a long association between pubs and literature (of whatever quality). They appear in Langland and Chaucer and almost everyone has heard of the *Mermaid* frequented by the great writers of the Jacobean age and most people know that Kit Marlowe was killed in a tavern brawl and 'died swearing'. In *Bartholomew Fair*, Ben Jonson speaks slightingly of the dull wits of his days as

'*Three Cranes, Mitre* and *Mermaid* men'. His own favourite drinking house was the *Devil* into which he was followed for centuries by other great literary men until that house was significantly replaced by a bank in 1788. Pepys and Sam Johnson were great tavern-haunters and many writers have continued their praise of inns.

Inns have been 'characters' or settings in many novels from the many references in Dickens through G.K. Chesterton's *Flying Inn* to Daphne du Maurier's *Jamaica Inn* and Patricia Wentworth's *Catherine Wheel*. Furthermore they have provided congenial places where writers, including Dickens, R.L. Stevenson among others, have found the right conditions for creative work. Alec Waugh worked at *White Horse*, Shenley, Herts. and *Burford Bridge*, Box Hill, Surrey seems to have been particularly inspiring in C19; Keats finished *Endymion* there, R.L. Stevenson wrote parts of *New Arabian Nights* and ealier it had been used by W. Hazlitt, G. Meredith, R.B. Sheridan, R. Southey and W. Wordsworth. Thomas Hardy has the rare distinction of having an excellent but infrequently available bottled ale named after him. In 1930s *Easton Court*, Chagford advertised in 'The Author' and subsequently offered hospitality to a galaxy of successful writers including S.N. Behrman, Louise Brogan, Patrick Leigh Fermor, Pamela Hansford Johnson, C.P. Snow and Evelyn Waugh.

Literary men have also used inn for its prime purpose: E.V. Lucas praised *George*, Stamford and *Royal George*, Knutsford with its *Cranford* associations (it was also a chosen stopping place for Sir Walter Scott). Scott is said to have used *Swan* near Grasmere to compensate for the Wordsworth's exiguous hospitality; Swinburne had a daily glass at *Green Man*, Putney; Thomson wrote *The Seasons* at '*Doves*', Hammersmith and Dickens wrote part of *Dombey and Son* at *Albion*, Broadstairs. Tennyson is said to have found materials for *Idylls of the King* while staying at *Falcon*, Bude, while in a different century Paul Brickhill researched 'Reach for the Sky' at *Lizard*, Cornwall. Joseph Addison is associated with *Talbot*, Lostwithiel while *Webbs*, Liskeard has a more dubious association with Edward Gibbon. Graham Greene's autobiography *A Sort of Life* (1971) recalls with pleasure *Noel Arms, Volunteer* in Chipping, Camden and *Live and Let Live* and the parsnip wine of the landlord at *Seagrave Arms*, Weston sub Edge. It is said that D. Defoe wrote part of Robinson Crusoe at *Old Cock*, Halifax; and at nearby Luddenden *Nelson* has associations with Branwell Brontë. The *Hare & Hounds*, East Morton (W. Yorks.) is mentioned in 'Jane Eyre'. It was once the family home of the Busfields and is now known as *Busfield Arms*. At *Barley Mow*, about two miles from Wimborne on Cranborne road, Evelyn Waugh wrote much of *Decline and Fall* in 1928.

With this background, it is not surprising to find dozens of inn names with literary associations. Authors include *John Bunyan, Byron, Johnson, John Evelyn, Sir Richard Steele, Tim Bobbin* (C18 Lancashire dialect poet). Characters include *Balancing Eel, Billy Bunter, Eliza Doolittle, Heathcliff, Hobbit, Goldfinger, Scarlet Pimpernel, Sherlock Holmes*. Inns named after novels include *Cruel Sea, Barnaby Rudge, Our Mutual Friend, Rob Roy. Land o' Cakes*, Manchester is Burns's name for Scotland and *Twa Dogs* is from his poem with that title. *Wurthering Heights* is on road from Haworth to Top Withens and *Fletcher's Arms*, Angmering, Sussex allegedly commemorates playwright John Fletcher, born at Rye (much more likely that it is derived from craft of arrow-making).

LITERATURE OF INNS

Dickens is the first name that springs to mind but there are others; Chesterton, J. Fothergill *('Inn-Keepers's Diary')*, Linklater *('Poet's Pub')*. The inn is an important character in the development of H.G. Wells's *Mr Polly*; Daphne du Maurier's *Frenchman's Creek* is said to be based on *Ferry Boat*, Helford Passage and *Jamaica Inn* was inspired by the inn at Bolventor. T. Burke's *Winsome Wench* (1938) is the story of a London inn from 1825 to 1900. There is much poetry in praise of inns and alcoholic drinks and Dr Johnson's famous remarks are quoted elsewhere.

LOCAL

Affectionate and somewhat possessive name for one's favourite pub in the neighbourhood. See M.A.C. Gorham's books: *The Local* (1939) and *Back to the Local* (1949). There is a *Local* in Leeds.

Pubs are not only natural centres of local life but their very name may refer to a local sight (see Natural Phenomena) or they may commemorate some village Hamden or a local worthy who has made good on a wider stage. (see also Local Pride)

LOCAL BREWS

Until brewing became very big business and the Big Six obtained a near monopoly in some areas, beer, like architecture, retained a local flavour. John Freeth, the C18 'Birmingham Bard', *c.*1798, sang in praise of 'fam'd Birmingham beer'. In early C19, Edinburgh ale (Mr Younger's) gained high fame as can be seen from William Hone's Year Book, 1839. Conversely, about the same time Chester ale was described as 'not lap for a dog, far less drink for a man' (George Borrow: *Wild Wales*). The same author mentions 'the celebrated Llangollen ale' but finds it excelled by the home brew at *White Lion*, Bala. He also described Allsop's as 'suitable for July and August, but scarcely for the end of October', though at any time it was preferable to porter. In C18 Ashburton, Deveon was famous for its 'pop': 'far richer than the best small beer, more of the champagne taste . . . The pop was but 2d. a bottle. It is a great novel loss to the town; because its recipe died with its brewer about 1785' (William Hone, *Table Book*, 1838). Local brews from small independent breweries still exist and even the mass producers make some attempt to meet local taste.

Mr Younger

LOCAL GUIDES

Many breweries produce pamphlets featuring their tied houses in a particular area and there are a number of publications dealing with a specific locality. 'Better Pubs' of Crediton publish guides to Devon, Dorset, Cornwall, Somerset, Hants, 'Inns of Character' have booklets on each of the old Yorkshire Ridings, etc. For East Anglian Pubs see V. Jones; A. Crawford and R. Thorne have dealt with (mainly C19) Birmingham Pubs. Books about London pubs include: T. Burke, *Will Someone Lead Me to a Pub?* (1936); T.E.B. Clarke, *What's Yours?* (1938); T.M. Richards & J.S. Curl, *City of London Pubs* (1973). There is also Nicholson's *Real Ale Guide to the Waterways*.

LOCAL PRIDE

Is often reflected in a pub name or sign which may celebrate local worthy, (which may not be human), local regiment or just the locality, e.g. *Craven Heifer, Yorkshire Rose, Yorkshire Terrier, Broad Acres, Yorkshireman*.

LOCAL 'SIGHT' see also *Physical Features*

A wide variety of examples which can range from *Cemetery*, usually in close proximity to this amenity, *Crooked Spire*, Chesterfield; *Cow and Calf*, Ilkley from distinctive rocks opposite; *Glover's Needle*, Worcester from spire of St Andrews; *London Stone*, Cannon Street, London; *Nine Saxons* from archaeological discovery; *Piltdown Man* from archaeological hoax; *Temple Bar*, Waltham Cross; *Three Arrows*, Boroughbridge from neighbouring monoliths; *Three Hills*, Bartlow, Cambs., from nearby burial grounds; *Three Willows*, originally landmark, now interpreted as cricket bats (there are many examples of pubs named from distinctive tree); *Millstone*, Hathersage; South Gosport is as likely to refer to local 'grit' as to basic element in grinding mill. Perhaps most charming example is *Love Pool*, Sellack, Herfs.

LOCATION
Some pub names are simple, but not very helpful, indications of their whereabouts, e.g. *Bridge, Hill Top, Pub on the Green, Toll Gate*. More specific locations are more helpful such as *Tan Hill* and some pubs have even given their name to the hamlet which has grown up as a result of their initiative. Simplest form of location is, of course, by prefixing name of town, village, locality or even street to Hotel, Tavern, Inn, Vaults.

LONDON
Has the following independent breweries: Fuller, Smith & Turner at Cheswick with slightly more than 100 tied houses in vicinity and a flourishing club trade. Produces London Pride and ESB among its four draught beers and the bottled range includes Golden Pride and Strong Ale.

Truman claims to have been operating in the East End for over three centuries and now has over 1,000 tied houses including a large group in the Swansea area. Produces four draught beers, a keg lager, cans and other take-home packs, together with bottled range which includes Ben Truman and Barley Wine. Youngs of Wandsworth is one of few breweries which publicly declares OG of its beers which number four draughts including a (seasonal) Winter Warmer, two kegs and a bottle range in which are Strong Export and Old Nick. It has about 140 tied houses, mainly in SW. London and extended free trade. Guinness at Park Royal are unique in relying entirely on free trade for distribution; even *Castle*, Bodiam – the only inn they own – is free apart from stout.

LONDON PUBS
Present a considerable problem for the arranger. There are questions whether to confine examples to City, extend to County or even to the new Greater London Area as well as how to place them in the Gazetteer. Furthermore, though there are a very large number concentrated in a comparatively small area, many of them – to the outsider at least – seem strangely alike in offerings, architecture and clientele. There are many books on the subject including J. Thirkell's *400 Glorious Pubs* (1973) and the follow-up *Top of the Pubs* which are pretty exhaustive and detailed in a way which is impossible in a guide trying to sample the whole country. My own much briefer selection is narrowed to houses which I consider to be of some particular interest.

LONGEST BAR
Claimed by *Heneky*, High Holborn, London which certainly seems to have the longest bar in London. Provincial competitors for this dubious honour might include *Downham Tavern*, Bromley.

LONGEST NAME
Competitors include *Fort St George in England*, Midsummer Common, Cambs., *13th Mounted Cheshire Riflemen*, Stalybridge, Gtr. Man. from which 'Mounted' has recently been deleted and *Ye Olde Tippling Philosopher, Rising Sun Real Ale Bar*, Frampton Cotterell, Glos., is a recent entrant.

LONG ROOM
A Georgian amenity with a number of alternative names: Great Room, Big Room, Assembly Room. It was nearly always on first floor with a window giving access to the porch roof from which distinguished visitors, successful MPs *et al.* could show themselves or address the crowd.

It was used for great social functions: dinners, dances, etc. and usually had a movable partition or folding doors so that it could be divided when convenient. It was normally provided with a pair of matching fireplaces, one at either end and often had an annexe or antechamber leading from it. This room may still exist as a dining-room or lounge or it may have been broken up to provide smaller accommodation (often bedrooms). This adaptation can be discovered by the existence of an over-large fireplace or the fact that bedroom walls are flimsy partitions and sometimes a dado or frieze continues through the new rooms.

LOST NAMES
The following are some pub names recorded in the past but which no longer seem to occur: *Two Pots, Old Pick-my-Ties, Shoe and Slap, Blue Last* (it was at the pub with this name in Shoreditch where porter was first sold), *Ham & Firkin* (formerly in Walmergate, York).

LOST PUBS
The serious inn explorer should be on the look-out for and be able to recognise a building which was once a pub but now serves other uses. Something of the size of the problem and the opportunities for discovery might be exemplified in the small town of Otley, W. Yorks. whose centre has recently and properly become a conservation area. There is the former *Queen's Head* (1774) in Kirkgate, *Green Man* of about same date in same street, *Half Moon* (before 1759) in Beech Hill, *Vaults* (C18) in Market Place, *Royal Oak* (C18 extended C19) in Clapgate, *Carpenters' Arms* (before 1822) later *Wharfedale*, Boroughgate and *White Horse* (1876) later *Royal White Horse*, Manor Square. Notable examples elsewhere include: C 16 (?) *Anchor* with neighbouring malt-house has been incorporated into Leycester's Hospital (ref. 1571), Warwick, *Sun*, Saffron Walden with magnificent C17 pargetting, *Lion*, Dunchurch, Warks. has Gunpowder Plot associations, *Red Lion*, Simonburn, N'land was suppressed by f18 squire.

LOUNGE
Really a hotel facility, contemporary with the arrival of lounges into private houses, presumably to replace the drawing-room.

In the 1930s the name was normally given to the pub's third room – the only one usually carpeted. The carpet justified increased prices in this room and therefore it was in the interests of profit to turn the second room into a lounge too. The name and furnishing were also probably attempts to attract the middle-class customers who may have been used to this appellation in hotels or on ships.

LOWEST see also *Geographical*
The claim to be the lowest inn in England is made by *Bridge*, Wilburton, Cambs. which stands some eight feet above sea-level.

MALT
Is produced by soaking barley in water until it begins to germinate when it is spread out on the floor of the maltings. When the malster judges that germination has proceeded far enough the process is stopped by lightly cooking in a kiln. (There is a *Malt Kiln* e.g. in Bradford). The rootlets are removed and the malt is ready for the next processes which include the conversion of the soluble starch into sugar by mashing and the sugar to carbon dioxide and alcohol by fermentation.

Adam & Eve

MAN
A surprisingly rare element in inn names. There is *Adam (and Eve)*, the common *Green Man* an uncommon *Red Man* (Kidderminster), and the unique (?) *Mortal Man*, Troutbeck. *Wild Man* is the medieval Wodewose also found in ecclesiastical carving. *Wise Man*, West Stafford, Dorset has doggerel (q.v.) attributed to Thomas Hardy:

I trust no Wise Man will Condemn
A Cup of Genuine, now and then.
When you're faint, your spirits low,
Your string relaxed will Bend and Bow,
Brace your Drum-head, make you Tight,
Wind up your Watch and put you 'Right'.
But then acquire, thro' too much Use
Of all Strong Liquors, 'tis the Abuse;
'Tis Liquid makes the Solid loose;
The Texture and whole frame destroys:
HEALTH lies – in the EQUIPOISE!

There was a *Naked Man* in Settle, now a café but sign (dated 1663) survives as does that of *Naked Woman* (dated 1660) at nearby Langcliffe.

MANORIAL INN

The medieval manor house had a tradition of hospitality and regularly provided accommodation for the peers of their owners together with the servants of their guests. The Dissolution of the Monasteries brought much land speculation and frequent increase of wealth among those who had acquired monastic lands. Sometimes the landowner converted his former home (having built a larger residence) or built a new house comparable to his original manor but intended as a profit-making inn from the beginning. *Spread Eagle*, Midhurst is an example of manorial inn and former manor-houses including *Oxenham Arms*, South Zeal; *Lygon Arms*, Broadway, originally *White Hart*. More recently landowners have found their resources lessening and have sold their houses which have been developed into inns e.g. *Old Hall*, Threshfield, N. Yorks. *Stanshawes Court*, Yate, *Grinkle Park*, Loftus, Cleveland.

MAPS

It is rare for an inn to appear by name on any but the largest scale maps but there are a number which appear on ordinary motoring maps of a scale of about 5 miles to the inch. The explorer might like to collect examples of which a few are given below: *Castle Comfort* on Mendip Hills; *Saltersgate* on edge of Pickering Moor; *Moorcock* in Ribblesdale; *Trouble House* nr. Tetbury, Glos.

MARQUIS

A peer, ranking below a duke and above an earl. Those commemorated in pub names include *Anglesey*, cavalry commander at Waterloo; *Lorne* who served with Marlborough and was involved in negotiations leading to Act of Union; *Westminster*, a property developer; *Granby*, a distinguished commander in Seven Years' War who is said to have established many of his discharged NCOs in inns; *Queensberry* associated with the codification of boxing.

MEAD

Ancient brew based on fermented honey. It is still made at *Mead House*, Newlyn; *Waterside Meadery*, Penzance; *Meade*, Gulval where it is sold. It also may be obtained in several Cornish pubs.

MEALS

Until C18 at least, beer was an important element in all meals. Even C16 Lenten fare for a Northumbrian household provided a quart of beer and a quart of wine to accompany the Earl and Countess's breakfast, their two boys shared a pottle (2 quarts), while the lady's gentlewoman had a pottle to herself and the two children in the nursery had a quart of beer between them. The allowance seems to have been quadrupled for the evening meal. At Court later in same century, maids of honour were allowed two gallons of ale and half a pitcher of wine to accompany their breakfast while another gallon was provided for supper and a further gallon for dinner.

Preparing Inn Food
(Medieval)

Between breakfast and dinner there was generally a 'nuncheon' or 'noon draught' which later was corruptly combined with 'lunch' (a hunk of bread) to produce the incorrect hybrid 'luncheon'. At other times the drink punctuating the intervals between meals was called a 'russin' and in religious houses the evening draught was called 'potatio'. In C16 even the English army seems to have marched on a beer-filled stomach since there are contemporary complaints of 'the greatest lack of vyctuals' being the unavailability of beer which was accepted as being much better for the army than wine or cider.

From meals accompanying some drinks we have advanced to drink accompanying some meals but, since 1950s there has been a real and welcome return to the notion that pubs might well be concerned again with 'vittles'. Many pubs have added restaurants, some of which have acquired modest fame and the patronage of the new 'coaching' trade. Perhaps even more welcome is the notion of 'pub food' provided at the bar and it is now becoming increasingly rare for the traveller to be unable to find some form of solid refreshment at a pub, though there are some curmudgeonly survivals behind the bar who seem outraged at a request for food and many seem to have problems on Mondays.

Basting

MEASURES
Early communal vessels (q.v.) were marked with pegs to indicate an appropriate measure for each draught. The volume between these marks seems to have been about half a pint. Besides pegs, hoops were also used to indicate levels. A hoop may have indicated a third of a pint but, more accurately, it indicated a third of a pot. The three-draught pot survived in Essex to C19 – the first draught was called 'neckum', the second 'sinkum' and the third 'swankum'. Hull has two pubs named *Full Measure*, there is a *Jack & Gill* at Allerton, Leeds.

Traditional measures ascended from nipperkin through quarter-pint, half-pint, pint, quart, pottle, gallon, half-anker, anker, half-hogshead, hogshead to pipe: each being double in quantity to its predecessor. Nipperkin is origin of 'nip' (third of pint), 'whiskin' seems to have meant pint in C17; in North a half-pint equals a gill. Wine bottles work on a different system but the multiples of an ordinary bottle of champagne have interesting names: Jeroboam, Rehoboam, etc.

'Schooner' seems to have originated in C19 USA as a tall glass containing double the quantity of a tumbler. By the end of C19 it had become a customary local measure in British pubs, containing 14 fluid ounces.

Apart from beer and cider, only whisky, gin, vodka and rum must be sold by fixed measure. Therefore, e.g. brandy, fortified wines, ordinary wines and liqueurs may be sold in unspecified quantities. A 'glass of wine' might vary in volume between 80ml and 168ml and there is no necessary correlation between price and quantity.

MECHANICAL see also *Inventions, Ships*
Machines, especially those involved in transport, have traditionally provided material for inn names and the practice has continued. Examples cover an extremely wide range and produce some unexpected names e.g. *Bluebird*, record-breaking car of 1935; Concorde aircraft under alias of *Double O Two, Bullnose Morris* in its home town, the flying boat *Canopus*, the slang name for a helicopter – *Chopper*, the boat-train *Golden Arrow*, Military aircraft include *Spitfire* and *Harrier*, Rolls Royce has provided the legendary *Silver Ghost*, while *Snowcat* is a somewhat slower mehanical sledge. *Victoria* can refer to the light four-wheeled carriage while *Woolwich Infant* commemorates the heaviest gun (35 tons) of its day (1870). *Bugatti* has been rightly honoured in former *New Inn*, Gretton, Northants and other vehicles include *Bicycle, Tramcar, Fire Engine* and a tube train under the name *Metropolitan*.

MEDIEVAL DRINKS
A number of intriguing names have come down to us including: Angel's Food, Dragon's Milk, Father Whoresonne, Go toe Wall, Huffe Cap, Lift Leg, Mad Dogge, Stride Wide. Some of these may have been mixtures but unfortunately the recipes do not seem to have survived.

MEDIEVAL INN see also *Pilgrim*
Often designed on H-plan, centred on the great hall, with a cross passage. Private chambers were usually provided on the first floor. A very good example (built 1350–60) survives in *Old Swan*, Saffron Walden which, unfortunately, in spite of retaining its name is no longer operative. It has a highly decorated doorway and windows with decorated tracery all within a timber frame. The finest stone-built survivors are C15 *George*, Glastonbury and *Angel*, Grantham. Such inns were provided by the great religious orders since hospitality was preached and practised by religious communities of both men and women. They served administrators, pilgrims, merchants, soldiers and vagabonds (see J.J. Jusserand: *Wayfaring Life in Middle Ages* (1961); E.L. Guildford: *Travellers and Travelling in Middle Ages* (1924); D.J. Hall: *English Medieval Pilgrimage* (1965)). *George*, Salisbury, originated as hospice for pilgrims to shrine of St Osmund; *Angel*, Lacock was probably once abbey guesthouse as was *Pilgrim's Rest*, Battle; *George*, Winchcombe still shows the carved initials of abbot Richard Kidderminster. Other surviving inns which are wholly or partly medieval include *Bell*, Hurley; Tewkesbury; Thetford; *Chequers*, Canterbury; *Crown, Old Bell*, Oxted; *New Inn*, Gloucester; *White Hart*, Bletchingley; *White Horse*, Romsey; *Star*, Alfriston.

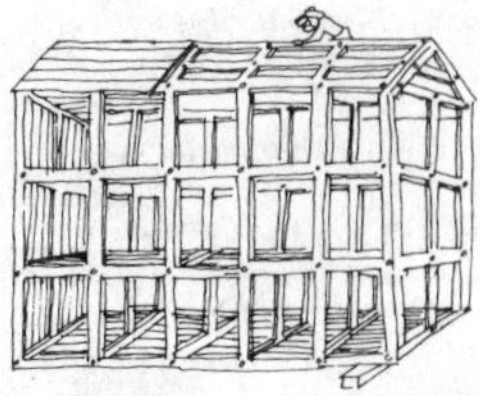

Constructing Medieval Inn

MEN ONLY
Many pubs, particularly in towns, used to have a club-like provision in a 'Men Only' room. It seems a natural equivalent to the Ladies' Room but it seems to have been a casualty of the Sex Discrimination Act.

MERSEYSIDE
Frederick Robinson's brewery in Southport controls about 3,300 tied houses, mostly in NE. Cheshire and Manchester but extending to Derbys. and N. Wales. It produces two draughts, two kegs and a range of cans and bottles including Old Tom and a stout.

Liverpool has had Higsons since 1780, now with about 160 houses, mostly in Merseyside, supplemented by considerable club trade. It is one of the few breweries that publishers OG of its beers which include two draught, two keg, canned and bottled including Stingo Gold.

MILLS
Wind and water mills have given their names to pubs either because a nearby mill was a good 'marker' e.g. *Wicor Mill*, Portchester or because the building now used as a pub was a former mill e.g. *Corn Mill*, Stamford Bridge. *Pandy* is apparently Welsh for fulling mill e.g. at Tonypandy.

MILD ALE
Milds are usually of lowish gravity (and cost) and sweeter than pale ales. Dark milds result from a greater proportion of darker malts and perhaps added caramel. They are less hopped than pale ales and often heavily primed (sugar added after fermentation).

MILITARY see also *Battles, Generals*
Large number of inn names have military associations: the inn sign at Bathpool, Som. depicts local volunteers mustering on green by inn in preparation for the arrival of the Spanish Armada; *Battle*, Reading, is derived from nearby former Battle hospital once a dependency of Battle Abbey; *Battle of Britain* (1954) is a popular (re)name in Kent; *Battledown*, Cheltenham commemorated a Civil War skirmish; *Blue Backs*, Warrington, bears nickname of local volunteers who used inn as HQ in C18; *Cherry Pickers* is also a nickname (11th Hussars). *Chindit* refers to General Wingate's troops (1939–45) and *Desert Rat* to 7th Armoured Division in same war. *Fencibles* were a local militia raised for home service in later C18; *Gurkha* commemorates the famous Napalese regiments first raised in 1915; *Inkerman* (1854) was a Crimean battle; *Martello* was a coastal fort against feared French invasion (*c.* 1804); *Milecastle*, was part of Hadrian's Wall defences against invaders from North; *Pike & Musket*, Walton, commemorated battle of Sedgemoor (1685); *Rifleman* occurs, as does *Volunteer*. The latter usually applies to old militia but at Exmouth it commemorates lifeboatmen. Local regiments are often remembered e.g. *Yorkshire Dragoon, Yorkshire Hussar*.

MINERS' ARMS see also *Colliers' Pub, Trade Signs*
Sometimes an inn with this name may appear in an unexpected place as at North Molton, Devon, a reminder of the copper mines worked in later C19; or on Greenhow Moors between Pately Bridge and Grassington which was a lead-mining area from Roman times until C19. There is a rare *Jet Miner's Arms* at Great Broughton, N. Yorks.

MINT
Name may be from royal mint for coinage as at Exeter or from the sweetmeat popular in Restoration period e.g. Southam, Warks.

MISERICORDS
The tip-up seats found in collegiate churches and churches which were formally monastic. Their undersides are often elaborately carved and it is an interesting fact that their subjects include nearly all ancient inn names *Cat & Fiddle* (Hereford cathedral), *Elephant & Castle* (St George's, Windsor), *Fox & Hare* (Beverley Minster), *Pig & Whistle* (usually bagpipes), etc.

MISLEADING NAMES see also *Corruption*
Inn names are not always what they seem to be. Examples might include *Cat & Cracker* (Catalytic cracker), Grain, Kent; *Chieftain* (a ship's figurehead), Morecambe, Lancs.; *Last Inn*, where the last is shoemaker's; *Union*, Leek, Staffs. where the conjunction is marital rather than political; *Ship Inn*, Styal, Chesh. from 'shippen' meaning 'cowshed'; *Twin Foxes*, Stevenage commemorates poacher twins called Fox; *Cock*, by itself may refer to tap not bird as always in association with *Bottle*.

MITRE
Ceremonial episcopal headgear but many medieval abbots had the privilege of wearing the mitre. Its use as an inn sign may indicate that the house was once episcopal or abbatial property e.g. *Mitre*, Glaisdale once belonged to Whitby abbey.

Mitre

MIXTURES
From the Middle Ages it was customary to mingle brews of different strengths and tastes to achieve more subtle flavours and balances. In C18 simplest mixture was 'half and half' which could mean equal quantities of ale and beer or of ale and 'twopenny' (strong ale) or of beer and 'twopenny'. More

elaborate was the pot of 'three thirds' or 'three threads' which contained equal proportions of ale, beer and 'twopenny'. This 'twopenny' was rather slow to serve and the problem was met by one Ralph Harewood *c.*1730 who produced a drink called 'Entire' which combined the several virtues of ale, beer and 'twopenny'. This drink was eventually called porter. Today 'half and half' usually means a mixture of mild and bitter. The other commonest mixtures are Shandy (unfixed proportions of bitter and lemonade) with variants involving mild and ginger beer. Black and Tan is Guinness and bitter; Mother-in-law is old and bitter; Boiler-maker is brown and mild; M & B is same as 'half 'n half' (and 'mix'); 'narfer narfer narf' is a half-pint of mild and bitter; 'across taps' is best and ordinary mixed; Granny is old and mild; Lightplater is light and bitter; Brown Split is draught mild and bottled brown; Light Split is draught bitter and bottled light; Blacksmith is barley wine and Guinness; Black & Velvet is champagne and Guinness. Apparently port is sometimes mixed with Guinness as well as with lemon. Happy Days is applied to a measure of whisky poured into a half of bitter; Dragon's Blood can mean barley wine with an added measure of rum; a Fast Lady is gin and Campari and Dog's Nose in C19 was a compound of warm porter, sugar, gin and nutmeg; later it was applied to gin and nutmeg: and even later it denoted gin in bitter. There are noxious mixtures which have blackcurrant as an ingredient and tales are told of Vimto, Coca Cola and such being added to honest drink.

MODERN NAMES see also *Mechanical*
Include persons alive or lately dead, reminiscences of 1939–45 War and recent developments such as *Early Bird, Man in Space, Cat & Cracker*. Brough has *Buccaneer* commemorating military aircraft manufactured locally and *Pathfinder*, Maltby, commemorates squadron which illuminated bombing targets in World War II. *1900th*, York refers to anniversary of city's foundation (AD 71).

MODERN PUBS
Some die-hards will never be convinced that a modern house can provide the atmosphere of the traditional and unique English pub. But even our most ancient hostelries were modern once and new buildings do allow an opportunity, however ill-taken, for architects and designers to show their skill. A few random examples: *Ridge Farm*, Bedlington, N'land; *Roundabout*, Birmingham; *Derby Turn*, Burton; *Parkfield*, Eastbourne; *Firebird*, Edgbaston; *Tern*, Chipping Sodbury; *Podium*, London EC2 (part of Barbican project); *Old Oak Stave*, Newport, I.o.W.; *Drawbridge*, Rotherham; *Sarah Siddons*, Warwick.

MODIFICATION
Old houses bear the marks of history and of fashion and old inns had to move with the times, updating their facilities, providing new or different accommodation and keeping step with changing taste. Medieval wall-paintings might be covered with oak panelling (*White Swan*, Stratford-upon-Avon), oak beams boxed in, ceilings plastered and wallpapered.

The great re-building period was in the coaching era when inns were added to, sometimes completely restructured and, at the least, were usually provided with a new frontage. The history writ in architecture can add an additional dimension in pub exploration: the persistance of old fittings, the signs of modification and clues for their date. The remaining evidence is often in the less obvious parts of the inn – attics, cellars, top-floor rooms and round the old yards which were once thronged with horses and their servants but even public rooms will give information to the perceptive: windows newer than walls, blocked openings or new openings indicated by support walls, remains of decoration or varying levels.

MONARCHS see also *Kings*
A selection of the less common monarchs who appear in inn names might include *Albert Edward* (later Edward VII), Eccles; *Merry Monarch* (Charles II also associated with *Royal Oak, Rose Revived*), *Nautical William* ('Sailor Billy', 'Sailor King', William IV); *Ordinary Fellow* (George V); *William the Conqueror* (William I); *Rufus* (William II killed in New Forest); *Shah* (Nadir Shah or Kuli Khan who became emperor of Persia in 1746, gave England trading rights and visited this country). There is a rare *James I* at Norwich.

George, Norton St Philip, Somerset (really St George)

MONASTICISM see also *Dissolution*
The mother of inns and hostelries. Besides the great pilgrimage inns, a few of which survive, quite a number of present-day hotels and inns incorporate some part of a former monastic building e.g. Blanchland, Furness, Kirkstead, Helston, Launceston, Malmesbury, Malton, Stamford, Tewkesbury in England and Llanthony in Wales.

MOON
Perhaps the moon is too changeable to compare in popularity with *Sun* as an inn name but it does occur in a variety of forms: *Rising Moon, Full Moon, Crescent, Half Moon* – even *Blue Moon*. There is also *Man on the Moon*.

MOTEL
The motel or 'Post House' is perhaps the most significant inn development since World War II. It is designed to exploit the motor car by providing comparatively inexpensive lodging of a highish quality but transitory nature with plenty of associated parking space and so located as to obviate the need for the motorist going far off the main routes. There are few signs of the English version becoming the all-pervasive institution originating in USA, partly because the distances are not so great, partly because it is not economically a strong competitor with the small hotel and finally because, though it may be convenient, it tends to lack the character (particularly that provided by the 'locals') which the English traveller expects in his stopping place.

MUG HOUSE
A popular C18 institution, a combination of ale-house and popular 'club'. These houses were distinguished by rows of pewter mugs placed in window or hung up outside. Rare survival of name at Claines, Worcs.

C18 'Pot House'

MULLED ALE see also *Ale Warmer*
A warming winter drink whose main ingredient is heated ale to which are added, at least, sugar, nutmeg and ginger. In C17 this concoction seems to have been called 'Lamb's Wool' and is in the line of descent from the medieval Wassail Bowl (q.v.).

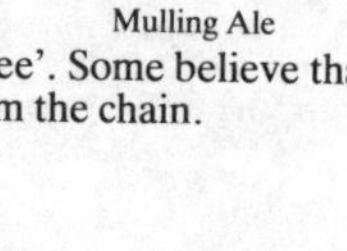
Mulling Ale

MULTIPLES
A term for pubs which are not Free Houses nor yet owned by breweries. They belong to a chain but the owning company does not itself brew. Some of them may be leased from a brewery and those which are not leased but belong to the operating form may, misleadingly, be described as 'Free'. Some believe that the larger the chain, the worse the individual houses that form the chain.

MUM
A Brunswicker concoction of ale brewed from wheat apparently introduced during the Commonwealth. It was a strong ale with various aromatic herbs added.
Its name is explained as: derived from its alleged inventor (Christopher Mumme); from the German 'murmmeln' – to mutter; or from 'mum' – silence.

MUSIC
From the medieval minstrel to the itinerant musicians of the Victorian period, musical entertainment has featured in pub activities. Later, special rooms were assigned for the purpose which also required an extended licence and these sometimes developed into Music Halls. Canned music began in London in 1890 with mechanical music boxes grinding out metallically the hits of the day for the insertion of a penny. At the opposite end of this theme there is a house at Parkgate, Cheshire, formerly *George* where Handel is said to have composed part of 'Messiah'. Inn names with musical associations (see also Musical Instruments) include: *Flash Harry* (nickname for Malcolm Sargeant), *Gilbert and Sullivan, Jenny Lind* (an operatic singer, 1820–87), *Louis Armstrong* (jazz trumpeter) and *Student Prince* (operetta).

MUSICAL INSTRUMENTS
Almost enough occur in inn names to provide a symphony but many of them originated as signals rather than for the melodic possibilities. *Bugle*, Hamble, Hants. is said to be one of the oldest inns in county and there are a number of namesakes. *Horn* may be hunting or it may be *Coach Horn*; there is also a rare *French Horn* and a *Buglehorn*. Besides the *Cat and the Fiddle* there is the *Cat & Fiffle* and the *Whifflers Arms*. There is the combined *Horn and Trumpet* and the amalgamated *Crown and Pipes*. The *Pig & Whistle* is almost a synonym for pub and other instruments occurring on signs include *Bag-pipes, Harp* and *Organ*.

MYTHOLOGY see also *Folk Lore, Gods*
Roman gods seem to have been quite popular in C18. Besides the expected *Bacchus*, there is *Apollo, Mars* and *Neptune* and the dock area of Hull possesses both an *Oberon* and a *Minerva* and there is a *Black Venus* at Challacombe, Devon. Local myth and legend are not forgotten in names such as *Arthur, Merlin, Bladud* (legendary father of Lear and builder of Bath) and *King Coel* (Cole). The *Lambton Worm* was a monstrous serpent allegedly slain by the young Lord Lambton and *Dun Cow* may refer to ferocious beast killed by Guy of Warwick. The *Mermaid* is nearly as common in seaports as the *Dolphin* and inland there is the rare *Griffin*, Dragons of various hues and the *Unicorn* whose horn was a panacea against all poisons. *Tom Thumb* occurs at Blaby, Leics. Good signs at Paignton and Christian Malford (Wilts.).

NAMES see also *Signs*
There is an extraordinarily rich variety of pub names, bearing many associations. The subject is a study in itself and yet there still seems to be no exhaustive study or even completely reliable minor treatments. There are names which defy interpretation, names which have only local significance and names which testify to almost every aspect of national life and character.
No really old inn called itself the Something Arms, described itself as Old or misinterpreted the 'thorn' letter (th) as 'y' to produce a word pronounced 'yee'. It was content to be known bluntly and simply as *George, Bell, Red Lion, White Horse, Unicorn*, or by whatever bold and prominent sign it distinguished itself for a largely illiterate public. Later, bad

Bell, Woodbridge, Suffolk

workmanship and a breakdown of tradition could make even signs misleading so that a former *Swan & Harp* could become a *Goose and Gridiron* (or vice versa).

There is a pleasing play on inn names in a ballad introduced into T. Heywood's 'Rape of Lucrece':

The Gintry to the *King's Head*,
The Nobles to the *Crown*,
The Knights unto the *Golden Fleece*,
And to the *Plough* the Clown (rustic).

The Churchman to the *Mitre*,
The Shepherd to the *Star*,
The Gardiner hies him to the *Rose*,
To the *Drum* the Man of War.

The Huntsman to the *White Hart*,
To the *Ship* the Merchants goe,
And you that doe the Muses love,
The sign called *River Po*.

The Banquer out to the *World's End*,
The Fool to the *Fortune* hie,
Unto the *Mouth* the Oyster-wife,
The Fiddler to the *Pie*.

Ships and racehorses are so frequently commemorated in pub names that they are treated under separate headings but this too can be misleading e.g. *Old Success*, Sennen Cove, refers to a prosperity-bringing fishing smack but *Victory* at nearby Towan Cross refers not to Nelson's flagship but a commercial triumph over a rival pub in 1903 or thereabouts.

A few 'difficult' names may be included here e.g. *Artichoke* is probably a compliment to Elizabeth I who was fond of this vegetable introduced in her reign; *Lubberheads* is said to be a corruption of 'libbards' (a variant of leopard's) heads and therefore derived from royal standard; *Stowponey*, if it still exists between Kinver and Stourbridge, is derived from Stourpont = Stourbridge; *Two Puddings*, Stratford E15 commemorates the generosity to the local poor of a former landlord; Bradford, Yorks. has *'Bod'* (person, fellow) as well as the nice double entendre of *Yarn Spinners; Three Cranes* is derived from arms of Vintners' Company and originally refers, not to birds, but to hoists used by draymen for lifting barrels; *Pepper Box* may be designated storage place for contraband pepper or other spices but it is also C18 slang for pistol.

NATURAL PHENOMENA see also *Physical Features*

Have given name to number of inns, particularly the phosphorescence of marsh gas which produced *Jack o' Lantern, Floating Light, Will o' the Wisp*. The *Slip*, Much Marcle, Heref. & Worcs., recalls a miniature landslide of 1575. Perhaps *Windwhistle*, Chard, Som. (together with *Wuthering Heights*, nr. Haworth) should also be in this category. Other natural phenomena are referred to in names such as *Mallyan Snout* (waterfall), Goathland; *Salmon Leap* (formerly *Midland*), Sleights, N. Yorks. and *Great Stone*, Northfield, W. Mid. (glaciated boulder preserved in nearby pound). *Blue Lias* (hard calcarious stone), Stockton Locks, Warks.

NEW INN

There are probably hundreds of inns so-called which are usually very old (convesely *Old Ball*, Horsforth, W. Yorks. is very new). Generally, they represent a replacement on the same site of a former monastic hostel destroyed by the Reformation. Occasionally it indicates a replacement, extension or improvement before this event. The most famous example is *New Inn*, Gloucester which was built originally in 1457 as a hostel for pilgrims.

NINETEENTH CENTURY see also *Gin Palace*
From the pub point of view falls into two eras. The first decade saw the work of Telford and McAdam with vast improvements in road communications producing over 1,000 miles of new roads and new bridges and by 1835 most main roads had been macadamised. Hence the first three decades were the golden years of coaching and the most prosperous times for keepers of roadside inns.

C19 Inn Kitchen Servant

The later decades produced the 'brassiest' age of the town pub expressing itself in the swank of London's West End and the grandeur of the great Northern towns. There is 'style' in both the magnificence of the building and the lushness of the furniture. The process began quite early in the century when the pubs set themselves up to be in the new industrial towns what they had been in the rural communities from which town populations were but recently removed – focal points, places of entertainment and sociability. Of course, there were differences related to the differences of culture and tempo between town and country and perhaps, above all, differences due to the attempt to compensate for the change from the natural rhythms of the land to the mechanical rhythms of the driving machines, a difference between recreation and 'escape'. Examples of C19 pubs might include *Sawyer's Arms, Lord Clyde*, Manchester; *Philharmonic, Vines*, Liverpool; *Bridge*, Salford; *Whitelocks*, Leeds.

Bar Furniture (Loudon)

NOBILITY
Many pub names and signs are derived, directly or indirectly, from the nobility and examples will be found under Aristocracy, Heraldry, Marquis, Princes.

NOPPY, NAPPY
An ancient adjective much used of good ale. It seems to have included the connotations of heady, foaming, strong.

NOTTINGHAMSHIRE
Hardys and Hansons have a brewery at Nottingham and about 230 tied houses largely in N. Notts. and Derbys. with free trade in the area. They produce two draughts, a keg and bottled range which includes a stout and Old Kim.

Home Brewery at Daybrook controls over 400 houses, concentrated round Nottingham but with some in neighbouring counties. it produces two draughts, a keg and bottled range including Bendigo.

Mansfield Brewery has about 180 tied houses in Mansfield and Chesterfield area and flourishing free trade. It produces two draught and three bottled beers.

Shipstones, New Basford, Nottingham have several hundred tied houses mainly in Notts., Leics., and Derbys. but spilling over into Lincs. and Yorks. with wide free trade. They produce two draughts, a keg and bottled range which includes Strong Ale.

NUMBERS
In inn names are usually adjectival: *Six Bells, Three Horseshoes, Three Cranes* and often refer, as in last case, to heraldry. Very occasionally, they occur as ordinals as in *One and Three*, Oldham where name is a superstitious attempt to avoid the thirteen which is the house's number in the street.

NURSERY TALES see also *Folk Lore, Mythology*
There is *Mother Hubbard*, Loughton, Essex; *Puss in Boots*, Hazelwood, Derbys.; *March Hare*, Ashton, Chesh.; *Jack & Jill*, Brimington, Derbys.; *Tom Thumb*, Stockport, Gtr. Man. as well as many Robin Hood characters. There is also *Hoop & Toy*, Thurloe Place, London SW7 whose sign portrays these children's articles but the name may be a corruption.

OAK
Extremely common and by far the most popular tree used in pub names. The most frequent adjectival form is *Royal Oak* commemorating Charles's escape at Boscobel and rejoicing at Restoration. Rare are *Original Oak* and *Hainault Oak* but *Hearts of Oak* in praise of Royal Navy in C19 is more frequent. There is also *British Oak, Gospel Oak, Land Oak* (Kidderminster), and, naturally, *Old Oak*.

OCCUPATIONAL HAZARDS
Death through drinking was a real danger for the early music-hall artist and remains one for the servants and owners of inns and public houses. In the last decade of C19 the death rate from alcohol was three times as great for publicans than the average for employed males. The peak was reached *c.*1900, declined to a low in 1935, but since World War II has begun to rise again.

ODDITIES
Some pub names are difficult to classify and every alert traveller must have his own favourite examples which might include *Brick Wall*, Skipton, N. Yorks.; *Burnt Post*, Coventry; *Candlestick*, nr. Hatfield, Herts.; *Fool's Nook*, Sutton, Chesh.; *Frying Pan*, Spitalfields, London; *Glue Pot*, Harrogate; *Mountain Dew*, Atherton, Gtr. Man.; *Mousetrap*, Bourton-on-the-Water, Glos.

Burnt Post, Coventry

OFFICIALS
Among the less usual officers who have given their names to pubs are *Bailiff's Sergeant, Beefeater, County Members* who were trustees of Cinque Ports, *Pindar* who impounded stray farmstock; *Twelve Knights* who maintained order on Welsh Border, *Twenty Churchwardens* who represented their parishes in maintaining pub at Cockley Cley, Norfolk, *Tything Man*, the manorial official who collected 'tenths'; *Wakeman*, Ripon – the city watchman.

OLDEST
There are a number of claimants to be the oldest inn or licensed premises in the country and, apart from lack of records, establishing the truth is complicated by such questions as do we mean the site which has supported an inn for the longest time? the longest continuous use as an inn? the oldest surviving building now functioning as an inn? etc. *Fountain*, Canterbury, had a strong claim until it was destroyed in World War II. Other competitors in the same city include *Falstaff*, formerly *Pilgrim's Rest* (heavily restored in C17). All the houses on west side of Mercery Lane once formed part of *Chequers*, a hostelry belonging to cathedral with beds for 100 pilgrims. *House of Agnes* is a well-preserved C17 house with long history as inn and Hepworth's in St Margaret's Street was originally a pilgrim's hospice.

Leaving Canterbury there are strong claimants in Nottingham's *Trip to Jerusalem* (partly C11?) 'Against the rockface leant the oldest pub in England with all the grades of a social guide: the private bar, the saloon, the ladies', the snug, the public.' (*c.*1930 as described by Graham Greene in *A Sort of Life*, 1971, p. 157), Manchester's *Seven Stars* and Chiddingfold's *Crown* while the site occupied by

Fighting Cocks, St Albans

Bingley Arms, Bardsey, W. Yorks. has allegedly been used as an inn since AD 953! Other competitors are *Angel*, Grantham, C15, cellars from early C13; *Ostrich*, Colnbrook may be C14; *Star*, Alfriston has been given a date of 1520 and its other ancient inns, *George* and *Ship* have been placed a century earlier. *Fighting Cocks*, St Alban's, occupies a monastic building (water gate?) but can only have been an inn from C16 at earliest. *Turk's Head*, Exeter, also seem C16 but may occupy earlier site. *Old Bell*, Hurley, Berks. may have been guest-house of priory which was destroyed in 1536. *White Horse*, Dorking, is largely C18–19 but incorporates elements of an earlier timber-framed houses which may date back to the C13 hospice of Hospitallers. *George & Dragon*, Codicote, Herts. is medieval and is claimed to date from C13; *Artichoke*, Christow, Devon, makes similar claims as does *Chequers*, Tonbridge, though the latter's present building can hardly be older than C15. *George*, Norton St Philip, Som. is probably early C15. Thatched *Star*, Harome, nr. Helmsley, N. Yorks. claims to be C13.

ONE BAR PUBS

Up to 1964 there was a regulation that pubs possessed of a single bar could only be granted a beer and wine licence. Permission to sell spirits as well (Full On Licence) was confined to premises which had at least two bars. When this restriction was removed, owners began to knock their bars into one giving them several advantages: the right to charge higher (lounge) price throughout licensed area, reducing bar staff and increasing drinking area.

OPTIC

Glass fronted dispenser inserted in neck of inverted spirit bottle, operated by spring-loaded valve to emit one measure at each pressure.

ORIGINS

Medieval Tavern

The earliest ale-houses were ordinary houses, cottages or farmhouses where the ale-wife brewed in her own kitchen and, weather permitting, served it outside at a bench, otherwise in her own living-room. As demand increased, ale would be brewed in an outhouse and some seating provision made in a downstairs room with direct access from outside.

Inns originate in the monastic guest-houses in the outer court of a religious house which also contained cellars and brew houses, hall, chambers and stables.

Taverns, being only concerned with the sale of wine and provision of food but not with accommodation would generally be smaller than inns but, as the Middle Ages progressed, it probably became increasingly difficult to distinguish the large tavern from the small inn. In C15 and C16, secular inns were able, in some cases, to imitate the provision of the great religious houses and would have their courtyard, timbered galleries, stables and barns, privy, oven-house, brewery and still-room. The hall tended to remain for communal entertainment, the great bedchambers were provided on the first floor with garrets or cock-lofts for the servants of guests, servants of the inn and perhaps even the host. On the ground floor were the kitchen, sometimes separate, and its own ancillary rooms: pantry, buttery, larder, scullery, etc. The tradition of manastic hospitality, especially its standards, continued after the Dissolution in regard to service, cleanliness and hospitality (indeed it is possible that some of the abbey personnel extruded from their old home and living found subsidence in continuing some aspects of their old 'trade' in inns). In C17 a guest seems to have had the choice of either eating at the common table with the host or ordering what he liked from the kitchen to eat in his own chamber (origin of distinction between 'table d'hote' and 'a la carte'). Music also seems to have been provided for the entertainment of guests in the larger inns. Sometimes the furnishing of inns seems to have been so remarkable as eventually to provide even a small house with an identifying name e.g. *Old Corner Cupboard*, Winchcombe.

C18 Inn Kitchen

OWNERSHIP
Besides the usual forms of ownership such as Free House, Tied House and Multiples there have been less common forms as e.g. Tontine (q.v.). Occasionally the established church perpetuates the ownership of medieval ecclesiasticism and occasionally advances e.g. *Plough*, Horbling, Lincs. has been owned by the parish since it was built in C19. It is rented to a brewery and the rent goes to rate relief. From about 1915 until recently there was a not unsuccessful experiment in State ownership in the Carlisle area.

OX
May originate as ecclesiastical symbol of St Luke but in some cases it certainly commemorates a real animal as in the *Ketton Ox* and *Durham Ox*, a gigantic beast which died early in C19.

OXFORDSHIRE
W.H. Brakspeare have a brewery at Henley with about 130 tied houses in the surrounding district. Their good selection of draught beers includes XXXX, they have an unpasteurised keg and a variety of bottled. There is a smaller brewery at Hook Norton with about 30 local tied houses and a more extended free trade. They produce two draught beers and three bottled. Morrells at Oxford have some 140 pubs in city and county and make three draught beers including College Ale, two unpasteurised kegs and a range of bottled.

Packhorse

PACK-HORSE
A common conveyance for small trader and generally used to carry fleeces to the domestic weaver and to convey woven cloths to the nearest market. Inn signs have frequent reminiscence of this trade, e.g. the small market town of Kendal has both *Fleece* and *Woolpack*, old inns which once served this traffic. The *Black Swan*, Helmsley and both *Swan* and *Packhorse* at Lavenham, Suffolk have similar origins.

PAINTINGS
Apart from the much neglected art involved on pub signs which now tend to yield a poor second or third place to the owning brewery, pubs possess their own paintings and sometimes act as an art gallery. They also occur in paintings and 'Outside the *Red Lion*' by William Shayer Sr. sold for nearly £7,000 in 1968.

Morland (Brewer)

PALE ALE

Usually pale in colour and well hopped but there are considerable variations since the term embraces a whole family of beers including:

Bitter

Best Bitter should be stronger than ordinary and may be sweeter.

Bottled Pale Ale and Light Ale are almost always the same thing but if a brewer makes both, the pale will be the stronger.

Indian Pale Ale or IPA is often above average strength, and was a name used by Bass in early C19 for beer they brewed specially to export to East India Company.

AK may refer to a light bitter or to a mild, either light or dark.

Export is a name often given to a strongest pale ale.

College Ale an old name given to a strong beer produced by monasteries, ecclesiastical colleges, etc. and was continued in the academic colleges of Oxbridge after the Reformation.

Audit Ale originally also had learned associations and was a special brew produced for drinking on audit days.

PARLIAMENT CLOCK

In C18 clocks and watches were subject to a special 5/- levy, hence private ones diminished in number and there was more need for public provision, especially in coaching houses. These latter are sometimes called Parliament Clocks and have certain characteristics: they are attached to wall, have a black japanned case and a large clear dial, similar to that of the later railway clocks which served much the same purpose. A few survive in former coaching inns e.g. in *Ship*, Lime Street, London EC1.

PATRIOTISM

Inn names often express patriotic sentiments e.g. some *Georges, Imperial, Commonwealth, British Oak, British Grenadier, Britannia*. The latter in Camden commemorates William Camden whose most famous work bore this title and in some places has a primary reference to ship of that name e.g. at Dover, Elterwater, Nailsworth.

Britannia

PEG

The large wooden tankard used for communal drinking from C10–14 was marked at roughly half-pint intervals by pegs which measured an individual draught, hence: 'Have a peg', 'take him down a peg'. Communal drinking from one container was common until C19. An alternative name for 'peg' was 'pin'.

> So extremely anxious was he (great reforming king Edgar) (fl. *c.*973) to preserve peace even in trivial matters, that, as his countrymen* used to assemble in taverns and, when a little elevated, quarrel as to the proportions of their liquor, he ordered gold or silver pegs to be fastened in the pots, that whilst every man should know his just measure, shame should compel each neither to take more himself, nor oblige others to drink beyond their proportional share. (William of Malmesbury, Chronicle, II, 8 – p. 147 in Bohn ed.)

* The same author blames an inrush of foreigners for bringing bad influences to bear on the native English including the Danes 'who taught them drunkenness' (ibid.).

PEOPLE see also *Monarchs, Politicians, Sportsmen*
Individuals from all social classes and all periods have achieved the rare honour of having a pub perpetuate their name. They include *Coverdale*, a C16 translator of the Bible; *David Brewster* (1781–1868), inventor of kaleidoscope; *Francis Bacon*, C13 Franciscan scientist and philosopher, *Gay Gordon* who raised Golden Highlanders in 1795 alias *Hieland Laddie, Cock o' the North* and the *Huntly* of *Huntly Arms*; *Giles* the cartoonist; *Henry Jenkins* who survived from 1501 to 1667; *Kossuth* alias *Independent*, C19 Hungarian nationalist; *Margaret Catchpole*, C18 adventuress; *Honolulu*, flamboyant racing tipster who died in 1965; *Mother Shipton* (1488–1560) prophetess; *Oily Johnnie*, a popular inn-keeper who also peddled paraffin; *Old Parr* who is said to have live from 1483 to 1635!; *Paxton* (1801–65), designer of Crystal Palace; *Robert de Mortain* brother of Conqueror and builder of Hastings Castle; *Shakespeare*, perhaps the most popular commoner; *Simon de Montfort* (1208–65), baronial leader, developer of Parliament and popular saint; *Sir Isaac Newton* (1642–1727), physicist; *Sir Walter Tyrrell*, alleged slayer of Rufus in 1128; *Van Gogh*, painter who spent a few months in Ramsgate in 1876; *Vermuyden* (1595–1683) engineer who drained much of S. Yorks. and Lincs.; *Whittington*, Lord Mayor of London in late Middle Ages; *William Dighton* who smashed Halifax coining gang in C18.

Mother Shipton, Knaresborough

PERMITTED HOURS
The times when licensed premises may legally be opened for the public sale of intoxicating liquors.

Permitted hours were introduced in 1550, during the reign of Elizabeth I when there was a closing time of 9 p.m. in summer and 8 p.m. in winter. The major reduction was under the Defence of the Realm Act of 1915 which has set the current pattern. There are regional variations but generally there are two periods: one from mid-morning to early afternoon, another from evening to night with both periods shortened on Sundays. As an example, the London hours are:

Weekdays:	11.00–15.00; 17.30–23.00
Sundays:	12.00–14.00; 19.00–22.00

There are, of course, occasional extensions of which Christmas Eve and New Year's Eve are standard and pubs near markets have special concessions. Drinks served after hours are sometimes known as 'later'.

PHYSICAL FEATURES see also *Local 'Sight'*
Both as a means of identification and as a 'selling point', notable features in the locality have often been used in pub names, e.g. *Brentnor*, Devon; *Bunch of Carrots*, Hampton Bishop, Heref. & Worcs.; *Bunker's Nob*, Addington, Surrey; *Devil's Elbow*, Princetown, Devon; *Devil's Stone*, Shebbear, Devon; *Ploddy House*, Taynot, Glos. – 'plodde' is puddle, pool or swamp; *Dog & Bacon* (Dorking Beacon), Tarn, Yeadon, W. Yorks.; *Tumble Beacon*, Tadworth, Surrey. Such names as *Calder and Hebble*, Halifax might be included in this category.

PIG & WHISTLE
One of the oldest pub names, probably Anglo-Saxon. There are many theories about its origin but there is fairly general agreement that the second element is a corruption of 'washael' – 'good health'. The former element may be derived from the word for 'pail' and refer to beer served from buckets into which horns or mugs, sometimes called 'pigs' were dipped. Another theory is that the expression is a

Pig & Whistle

corruption of the angel's greeting to Mary: 'Pige washael' – 'Health to the maiden'. Finally, one cannot help wondering if the name or sign is connected with the musical pigs which frequently occur on misericords (q.v.).

'*Pig*' alone, often found in Derbyshire, refers to the oblong ingots into which lead was cast. The reservoir from which they were 'fed' was called a 'sow'.

PILGRIMS see also *Ecclesiastical*

Hostels provided for these devout wayfarers can indicate a route or Pilgrim's Way e.g. *Stepping Stones*, Westhumble, Surrey. The '*Trip to Jerusalem*', Nottingham, perhaps the oldest inn in the country, was originally *Pilgrim*, changing its present name in 1189 when it was served from the castle above and possibly provided a staging point for soldiers assembling for the Crusades (q.v.). 'Tryppe' is said to be Old English for 'Halt'. Inns which were created for the benefit of pilgrims include *George and Pilgrim*, Glastonbury; *Angel*, Grantham, serviced by both Templers and Hospitallers; *George*, Norton St Philip; *George*, Winchcombe, for pilgrims to Winchcombe and Hailes; *Old Bell*, Hurley; *White Horse*, Dorking; *New Inn*, Gloucester, for pilgrims to shrine of Edward II. Some inns called *Bull* may derive their name from 'bulla' the corporate seal of religious houses as may *Ball* in some cases. The bells of Canterbury pilgrims may have given some hostels their name *Bell* and Jerusalem pilgrims who carried palms and were known as palmers may have provided the name for the original *Palmer Flatt* hotel in Wensleydale.

Wealthy Pilgrim

PINT

The traditional measure (derived from corn measure) for all types of draught beer. The law demands that the beer be poured up to the brim into a glass which bears the stamp of the Weights and Measures Department. If there is to be a 'head', it must stand out above the top of the glass or above the 'Plimsoll line' if the glass is marked in this way.

When people 'go for a pint', they invariably go to a pub and almost invariably consume more than a pint.

PLACE NAMES

The curious explorer may have wondered about such place names as Beer Charter, Beercrocombe, Beer, Beer Hackett, Beer Head and may be disappointed to learn that the Devon Beers seem to be derived from an Old English word meaning 'grove' while the Dorset and Somerset ones seem to come from a similar Old English word meaning 'pasture'.

PLANS

The plan of an old inn is as typical as that of a church and for much the same reasons; it is functional and was only modified to suit changing needs. The interested explorer, with the permission and help of the landlord, can, if he chooses a suitable time, trace the plan from room to room. It is perhaps best to begin with the massive main chimney, frequently the oldest part of the house and often with its base supported on a kind of buttress in the cellar. Old beams and cornices disappearing through partitions will tell of rooms divided, though the modern practice is rather to 'open up' the old small rooms on the ground floor to provide 'open plan' drinking areas which can accommodate more consumers and require less servers. Look also for blocked-up archways and doors which are often more discernible from outside and don't forget the yard. C19 pubs were increasingly designed on the 'open plan' principle with variants on the dispensing area which might be a 'promontory', 'circular' or other form of central bar.

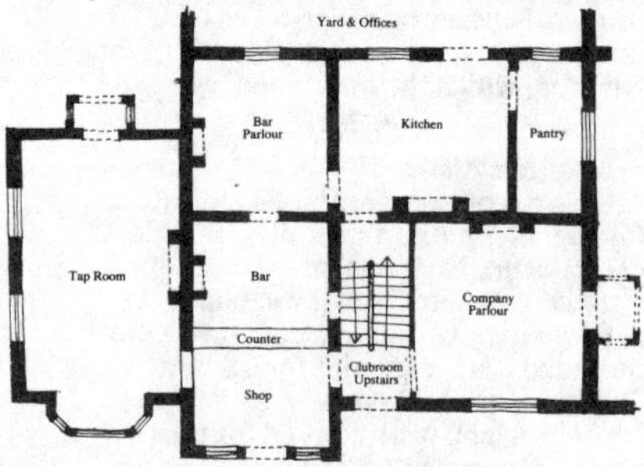

Ground Floor Plan, Suburban Pub, C19/20

PLOUGH
As inn name may refer to constellation 'Ursa Major' but almost aways it is the essential agricultural instrument which in Middle Ages was seen as semi-sacramental. The plough was blessed on the Sunday or Monday following the twelve-day Christmas holiday and the decorated plough was later processed from church to raise a collection ('plough money') which then financed the 'Plough Ale'. The plough is sometimes combined with other instruments e.g. *Plough & Harrow, Speed the Plough*, Barton-le-Clay, Beds. There is a rare *Plough & Sail*, Crossbush, Surrey which may refer to the harvest of land and sea or to the beginning and end of the basic process from ploughing of land to milling of resultant grain.

The Plough

POETS' PUB see also *Literary*
Apart from Eric Linklater's novel, pubs have provided a refuge, if not an inspiration, for a number of creative writers – a service which goes back to the Mermaid or earlier. As a minor example, *Bell*, Clare, Suffolk accommodated E.H.W. Meyerstein in 1936. *Lady of Shallot*, Louth, Lincs. reminds us that we are in Tennyson country.

POLITICIANS
Have received mnore than their mede of memorial in pub names. They range from *Beaconsfield* (Disraeli) to *Herbert Morrison*, include *Cobden* and *Peel* and among the prime ministers honoured are *Walpole, Palmerston, Gladstone* and *Lloyd* George under the soubriquet *Pride of the Valley*.

POLITICS
Pubs have often been involved in politics: providing a platform for speeches, reward for voters and a rostrum for Parliamentary results. In C18 pubs were deliberately used for political ends: proprietors were chosen by the landowners for their political affiliation, their houses became propaganda centres and gathering-places for those of like mind who would sally out to attack street demonstrations by those of a different party. Inn signs became symbols of political sympathy (a tendency which had begun at the Reformation) and names were changed to reflect the support of the owner. Even certain drinks acquired political implications (cf. below). Something of the variety of reflections given by inn names may be seen in the following examples: *Daylight Saving, Free Trade, French Revolution, Reform. Land of Liberty* commemorates a Chartist agricultural experiment of 1846–51; *Spanish Patriot*, remembers Spanish Legion which fought against Franco (1936)

while Tolpuddle has its *Martyrs* who tried to form a Union (1834). *Man of Steel* recalls the Sheffield steel-workers admiration for Stalin, *John F. Kennedy* has been honoured, while *Red Jackets*, Camborne, Cornwall recalls imposition there of martial law in 1880s. Older events are remembered in *This Ancient Boro*, Tenterden, Kent and *Wat Tyler* led the Peasants' Revolt of 1381.

POLITICAL DRINKS
In C18 punch was so favoured a drink among the Whigs that *Punchbowl* became almost a party badge and inns with this name were generally centres of Whig activity, meeting places for their supporters, etc. The Tory preference was more for sack, claret and canary. There is *Punchbowl & Ladle* at Penelewey, Cornwall.

PORCHES
C18 coaching houses are distinguished by prominent porches with flat roofs supported by sturdy columns. Above the roof there is usually a full length opening window. These porches were sometimes used as a platform for loading and unloading the considerable luggage carried on the top of coaches (though some inns provided special 'loading bays' in the yard which gave direct access to bedrooms along a corridor or gallery). The porch roof was frequently used as a podium from which speeches (particularly political) could be made to the crowd assembled below and from which important announcements, election results, military victories, etc. could be made.

PORT
England acquired advantageous trading relations with Portugal in C18 (q.v.) and, as a result, port became very popular especially in view of the increased duty on French wines.

PORTER
Gone, but not quite forgotten; porter was first brewed in Shoreditch in 1722 and last brewed in Dublin in 1973.

Porter was the first national beer since it travelled well whereas local styles did not (see Entire). The drink is said to have acquired its name either because it was particularly popular with the porters of Covent Garden or because Harwood's delivery man announced his arrival with a stentorian call for a 'Porter'! It was notably bitter, probably brewed with roasted malt, well fermented, dark and thick and it mixed well with London water. The Dublin brewers, Guinness, was founded in 1759 and switched entirely to porter production in 1799. Its 'plain porter' became the drink of the Irish working man until it was slowly superseded by the slightly heavier 'extra stout'. The final evolution is the bitter stout which has not only become synonymous with the name of Guinness (q.v.) but a monopoly.

POST HOUSE
Inn providing a staging post, usually 12 or 15 miles (depending on road conditions) from the next. It provided a change of horses and postillion for the lucrative posting trade. The transport was usually a chaise, a light carriage with an opening hood and pulled by a pair of horses. This C18 development probably originated in the Tudor period when documents and letters of State were carried by royal posts along the four main post-roads: London–Dover for France; London–Plymouth for navy; Great North Road for communication with North and Scotland, while Wales was reached via Chester. In C17 the posts carried occasional private letters which were delivered at inns where the inn-keepers acted as postmasters and were responsible for local delivery. National post office was established in 1657 with a monopoly for both letter carrying and for furnishing the post-horses.

POST WORLD WAR II

Pub developments from the 1940s to present have been fast and varied. 1948 saw the nationalisation of the New Town pubs under Labour and 1952 saw their denationalisation under the Conservatives. There were massive mergers and amalgamations between breweries and the period saw the introduction of plastic hoses, metal pressurised kegs, lighter beers which were indistinguishable apart from their labels, the disappearance of choice and local specialities on the Lowest Common Denominator principle by 'chemicalisation' and standardisation.

The houses were affected by the increased 'coach' trade, producing more faked interiors and demolition of the small cosy rooms to provide mass consumption for mass production while juke boxes and gaming machines increased their profits at the expense of conversation and privacy. It was an era of fake beams and fake horse-brasses, pin-tables, soft drinks and Muzak. There were more managers and fewer landlords, less stability and more change, more expensive but weaker beer. The alleged dangers of State monopoly and lack of choice were replaced by the fact of near capitalist monopoly and lack of choice. This situation led to rise of CAMRA (q.v.).

PRICES

In 1400 best ale was sold at 1½d. a gallon.

In 1500 the price had doubled.

In 1600 West Riding Quarter Sessions ordered that no ale was to be sold at more than 1d. a quart.

Modern prices are, of course, savagely affected by Excise Tax which e.g. is more than £5 on a bottle of whisky. They also can vary quite considerably between pubs, less between rooms in the same pub but more again between different beers in the same room. One advantage of the EEC has been the public display of bar prices.

PRIME MINISTERS   see also *Politicians*

It has been noticed that all prime ministers between 1839 and 1895 have a place among inn names but from 1895 to the present only three have been so commemorated.

PRINCES   see also *Feathers*

Among the Princes remembered in pub names are the frequent *Prince of Wales, Black Prince*, Farnham; *Prince of Teck*, London SW5 and Prince of Orange alias *Brave Maurice*, Whitechapel Road, London, also *Regent*.

PRIVATE BAR

Originally meant a private part of the house where the stocks were kept, later it was used for orders only (the antecedant of Jug and Bottle, q.v.). By 1870s, 'Private Bar' had acquired a new meaning: it was literally a bar into which people went to be private. It had not only partitions which screened it from other bars but it was even screened from the counter and its drinks were served through a gap below eye-level. Naturally, customers paid a little more for this privacy. By last decade of C19 it was quite common for pubs to have a couple of public bars and a couple of private ones, perhaps a smaller and larger in each category. Private rooms for individuals had always been available at a price but the Industrial Revolution seems to have had the effect of screening classes or minor sub-divisions of classes from each other (see Snob Screens).

Private Bar (late C19)

PRODUCTION
UK is third largest producer of beer in the world with over 38½ million barrels a year, coming third to West Germany and the USA. We are lower in rank of consumers, and declining, coming about tenth with something like 190 pints per head per year.

PUBS
The commonest and peculiarly English name for a licensed house with one or more public bars. There is a joke that in York the streets are called gates, the gates bars and the bars pubs. Though it is estimated that there are some 70,000 examples of the genus 'pub', the word is a surprisingly recent expression only coming into common use, as not only an abbreviation of 'public house' but the familiar expression, in the latter half of C19 which has been described as the pub's 'brassiest age'.

PUBABLE
On analogy with Dr Johnson's 'clubable' man, one might attempt an analysis of the 'pubable' one. He likes to feel welcome, whether he is introvert or extrovert and he likes to feel at home. In other words, he asks for two relationships: one with the gov'nor and/or his staff, the other with the institution itself – he likes to be at ease in a friendly and sympathetic atmosphere. He likes a sense of continuity and tradition. He likes some choice in his drinking and a respect for beers in the licensee. He likes the possibility of variety in the size and nature of the groups which he may join and the feeling that he may join in even if, for the moment, he prefers to be by himself. In short, he likes to be able to decide for himself the extent of his privacy or his communality. He likes to be warm and comfortable and have the possibility of conversation and to choose between friends and strangers in the range of his conversation. If he wants comparative silence he should be able to find it and not be assaulted, willy-nilly, by juke-box or the mechanical or electronic noise of games machines. Of course he wants good beer but he also appreciates the permanent availability of 'small chop' with some variety if it is only limited to nuts, cheese, crisps or a sandwich.

PUBLICAN
A useful but not very accurate word. It meant first a tax-farmer and then, by extension, a gatherer of taxes. With excise duty what it is, perhaps the word is not so inaccurate after all but it hardly defines what the man or woman who runs a pub would regard as their central function. Technically, he might be owner, tenant or manager (q.v.). There is no defined route to this job, though most 'gov'nors' have had some preparatory experience and the brewers run short training courses for their employees. It is often a family tradition and there are some free-holders who owned more than one pub. Some make a ladder for themselves as they ascend from manager through tenant to owning their own free house. Others find promotion in rising to responsibility for bigger houses with higher financial rewards. Very often, running a pub is a second career after lengthy experience in some other form of work – perhaps most frequently in the police or armed forces but by no means necessarily so and the man behind the bar may have come from almost any other trade or profession.

PUBLIC BAR
The basic pub room, sometimes referred to simply as the Bar but with alternatives such as Tap Room, Vault(s). It is directly descended from the kitchen of the inn or the tap-room of the tavern where the casks were stored. This room was open to the 'general' – labourers, pack-horse drivers, waggoners, etc., while those with some social pretensions were received in the parlour, private room, or later, in the coffee room. The public bar has a special character, well described in B. Davis (op. cit. 73f) as having 'a rather sophisticated hardness and smoothness appropriate to its

kitchen tradition. It has an honest-to-goodness, down to earth, character, a restrained masculinity and a controlled strength'. It should give an impression of warmth, both actual and human and of shelter and seclusion from the outside world. However simple the furniture, there should appear to be plenty of it with no sense of vast areas of empty floor. There should be no internal divisions but there might well be nooks and corners. There should be no 'colour scheme' but the prevailing note should be a 'symphony in brown'. Neither should there be any frills or fuss but a certain hardness and spareness – it is a room where the pleasures of social drinking more than compensate for the unnoticed lack of interior springs or padding in the furniture.

PUBLIC HOUSE

Up to C19, the tavern was literally a 'public house', i.e. a private residence whose occupant made some of his rooms available for the entertainment of the public. His relation to them was that of host to guests, the rooms were furnished as they would be in any equivalent private house, visitors were looked after, as they would be in a private house, according to their status: upper ranks by waiters (footmen) in the parlour, lower by pot boys in the tap room (equivalent to the servants' hall). The original bar was a form of the housekeeper's (or chamberlain's) room. The exterior was exactly the same as that of a private house except for a more or less distinguishable sign-board, hence the possible confusion exploited in C18/19 drama.

Malt Shovel, Spondon

Today, the point about public houses is still that they are public. Unlike a club with which it has some similarities, the pub is essentially open to all – absolutely anyone (above a certain age) may come in. If a pub becomes invaded or monopolised by any sort of exclusive clique who freeze out either locals or the chance customer that house has, in fact, ceased to be what it was licensed to be.

PUBLIC ROOMS

The rooms for drinking as distinct from the private accommodation of the proprietor. They are usually confined to the ground floor, at least in a small house. Their names proliferated, particularly in C19 so that there were Public Bars and Private Bars, Men Only and Women Only, Taps, Vaults, 'Spit & Sawdust', Snugs and Saloons, Jug & Bottle, Smoke Room and Parlour. Sometimes there were special rooms which accommodated a particular facility: Billiard Room; Music Room; Coffee Room; News Room; etc. These names changed with fashion, function and (to some extent) geographical location e.g. in North the Public Bar is sometimes known as the Vault(s). Similarly the News Room might be called the Tap Room and the Smoke Room, the Best Room, Music Room, Snug, Parlour or (in our time) Lounge. On the whole, women were allowed in Jug & Bottle, certain Private Bars and the Smoke Room but not in the News Room or the (Public) Bar.

'PULL'

The handle of the old-fashioned beer-pump and perhaps the most universal symbol and indication of an English pub. It is perhaps the only item of visible pub furniture which does not occur in some other context. 'Besides this, they have a sculptural strength and elegance which, even regarded as an abstract form, gives delight' (Davis, op. cit, 61). In the '20s and '30s there was an unfortunate attempt to modernise their traditional form into a cylinder mounted on a cone but worse was to come. In '60s thousands of engines were torn out of

Pull

pubs and their pulls sold for 7s. 6d. (37½p) each in a characteristic surge of brewers' vandalism cf. previous 'face lifts' which have altered frontages, changed signs and letterings, ousted Victorian furniture, removed Edwardian glass, etc.

One of the many benefits of CAMRA (q.v.) was to rescue and restore many beer-pump handles, though now they are not always functional. The normal assemblage is two but three is quite common and there are occasionally splendid units of five or more pulls.

Keg beer and pressure service banished beer engines and their splendid handles, pleasing in shape and often embellished in brass or painted ceramic, and replaced these noble artefacts by 'a squalid row of deformed and strident boxes', garish in colour, sometimes internally lit and often tortured into some sort of trade mark.

PUMPS
Electric pumps, often via a metered dispenser, are increasingly used to raise beer from the cellar to the dispensing point but traditionalists prefer the manual bar pumps or beer engine (q.v.).

PUNCH see *Political Drink*

PUNCHEON
Large cask for liquids, fish, etc., usually of a specific volume according to the commodity it was intended to contain, e.g. rum puncheon holds about two gallons. *Rum Puncheon*, Boston, Lincs. was birthplace of John Foxe, martyrologist.

PURITANISM
Powerful religious and social forces increased their influence in England from the last years of Henry VIII until their triumph rather more than a century later in the establishment of the Commonwealth. The purification of church and state also involved individual behaviour. Drinking has always been abused but the Puritans made some previously innocent practices sinful. Sunday which the Christians had made a holy day which had always been celebrated with a little drinking became, under the Commonwealth, the very day on which drinking was not allowed. Landlords could be fined such large sums as 30s. for permitting it on their premises and the drinkers themselves were fined sums varying from 1s.4d. (itself a considerable sum) to as much as 5s. Brewing itself was forbidden on the Fast Days ordained by the Commonwealth and offenders were fined e.g. 2s. People resisting the inspectors were also fined e.g. 10s. Christmas was (rightly) seen as incorporating pagan elements and was therefore 'abolished'. The Restoration brought a reaction celebrated by restoration of old inn sings and erection of new ones: *King's Head, Royal Oak, Rose Revived, King's Arms*.

PURL
A very popular drink in early C19 which was a sort of fortified beer. To a barrel of strong ale was added a variety of herbs, roots and fruits and this mixture was left to mature for some months before being tapped. Later in the century 'purl' seems to have been equated to 'dog's nose' = hot beer with a dash of gin.

PUZZLE VESSELS
C17 ale-house humour produced a number of challenge or puzzle vessels including: Wager or Puzzle Jug – usually with many spouts, some with perforations in the neck but it was possible to empty them by sucking if you knew the trick. Some of them were inscribed with a challenge.
Ale Yard or Long Glass – this was a trumpet-shaped vessel, a yard in length with the narrow end enclosed and expanded into a large bowl. The challenge was to empty it without taking the mouth away from and the problem essentially consists in the change of flow when air reaches

Ale Yard

the bulb, displacing its content with a splash, tending to startle the drinker and cause him to withdraw his mouth under the shock of the cold liquid on his face and perhaps on his clothes.

QUEEN, QUEEN'S HEAD
A fairly common pub name but its exact application is far from clear. The earliest of these signs may be derived from Our Lady, Queen of Heaven cf. *Seven Stars, Maid's Head*. When they have been made to refer to an earthly Queen, Queen Elizabeth I is often portrayed and there is a *Queen Bess*, Scunthorpe. Others mentioned by name include *Queen Edith*, Cambridge – wife of Edward the Confessor – and there is a *Queen Catherine* (Parr), Osmotherley, a wife of Henry VIII and a *Queen Adelaide*, consort of William IV, Rye. Usually the Queen is nameless and only indicated by the picture on the sign e.g. at Box, Ane Boleyn; at Colney Heath, Jane Seymour.

Queen Victoria is expectedly popular and her likeness appears e.g. at *Queen*, Penzance; *Queen's Head*, Bermondsey and London also has a rare *Queen & Prince Albert* in Great Titchfield Street.

RACEHORSES
Particularly in Northern England, racehorses have provided a fruitful source for pub names. Examples include *Alice Hawthorn* (1842–5), *Altisdora* (1813), *Beeswing, Charles XII, Little Wonder* (1840), *Non Plus*. *Revellers Arms*, Yafforth, is named after 1818 winner of St Leger; *Running Horses*, Mickleham, commemorates dead heat of 1828 Derby; *Smoker, Why Not* and *Young Vanish* were all racehorses but *Sir Tatton Sykes* was an enthusiastic race-goer. *Gimcrack*, York does not refer to inn building but commemorates the famous Gimcrack Stakes run on local racecourse. Other 'event' names include *St Leger, Chase*.

RAILWAY
The increased popularity of rail travel had two effects on regard to inns. Positively, the railway companies built their own hostelries, particularly in proximity to the great termini and smaller houses often acquired the name *Railway* or *Station* by association. The negative effect was on the old coaching inns whose trade was hit so hard that many shrank in size and some disappeared altogether.

But increased (and cheaper) travelling led to the development of a holiday trade in suitable localities and some hostelries became holiday inns providing accommodation over extended periods e.g. *Morritt Arms*, Greta Bridge. Others provided stop-over board and lodging for railway users or a social centre for those concerned with the building or maintenance of the system.

Inn names are most frequently *Railway* but there are references to the great companies such as *Great Northern, Great Western, Midland*, etc. and there are less obvious railway associations such as *Marlow Donkey*. *George and Dragon*, Yarm has a plaque commemorating meeting which initiated first passenger railway in the world. Famous locomotives are commemorated: *Flying Scotsman, Silver Link*, expresses like *Royal Scot* and routes like *Silver Arrow*. The 'Beeching Axe' (closures of 1963, 1965) produced many *Silent Whistle*(s). There is an *Engine & Tender* at St Neots, Hunts. while Spennymoor, Durham has a 'set': *North Eastern, Railway* and *Station*.

A recent development in railway catering, 'Tavellers-Fare' has been the introduction of real ale into buffet-bars with special advertising.

RAM
A common sign in cloth-making areas. It was the crest of the Clothworkers' Company. The rare *Ram & Teazle* has a double reference since the latter was used to raise up the nap on cloth.

RARITIES see also *Corruption, Oddities*

Rare inn names can fall into very different classes and every explorer will be tempted to make his own collection. They might include such varieties as *Cardinal*, Francis Street, Westminster; *Stephen Langton*, Friday Street, Surrey; *Friar's Oak*, Hassocks, Sussex; or *Cat & Custard Pot*, Shelton, Beds.; *Leg of Mutton & Cauliflower*, Ashtead, Surrey or *Voyager*, South Shields, Durham; *Oasis*, Redcar, Cleve.; *Portcullis*, Chipping Sodbury. There is *Royal Standard of England* at Forty Green, Bucks.; *Free Library*, Queensway between Birkenhead and Liverpool; *Catash*, North Cadbury, Som. from the ancient 'Hundred' in which it stands, *Tyacks*, Camborne, Cornwall from the Cornish for 'farmer', *Hammer & Stithy* (anvil), Ossett, W. Yorks., *Spacey Houses*, nr. Harrogate.

REAL ALE

The campaigning name for traditional draught beer which is brewed only from the finest natural ingredients: malted barley, pure water and hops fermented into alcohol by yeast. These same simple ingredients can produce all the varieties of bitter, mild, winter brews, old ales, barley wines and porter. The dispensing system should avoid pressurised CO_2 or carbonic acid gas. Compare the old rhyme:

He that buys land buys many stones
He that buys flesh buys many bones
He that buys eggs buys many shells
But he that buys good beer buys nothing else.

BR Real Ale Sign

'REAL' SIGNS

There are occasions when the sign of the inn is replaced by the actual object corresponding to the pub's name. A well-known example is *Beehive*, Grantham. There is also the water wheel at *Water Mill* nr. Pately Bridge and there are occurrences of coaches, etc. as well as the unique hanging sign of *Bath*, Dewsbury.

REBUILDING see also *Modification*

The posting or coaching era was the time for large scale modification in a very large number of inns but an old house was rarely rebuilt in its entirety unless, as too often happened, it was burnt down. The usual practice was to rebuild the central or front portion in the contemporary (Georgian) style and the older structure can often still be traced in the wings or by the roof line.

RECORDS

Inns are centres of lively general competitiveness and there has, inevitably, been much rivalry in liquor consumption. Space permits of only one competitor for the 'Book of Records'. An obituary in the 'Gentleman's Magazine' of December 1810 recorded the death 'at Ewes farmhouse, Yorkshire, aged 76, of Mr Paul Parnell, farmer, grazier and maltster who, during his lifetime, drank out of one silver cup upwards of £2,000 sterling of Yorkshire Stingo, being remarkably attached to Stingo tipple of the home-brewed best quality. The calculation is made at 2d. per cupful (i.e. nearly a quarter million cups!). He was the bon-vivant whom O'Keefe celebrated in more than one of his bacchanalian songs under the apellation of 'Toby Philpott'.

In a different field, the sporting squire Osbaldestone celebrated his feat of riding 200 miles in less than nine hours by drinking at *Rutland Arms*, Newmarket all night until the sun rose high above the Rowley Mile. Osbaldestone, whose Arms used to be born by the pub at Allenston, N. Yorks. was no mean record-breaker: his record ride was for a bet of 1,000 guineas; he fought and beat the army's boxing champion; he caught a fox, badger and otter within 24 hours to win another wager and he also claimed to possess the best pack of fox-hounds in the country.

RED LATTICE
In C16–17 it was the almost universal custom for ale-houses to have open windows to allow fresh air into their crowded and smoky interiors. Some privacy was provided by a trellis or lattice, coloured red, fixed in front of the windows which enables the inmates to see out but prevented outsiders from seeing in. (There is a reference to this in Shakespeare's Henry IV.)

This provision led to an almost total identification between red lattice and inn: 'As well known by my wit as an alehouse by a red lattice' (Marston: Antonio and Mellida) cf. Decker's: 'a whole street is in some places but a continuous ale-house, not a shop to be seen between red lattice and red lattice' (1632). Sometimes, unusually, the lattice was coloured green and this is allegedly the origin of *Green Lettuce*.

RED LION
There are hundreds of pubs with this name and sign of which many may be derived from the badge of John of Gaunt (1340–99), 'time-honoured Lancaster' whose estates covered vast areas of the country. There are a few signs which show the man himself.

Red Lion

REGENCY see also *Prince*
It was probably in this period that the pub reached its zenith in terms of popularity, prosperity and social function. It saw the climax of the coaching era and was a great age for clubs and associations which found their first homes in inns which were also the centre for a variety of recreational activities in both town and country. Indeed, they were often the only available accommodation. The Regency period was the age for balls in the Assembly Rooms and saw the inn become the host for increasing numbers of private coaches, a stopping place for chaises and developing its posting and coaching trade. Inns were the scene of hunt breakfasts, gambling and wagers but above all cards, smoking and intoxication. It was this era which saw the transition from the old inn to the modern hotel as in the case of *Stamford* Hotel, Stamford with its distinguished classical front designed in 1820.

REGULATIONS see also *Legislation*
'No priest to be an ale-scop (i.e. reciter in an ale-house) nor in any wise act the gleeman' (St Dunstan *c.*965 AC).

'All alehouses to be forbidden except those which shall be licensed by the Common Council of the City of Guildhall . . . And that no . . . alewife brew by night, either with reeds or straw, or stubble, but with wood only' (City of London, 1189).

'There shall be standard measures for ale, wine and corn' (Magna Carta, 1215).

'No brewster shall henceforth sell except by true measure, viz. the gallon, the pottle (or half gallon) and the quart . . . the tun to be 150 gallons' (Assize of 1277).

RELIGIOUS NAMES see also *Boot, Crusades, Ecclesiastical, Saints*
In view of the religious origin of inns, it is not surprising that many still bear names and/or signs which are reminders of this fact. *Adam & Eve* is suitably situated in Paradise, Glos. For *Anchor, Angel and Bell*, see separate entries. There is an *Ark* and a *Catherine Wheel* which may be related to a small and obscure order called the Knights of St Catherine. *Cock* is frequent as is *Cross Keys*, both symbols of St Peter. There is a *Crutched Friar, Black Friar, Friar's Oak* as well as a *Shaven Crown. Jacob's Ladder,*

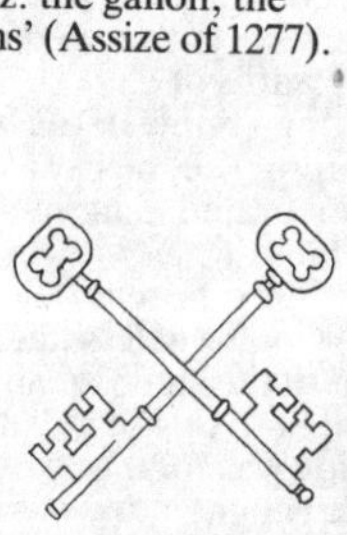
Cross Keys

Noah's Ark, and a rare *Bell & the Dragon* and *Samson & the Lion* all occur as do *Lamb, Lamb & Flag, Lion & Lamb*. The *Three Crowns* may refer to the Three Kings or Magi who followed the *Star*, alias *Star in the East. Manor of God Begot* reminds us that it was once a religious hospice as *Mitre & Keys* refers to former property of Petrine see. The frequent *Ship* may once have been the *Ark, Salutation* is old name of Annunciation and in this grouping we might include *Good Samaritan* and *Holy Well*. Many religious names were obliterated by design at the Reformation, some were lost by accident later while others disappeared with the house that bore them.

RELIGIOUS HOUSES see also *Monestery*
Many present inns were once part of a monastery or provided by a religious house for its guests e.g. *Lord Crewe Arms*, Blanchland; *Red Lion*, Wingham, Kent; *Manor of God Begot*, Winchester. *Angel*, Grantham was founded by Templars and *Rothley Court*, Leics. occupies a Templar site.

REMOTE INNS
One can be firm about the highest inn but remoteness is more difficult to estimate. Should one look on Exmoor, Dartmoor or in the High Pennines? Frequently *Moorcock* occupies a remote location. A likely contender for the remotest inn would be *Green Dragon*, Hurst, W. Yorks. at end of cul-de-sac and five miles from the nearest village (Reeth).

RENAMING see also *Changed Name*
Pubs have been renamed for a variety of reasons: distinction, fashion, amalgamation, religious or political expediency. Occasionally, tradition has been too strong as in the attempt at Bamford, Derbys. to rename *Golden Fleece*, Sir Winston Churchill. White Hart, Chelsea has recently been renamed *Drug Store* and strangely combines bars with boutique and chemist's shop.

REST cf. Halfway House
Traveller's Rest usually occurs after a difficult section of road or a long way from the next inn. There is one at the summit of Kirkstone Pass in the Lake District. There is *Hunters Rest*, Clutton (Som.); *Woodmans Rest*, Shirley, W. Mid.; *Miners Rest*, Long Ashton. There is a rare *Boatman's Rest* at Barnsley, near the canal. *Rest and be thankful* is often in barren or hilly terrain and represents a haven after an arduous or perilous journey.

Traveller's Rest, Crimple, Nr. Harrogate

RESTRICTION
Of public drinking places is chiefly effected by licensing (q.v.). The first close control of numbers of houses seems to have begun in 1552 but it does not seem to have been very effective and the situation was complicated by the connection between religious reformation and antipathy to pubs. A 1591 report on Lancashire and Cheshire, centres of Catholic resistance, states that the streets and ale-houses were so crowded during (Anglican) service time that there was no one in the Established church except the Parson and his clerk. It went on to say that ale-houses were innumerable and that great abuses prevailed.

In 1618 a letter to Lords in Council complained that though London's taverns had been limited to 40 in 1552, there were now 400 in the City alone. About 20 years later, the Middlesex justices reduced the ale-houses in Covent Garden from 24 to four. Fairs and markets also increased the pressure for more drinking provision and in early C17 John Taylor, a supporter of this facility, argued for the 'fruitfulness' of ale by stating that during the annual fair in the small town of Kinbolton, Northants., its 38 dwellings became 39 ale-houses as one house was divided into two in order to serve more.

Ale House

RETAIL OUTLETS
By C15 there were three main types of houses selling fermented liquors to the public:
Alehouses, sometimes called tippling houses (q.v.) where beer and ale were brewed and sold on the premises.
Taverns where wine as well as beer and ale could be sold.
Inns which provided shelter, stabling, etc. as well as food and drink.

ROADS & ROUTES see also *Communications*
Former ways for farers by foot or with beasts are commemorated by *Carriers, Waggoners, Packhorse, Drivers*, also by various *Rests, Turnpikes, Bridges* and *Gates* and the unusual *Portway*, Staunton-on-Wye, Heref. & Worcs. which marked the way to town for carriers. Other examples would include the various *Junctions* (the one near Holmfirth has a good modern sign), *Broad Highway, Roundabout* and *Old Roundabout* and the more recent *Flyover* and *Turnpike Motor Inn*.

ROLLING WAY
The steep incline down which barrels are run from immediately under the cellar flaps outside the pub to the level of the cellar floor inside.

ROMANS
Were responsible for the introduction of inns to England and Wales. They were originally halts on their great roads but they often also grew in their towns as well as the taverns which existed there and on the fringe of their camps. The Roman inn was called a 'mansio' (cf. 'In my Father's house are many mansions' which means 'rest house') providing food, drink and sleeping quarters and usually situated a day's march from the next. The larger examples had a 'warming room' with a fire, sometimes baths and usually stabling. One excavated at Housesteads seems to indicate a murder and the secret disposal of the resulting body. Besides the inns, there were also taverns or 'tabernae', designed by the bush of vine leaves which also passed into English inn signs.

Mansio

ROOMS
Inn rooms were of two main kinds: the private guest rooms and the more public rooms for eating and drinking. In a lease of 1473, *George*, Salisbury was stated to possess 13 guest chambers: Principal Chamber, Earl's Chamber with adjoining pantry, Oxford Chamber, Abingdon Chamber, Squire's Chamber, Lombard's Chamber, Garrett, George, Clarendon, Understent, Fitzwaryn and London Chamber. (It is interesting that some of the names of these individual rooms are also found as the name of an entire inn.) Besides these private chambers, the inn also possessed a 'taberna', Buttery, Tap House, Kitchen, Hostelry and Parlour. The practice of identifying all rooms by names continued into the Tudor period when we find such designations as 'Darke Parlour', 'Corner Chamber', 'Maister Hussye's Chamber', etc. Later, more fanciful names honouring distinguished guests or derived from the room's decoration occur such as 'Reine Chamber', 'Flower de Luce Chamber'. This distinguished accommodation was, of course, confined to the quality; less important guests were lodged in anonymous garrets or 'cock lofts' under the roof.

The principal rooms at *Duke's Head*, King's Lynn were originally known as 'Wainscot Room', 'Great Parlour', 'Hare', 'Parlour' and 'Cockfighting Room'. *Royal Fountain*, Sheerness still possess door labels with designs of gilt on a grey-green background indicating 'Rose', 'Crown', 'Star' and 'Sun' rooms among the private accommodation. For the later names of public rooms (q.v.) and individual entries.

ROUND
If two people meet in a pub, convention requires that each buy the other a drink in an order decided by first arrival, argument or whatever. Thus two in a group means two drinks and these are paid for as bought, unlike the Continental system. Three means three drinks and the larger the group, necessarily the larger is the amount of drink consumed since a member who misses his round tends to be 'persona non grata'. It is almost a matter of honour not to leave a group without paying for a round, 'standing one's whack', 'claiming my throw', 'making my shout', 'paying my Wally (Grout)' or whatever is the current phrase. Since the unit of drink is customarily a pint, the practice of 'rounds' has been (wrongly) held to explain the necessary weakness of English beer since otherwise, in a large group, incapacity would prevent completion of a round by all its members.

ROYAL
An inn name may commemorate a regal visit but more often it is simply a loyal compliment. The Royal Arms in inns called *Kings Arms* (q.v.) may if they have been correctly delineated, give a clue to the age of the house bearing this sign. *Royal Children*, Nottingham refers to legend that James II's children played with those of the contemporary inn-keeper. *Royal Oak* commemorates the future Charles II's escape from his enemies at Boscobel in 1651 by hiding in an oak tree. This happy event was remembered in Oak Apple Day and by numerous inns which adopted this name after the Restoration in 1666.

SACK
Dry Sherry was a well-established drink in C16 but by about 1600 some medical men were viewing it with considerable doubts:

> Sacke doth make men fat and foggy, and therefore is not to be taken of young men. Being drunke before supper with a store of sugar, it provoketh appetite, comforteth the spirits marvellously and concocteth raw humours. Canary sacke is more full of spirits than any other.
> (William Vaughan: Directions for Health, naturall and artificiall, 1600)

SAILORS see also *Admiral, Ship*
Besides *Jolly Sailors* and (unique) *Tumbling Sailors* at Kidderminster, many inn names celebrate individual maritime exploits. Apart from *Nelson* (see Hero), there are pubs bearing the names of *Captain Cook*, discoverer of Australia; *Drake* and *Hawkins*, Elizabethan buccaneers; *Captain Webb*, the first Channel swimmer. Admirals include *Rodney, Duncan* and *Hawke* and one wonders if some of these are not acts of gratitude by sailors using their prize-money to set up a pub. Perhaps the most recent sailor to be honoured is *Lone Yachtsman* for a single-handed crossing of the Atlantic.

SAINTS see also *Bishops, Religious*
In consequence of their ecclesiastical connections many inn names are associated with Christian saints. The chief saint appears in *Maid's Head, Salutation* (q.v.) and *Seven Stars*. Other survivors include *Bishop Blaise*, patrol of woolcombers, *Catherine* of the wheel, *St John*, Torpoint and Blackburn – probably the Baptist, patrol of Templars; *St John of Jerusalem*, London EC1, patron of Hospitallers; *St Peter's Finger* is probably a corruption of St Peter ad Vincula to whom nearby church is dedicated; *St Loyes*, Exeter is patron saint of blacksmiths and the favourite oath of Chaucer's prioress. Some saints are hidden under their symbol: St Peter's Keys, St Lawrence's Gridiron, etc. *Startled Saint*, West Malling has a modern sign showing St Lawrence (?) 'buzzed' by a plane from the wartime station.

SALOON BAR

Swan, Bridgnorth

Name came into use in last decades of C19 but its original connotation is unclear. It tended to become a larger and more dominant feature in pub planning in 1890s and at this time and subsequently was characterised by being larger than the other bars, always having a fireplace and usually better furnished: carpeted, leather-upholstered seats, heavy wallpaper, pictures and even vases of flowers. In short, it was designed to make the (lower) middle class feel at home.

Its ancestry lies rather in the parlour of the inn than the kitchen of the tavern and together with the Public Bar it came to form the pub rooms proper. There is no real distinction between Smoke Room and Saloon Bar, they are regional names for the same thing: the former being the preferred Northern name.

SALUTATION

Once a very popular sign – the old English word for Annunciation and should represent the archangel Gabriel saluting the Blessed Virgin with the words 'Ave Maria' (Lk.i.28). During the Commonwealth, many inns with this sign were renamed 'Soldier & Citizen' presumably requiring a minimum reworking of the sign.

SEA see also *Battles, Sailors, Ships*

There is a *Lighthouse*, Wallasey; *Pilot*, Exmouth (fine modern sign) and *Cruel Sea*, London NW3 opened by Nicholas Montserrat.

SEASONS

Rarely occur in inn names, but there is *Flowering Spring*, Shiplake, Oxon., and *Four Seasons*, Yate, Avon (with a good sign).

SERVANTS

Medieval Inn Servants

From C16 the servants of an inn included ostlers (who saw to horses), chamberlains (male forerunners of chambermaids but with higher status), tapsters (men who tapped barrels and drew ale or wine) and pot boys who ran between cellars and drinking room with pots of ale or beer. The service by C19 was not all it might be when inn was described in Torrington Diaries as:

> seat of all roguery, profaneness and debauchery . . . the innkeepers are insolent, the hostlers are sulky, the chambermaids are pert, and the waiters are impertinent; the meat is tough, the wine if foul, the beer is hard, the sheets are wet, the linen is dirty and the knives are never clean'd.

Servants in general have given their name to a number of pubs e.g. *Black Boy*, popular in C17–18; *Running Footman, Two Chairmen* (Sedan Chair carriers); *Ram Jam* (Indian Table servant credited with drink recipe), *Trusty Servant* (with unique sign).

SERVERY

Area from which drinks are distributed and therefore related to drinking area. In larger houses it tends to be either a single 'corridor' running through each licensed room or a central point in an open-plan design.

SERVICE
The disappearance of pot boys and waiters and their replacement by the bar (q.v.) was contemporaneous with other changes associated with mass production and industrialisation. A bar fitted with pumps and cocks produced much quicker turnover than servants scuttling in and out of cellars and stores. C19 pub was rapidly tending towards a shop serving passing casual trade or off-sales for home consumption. The tempo of life was speeding up: counter clerks and industrial workers were travelling further to their work and increasingly deprived of spare time as they became more servants of machines and subject to time-tables. More money could be made by providing less service and encouraging quicker turnover. Tavern-keeping became a business rather than a service and customers consumers rather than friends.

SETTLE
Perhaps the oldest survivor of traditional pub furniture: usually fixed or built in with high back and sometimes solid ends to eliminate draughts. Later versions are normally slightly curved in plan and placed to one side of tap-room fireplace so that most remote occupants are brought forward to bring fire within their view. The curve is also sociable, tending to bring occupants into sight of each other and encourage talk and companionship. The shaped 'settle ends' are often attractive.

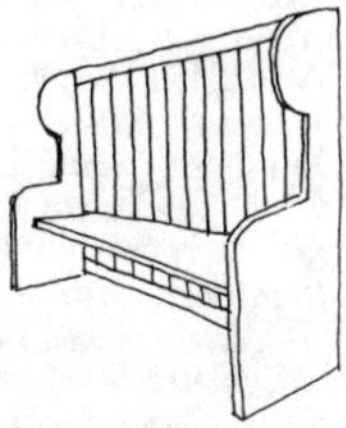
Traditional Settle

SEVENTEENTH CENTURY
Many taverns of this period occupied the first floor of a building whose ground floor was given over to other purposes. One arrangement was to have the inn above and an associated ale-house below: a custom which is reflected in contemporary hotels where the private part with its own lounge and bar is on the first floor while the public rooms (including bars) are at ground level.

This century saw the Great Rebellion of the rising bourgeoisie against the king and its success brought in the Protectorate, the nearest thing to a dictatorship that this country has ever endured and the associated ideology brought attacks not only on traditional religion but also on traditional pleasures. Christmas was abolished and the whole trade and custom of drinking and hospitality suffered a severe set-back. The Restoration was a reaction with more indulgence which not only brought more trade to inns but also effected a revival of tavern life:

> All ranks and conditions of people gathered there for every conceivable social purpose. It was a rendezvous, a business office, a postal address. professional men and court officials were 'to be heard' at such and such a tavern. Men went there to sit in the warmth, to read, to gossip and to smoke. (B. Davis: op. cit. p. 9)

A French traveller in the reign of Charles II described the customary entertainment in inns of the time. They sent for a band of all kinds of instruments ('among these the harp is most esteemed by the English') to accompany their supper where they were joined by the landlady and her daughters 'to entertain the guests at table with pleasant conceits, where they drink as much as the men'. The reporter mentions the 'disgusting' habit of drinking healths from a common cup and that of providing, after supper, a packet of tobacco and pipes 'which is a general custom, as well among women as men, who think that without tobacco one cannot live in England because, they say, it dissipates the evil humours of the brain'.

SHANDY
A refreshing and weak drink, often taken in hot weather, consisting of a mixture of bitter beer and lemonade. Trading standards have not fixed the relative proportions but it is generally assumed that the beer should be at least half.

SHERRY see also *Sack*
Sack or Seck came to England in early C16 as a dry, yellowish wine, sometimes made more attractive to local taste by the addition of sugar, spices, eggs or toast. 'Bristow milk' in 1634.

SHREWSBURY
The brewery at Wem belongs to Greenall Whitley (see Lancs.).

Swan, Bridgnorth

SHIPS
Occur in inn names both as types and as individual vessels. *Ship* is by far the commonest. There is a rare *Ship Ahoy* at Bridlington, but there are also *Bombay Grab* (used to transport IPA in C18), *Foy Boat* (serving vessels becalmed in Downs), *Hoy* (river and coastal boat) also (Llandoger) *Trow* (small river craft), *Steam Packet, Newcastle Packet, Sloop, Frigate, Bonny Boat* (early form of kayak). Particular vessels include *Antigallican, Bounty, Chieftain, Cutty Sark, Discovery, Flying Dutchman, Fortune of War, Gipsy Moth IV, Golden Hind, Good Intent, Great Harry, Old Albion, Prospect of Whitby, Royal George, Shiny Sheff, Short Blue, Turbinia, Victory, Vauxhall, White Bear. Two Queens*, Upton Park, London E13 refers to Cunarders.

The Albion

SHORTEST NAME
CB is in Arkengarthdale, N. Yorks. The initials are those of Charles Bathurst, lord of the manor in C18 who opened up some of the local leadmines stamping his inials on each pig. Other competitors are *XL*, Garstang and *Ox*, Lebberston, N. Yorks.

SHOVE HA'PENNY
A traditional pub game, dating from C16, surviving mainly in south-west and East Anglia. The object of the game is to nudge with the fleshy part of the palms brass discs into each of nine 'beds' marked on a highly polished board. There are local variants, notably in the Isle of Purbeck, which use a bigger board with different markings.

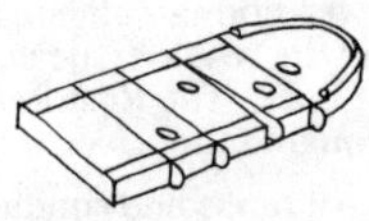
Shove Ha'penny

SIGNS see also *Real Signs*
Tavern signs began with the Romans: 'Vino vendibili suspensa hedera non opus est' – 'there is no need for ivy to indicate a saleable wine' or 'a good wine needs no bush'. The sign of *Bush* (q.v.) is a lineal descendant of the Roman bunch of ivy, a symbol of Bacchus. The Roman sign for a vintner depicted two men carrying on poles a large amphora and this is the iconographic ancestor of *Jolly Brewers*, showing two men carrying a barrel on long poles. The Romans also seem to have used the Chequer Board and *Chequers* was, for centuries, the commonest English sign, often painted at the tops of the door posts at the bar entrance. There is a rare survival at *Methuen Arms*, Corsham. On sign boards it may be the device of the Earls de Warrenne who are said to have had the privilege of licensing ale-houses in Middle Ages but it could also be the Cellarer's Checker. Inn signs seem to have originated from two main traditions: the signs used by monastic hospices and the custom of distinguished visitors displaying arms outside an inn during their temporary residence. Trade signs were of course common to all retail establishments but an enactment of Richard II (1393) required: 'Whosoever shall

brew ale in the town with the intention of selling it must hang out a sign, otherwise he shall forfeit his ale'. This was, of course, to bring the brew within the ambit of the ale-connor (q.v.) but signs were also advertising agents and 20 years earlier there had been a decree against signs extending more than seven feet over the roadway. Nevertheless advertising continued and became particularly ostentatious in C17 e.g. the prodigious sign of *White Hart*, Scole erected at the astronomical cost of over £1,000 in contemporary money. The signs had become so closely associated with the service that a century earlier the loss of licence meant the official removal of the sign and a century later unpopular signs were changed to avoid loss of trade. Taverns seem to have kept to simple signs: stake, barley, sheaf, garland or red paint (see Red Lattice) but inn signs proliferated with increasing diversity during C17 and C18 and were often suspended across the road (see Gallows). Earlier they were simple paintings on board or more rarely on wall or carved on stone slab (examples in Guildhall Museum, London, including *Ape & Apple, George & Dragon, Three Bells, Three Crowns, Three Kings, Goose and Gridiron*) or plaques made from iron or tiles. Recently the individual name of pub has given way to prominent name of owning brewery but there are signs of a welcome tendency to renew the art of the inn sign. Among good examples of signs might be included the fine relief of *Grapes*, Shepherd Market, London and the three-dimensional *Black Friar* in Queen Victoria Street (though the painters might have depicted the Dominican habit more accurately), then there are *Knight*, Avely, Essex; *Redesdale Arms*, Moreton in Marsh, Glos.; *George*, nr. Uldale, Cumb.; *Angel*, Wootton Bassett, Wilts., *Butchers Arms*, Sheepscombe, Glos.; *Coach & Horses*, Gloucester; *Edinburgh Castle*, Hastings; *Flying Machine*, Gloucester; *Green Dragon*, Carlisle; *Lancelot*, Brompton, London; *Quicksilver Mail*, East Coker, Som.; *Sherlock Holmes*, Charing Cross, London; *Squinting Cat*, Harrogate; *Squire*, Chipping Sodbury; *Volunteer*, Chipping Camden.

Inn Sign Board

SIGN PAINTERS

Most are anonymous and, perhaps, deservedly so but some were first-rate artists such as William Hogarth, Richard Wilson, George Morland, 'Old' Crome, Millais and David Cox. In late C18 and early C19, the painting of inn-signs were often a side-line for coach-painters who emblazoned the owners' crests and arms on the panels of their coaches. One such was J.F. Herring (b.1795) who was a coach-painter at Doncaster who branched out into into signs, particularly representations of St Leger winners. Most were painted by itinerant artists, probably in return for a drink and a meal and later in C19 they were executed by sign-writers who painted owners' names over shops and brewers' names over pubs. Recently, brewers have taken an interest in signs, some maintaining a department for sign-painting, others employing freelance artists but much remains to be done to restore this 'genre'.

SIXTEENTH CENTURY

At this period no one drank water, except in dire necessity but only peers, vintners, taverners and religious kept wine in their houses. Wine cost fourpence a quart (remember Falstaff's bill?) but corks had not been invented and bottles were only used to convey the young wine, drawn from the wood, from cellar to table. If you could afford it, you drank (small) beer for breakfast and at midday and wine in the evening. Taverns in the second half of the century were becoming increasingly clubs and meeting places for males – the female element was supplied by the brewsters and serving wenches.

Travelling was still mainly on horseback but there were still the great lumbering wagons in which the rich sometimes travelled. These were served by inns which, following the medieval tradition, were built around galleried courtyards with another yard behind for stabling the horses and standing for waggons. Similar, but less ornate, vehicles were used for the transport of goods by road. Their waggoners had neither the means nor the social status to seek lodging in the new inns and it is not entirely clear where they found their food and shelter. The latter could be found under their waggons or in a hedgebottom but there is some evidence that the less inhospitable of the tavern-keepers occasionally provided it since there is late C16 legislation against this practice. They would certainly find food, drink and company in the tavern kitchen but the parlour was reserved for their betters – the origin of the two-bar pub.

SKITTLES
Once as closely associated with beer as fish is with chips. The word covers a variety of games including Nine Pins, London Skittles and Aunt Sally. Some are played outdoors, some require a purpose-built alley. Skittle alleys have mostly disappeared with bar extensions but a few survive, particularly in West Country e.g. *Red Lion*, St Columb Major; *Red Lion*, Newquay. The one at *Falmouth Arms*, Laddock is used as a bottle store. Some used the road outside for skittles or kayles and it was swept and watered before play. At Lamorna, Cornwall, a diamond-shaped frame was let into the road to assist in the placing of the pins.

Skittle Alley

SMALLEST
It seems generally agreed that the smallest pub in England is *Smith's Arms*, Godmanstone, Dorset. It measures 20′ × 10′ with its thatched eaves reaching within 4′ of ground. Another contender is *Nutshell*, Bury St Edmunds whose bar measures 12′ × 7′.

SMOKING HOUSE (Smoke Shop)
A late C19 term for hostelries which provided the combined pleasure of drink and tobacco-smoking (which was not always allowed in a middle-class home).

SMUGGLING
As a prosperous and general trade, smuggling seems to have begun during the French War (1692–7). Brandy was the chief item on the 'free-traders' list but it was soon supplemented with wine, silks and 'haute couture'. Once started the practice continued and one of Queen Anne's first Acts (1703) was 'for encouraging the consumption of malted corn for the better preventing the running of French and Foreign Brandy'. Quite a number of coastal or remote inns have 'hidy holes' to conceal a variety of untaxed goods (including salt). Pubs with a smuggling connection include *Angel*, Thameside, London; the *Mermaid* and *Old Bell* in Rye were connected by a tunnel; *Star and Eagle*, Goudhurst, Kent has a passage to church; *Old Albion*, Crantock, Cornwall had smugglers' hole by fireplace; *Oak & Ivy*, Hawkhurst, Kent; and *Ship*, Saltburn were smugglers' HQs. There is a *Smuggler's Rest* and *Revenue* at Devonport reminds us of the revenue men who were the smugglers' great adversaries.

SNOB SCREENS
A late C19 development which provided both privacy for the customer and control by the licensee. They were frosted glass panels with hinged panels (not fixed as in private bars). Rare examples survive in undeveloped pubs e.g. *Prince Albert*, Formosa Street, London. The fixed screens are even rarer and worthy of note for the pub explorer.

SNUG

Snug (from C17 woodcut)

Term seems to be mid C19 and describes very small, completely detached room giving complete privacy. It was probably derived from the private parlour and used for business or other confidential purposes including the discreet entertainment of ladies. Often this accommodation was only adequate for two, though in Lancashire the term is sometimes attached to Parlour. Sometimes they were private appartments next to the counter but screened with only a low opening to pass drinks through. Nowadays, where 'snugs' survive they tend to be reserved for regulars of long standing with users either nominated by landlord or by selection of existing users. Ideally, the snug should have its own open fire, no external window and only be accessible via the servery.

SOCIAL DISTINCTIONS

In spite of romantic ideas, inns always seem to have made distinctions in the treatment of their guests. Even medieval hospitality recognised three classes of guests and provided for them accordingly. The difference then was a much wider spectrum, ranging from the completely penniless to the highest in the land whereas modern hostelries cater for a much narrower band but seem to make finer distinctions. The later Victorian period made the habitués of one bar invisible to the users of another and assumed three social levels, provided for in three bars. There was the Public Bar for labourers, Private Bar for superior artisans, small shopkeepers, etc. and Saloon for the lower middle class. Entire houses affected distinction by use of title 'hotel' prefixed by 'County' or, especially, 'Grand'.

SOCIAL FUNCTION

Besides providing a location for many communal activities: meeting of sports clubs, friendly societies (cf. *The Friendly*, Stanbury, W. Yorks.), political associations, etc., the inn, particularly that of the village, was the natural place for advertising local forthcoming attractions. Inns are still used by Rotary, Round Table, Friendly Societies (some are even named *Oddfellows Arms*) but their social function probably reached its height in C18.

In C17 Bishop Earle commented:

> To give you the total reckoning of it, it is the busy man's recreation, the idle man's business, the melancholy man's sanctuary, the stranger's welcome, the inn-of-court man's entertainment, the scholar's kindness, and the citizen's courtesy. It is the study of sparking wits, and a cup of comedy their book, whence we leave them. (Cosmographie)

Even the Sociologists have investigated this function in Mass Observation: *The Pub and the People* (London 1970), see also the earlier '*English Inn, past and present*' by A.E. Richardson & H.D. Eberlein.

SOLDIERS see also *Heroes, Military*

Do not seem to figure as prominently in inn names as sailors but include *Grave Maurice*, C17 leader of Netherlands v. Spain; *Picton*, hero of Peninsular War, killed at Waterloo; *Raglan* involved in Peninsular and Crimean wars; *Sir Colin Cambell*, also *Lord Clyde* of Peninsular, Crimea and Indian Mutiny.

There are plenty of unnamed soldiers like *Dragoon* (Bromsgrove), *Retired Soldier* (Malvern) and the pub which once served the defunct barracks at Norton, Glos. is fittingly called *Retreat*.

SONGS see also *Music*

Drinking songs are a genre on their own. One of the best English medieval examples occurs in Sloane Collection: 'Bryng us in Good Ale' each of whose eight verses, after declaring what the singers do not want, has the refrain: '(But) Bryng us in good ale, and bryng us in good ale, For Our Blyssyd Lady sak, bryng us good ale.' There is a catch to accompany drinking in Shakespeare's 'Twelfth Night' and C17 produced many examples, often with a political or loyal reference e.g. 'Here's a health to the King and a lasting peace', 'Here's a health unto his Majesty', 'Now since we've met, let's merry, merry be'.

A variety of songs have produced inn names including: *Auld Lang Syne, David of the White Rock, John Peel, Polly Perkins* and, inevitably *Nellie Dean*.

SOVEREIGN see also *King, Queen*

As an inn name, usually refers to monarch but may commemorate ship 'Royal Sovereign' and *Sovereign* nr. Denby Dale, W. Yorks. has gold coin on its sign.

SPARKLER

Adjustable screw to reduce opening on spout of hand pump to give tight 'head'.

SPILEPEG

Combined tap and bung used in broaching a barrel.

SPIRITS

Distillation seems to have reached Europe from the East in C12 and became common by c15. 'Aqua Vitae' seems first to have been valued as a love-potion and aphrodisiac but by C16 it was regarded as a medicine, taken a few drops at a time in a glass of wine. The earlier monastic cordials distilled from herbs, etc. were much more palatable medicine and some have survived e.g. Benedictine and Chartreuse.

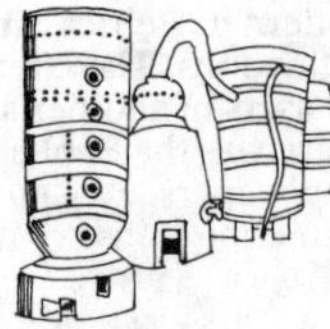

Spirit Still

Gin, Geneva, Ginever (flavoured with juniper berries) seems to have been introduced as a result of Leicester's expedition to Holland in 1586 which also produced the expressions 'Drunk as a Dutchman' and 'Dutch Courage'. In 1690, partly as a result of the war with France and also to protect English corn-growers, an Act as passed allowing any Englishman to distil spirits from home-grown corn.

The taste, thus encouraged, grew apace. In 1694, with a population of six million, England consumed 750–800,000 gallons but by 1734 with an increase of only a quarter million in the population, it was consuming six million gallons, rising in 1750 to over eight! None of these figures take account of smuggled or illicitly distilled spirits.

SPIRIT URN

A decorative china urn, usually with the name of the contained spirit in flamboyant (often gold) lettering. It was normally installed on the bar and fitted with a tap for dispensing spirits. Where these attractive bygones survive, they only serve a decorative purpose, their utilitarian function having been displaced by the 'optic' (q.v.).

SPIT & SAWDUST

C19 and C20 name for the public bar, dating from the time when its floor was covered with absorbent sawdust and each corner was provided with spitoons. This was the basic drinking area where the working class were served by men, often in baize aprons (the barmaids were confined to the more 'select' areas).

Victorian Spirit Fountain

SPORTS & PASTIMES see also *Games*

A long association between pub and sport is evidenced in many names e.g. *Dog & Duck* which may have sentimental echoes for some but in fact it is a reminder of one of the many barbaric sports of our not too distant forefathers. In C19 there was a close connection between pubs and horse-racing and boxing in particular. Many publicans were ex-boxers and one of them founded the National Sporting Club in 1891. Others were ex-jockeys, many were book-makers and pubs provided general opportunities for passing bets. By this time cock-fighting and ratting were on the wane but pigeon-fanciers often met in pubs.

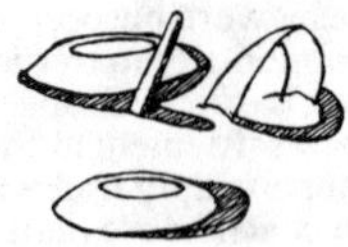

Quoits

Associated names might include *Anglers Arms, Angler's Rest, Three Fishermen; Cricketers* (often 'Jolly'), *Kentish Cricketers, Ball & Wicket, Bat & Ball, Maiden Over, Yorker*; there are many *Horse & Hounds* and racing has provided *Jockey, Scales, Whip & Saddle*, etc. There is *Noble Art* (of boxing), the unique *Bareknuckle Boys* (Holmfirth) and *Wrestlers, Touch Down* for rugger fans and *Treble Chance* for soccer speculators. *Red Grouse* reminds us of game-bird shooting; *Top of the World* commemorates conquest of Everest in 1953 while *Whoop Hall* nr. Settle is reminder of local squire's joy in fox-hunting. For those who prefer a quieter and gentler sport, there are plenty of *Bowling Greens*. On this subject, see; J.W. Day, *Inns of Sport* (Whitbread 1949).

SPORTSMEN

There are numerous *Sportsmen's Arms* and *Sportsmen*, Stratford-upon-Avon (formerly *Bull*) has a new and whimsical sign while that of *Cricketers*, Meopham, Kent portrays four famous county players. *Bob Fitzsimmons* recalls a champion boxer and Gordon Richards is remembered in *Champion*, the prize-fighter *Tom Cribb* has his name perpetuated and *Cumberland Wrestlers* was so-called in honour of the local champions Steadham and Clarke.

Cricketers

STAFF

The traditional staff of a public house, apart from the host, his wife and family, included tapsters, pot-boys and serving wenches. Later the non-family staff were called waiters and barmaids. There seem to have been two developments since World War II: first, the almost universal practice of bar service only and the increasing number of pubs whose serving staff are limited to husband and wife.

STAGECOACH see also *Coach*

This passenger service was established in later C17 and its vehicles started from a well-known point, usually an inn, and proceeded by 'stages' where they stopped to allow embarkation and disembarkation, refreshment and change of horses. The stages were always inns.

The pubs at 'stages' and termini had a variety of names: Coach Stations, Stage Posts, Change Houses. They provided waiting rooms, toilet amenities, meals and beds as well as storage and repair facilities for vehicles, stabling and farriers for the horses. The intermediate Stage Posts or Change Houses were usually at 15-mile intervals and marked fare stages. They naturally developed at critical points: beginning of turn-

Loading Stagecoach

pikes, road junctions or intersections of coach routes, bridges, hill-tops or hill bottoms. Sometimes old houses at a suitable site were extended, in other cases new houses were purpose-built. In either case, landlord often ran his own post-chaises or omnibuses to towns and villages off the main routes and his house acted as a parcels office. Change-houses in out-of-the-way places often became the nucleus of a new settlement as they attracted wheel-wrights, blacksmiths, farriers, etc. and other ancillary trades and suppliers. *Falcon*, Bude deserves recording as it survived as a coach house until 1912 and even ran a horse omnibus to the new railway station until 1920.

STAR
As an old inn name its reference is usually religious (q.v.) but later it can refer to orders of chivalry e.g. *Leg & Star, Star & Garter, Star of India. Star & Wagon* probably refers to Pole Star and King Charles's Wain (Ursa Major) or *Plough*. There are also: *North Star, Morning Star, Three Stars, Shooting Star* and unique (?) *Black Star* (Stourport-on-Severn).

STILLION (STILLAGE)
Originally seems to have been support for cask or barrel, later bench or frame to keep variety of articles (including casks) off the floor. A cask is on stillage when it is held immovable by frame or chocks to allow sediment to settle before being broached. Later still, it was synonym for 'wagon' – the central fitting in an island bar providing a complete drinks dispensary. Few of these complex appliances seem to have survived though Girouard (op. cit.) has a photograph of the magnificent appliance of 1899 which served *Elephant & Castle*, Newton, Bucks. until its demolition.

STINGO
A name which for at least two hundred years was particularly applied to strong Yorkshire Ale.

STOCK ALE
A strong ale matured over a long period, since it was well-hopped and fermented almost to the limit. It was stable and therefore could be held 'in stock' almost indefinitely. Its counterpart was 'Running Ale', beer that was moved quickly through high consumption and therefore did not remain in stock (nor could it without deterioration). Stock Ales are rare nowadays but Whitbread Fremlins still produce a Stock Ale and some Strong and Best Bitters made today may still approach Stock Ales in quality.

STOUT   see also *Guinness*
The final evolution, which began with 'Entire' (q.v.) of a family of dark brown to black top-fermented beers which were characterised by thorough mashing, blending of several worts, an extremely high hopping rate and the use of roasted (and sometimes unmalted) barley. One result of this process was the ability to travel and the consequent dissemination of a local brew far from its birthplace. Milk Stout was the common name for sweet stout because lactose is used in its manufacture. It is said that Mackeson, now part of the Whitbread group, allowed neighbouring farmers a right of way through its brewery so that visitors were impressed by the sign of cows passing through the brewery yard.

STRONG ALE

> He who drinks small beer, goes to bed sober,
> Falls as the leaves do fall, that fall in October;
> He who drinks strong ale, goes to bed mellow,
> Lives as he ought to live, and dies a jolly fellow.

(Anon. C17?)

Old names for Ale include Barley Broth, Oil of Barley and Barley Wine and it seems that all these indicated a strong ale. Traditionally beer and ale were brewed at three strengths (see X) – single or small, double, and half way between. A variant was single, double and triple strength and there were mixtures of the various strengths.

Today, most brewers produce a high gravity beer of one kind or another: pale or dark, sweet or dry, draught or bottled. The strongest beers are the Barley Wines whose maturation may take as long as 18 months. They have a characteristic 'fruity' and satisfying flavour and a strength of 10–11 per cent. Their flavour is related to generous hopping which also helps to preserve them. A selection of draught strong beers whould include: Ruddles County; Fuller, Smith & Turner's Extra Special Bitter; Theakston's Old Peculier; Timothy Taylor's Landlord; Young's Winter Warmer; Wadworth's Old Timer.

SUFFOLK

Southwold has Adams with a number of tied houses in east of county and wider free trade. It produces three draught beers (including a Strong) and two strong bottled ales: Fisherman's Strong, Broadside. Greene, King are at St Edmundbury with subsidiary breweries at Biggleswade, Beds., and Huntingford, Herts. They have some 900 tied houses and expansive free trade offering a remarkable range (eight) of draught beers, four kegs and bottled beers including St Edmund's Ale, Suffolk Ale, Audit Ale. Tollemache Cobbold are in Ipswich with about 380 tied houses in Suffolk and Cambs. with extensive free trade. They produce three draughts including (winter) Old Strong, a good keg which is not always available and bottled range including Cardinal Ale, Tolly Royal Barley Wine.

SUN

As inn sign seems to originate in badge of Edward III, 'the Sun of York', variants of which include *Rising Sun, Sun in its Splendour*. Other usage may be response to the rather prominent natural object. There is *Sun & Star*, Westhill, Surrey; *Old Sun* at St Neots, Hunts. and *Sun*, Long Marston, Yorks. has a good sign.

Sun

SURFACE TREATMENT

An important element in pub decor which includes exposing structure (beams, masonry or brickwork – often carefully pointed), wallpaper (especially Victorian Anaglypta and more recent flocked paper), painting including brush-graining – a traditional way of painting soft wood to imitate natural grain, and such things as beaten copper, etc.

SUSSEX

Lewes has Beard's brewery with about 25 tied houses. It produces a draught XXXX, a strong dark ale. There is also Harvey's with about the same number of houses and issuing five draught beers (including XXXX and Elizabethan Ale), one keg and a bottled range including stout. In Horsham is King & Barnes with about 60 tied houses. They produce three draught beers (including winter Old) and a good range of bottled with a strong pale, a strong brown and a barley wine.

Pump House, Brighton, Sussex

SWAN
A sign which has been long popular. It is said, dubiously, to originate from the chivalric Order of the Swan instituted in 1440 by Frederick II of Brandenberg but it seems much older than this and Frederick's order itself is probably based on older associations. It may be a Marian symbol – the *Silver Swan*, alias *White Swan* or it may be heraldic* since there was a medieval romance about the Swan Knight (also referred to on misericords). *Black Swan* alias 'Mucky Duck' is of frequent occurrence. *Swan Revived* may commemorate a reopening after the Commonwealth experience. *Swan with Two Necks* is generally accepted as a corruption of 'two nicks' which were marked on the bills of birds belonging to Dyers' and Vintners' Companies. Other swans were royal and marked with five nicks.

* White Swan was badge of Edward of Lancaster who fell at Shrewsbury.

TABOOS
Busby Stoop near Thirsk has a chair which is alleged to bring sudden and tragic death to anyone who sits in it. *Old Cross*, Alnwick has bottles whose disturbance allegedly brings death. *Roundstone*, East Preston, Sussex is named from weight 'holding down' a suicide.

TANKARD see also *Vessels*
Originally a medieval container used for carrying water and holding three gallons. Later became smaller and made of metal (commonly pewter in C15) when it seems to have settled at either a pint or a quart. 'Hanap' was a relation to the tankard, its name being derived from OE for 'cup'. The basket for carrying these fragile cups was a 'hanaper' or 'hamper'.

TAP ROOM
The room where casks were 'tapped' by inserting a spilepeg (q.v.) so that contents could be extracted for retail consumption. This room (sometimes called vault(s) became the common drinking room of a public house and the ancester of the public bar. Its name has survived occasionally as a designation of the pub e.g. *Coronation Taps*, Clifton, nr. Bristol.

Tap Room (Loudon)

TASTE (in Beer)
Recent statistics indicate roughly the proportions of different types of beer consumed in British Isles:
Lagers, 20 per cent; Draught Bitter, 40 per cent;
Draught Mild, 12 per cent; Bottles (and canned) Light Ales, etc., 10 per cent; Bottled Brown Ales, 4 per cent; Bottled extra strong ales, 1 per cent; Bitter Stout, 8 per cent; Sweet Stout, 4 per cent.

TAVERNS
Inns (q.v.) were basically for wayfarers whereas taverns were 'locals', places for social drinking with friends and neighbours. A Roman alternative for 'taberna' was the appropriate 'bibulia'. Taverns proliferated in the Middle Ages, often only distinguished by their 'bush' when the alewife had a ready brew. By C16 there were 40 taverns in the City of London defined as being 'for the leisure hours of those about them'.

Medieval Taverners

TAX
First imposed on beer in 1642 and, once imposed, it was not only retained by successive governments but was raised sharply from the original 2s. a barrel to 3s.3d. in 1689. With the outbreak of the French War in 1690, it jumped to 6s.6d. (Malcolm Boyes in *Yorkshire Inns* (1977) records that in 1341 there were two breweries in Tadcaster, 'one of which paid 8d. in imperial taxes and the other paid 4d. for the year'). In 1756 the tax on 'brewing victuallers' was applied at the same rate as that on wholesale brewers which had the effect of sharply reducing the numbers of the former and therefore of increasing the number of 'tied houses'. Whether it was cause or effect, contemporary records complain of increasing 'insolence' in inns and a depreciation of their service.

TEMPERATURE
American's complaint about 'lukewarm' British beer is due to the fact that all American beer is lager and warm lager is repellant but top-fermented beer loses much of its character if it is served at too low a temperature. The best temperature for drinking is related to the fermenting temperature. Even lager can be served too cold and it should be drunk at 40–50°F (7–10°C), the right temperature for top-fermented beer is 50–60°F (10–15°C) with the ideal at the mean of 55°F (13°C). Guinness, according to its makers, should be served at 54°F.

TENANT
Pays a rent to owning brewery, buys stock from same source and then may make what he can through catering, accommodation, extra facilities, etc. Lack of encouragement on the part of brewer may inhibit an imaginative tenant from developing the pub's full potential but, on the other hand, its wise guidance may restrain him from unsuitable transformations or modifications. Whatever the tenant spends on furnishing and decoration is usually paid back on valuation by the brewery when he leaves their house.

THEATRE
There is a long association between inns and the stage and many Elizabethan and Jacobean plays had their 'first night', or at least their first public performance, in an inn yard. C17 inns often provided a theatre for wandering players and troupes sponsored by the nobility e.g. *Belle Sauvage*, Ludgate Hill; *Boar's Head*, Whitechapel; *Cross Keys*, Gracechurch Street. Perhaps their successors are in the theatre pubs which offer a home for fringe drama and music-hall type of entertainment such as *Bush*, Shepherd's Bush; *King's Head*, Islington; *Pindar of Wakefield*, Gray's Inn Road.

Pubs all over the country often provide a variety stage in their music or concert room or even in the 'lounge' and others have a close association with a nearby theatre, its patrons and players. The concentration of theatres in London has produced a number of 'Stage Door' pubs including: *Nag's Head*, Covent Garden; *Opera Tavern*, Drury Lane; *White Swan*, New Row; *Salisbury*, St Martin's Lane.

'THEME'
As a reaction against the sterile Modern Movement some pub designers attempted to give individuality by a 'theme', often based on the name of the house. Sometimes this idea was perverted into a 'gimmick':

> 'Commercial firms in the pub-decorating business encouraged by certain brewery commercial staff, indulged in every kind of extravagant absurdity in the invention of gimmicks, racking their brains to think of a new nonsense whenever a pub was built or an existing bar renovated. The atlas was combed from Spain to the South Seas, the compendium of trades and occupations from whaling to wheel-tapping, the sporting calendar from ice-hockey to hurling. A bar must never, on any account, look like a bar; "What should we make it look like instead?" ' (Davis, op. cit. 16).

The name 'thematic pubs' has been given equally to such absurdities as Davis castigates and to the intelligent use of an idea to give interest and decorative unity. These are particularly common in London: there are nautical themes at *Ship*, Talbot Court; Lime Street, and Fenchurch Street, EC3 perhaps less suitably at *Smuggler's Tavern*, Warren Street, SW1. There is a military theme at *Ordnance Arms*, St John's Wood, NW8; a police one at *Copper*, Tower Bridge, SE1 though name refers to brewing utensil; motor car at *Horseless Carriage*, Chingford, E4 and railway at *Railway*, Liverpool Street, EC2. The maritime theme recurs at *Queens*, Upton Park, E13 and *Trafalgar*, Greenwich and is part of the multifarious associations of *Samuel Pepys*, Brooks Wharf. There are 'literary' themes at *Punch*, Fleet Street; *Sherlock Holmes*; *Edgar Wallace*, Essex Street, and crime naturally figures in *Jack the Ripper*, Fournier Street, E1. A former brewery in St Katherine's dock area makes a theme of *Dickens* and theatrical associations are prominent in *Nag's Head*, Covent Garden and *Rule's*, Maiden Lane. *Clanger*, Houndsditch features the Great Fire of London, while *Yorker*, Piccadilly has cricket and *Colonies*, Little Chester Street, Belgravia adopts a colonial theme.

Outside London there is the extraordinary *Covered Wagon*, Moseley, Birmingham; *Brown Derby* in same city makes use of theatrical world of 1920s and less exuberant provincial examples might include *Station*, Welling, Kent with its Roman theme; *Doffcocker*, Bolton – times and seasons; there is also *Hourglass*, Nelson; *Red Cat*, Greasby, Cheshire (features cats); *Shiny Sheff*, Sheffield, its adopted cruiser of World War II; *Hayling Billy*, Hayling Island, Hants., its local railway; while *Ghurka*, Ivor, Bucks. and *Royal Marine*, Combe Martin, Devon honour fighting men. An extreme example is *Westerner*, Taunton, Devon, with its courtyard perverted to simulate a frontier town of the Wild West.

TIED HOUSE

Originated in the growing separation of brewers and alehouse-keepers, from mid C17 to mid C18. The competition of cheap spirits led the latter into their suppliers' debt and when they became bankrupt the brewers took possession of their houses. The more money the brewers lent to maintain their outlets, the more the process accelerated e.g. in 1746, Whitbreads owned 13 alehouses, in 1756 they owned 24. Outside London the takeover was slower but generally the wholesale brewers increased their outlets to keep pace with expanding production. By 1916 nearly half the 'victualling houses' in London were in the brewers' control and in Reading it was 66 out of 68 inns and alehouses.

A tied house is usually owned by a brewery company but sometimes it is leased to them by an individual or institution. The essential feature is that it is 'tied' by a trading agreement to serve as an outlet for the products of a particular brewery, usually of a monopolistic character in a range where there might be competition but most tied houses do sell other products if only Guinness whose known quality precludes the need for tied houses.

TIMBER FRAMED

The 'half-timbered' inn is perhaps the one that occurs when one pictures in imagination the ideal hostelry. Certainly the brewery modern imitation seem to suggest a sincere form of flattery. The details involved in this building skill have been authoritatively described in C.A. Hewitt's *English Historic Carpentry* (1980) and his discoveries have helped to give a more precise date to the following: *Boar's Head*, Braintree, Essex (*c*.1370); *Old Sun* (no longer operational), Saffron Walden (*c*.1355); *Woolpack*, Coggeshall (early C14); *Red Lion*, Colchester (*c*.1500 or earlier); *Punchbowl*, High Easter (*c*.1540 30 years); *George*, Southwark rebuilt 1677.

TOASTS
The word (in this sense) seems C18 and was used for the ancient practice of drinking health and may originate from the toasted bread put in wassail bowls, etc. An alternative explanation is that it is a corruption of German 'stoss an!' – 'knock glasses'. The practice is less formal and much reduced but it is still customary to precede the first drink of a session with a quietly murmured toast to its buyer, or to the barman if you are unaccompanied. The words have become less serious and less exotic and the contemporary one seems generally to be 'Cheers' though 'Cheerio', 'Good Luck' and 'Your Very Good Health' are frequently heard.

TOBY JUG
Originally a beer-pot closely allied to the Bellarmine or Greybeard. It was rather more elaborate in that instead of being formed into a mere face, the jug embraced the entire figure of a portly toper in C18 costume. Its original has been identified as Toby Philpot, fond of Old Stingo and with the aim and reputation of being able to outdo anyone in the consumption of ale. He died 'full as big as a Dorchester butt' and the jug is his memorial 'sacred to friendship, mirth and ale'. According to the legend the archetypical Toby jug was baked from earth taken from Toby's grave. Also Charrington's trade mark.

Toby Jug

TONTINE
A form of fund raising, named after the Neapolitan baker, Lorenzo Tonti, who invented it. Money was invested by a number of stake-holders and accrued until there was one survivor who inherited the lot. Several inns were built by this method and have the word tontine in their name e.g. *Cleveland Tontine* on A19. The Thirsk–Yarm turnpike was built in 1804 and a tontine was set up to provide an inn to serve the coaches using it.

TRADE AND CRAFT SIGNS
There are few craft skills or trades which have not received commemoration in inn names or signs. They include *Axe & Compass* (Carpenters' Arms); *Bay & Say* (types of cloth related to settlement of Flemish weavers in C16); *Beetle & Wedge* (tools for spliting timber); *Basket-Makers*; *Bettle & Chisel* (slate-cutter's tools); *Bushel & Shrike* of cornchandlers – 'heaped bushel' and 'struck' bushel, levelled with rim; *Chalk Drawers* are chalk carriers; *Clickers* are shoe-workers as *Cobblers* are shoe-repairers. There are *Electricians* at Huddersfield, *Fellmongers* who trade in sheepskins, *Flemish Weavers* and *Flint Knappers, Foresters* and *Hufflers* who ferry goods from ship's chandlers to off-shore vessels, while *Lathcleeves* are lath-splitters. There are *Limekilns* for mortar makers, *Pestle & Mortar* for pharmacists and *Plummet Line* for builders as well as a *Potter's Wheel*. Workers include the apprentice *Printer's Devil* and *Porter & Sorter* which serves both station and post office at East Croydon. *Ram* is crest of Worshipful Company of Clothmakers and *Showman*, Cullopton, Devon is a changed sign resulting from the use of a neighbouring field by travelling fairs as winter quarters. *Slubbers* and *Scutchers* are workers in cloth and linen while *Spade & Beckitt* are turf-cutters' implements as *Square & Compass* belong to stone-masons. Rare is *Spinner & Bergamot* (a kind of rough cloth). *Sugar Loaf* is a trade-sign of grocers (occurs in combination, e.g. *Swan and Sugar Loaf, Three Sugar Loaves*) as *Three Horseshoes* is of Farriers and *Three Tuns* of Vintners. There is a *Tinmans* in Forest of Dean and *Turf Cutters* at East Boldre, Hants. The *Two Sawyers* are the operators of the two man frame-saw for shaping timber and *Old Saw* occurs at Gomersal, W. Yorks. There is a *Yuttick's Nest* at Blackburn. 'Yutick' was a 'drawer-in' at the mill, named after local name for whinchat whose posture seemed to be imitated by these workers. There are *Tile Sheds*, Great Ayton and *Crossed Scythes* at Totley where scythes were made.

TRADE 'ARMS'

Probably in reaction to pretensions of old inns with other names adopting aristocratic family arms, many humbler establishments adopted 'Arms' preceded by names of manual occupations such as *Blacksmiths, Boilermakers, Boltmakers, Brassmoulders, Bricklayers, Brickmakers, Bricksetters, Butchers, Carders, Carpenters, Carriers, Cloggers, Clothiers, Cobblers, Colliers, Coopers, Cordwainers, Crofters, Cutlers, Dressers, Drovers, Drysalters, Dyers, Engineers, Farmers, Fellmongers, Fishmongers, Flagcutters, Flaxdressers, Fletchers, Foresters, Gardeners, Glovers, Graziers, Hingemakers, Horsebreakers, Jet Miners, Joiners, Limeburners, Malsters, Millers, Miners,* (Machine) *Minders, Moulders, Nailmakers, Ostlers, Papermakers, Paviers, Plasterers, Plumbers, Pressers, Printers, Ropemakers, Shepherds, Sheepshearers, Skinners, Spindlemakers, Spinners, Stonemasons, Turners, Weavers, Welldiggers, Wheelwrights, Waggonmakers, Waste Dealers, Whitesmiths, Yarnspinners.*

TRADE TOKENS

Issued in mid C17 to offset great lack of small change at this period. They were unofficial coins guaranteed by men of standing and redeemable in coin of the realm at their face value, usually half-penny or farthing. They circulated freely, not only in the towns where they were issued but often for many miles around. The existence of an inn-keeper's token is proof that the inn was of considerable importance and of very sound economic reputation at the time of its issue. Quite a number of old inns display such tokens.

TRADITIONAL ALE

see also *CAMRA, Keg, Real Ale*

Beer brewed in the traditional manner, a process occupying seven days of which six are usually required for fermentation. The process requires close and careful attention at each stage and the resultant product requires continuing care in transport, storage and serving. It can easily be 'bruised' by rough handling and 'soft-pegging' and 'hard-pegging' processes were needed in their broaching so that they could be dispensed by engines which required some physical effort and skill. Increasingly, more and more pubs are proud to advertise that once more they have traditional ale on their premises.

TRADITIONAL TAVERN

Up to C19 the public house was almost indistinguishable from a private house. Its ground floor usually had five rooms: public parlour, tap room, bar, kitchen, private parlour. The last two were not accessible to public except in small country pubs. The tap room was frequented by the working class and usually furnished with wooden tables, fixed benches round walls and a large open fireplace. The public parlour was more genteel with pictures, better furnishings, chairs rather than benches and a more elaborate chimney piece, sometimes with a mirror above. Food was usually served in tap-room or parlour but superior taverns often had a coffee-room which, in spite of its name, functioned as a restaurant. There was no bar in the modern sense.

C18 Tap Room

TRANSPORT

see also *Communications*

The provision of inns was much affected by the improved passenger transport of the coaching era and the general increase in the carrying trade whether by land or water. Hence, besides the obvious coaching houses, we have such names as

Waggoner's Arms, Wait for the Waggon (Wyboston, Beds.), *Mailcart* (Spalding, Lincs.), *Carter's Rest, Van & Horses, Waggon, Tradesman's Arms* (Stokenham, Devon). Improved transport produced the commercial traveller and hence the '*Commercial*' inn (q.v.). Wider associations are indicated in e.g. *Coal Exchange*, Fareham, Hants., *Coal House*, Apperly, Glos., *Ship & Shovel, Coal Hole*, London. There are many *Ferry* inns, some *Piers*, while vehicles (q.v.) include *Hansom Cab*, the 'gondola' of C19 London and *Selsey Tram* while 'P' and parking meter occur on a pub sign in Tottenham.

TRAVELLERS' REST
Their 'dedication' must have seemed particularly appropriate to exhausted man and beast before the days of mechanical transport. The *Travellers' Rest* on the heights above Sowerby Bridge, W. Yorks. is precisely located at 1,033′4″ above sea level. This accuracy derives from the fact that an OS datum point is on the inn.

Traveller's Rest

TREES
There is a surprising range of trees occurring in inn names but by far the most dominant is *Oak*, often with the prefix *Royal*. There is an appropriate *Cotton Tree* at Bolton, *Plum Tree*, Pershore, Worcs. and a rare *Lemon Tree*, Chandos Place, London which may be due to the nearness of former Covent Garden fruit market. Many tree signs no doubt originated from a landmark but *Three Willows*, Birchanger, Essex has been given a new twist by portraying three styles of batting.

TRIPLE PLEA
There are various explanations of this curious name/sign but that at Halesworth represents a man on his death-bed surrounded by parson, doctor and lawyer with devil lurking in background, all trying to get the last out of the dying man.

UNDERGROUND PASSAGES
Many ancient hostelries claim to have underground passages leading from their cellars and sometimes from their well. Many such traditions should be viewed with suspicion though such passages have existed and occasionally remain, usually with their ends blocked up. There seem to be entrances to such tunnels at *George*, Stamford and *Mermaid* and *Old Bell*, Rye have an underground connecting passage. Some claimants are also recorded in Gazetteer.

Mitre & Keys, Leicester is said to have a tunnel under it, connecting both St Nicholas' Church and castle; *Whately* (formerly Three Tuns), Banbury, Oxon. claims an underground passage from its cellars to the Cross; *Lad in the Lane* (formerly Green Man), Erdington, Birmingham has entrace of tunnel leading to manor house opposite; *Rutland Arms*, Newmarket, Suffolk once occupied by Charles II is said to be connected to Nell Gwynne's house in Palace Street; *Queen's Lard*, Queens Street, London WC1 has a passage to nearby house once occupied by George III.

UNION
Name usually derived from one of the Acts of Union, either between England and Scotland (1707) or England and Ireland (1801).

UNIQUE see also *Rareties*
Everyone has their collection of unique names but often they tend to have duplicates and it is safer to call them rare. Nevertheless, among doubtless many others, the following are said to occur only once: *I am the only running footman*, Hay's Mews, London W1; *Corporation Brewery Taps*, Doncaster; *Flying Monk*, Malmesbury; *Guinea Pig*, East Grinstead; *Gunners*, nr. Liverpool; *Hadrian's Wall, Karozzin* (Maltese horse-drawn cab), *Mazeppa*, Wednesbury, Salop (said to be derived from former maze in vicinity but this would only be a secondary explanation); *Peat Pitts*, Ogden, N. Yorks.; *Windwhistle*, Chard, Som.

UTENSILS see also *Vessels*
The tools used in brewing and dispensing have often become pub names e.g. *Malt Shovel, Tankard, Toby Jug, Thimble* (spirit measure), *Leather Bottle, Copper*. Other utensils sometimes occur e.g. *Frying Pan*.

VAULTS
Originally a synonym for cellar since the archetypical medieval cellar was vaulted but the word developed into an equivalent for store, particularly a cool room and eventually as an alternative name for 'Tap'. It seems to have narrowed its meaning to a wine and/or beer and spirit store in C19. Vaults with a personal name in front of it was commonplace in Victorian London when a licensed house tended to be called by the name of the owner and described as a wine and spirit vaults. Such pub names are fairly common in the North but less so in the South except for London with the houses belonging to the big chains like Henekey's and Finches. (In this connection, it is sad to record that Yate's Wine Lodge in the Strand with its famous 'Tram Shed' bar closed on 22 April 1981 after 77 years on site.)

Tapping Barrels

In many parts of Northern England, the word 'vaults' has shifted its connotation from the part to the whole and then from the whole to the part so that the public bar is known as the vault.

VEHICLES see also *Transport*
There are the ubiquitous *Coach and Horses, Horse and Waggon*, etc. but rarer examples extend to modern vehicles (see Mechanical) and recently *Burns*, York has been renamed *Hansom Cab* in honour of Joseph Hansom, architect and designer who was born in this city. There is an *Omnibus* in Queensbury, W. Yorks.

VESSELS see also *Gasses, Measures*
Drinking vessels include cups, bowls, flagons, horns, glasses, tankards. In ancient times they were often decorated with precious metals and also had the characteristic of lacking a flat bottom. Therefore, they could not be put down while containing liquid which consequently had to be consumed at a single draught. Later stands were designed to obviate this difficulty. Materials included wood, glass and there is even evidence of shell in early days but the commonest material among Anglo-Saxons was horn. The horn of Ulphus is still

Medieval Beer Jug

preserved among the treasures of the cathedral at York and the Mercian king Witlaf presented a precious drinking horn to Crowland abbey 'that the elder monks may drink from it on Feast Days and remember the soul of the donor' (cf. s.v. Health). An elaborately carved oak peg tankard was found in the ruins of Glastonbury abbey which could contain two quarts (divided by eight 'pegs' q.v.) and on its lid was a representation of the Crucifixion and round its sides were figures of the apostles. In the Middle Ages leather was a common material for drinking vessels for private or public use.

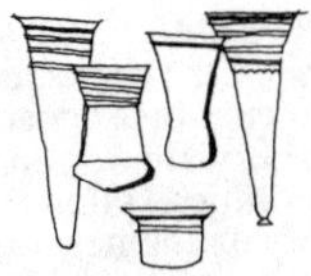

Anglo-Saxon Drinking Vessels

A C17 book lists the following: of wood (elm, box, maple, holly) – Mazers, broad-mouthed dishes, Noggins, Whiskins, Piggins, Crinzes, Ale-bowls, Wassail bowls, Court dishes, Tankards, Kannes (varying in capacity from a quart (pottle), through a pint to a gill; of leather (mainly used by country labourers, shepherds and harvest people) – simple pottles. Higher in the social scale were leather drinking mugs, sometimes tipped with silver as were the great Black Jacks that apparently started a French legend that the English drank from their boots (a possible origin of the sign *Boot*?). Drinking vessels were also fashioned from horn, cocoa-nut, gourds, ostrich eggs and shells of fishes. The middle class could apparently produce for their friends' entertainment flagons, tankards, beer cups, wine bowls (with or without covers), some parcel gilt, some entirely gilded, and of 'sundry shapes and qualities'.

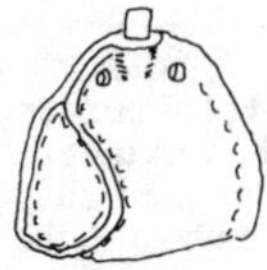

A Leather Bottell

Modern Glass Mug

Some drinking vessels occur in inn names: *Tankard, Leather Bottell, Black Jack, Blue Bowl* (for punch). There are also *Jug & Bottle, Full Quart*.

VICTORIAN PUBS see also *Gin Palace*

The characteristic Victorian pub is a town, and particularly an industrial town, invention. It goes with conspicuous expenditure, capitalism, industrialism, mass production, class distinction and middle-class respectability. It was the real dispenser of the 'opium of the people' (Victorian drinking was dreadful and in 1900 the death-rate for alcoholism was 100 per million as compared with e.g. 5 in 1965). It offered a dream combining the image of wealth with oblivion and was the antithesis of the medieval church: the latter was an earthly foretaste of future heaven whereas the latter was a present heavenly taste of earth.

Like all Victorian art their pubs were excessive: over-decorated, unoriginal (except by an idiosyncratic confusion of styles). They were pretentious without and riotous within: a world of fantasy, romance and the illusion of wealth. As Dickens pointed out, their number and splendour were not in proportion to the wealth of an area but to its poverty. Yet, whatever their origins and purpose, they are examples of significant social architecture (almost as much as the cathedrals of the Middle Ages) and as such have not perhaps received full attention. They were not the subject of serious study until 1975 when Mark Girouard produced his *Victorian Pubs*, largely limited to London examples. Others include *Borough*, Great Crosslands Street; *Vines*, Lime Street; *Goat Head*, Kirkdale Road; *Albert*, Sealt Street; *Lion*, Tithebarn Street; *Central*, Ranelagh Street; *Philharmonic* – all in Liverpool. Birmingham can offer *Gothic Stores*, Great Hampton Street; *Hen & Chickens*, Constitution Hill; *Brooks Vaults*, Jamaica Row; *St Martins*, St Martins Lane; *Woodman*, Albert Street; with *Barton Arms* at Aston almost a rival to Liverpool's *Philharmonic*. Manchester has *Oxford*, Oxford Road; *Crown & Kettle*, Oldham Road; and *Griffin* at Heaton Mersey. In Stockport Underbank Street *Turner's Vaults* preserves some very rare fittings.

VIDENDA see also *Collections*
One of the characteristics of a traditional pub is the collection of miscellaneous objects which adorn its walls: sporting prints, old photographs, horse furniture, copperware, bygones, antique drinking vessels, etc. These articles are not really decoration, often they are not a collection in that this word implies a person and a unifying theme, curiosa have other implications and they are not always antiques. I suggest 'videnda' for these items for they are things the explorer should not only look out for but look at.

VILLAGE INN
It could well be that the inn is the oldest institution in the village if the village is pre-Christian. Otherwise it would vie with the church and often originated in some kind of dependence. They were, and are, simple buildings, accommodating their customers on forms outside in summer and in settles round the kitchen fire in winter. The village inn did more than provide warmth, drink and pleasant company but it was also the place where:

> the labourer aired his grievances and first felt his way towards emancipation. It was the place where humble funds were accumulated out of pennies and half-pennies to pay for the sickness or burial of a contributor, or for clothing or coal. It was the countryman's own club, a place where, free from interference and patronage, he could call his soul his own. (English Village. V. Bonham Carter (1952) p. 214)

VOLUNTEER
As an inn name, most likely to be C19. It can occur simply as *Volunteer* but there is also *Volunteer Rifleman* with punning 'Arms' and *Naval Volunteer*.

WAGERS
Long association with pubs and particularly common in C18 and early C19 e.g. *The Times* records at beginning of March 1804 in *Bull*, near Tunbridge Wells 'a farmer's servant drank, for a trifling wager, a quart of Hollands [gin] in the space of three minutes and a half; the limited time was fifteen minutes'. He immediately left the inn, was found an hour later insensible in a field and, in spite of every assistance, 'expired within a few hours'.

WAGGONS
Heavy carts, with particularly wide wheels to lessen the probability of being bogged down, were for centuries the main form of transport for people and their possessions as well as for heavy commercial loads. These covered about three miles an hour and travelled about 35 miles a day resting at pubs which sometimes acquired such names as *Waggon & Horses, Waggoners Arms, Carriers*. The driver sometimes rode on the waggon but often alongside on a 'spare' horse with bells on its neck. Passenger traffic from C18 was taken over by coaches or lighter vehicles but waggons continued to carry heavy goods until the arrival of railways.

Waggon

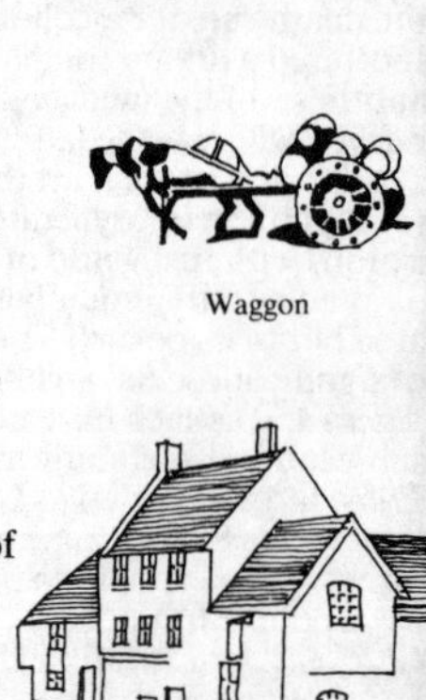
Waggon & Horses, Sleaford, Lincs.

WASH & TOPE
An inn notice indicating that a traveller could rest and attend to his toilet before 'toping'. An imaginative sign at Hunstanton plays on fact that 'tope' is name given to small shark found in Wash.

WATER
An important constituent in brewing where it is called 'liquor'. The Liffey has been given mythological attributes as providing the special characteristics of Guinness, though the water is actually obtained from wells (q.v.). The water of Burton on Trent has a good proportion of calcium sulphate (gypsum) very suitable for pale ales. Similarly, London stout depended on calcium carbonate and sodium chloride in the local water. The small Ventnor brewery of Burt & Co. is sited beneath the steep slopes of St Boniface Down, where there is an abundant supply of suitable spring water. Modern science has given power to adjust town supply to brewers' needs by addition or subtraction of particular salts and thus reduced importance of natural supply though some breweries have maintained their own private source.

WATERSIDE PUBS see also *Ferry, Transport*
Seem to have a common element warranting a particular entry. Logically, the category would include sea and lakeside houses but it appears better to narrow the connotation to riverside and canalside hostelries with the association of 'messing about in boats' or watching others doing so. In one sense, at least, such pubs are the aquatic equivalent of the coaching houses, waggoners and pack-horse inns which lined the land communication routes. It has been estimated that there are some 2,000 houses within a few yards of a river, canal or Broad and that though this category has been reduced by the decline of waterborne traffic there has recently been a new lease of life due to the increasing recreational use of inland waterways. On such pubs, see: R. Russel, *Waterside Pubs* (1974); A. Hill, *Nicholson's Real Ale Guide to the Waterways* (1980?).

WATNEY MANN LTD
Complex activity which is part of Grand Metropolitan Hotels. Originated in 1958 merger of three large London breweries to which Websters and Wilsons have since been added. Their nine breweries are in Mortlake, Halifax, Manchester and Edinburgh producing variety of draught, keg, canned and bottled which includes Export Gold, Stingo. Grand Metropolitan also owns International Vintners and Distillers (including Gilbey's, Smirnoff) as well as Peter Dominic, etc. They also own Club mineral waters, Taunton Cider and have a 50 per cent interest in Carlsberg.

WELLINGTON BEER ACT (1830)
To encourage beer drinking in face of the worrying over-consumption of cheap spirits. Allowed beerhouses to operate under a Customs licence instead of the usual Magistrate's whose only power over these beer shops was that of closing them in the event of riot. These were easily acquired and large, uncontrolled houses were allegedly haunts of thieves and receivers of stolen goods and this bad reputation was spread by keepers of taverns and inns, affected by loss of trade, leading to Act of 1869 which placed them under Magistrates' control.

WELLS
Good water was an essential element in good beer. Many breweries still require their own wells for the supply of 'liquor' e.g. Guinness Border Breweries, Forshaws. The same is obviously true of 'home brew' and inns and ale-houses often had their own supply. Inns still possessing their own well inside the house include *Red Lion*, Avebury, Wilts.; *Fox & Hounds*, Beauworth, Hants; *Old Albion*, Crantock, Cornwall; *Crown*, Evesham.

WHAT A WHOPPER!
Expression ingeniously explained as originating in executions at Old Wapping Steps, near *Town of Ramsgate* (formerly Red Cow). Sailors guilty of crime on the high seas in C18 and earlier were allegedly sentenced to death by having three tides wash over them at Wapping Basin. The bloated corpses were called 'Wappers' and expression became applied to other unnaturally large objects.

WEST MIDLANDS
Batham's have a small brewery at Brierley Hill with eight tied houses and some local free trade. All beers are draught from wooden casks. JPS Breweries are also at Brierley Hill with 17 tied houses and extensive free trade. They produce three draughts including a (winter) Old Ale, a distinctive keg, and bottled range. Wolverhampton and Dudley Breweries have about 800 tied houses, together with free trade. It is a combination of Banks (two draughts, canned and bottled beers including Old Ale) and Hansons which produces two draughts and a bottled stout.
Holdens brewery is at Dudley with eight tied houses and club free trade. It has a small range: draught mild, keg bitter and bottled Pale Ale.
Davenports are in Birmingham and they have about 100 widely scattered tied houses, many clubs and a home delivery service. They produce two draughts, two kegs and a bottled range including Top Brew.

WET
Going for a wet can be (1) getting some drink in (2) getting some drink out.

WHEATSHEAF
An inn sign borrowed from the arms of the Bakers Company. It has been suggested that its appearance indicates that the house so marked once combined a bakery with the sale of liquor.

Brewster-Baker

WHEELBARROW
A rare and obscure sign. There is *Wheelbarrow*, Southsea Common, Hants. and *Wheelbarrow Castle*, Radford. There is an anecdotal 'explanation' of the former relating to a drunken commander who had to be barrowed back to Southsea Castle which may be 'post factum'. There used to be a religious sign of *Boy with Wheelbarrow* relating to legend of obscure English saint, subject of Ronald Duncan's play 'The Boy with the Cart'.

WHEELWRIGHT
It was the custom of some carpenters and wheelwrights to provide ale for their customers who were waiting for a rushed job as repair to a coach or carriage. This facility may have been formalised by the establishment of a tavern or ale-house alongside or near the workshop and this situation could produce such names as *Carpenter's Arms, Wheelwright's Arms* and perhaps *Wheel*.

WHIMSY see also *Humour*
The explanation of such names as *Nobody Inn*, Duddisombleigh; *Dewdrop Inn, Slip Inn, Jack & Gill*.

WHISKY
Throughout C18 illicit stills had flourished in Scotland, particularly in Highlands. Law gradually established its demands in second quarter of C19 but there was little export of either Highland malt or Lowland grain whisky as neither were to the English taste. (There had been some consumption in C18 when duty on Cognac was increased.) In 1860s successful blending had been achieved but English upper classes were too addicted to brandy to change their habits. In 1880s the vineyards of Cognac area were

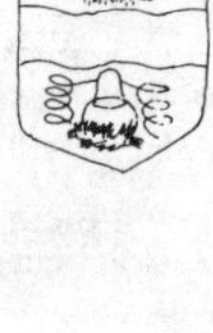

devastated by Phylloxera and by 1890s the stocks of brandy had been depleted so that the former spirit drinkers turned to whisky.

Spelling is important: a penultimate 'e' makes it Irish, otherwise Scotch. Hibernian whiskey was first on the scene in early C19 perhaps introduced by Irish fleeing from famine. Though Scotch was later it soon became dominant. The experienced drinker does not ask for 'whisky' but specifies his favourite brand.

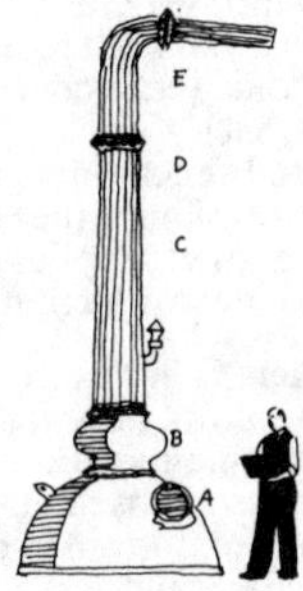

Whisky Still

WHITBREAD
A vast operation which has absorbed many formerly well-known brewers (including Bentleys, Nimmo, Duttons, Threlfalls, Flowers, Tivvy Ales, Fremlins, New Langton). It has 220 operating breweries, 19 bottling plants, ten mineral water factories and two hop farms. Whitbread produce two draught, several keg (including Stella Artois and Heineken), canned and bottled including Gold Label (one of country's strongest) and Makeson stout. A number of regional products are marketed under the name of the absorbed breweries.

WHITE HART
Popular and ancient sign, used as badge by ill-fated Richard II. Pepys mentions *White Hart*, Saffron Walden.

WHITE HORSE
Originally a pagan emblem, standard of Saxons and badge of Kent related to the White Horses cut in the chalk of hills. The Galloping White Horse was a device of the House of Hanover. Sign usually depicts a white farm horse e.g. Chard, Som. Perhaps most famous inn of this name is *Great White Horse*, Ipswich.

White Horse, Bingley, Yorks. (allegedly C13)

WILD MAN
Probably a variant of the medieval woodworse or wodehouse, often represented in carving e.g. misericords at Windsor; Exeter Cathedral; Hereford Cathedral; St Mary, Faversham; St Nicholas, North Walsham; Ripon Cathedral. Sign usually represents a naked savage e.g. Streethouses, nr. Tadcaster.

WILTSHIRE
Swindon has Arkells with some 60 tied houses, mainly in vicinity. Two draught and unpasteurised keg and a bottled Strong Ale. Gibbs Mew are in Salisbury with 50–60 tied houses in neighbourhood and more extensive free trade. Above average keg and bottled include Sarum Special. Wadworth brew at Devizes and have about 150 tied houses in country with more extended free trade. They produce five draught beers, including 6X and Old Timer, keg, canned and range of bottled.

WINE
Home-grown and imported from Angevin possessions, wine was almost as common as beer in the Middle Ages. Besides White and Red Bordeaux, there was Claret, Malmsey, Muscadel and Rhenish wines imported through Holland to Deal. Most wine was drunk young (six months to a year) before it turned to vinegar in the imperfectly sealed casks. on wine in C14

Medieval Wine Production

England, see Gasquet: *Monastic Life* (1904) p. 59f. Wine often had spices and other additions and was used as a tonic (cf. modern monastic production from Buckfast).

Arms of Vintners Company

The French wars of C18 had enormous effect on wine-drinking – the sudden cessation of long accustomed supplies not only produced smuggling (q.v.) but even led to the production of ersatz wines:

> There is in this city (London) a certain fraternity of chymical operators who work underground in holes, caverns and dark retirements, to conceal their mysteries from the eyes and observations of mankind. These subterranean philosophers are daily employed in the transmigration of liquors, and by the power of magical drugs and incantations raise under the streets of London the choicest products of the hills and valleys of France. They can squeeze Bordeaux out of a sloe, and draw Champagne from an apple. (Addison, 1709)

As real wine was often diluted, sometimes with Devon cider, so Port (advantageously available under C17 trade agreement) became a favourite with the upper classes though vintage port was not produced until 1775. It was often sold in newly created outlets which only sold wine or concentrated on its sale leading in later C18 and C19 to *Wine Bar, Wine Vaults*.

WOMEN IN PUBS see also *Ladies Only*
It certainly seems the pre-Reformation custom that wives followed their husbands into the ale-houses which, after all, were usually provided by a woman – the brewster. Later, this ancient custom seems to have been regarded as reprehensible:

> What women (even among the droonken Almaines) is suffered to follow her husband into the Alehouse or Beerhouse? (Gascoigne: A Delicate Diet . . . 1576).

On the other hand, later genial writers seem to have thought that the presence of women had the good effect of limiting the amount of beer consumed. The Chester Miracle Plays (C14–15) indicate that there was a custom of women, taking their own food with them, to meet convivially in an ale-house where they consumed copious draughts of 'merry-go-downe'.

Pubs degenerated in C18–19 and though their clientele extended through the social scale it did not seem to bring its wives. After a long absence, respectable women returned in later C19 where they were accommodated in the Jug and Bottle (q.v.) and later in their own Ladies Only Room. This return was the result of greater order, changes in style which encouraged sitting in small quite rooms rather than standing in large noisy ones and the greater possibility of privacy.

WOOD, BEER FROM THE
For centuries, beer has been matured in, transported in, and served from oak casks but metal drums are cheaper, last longer, can be mass produced and are easier to handle and sterilise and so they are replacing oak barrels. Conversely, wooden barrels are better insulators and can be left long hours in the sun without their contents being affected. Furthermore, wooden casks develop their own microflora, including various yeasts, which can have a very enhancing effect on their contents. There are micro-organisms with a deleterious nature but a well-hopped beer is its own protection against such. Many experts also believe that wooden containers confer longer life on true draught beer since they allow it to 'breathe'.

WOOL
The chief source of national wealth in C12–15, hence the Chancellor's Woolsack. This industry has naturally left its mark on inn signs such as *Woolpack* which reminds us of the transport of wool from the shearings to the processing plants. It is found on communication lines and in the vicinity of the great sheep-walks. *Sheers* occurs as does *Ancient Shepherd* (Bolton), *Shepherds Arms* and *Shepherds Rest. Fleece* is common and often Golden as an indication of the wealth it brought (*Golden Fleece*, Pavement, York has a fine gilded oak sign). *Ram* was the crest of the Clothworkers Company and deserves mention in this context.

Woolpack

WORLD'S END
There are a number of examples of this somewhat apocalyptic name e.g. Almer, Dorset; Chelsea, London. There is a suggestion that it is connected with Mother Shipton's prophecies and the inn bearing her name at Knaresborough had, until recently, an interesting sign showing collapse of nearby bridge, coach falling into river Nidd and pub itself decomposing. More likely, the name arises from hyperbole, since many inns with this title are found on parish boundaries and may date from the time when the local parish was the limit of most inhabitants' experience.

WROUGHT IRON
Occasionally occurs in the internal furnishings of pubs but the most impressive examples of this blacksmith's art are to be found in the brackets and surrounds of hanging inn signs e.g. *Golden Fleece*, Thirsk; *Ship*, Mere, Wilts.; *Three Swans*, Market Harborough, Leics.; *Swan*, Knowle, W. Mid.

Wrought Iron Sign Bracket

X see also *Cooper*
Many have originated in early C16 as a guarantee that the cask so marked contained the standard measure. But it was also used from an early time in monasteries as an indication of the strength of ale or beer so that Simplex (small beer) received an X; Duplex (double strength) received a double X and Triplex was appropriately marked XXX. Some brewers name their products by a number of Xs, even unto 6X but this should not be taken as a mathematical indication of their strength as compared with their ordinary brew.

YARD (COURT)
The inn yard provided accommodation for horses, coaches and sometimes their riders and drivers. It still may provide successful hunting ground for the explorer seeking relics of the past. The loose boxes may have been converted to garages but unused buildings often still contain interesting lumber. The harness rooms and ostlers' quarters are often identifiable and there is frequently a mounting block to help the less athletic into the saddle. In the larger inns there were quarters for the postboys above the stables and the old inn kitchen usually abutted on the yard.

Inn Yard

YARD OF ALE see *Puzzle Vessels*

YORKSHIRE

Darleys have a brewery at Thorne with some 100 tied houses in neighbourhood and free trade. They produce two draughts, keg, and range of bottled including stout. The small brewery at Selby has recently been resuscitated. It has one tied house, some club and free trade. Its strong traditional draught bitter is worth locating. Sam Smith of Tadcaster has some 300 tied houses in North but bulk of its business is free trade. It produces four draught beers (including a Strong Ale), a wide range of container beers and many bottled including Sovereign Pale, Old Samson and Taddy Golden. Timothy Taylor of Keighley have some 30 tied houses with free trade. They make four draught beers, including splendid Draught Landlord and a good bottled range including stout. Theakston of Masham have only 16 tied houses with wider free trade. They have recently acquired Carlisle brewery and produce good bottled range and two draughts including Old Peculiar, one of the strongest beers from the wood. Yorkshire Clubs of York has a similar origin to Northern Clubs and South Wales Clubs. It supplies over 200 clubs in Yorkshire and neighbouring counties with five draught beers and four bottled. There is Franklins of Harrogate and a new Bradford Brewery.

Tetley's Dray

GAZETTEER

arranged by counties and
with map reference
to facilitate discovery

Where a town has an inn or public house of interest, I have also included (some of) *Good Beer Guide's* recommendations.

Batchelor is D. Batchelor: *The English inn* (Batsford 1963)
P(evsner) is *Buildings of England*
Richardson is *Old Inns of England* (Batsford 1948) with appendix of selected inns.
GBG is *Good Beer Guide* (CAMRA) 1980 updated annually
Letts is *The Best of British Pubs* by P. Ear (1980)

INTRODUCTION

What interests people exploring pubs? Associations, curiosities, atmosphere, age and history, the building itself, the atmosphere and the provision, especially food and drink. The houses listed generally have interest under two of these headings and sometimes more. The information comes from a very large number of sources but three are mentioned. Batchelor, whose book on *The English Inn* is something of a classic and he provides a kind of yardstick. This function is supplemented by Richardson, an earlier book, which contains a lengthy list under counties, of distinguished inns. Mention of such listed inns, apart from providing confirmation of choice, has another interest for the person trying to find them – some have been destroyed by enemy action, others by demolitions of planners, others have been turned to other uses – and such discoveries add another dimension to pub exploration. Finally, there are the basic functions of a pub; first, the offering of good drink which should be universal and, secondly, the provision of good food which should be more extended. For the former I have made much use of GBG (CAMRA) and, for the latter, Letts Guide to the Best of British Pubs.

Some 4,000 pubs have been listed in the Gazetteer, arranged by counties and with a map reference for each. The name of the pub is followed by a brief entry indicating why it has been selected.

AVON

BATH 7464

Francis, Queen Street, formed from six former private houses of early C18. Associations with Shelley's wife. Much damaged World War II. *Pratts*, South Parade, Adam house of 1773 where Walter Scott once lived. *Royal York*, Georgian hotel of *c.*1760, visited by Princess Victoria in 1830, probably equivalent to *York House* listed by Richardson, together with *Angel*. Letts recommends Georgian *Crystal Palace*, Abbey Green and *Priory*, Weston Road, 1835. Among GBG offerings are *Belvedere Wine Vaults, Coeur de Lion* off Northumberland Place, *Farmhouse*, Lansdown Road, *King William*, Thomas Street, *Porter Butt*, York Place, *Star*, Vineyards.

BRISTOL 5872

Artichoke, Colston Avenue, C18 with nice early Georgian doorway. *Grand*, Broad Street, 1869, 'cool but competent essay in Venetian Quatrocento' (P). '*Hatchet*, Frogmore Street, contains some C16 material, much altered including C18 windows. Frequented by prize-fighters in C19. *King Dick*, same street, is recommended by Letts. *Llandoger Trow*, King Street, 1669, 'most spectacular timber-framed house in Bristol' (P). Associations with R.L. Stevenson and actors from Theatre Royal including Irving, Beerbohm Tree. *Rummer*, All Saints Lane, is successor to many inns on site. Gained present nme in C18 when it became coaching house with new frontage. *Shakespeare*, Victoria Street, may have originated as private house *c.*1636; timber-framed with C18 windows inserted. Among GBG's list are *Bay Horse, Bristol Bridge, Cattle Market Tavern, Kings Head, Naval Volunteer, Shakespeare Tavern, Ship*.

CHEW MAGNA 5763

Church House, fine early C16 building with very fine fireplace, at entrance to churchyard. No longer operational as pub.

CLAPTON-IN-GORDANO 4773

Black Horse, traditional village pub of character (C18?). GBG.

CLEVEDON 4071

Regent, in spite of name, has Spanish style public bar. (GBG). *Royal Pier* is typical of later C19 seaside hotel architecture.

CONGRESBURY 4363

Old Inn, claims to be C15. (GBG).

DUNDRY 5566

Carpenters Arms, rural house where 'Shut the Box' is played. (GBG).

HINTON CHARTERHOUSE 7758

Rose & Crown, Victorian Free House, recommended GBG and Letts.

LONG ASHTON 5470

Miners Rest 'excellent country pub with panoramic views' (GBG).

NAILSEA 4670

Friendship, 'stone-floored pub full of nostalgia' (GBG).

ODCOMBE 5015

Masons Arms, 'splendid C15 thatched pub' (GBG).

PRISTON 6960

Ring o' Bells, 'superbly renovated 300-year-old village local' (GBG).

RICKFORD 485
Plume of Feathers, 'charming pub in idyllic and picturesque hamlet' (GBG).

SOUTH STOKE 746
Packhorse, gabled with mullioned windows, dated 1674. (GBG).

STANTON WICK 636
Carpenters Arms, converted from C17 cottages, stone-built, slate roof, stone flagged floors, open fireplaces with bread ovens. Fine collection of pewter mugs.

WESTON-SUPER-MARE 326
The entire town is mainly early Victorian. *Royal, c.*1810 with additions *c.*1845. GBG gives *Britannia, Davenports, Long John Silver, Silver Jubilee*.

BEDFORDSHIRE

AMPTHILL 033
White Hart, Dunstable Street, transformed early C18 to cater for coaching trade with new bricked front and bay windows. Three storeys, seven bays.

BEDFORD 044
(Red) *Lion*, High Street *c.*1830 with earlier rear portion C17/18, impressive front of seven bays with giant pilasters. Picturesque courtyard. *Swan*, by bridge over Ouse, 1794, 'a remarkable monument' built by Holland for Duke of Bedford. Ashlar-faced, three bays with pediment. Preserved 1688 staircase from Houghton House. GBG gives, inter alia, *Castle, Devonshire Arms, Kings Arms, Windsor*.

BIGGLESWADE 1944
Crown, High Street late C18 'with enjoyable Art Nouveau lettering'. *Swan* 'fine old coaching inn'. *White Hart*, Market Place, restored timber-framed building of hall-house type (C16?). GBG gives *Coach & Horses, Rising Sun*.

BLETSOE 0258
Falcon, former coaching inn, courthouse and farmhouse backing on to Ouse. Associations with Thackeray and Omar Khayyam.

DUNSTABLE 0221
Sugar Loaf, 1717, nine bays, two and half storeys, blue and red brick. Stopping place for heavy coaches to north-west. Interesting sign. GBG gives *Horse & Jockey, Winston Churchill*.

ELSTOW 0547
Swan included by Richardson in 'select list of notable inns'.

GREAT BARFORD 1352
Swan – no architectural pretensions but interesting and worth visiting. GBG gives *Beehive, Golden Cross*.

LEIGHTON BUZZARD 9125
Swan, Market Place, *c.*1840, white building in classical style with central porch. *Unicorn*, Lake Street, late C17, brick front, three storeys, nine bays with recessed centre. GBG gies *Ashwell Arms, Black Lion, Roebuck, White Horse*.

LUTON 0821
Red Lion, unprepossessing front hides ancient hostelry (later C15) once belonging to Guild. After dissolution became inn, subsequently much altered: Georgian stables, front of 1880s. Issued trade tokens in 1666. GBG gives *Boater, George II, Harrow, Mother Redcap*.

POTTON 2249

Rose & Crown, Market Place, C18 with two canted bay windows. GBG gives *Bricklayers Arms, Red Lion, Rising Sun*.

TEMPSFORD 1653

Anchor in Richardson's list. A riverside free house. (GBG with *White Hart*).

TURVEY 9452

Five Fishes, not noticed by Pevsner but in Richardson's list. GBG gives *Three Cranes*, a comfortable spacious house dating from C17.

WOBURN 9433

Beford Arms, George Street, a quiet C18 building with long white front. Good early Georgian example: panelled rooms, Assembly Room, large stables. *Red Lion* small traditional High Street pub, C18?, with symmetrical bays and single dormer. GBG gives *Black Horse*.

BERKSHIRE

ASCOT 9168

Royal Ascot, C19?, seven bay centre with attachments. Brick and stone dressings. 'Homely and of no architectural merit' (P).

BEENHAM 5868

Three Kings (alias Jack's Booth), C18, two storeys, tiled. Alternative name commemorates prize fighter. Associations with eccentric Rev. T. Stackhouse.

BINFIELD 8471

Stag & Hounds, probably originally hunting lodge in Windsor Forest, Coaching House in C18, wing added in Regency period. Visited by Cobbett (1822).

BRACKNELL 8769

Red Lion, High Street, C17 'Brick with odd horizontal courses'. Timber-framing with brick in-filling visible at side. Murderous landlord in early C19. *Old Manor* much altered C17 gabled brick building. GBG gives *Market Inn, Royal Oak, Silver Birch*.

BRAY 9079

Crown, High Street, originally C15 hall-house. *Hind's Head*, originally village pub, up-marketed and made famous in late 1930s. GBG gives *Ringers*.

CHIEVELEY 4773

Hare & Hounds, C16 farmhouse, licensed in early C19 after occasional use as court house in C18. Hunt meet.

COOKHAM 8985

Bel & Dragon, former village inn, now up-market with restaurant. *Kings Arms*, according to Batchelor, has (had) trade tokens of Charles II, former coaching inn with superb garden, recommended GBG. *Royal Exchange*, possibly C16, licensed only from early C19.

DUNSTABLE 0221

Norman King, ancient site and medieval building seems to have used C12 materials. Heavily restored in 1960. 'Norman King' is Henry I, founder of priory. *Old Sugar Loaf*, two storeyed brick, 1717; former town-centre coaching inn. GBG gives *Horse & Jockey, Winston Churchill*.

ETON 9678
Crown & Cushion, C17, three storeys with oriel on cast-iron columns.

FARINGDON 2895
Bell, Market Place, with a mullioned window and some plaster work (early C17?). *Crown*, Market Place, Georgian front conceals much older, early C14 house with pretty courtyard and Jacobean staircase. Good plaster ceiling in front upstairs room.

HARTFORD BRIDGE 7757
White Lion, listed Richardson 'fine house of early Georgian character'.

HORTON 0307
Five Bells, originally a Church House and remained church property until 1927. Some C16 elements in present building which had attached smithy. GBG gives *Crown* 'low-beamed pub in village centre'.

HUNGERFORD 3368
Bear, low-white former coaching inn with Tuscan porch of Georgian period. Claims to have C13 origins. Much later associations with William of Orange. *John o'Gaunt* is probably C17 and has a rare name. *Three Swans* in Richardson's list. GBG gives both.

HURLEY 8283
Old Bell, originally guest house of Benedictine priory and mentioned in 1157 (Batchelor), claims tunnel to priory. Rebuilt C16? good panelling on landing and fine garden. GBG gives *Black Boy*.

LAMBOURN 3278
Red Lion in Richardson's list. GBG gives *Wheelwrights Arms*.

MAIDENHEAD 8881
Bear, listed Richardson. GBG gives *Cricketers, Hand & Flowers*, (two) *North Star*(s), *Prince Albert*.

NEWBURY 4666
Chequers, Jack o' Newbury, Pelican are listed by Richardson; P gives C16 *Eight Bells*, single-storeyed with three gables. GBG has *Bacon Arms, Catharine Wheel, Dolphin, Globe*.

PANGBOURNE 6376
George, C17 inn refaced with Georgian façade of three-storeys including upper range of imitation 'windows'. (Richardson who adds *Swan*). GBG gives *Copper* on A329.

READING 7272
Great Western, 1844 'a quiet small palazzo'. *Seven Bridge House*, Bridge Street is original Simonds house by brewery, *Ship* listed Richardson. P mentions *George* with its picturesque courtyard. GBG gives *Butler, Cap & Gown, Caversham Bridge, Cross Keys, Foresters Arms, Greyhound, Lion, Royal Albion, Wallingford Arms*.

SONNING 7575
Bull, half-timbered, tile roof, possibly C16. Fireplace with recesses for mulling ale. Bull said to be derived from arms of local squire. *White Hart*, by ancient bridge, up-market former coaching house.

THATCHAM 5167
King's Head, White Hart, listed Richardson. GBG recommends former described as 'old coaching inn with interesting collection of medals' and adds *Cricketers*.

THEALE 6371
Old Angel, listed Richardson. GBG gives *Falcon*.

TIDMARSH 6374
Greyhound, cottage-type, half-timbered with thatch, said to occupy site of C13 priest's house. Licensed in C17 as *Gridiron*, emblem of St Lawrence to whom local church is dedicated.

WALTHAM ST LAWRENCE 8276
Bell 'an impressive piece of C14 timber-framing' (P), one of external bells functions, also recommended by GBG which adds *Star*.

WICKHAM 3971
Five Bells, possibly C16 structure but not licensed until C19 when it accommodated travellers on London–Lincoln route (Ermine Street). Substantial rebuilding of 1976 demolished much of ancient structure.

WINDSOR 9676
Castle, late C18, 'with handsome early C19 cast-iron balcony' (P). Period rooms on upper floor. Fine lounge once belonged to private house recently incorporated. *Old House*, late C17, centre of seven bays with asymmetrical wings, pedimented porch (Tuscan). Wren is reputed to have lived here in 1676. *South Western*, C17 in spite of name, three gables with over-sailing upper floor. *Star & Garter* is listed by Richardson. GBG gives *Adam & Eve, Carpenters Arms, Stag & Hounds, Two Brewers, William IV*. *Three Tuns* built in 1518 as hall of Guild of Holy Trinity. *White Hart*, 1890, 'lifted straight out of Kensington' (P).

WOKINGHAM 8068
Old Rose, unprepossessing front masks older building of which some parts may be C15. Associations with Arbuthnot, Gay, Pope, Swift. GBG gives *Crooked Billet, Lord Raglan, Red Lion, Two Polars*.

YATTENDON 5474
Royal Oak, former village inn, claimed to date from C16, much developed and converted. GBG gives (uniquely named?) *Nut & Bolt*.

BUCKINGHAMSHIRE

ADSTOCK 7329
Old Thatched Inn – delightful village pub, C17?

AMERSHAM 9597
Crown, Georgian front conceals much older inn. Wall-paintings commemorating Elizabeth I's visit. Used as local court-house. Good yard. *Griffin*, listed Richardson, early C18 with three storeys, five bays in chequered brick. *Red Lion*, white late Georgian style. GBG gives *Elephant & Castle*.

ASTON CLINTON 8712
Bell, up-market hotel recommended Batchelor. C18 listed building which retains some original features. GBG gives *Rothschild Arms*.

AYLESBURY 8213
Bell, listed Richardson. *Bulls Head*, exterior is Victorian but interior has some interesting original features (C16?). *Dark Lantern*, C16–17, irregular, partly timber-framed, recommended GBG. *Derby Arms*, early Georgian, originally a private house, five bays, two and half storeys in red brick, recommended GBG. *George*, former coaching inn of *c.*1770 no longer functions. *Kings Head*, much altered but built C15 as hospice of Franciscan friary, three gables, fine window on left of archway into yard. Claims dubious distinction of entertaining both Henry VIII and Oliver Cromwell. National Trust. *Railway*, 1898, 'an engaging little horror' (P). Brewery in Walton Street early C19 red brick. GBG adds *Bricklayers Arms, Saracens Head*.

BEACONSFIELD 9490
Royal Saracen, listed Richardson, as is *Royal White Hart*. According to P former is 'an essentially modern half-timbered job'. In London End is Georgian 'Malt House'. GBG gives *Swan*.

BIERTON 8415
Red Lion listed Richardson.

BLEDLOW 7602
Red Lion, long and low with dormers, allegedly C14. GBG gives more modern *Boot* at Bledlow Ridge.

BUCKINGHAM 6923
Swan and Castle, attractive Victorian front, white with black trim, much altered former coaching house. *White Hart*, early Victorian front, Tuscan porch crossing pavement, once principal posting house of town. Buckingham arms in dining room. Recommended GBG which adds *Britannia*.

CHALFONT ST GILES 9993
Merlin's Cave, C17 tavern, much extended in C18. Name allegedly suggested by Milton! *Pheasant*, originated as C17 ale-house, dubious associations with Milton. New name supported by pair of birds in garden.

CHALFONT ST PETER 9990
Greyhound, described by P as 'most handsome house', red brick, five bays. Claims C14 antecedants but mainly C18 and possibly coaching house. Listed Richardson. *Jolly Farmer*, recommended Batchelor. GBG names *White Hart* a 'much altered old inn'. It originated in C16 and has some remains of this period. Allegedly haunted by C20 ghost.

CHESHAM 9601
Crown, listed by Richardson but not mentioned by P. *George* has rare wall-paintings of *c.*1715. *Kings Arms*, possibly C17 and protected by preservation order. *Swan*, old-world pub which may have originated as hunting-lodge. Preserves Georgian shove ha'penny board. Allegedly haunted. GBG gives *Queens Head*.

COLNBROOK 0277
George, Georgian with three bays on either side of arched carriageway. *Ostrich*, being across Colne is strictly in Middlesex. Timber-framed with over-sailing upper floor, allegedly former monastic hospice but possibly C16 and a former coaching inn on Bath route. Murderous landlord in its early inn days. GBG gives *Red Lion* which 'could be confused with an antique shop'.

DENHAM 0487
Falcon, late(?) Georgian of two storeys and five bays, also recommended GBG. *Swan*, a pleasant little Georgian inn is illustrated in Richardson.

ELLESBOROUGH 8306

Rule & Square seems to have originated in Jacobean annexe to farm. Much of C18 structure survives. Chimney-corner allegedly has female ghost.

FENNY STRATFORD 8834

Bull, Cock, Swan are listed Richardson. The two former were coaching houses and the alleged origin of a 'Cock and Bull' story. P finds 'nothing of real note'. GBG gives *Malsters Arms* as an 'ordinary town pub'.

FORTY GREEN 9292

Royal Standard of England, free house with unique name and only place where Owd Roger, originally brewed here but now at Burton, is available on draught. (GBG).

GREAT LINFORD 8542

Old Wharf is an attractive whitewashed canalside pub (C18?) on banks of Grand Union Canal. GBG recommended canalside house is *Black Horse*.

GREAT MISSENDEN 9801

Little Abbey, occupies site and fragments (much restored) of C12 religious house which had been converted to private house after Reformation. Minstrels' gallery survives of this transformed dwelling. *Nags Head*, stagecoach halt in C18 developed from earlier house which may have been C16. Associations with Turpin. Garden. GBG recommends latter, adding *Barley Mow, Cross Keys, Red Lion*.

HADDENHAM 7408

Beehive, early C18 but no longer functioning. *Dolphin*, opposite, C18 front of three bays, stone and brick. Good wrought-iron sign. GBG gives *Kings Head* 'with unusual signs'.

HIGH WYCOMBE 8593

Falcon, Red Lion are listed Richardson. Former is a scheduled building with dubious claims to date from C14. GBG gives *Masons Arms, Roundabout*.

LOUGHTON 8337

Fountain, former coaching house on Watling Street (A5) with stagecoach. GBG gives *Talbot*.

MARLOW 8587

Chequers is listed Richardson. *Compleat Angler* described by Batchelor as 'an exquisite inn'. In most beautiful situation. *Crown* was built as Town Hall in 1807. *George & Dragon* is C18 red brick, pedimented, two storeys, nine bays. GBG gives *Carpenters Arms, Clayton Arms, Ship*.

MEDMENHAM 8084

Dog & Badger, rambling, picturesque old inn with dubious claims to a C14 origin. (GBG).

NEWPORT PAGNALL 8743

Swan Revived but not enough to restore Chippendale furniture which once graced interior. Front of *c.*1835 but older interior preserves Jacobean staircase. (Richardson, with *Anchor*). In St John Street is former *Wrestler's* with C18 front on C16 building and Toll House. GBG gives *Cannon*.

OLNEY 8851

Bull, black and white front with deep columned porch, Georgian.

PENN STREET 9296

Hit or Miss, overlooks cricket field owned by landlord. Sign has cricketing allusion. Formed from pair of C18(?) cottages. Interior decoration includes allusion to local chair-making industry.

PRINCES RISBOROUGH 8003

George & Dragon, long history as inn on London–Oxford coach route. Well preserved stable yard and associated buildings.

SPEEN 8499

Plow (sic), dates from Tudor period and has associations with Charles I.

STEWKLEY 8525

Old Swan, some medieval elements in building but only seems to have developed as pub in C19 due to success of attached brewery.

STONY STRATFORD 7840

Bull, Cock, two noted Georgian coaching inns on Watling Street and most likely the real progenitors of 'Cock & Bull' story, rumours concerning contemporary wars. Both part of rebuilding after disastrous fire of 1742. GBG prefers *Bull*.

TURVILLE 7691

Bull & Butcher, half-timbered with brick in-filling. Cottage-type (C17) which traditionally gained licence to serve masons restoring church. Sign indicates possible associations with butcher's shop.

WEEDON 8118

Wheatsheaf, timber-framed with brick in-filling C16/17. GBG gives *Five Elms*, 'a lovely old pub'.

WENDOVER 8708

Corner House, early C18, nine bays with blocked central archway. *King & Queen* was built in the accession year of William and Mary and its original sign bore their representations. *Nag's Head, Packhorse, Red Lion* listed Richardson without details. R.L. Stevenson stayed at latter in 1875.

WEST WYCOMBE 8394

George & Dragon, early Georgian, the inn-sign bears the date 1726. Originally nine bays but reduced. Some earlier work survives. Fine lead oval sign without and good period staircase within. Claims two ghosts. Associations with Cromwell and Hell Fire Club.

WHITCHURCH 8020

White Hart listed Richardson.

WINSLOW 7627

Bell, early C19 with nice bay windows on ground floor. (GBG). *George*, early Georgian with 'fabulously ornate' (P) wrought-iron balcony brought from Claydon house.

CAMBRIDGESHIRE

ARRINGTON 3250

Hardwicke Arms, claims a C13 origin but has been much altered and developed over the centuries. Its structure shows traces of six building periods.

BARTLOW 5845

Three Hills, recommended Letts and described 'medieval/Georgian'.

BUCKDEN 1967

George, possibly originated in C17, developed in C18 when it became a coaching house on old Great North Road. In Richardson's list, together with *Lion*: may have developed from a medieval guest-house or hospice (*c.*1500) belonging to the bishops of Lincoln. It was called *Lamb & Flag*, later a coaching inn, then *Lamb* until mid C19 (boss in lounge). *Falcon*, also listed and GBG which describes it as 'a tiny, one-bar village pub'.

CAMBRIDGE 4658

Blue Boar, former coaching and carriers' inn, much altered C19 and C20 with only coffee room surviving of earlier period (together with old sign), apart from cellars. *Central*, Market Hill, 'a good example of a modest C18 red brick building' (P). *Eagle*, Benet Street, whose 'galleried courtyard reproduces in early C19 terms (cast-iron columns) the precedent of the earlier coaching inn' (P) (Letts). *Fort St George in England*, Midsummer Common, formerly on island with toll house and ferry. Originated C16, renamed and much developed in C19. *Garden House*, Victorian with recent additions and modifications. Large gardens extended to Granta (Letts). *Mill*, attractive L-shaped riverside inn, three bays, two and half storeys. C18 or early C19, originally *Hazard Arms*. *Mitre* and *Baron of Beef*, Quayside are further reminders of great days of Cam as inland waterway. *Pickerel*, former watermen's hostelry of C16 of which a portion survives behind C19 frontage. *University Arms*, Regent Street, formed from several early C19 houses with two extensions in C20, 'more like Bournemouth than Cambridge' (P). GBG gives none of above but its recommendations include *Cambridge Arms, Cross Keys, Free Press, Granta, Spade & Bucket*.

CAXTON 3058

Crown, Georgian five-bay front conceals early C16 rear also C16 carriageway to right. Recorded in 1545. *George*, Georgian front of seven bays with central carriageway. In rear is much Elizabethan brick and fine mullioned windows.

CAXTON GIBBET 2960

Caxton Gibbet at cross roads where A45 cuts Ermine Street. Large inn, possibly of C18 but later rebuilt and extended so that part of yard and its well have been covered.

CHATTERIS 3986

Old George listed Richardson. GBG gives unusually named *Honest John* which occupies former Labour Exchange.

CHESTERTON 4560

Green Dragon, mid C16, licensed by University Vice-Chancellor in 1630. Operated ferries. Popular bargemen's pub in C18–19, since reduced in size – adjacent cottages were once part of inn. *Pike and Eel*, opposite site of famous Stourbridge Fair. Formed from two (C17?) cottages.

CLAYHITHE 5064

Bridge may occupy site of former hostel of Hythe abbey. Present buildings partly C18 when it was *Pike and Eel*, became *House of Lords* for a short time after 1895 and has had present name since 1912. Free House with riverside lawn.

CONINGTON 1785

White Swan (GBG) 'excellent country pub with good selection of pub games'.

EATON SOCON 1658

White Horse, C18, early Georgian red brick, later five-bay addition with 'pretty doorway'. Interior may be older than front and has unspoilt chimney corner and much original C18 furniture. *Old Plough*, low, timber-framed, possibly C16. GBG gives *Bell, Old Sun, Waggon & Horses* – all on side of Old North Road.

ELM 4607
Black Horse with 'weird, humble, yet showy red brick front', dated 1665 (P).

ELTON 0893
Black Horse, (Over End), Georgian with five bays.

ELY 5380
Bell, listed Richardson, (together with *Lamb*) only mentioned by P for its 'gargantuan Egyptian lettering'. *White Hart*, late C18 front concealing much C15 work and a rear wing of early C17. Batchelor features *Cutter* on its fine waterside site. GBG gives *Minster Tavern, Prince Albert*.

FEN DITTON 4860
Harvest Home, rare survival of the service whereby beer is brought from the cellar and served at the table. (GBG). Letts gives *Ancient Shepherds*, described as 'medieval'.

FEN DRAYTON 3468
Three Tuns 'has a nice half-timbered gable and inside sumptuously carved beams' (P).

FENSTANTON 3168
King William IV (GBG), 'fine old pub, updated without losing its atmosphere'.

FOWLMERE 4245
Letts gives *Chequers* ('Elizabethan') and *Swan* ('Tudor').

GRANTCHESTER 4355
Red Lion listed Richardson. GBG gives *Blue Ball*.

HOLYWELL 3370
Ferry Boat, one of several claimants to 'oldest inn in England' title. Thatched and half-timbered (some fake) with remains of C13 material. Riverside Fenland pub popular with bargees in C19. Allegedly haunted.

HUNTINGDON 2371
George, historic house on Old North Road. Operational in Tudor period, sold to Cromwell family early in reign of Elizabeth I. Became famous coaching house in C18, largely burnt down in C19, rebuilt in 1865. American Red Cross centre in World War II. C17 remains in yard include very rare survival of open gallery. *Old Bridge*, rambling, partly C18, former coaching inn whose premises once included a bank whose vaults are under bar. Good doorway. *Bridge, George, Woolpack*, are all in Richardson's list and the first two are mentioned in Batchelor.

ICKLETON 4943
Red Lion, dated 1580 in Letts which recommends.

KEYSTON 0475
Pheasant, large thatched cottage-type inn (C18?). Free House. (GBG).

KIMBOLTON 0967
Half Moon, claims to be C16 and preserves some peculiar games. (GBG).

LEVERINGTON 2339
Bell, pre-Reformation. Half-timbered with interior newel staircase. GBG gives *Rising Sun*.

LINTON 5646
Letts recommends *Bell*, described as 'medieval'.

MARCH 4197
Griffin, old coaching inn in town market place. GBG gives *Cock, Rose & Crown, Seven Stars*.

MARHOLM 1402
Green Man, alias *Fitzwilliam Arms* has a 'living sign' – a box tree cut into human shape.

PETERBOROUGH 1999
Bull, Westgate: long, low, two-storeyed front, probably early C18. Interior houses a picture collection. *Royal*, Westgate: 'a handsome, plain Georgian house of five bays' (P). Richardson lists *Angel* and GBG gives *Gladstone Arms*, Gladstone Street, *Still*, Cumbergate. In near vicinity are *Blue Bell, Comet, Peter Pan* at Dogsthorpe; *Blue Bell*, Werrington; *Cresset, Silver Jubilee*, Bretton; *Dragonfly*, Orton.

POPE'S CORNER, Cambridge 4659
Fish & Duck, riverside pub at junction of Cam and Ouse, originally a little waterman's tavern, recently rebuilt as glossy establishment to exploit pleasure cruising.

RAMSEY 2885
Lion, modest High Street hotel in small town. Characteristic of type. (GBG).

ST IVES 3171
Golden Lion, probably originated in C16, later became a coaching inn when it was substantially rebuilt. Former courtyard roofed over to provide modern lounge; old balconies discernible as passages. *Pike & Eel*, two miles away at Overcote Ferry, a C17 inn, by side of river Ouse, popular with fishermen.

ST NEOTS 1860
Cross Keys, brick façade and bay windows added *c.*1730 to 'modernise' an older inn, profiting from coaching trade (GBG). In Richardson's list and mentioned by Batchelor, together with *Bridge* and *Royal Oak* (GBG which adds *Globe, Lord John Russell*). *Bridge*, is a riverside inn part of whose fabric is claimed to be C13.

SAWTRY 1683
Bell, 'a pleasant old village pub' (GBG). Richardson lists *Globe*, no details.

SOHAM 5973
Fountain, big village hotel with nearby weighing machine to assess loads on carts.

STILTON 1689
It is a tragic fact that this famous coaching centre seems no longer to have an ancient inn. Even the famous *Bell*, listed Richardson, entrepot for cheese, seems recently to have been abandoned.

TRUMPINGTON 4455
Green Man, ancient village inn of C16, half-timbered and with original king-post roof.

TURVES 3396
Three Horseshoes, free house in remote village. (GBG).

WANSFORD 0799
Haycock, posting house of 1632 on earlier site. Built of local stone and roofed with Collyweston flags, said to cover more than acre. Tethering rings in archway to yard. (Enclosed) gallery distinguishable. Sign depicts anecdote which gave inn its name. Features in Torrington Diaries. Listed Richardson.

WHITTLESEY 2797
Black Bull, mid C17, pedimented doorway, frieze, mullioned windows. GBG gives *Boat, Letter B*.

WILBURTON 4875
Bridge, one of the claimants to being the lowest inn in England. It is 6ft (about 2m) above sea level.

WISBECH 4609
Rose & Crown, early C19 grey brick façade masks older building containing fine C18 staircase. C17 building at back and C16 cellars. In town are excellent buildings of North Brink brewery of *c*.1790. *Ship* is listed Richardson. *White Hart* is early Georgian and was red brick with central archway but it has been disastrously cemented. GBG gives *Angel, Hare & Hounds, Riverside Tavern*.

CHESHIRE

ALDERLEY EDGE 8478
De Trafford Arms is listed by Richardson. GBG gives *Moss Rose* which has bowling green.

AUDLEM 6543
Bridge, interesting canalside pub in exceptionally attractive village. (GBG). *Crown*, former C17 coaching inn strategically situated at junction of A529 and A525.

BARTHOMLEY 7652
White Lion, typical 'black and white' house of area with thatch, dating from 1614. Pretty village was scene of Civil War massacre. (GBG).

BOLLINGTON 9377
Swan with Two Necks, modernised village pub at end of country lane and by side of river Bollin. GBG gives *Crown, Dog & Partridge, Meridien, Vale*.

BRERETON GREEN 0516
Bear's Head, dated 1615, timber-framed, attractive porch and interesting gable-end. *Cat & Fiddle* is also an interesting old inn. (Richardson, GBG).

BROXTON 4754
Travel, half-timbered inn with nice garden. Probably of C17 origin. GBG gives *Royal Oak*.

BUCKLOW HILL 7383
Swan – nucleus of this establishment is a medieval inn, now surrounded by 'motel units'.

CHEADLE 8788
George & Dragon, White Hart listed by Richardson. GBG gives *Printers Arms, Star*.

CHESTER 4066
Bear & Billet, three storeys heavily timbered, dated 1644 in spite of earlier appearance (Richardson and GBG). *Deva*, C18 frontage on much older house which still retains Elizabethan staircase and Jacobean chimney-piece. *Falcon*, possibly of 1626 but its crypt-cellar is much older, C13? (in Richardson's list as is *Feathers*). *Grosvenor*, Eastgate, *c*.1865, 'large and architecturally dull' (P). *Old Custom House*, timber-framed building of 1637 but with older elements e.g. crypt cellar (C13?), oriel window (GBG). *Old King's Head*, in same (Castle) Street, is

also C17. *Pied Bull*, Shoemakers Row has C18 façade built over pavement, masking older house, probably C16 with staircase of this period. *Queen*, Station Road, 1860, rebuilt 1862, 'stodgy' large and Italianate' (P). GBG gives *Albion, Bull & Stirrup, Liver Inn. Red House* on banks of Dee deserves mention because of its superb garden. *Talbot*, Lower Bridge Street, was originally a private house of 1715.

CHRISTLETON 4365
Ring o' Bells, characteristic country inn.

CLUTTON 4654
Bull's Head, pleasant village pub.

CONGLETON 8562
Duke of Wellington is allegedly Tudor. Free House with garden. *Lion & Swan*, large former coaching house, partly C17. Porch with Tuscan columns and square bay above. Listed Richardson (with *Bull's Head*) and GBG which also gives *Forester's Arms, Olde King's Arms. White Lion*, small High Street pub, C17 'black and white' with some interesting details on its front.

DARESBURY 5782
Ring o' Bells, unspoilt pub (C17/18?) in attractive village with Lewis Carroll associations. (GBG).

DELAMERE 5570
Vale Royal Abbey Arms, at road junction, late Georgian with three bay centre and one bay lower wings. Name is almost sole reminder of largest Cistercian abbey f. in 1281 under Edward I in great forest.

DISLEY 9784
Ram's Head, 'early Victorian Tudor inn with gables' which, with school and fountain distinguishes little town centre. GBG gives *Albert, Mousetrap*.

FRODSHAM 5177
Bear's Paw, large E-plan house of 1632, gables, mullioned windows, much restored 1902–3. GBG gives *Golden Lion*.

GAWSWORTH 8869
Harrington Arms, unspoilt old pub, still attached to C18 farm from which it originated. (GBG).

GOOSTREY 7769
Crown, attractive country pub near Joddrell Bank radiotelescope. (GBG).

GREAT BUDWORTH 6677
George and Dragon, 1875 with elaborate wrought-iron sign, in attractive village with one of best perpendicular churches in county.

GREAT SAUGHALL 3569
Swinging Gate, probably of *c.*1490, brick with stone newel stair inside, unfortunately now a private house but *Greyhound* opposite is operational. GBG gives *Egerton Arms*.

GREAVE 9390
Foresters Arms (sic), *Romiley* is recommended by Letts who states that this is a Tudor house (not noticed by P).

HALTON 5381
Castle, monumental building of 1737–8 with entrance staircase, coat of arms over, designed as Court House for Duchy of Lancaster.

HASLINGTON 7355
Hawk, recently extended but nucleus said to be C15. (GBG).

HOOLE BANK 4167
Royal Oak traditional country inn with notable fireplace only a mile from city centre.

KNUTSFORD 7578
Angel, C18 coaching inn, mentioned in 'Cranford'. *Royal George*, once principal posting house, Georgian brick with ashlar quoins. Fine Assembly Room, added later in C18, circular card room and good staircase. Both mentioned by Batchelor and Richardson. *Rose & Crown* is former coaching inn of 1647, restored 1923 'retaining Tudor style'! Notice King's Coffee House (1907). GBG gives *Builders Arms, Freemasons Arms, Lord Eldon*.

LITTLE BOLLINGTON 7286
Nag, stone and slate with bow windows on either side of porch, formerly an C18 coaching house on A56.

LITTLE BUDWORTH 5965
Shrewsbury Arms, unspoilt country inn of same period as rare church of *c.*1800. GBG also gives contrasting *Red Lion*.

LITTLE LEIGH 6175
Holly Bush, 'unspoilt, thatched farmhouse pub' (GBG).

LOWER PEOVER 7474
Bells of Peover began as C14 clergy-house, much altered and developed. Called *Warren de Tabley Arms* until 1895 when it was renamed in honour of licensee named Bell. Much used in World War II by American officers and guests including Patton and Eisenhower.

LYMM 6786
Dane Bank – fine pedimented building of two storeys, Georgian. GBG gives *Jolly Thresher, Railway, Spread Eagle*.

MACCLESFIELD 9173
Macclesfield Arms, large Georgian (1811) five bays, three and half storeys, reflecting town's silk wealth. Older and much smaller is *Castle*, Churchwall gate (GBG which also gives *Evening Star, Jolly Sailor, Star, White Swan*, among others).

MOBBERLEY 7880
Chapel House, small pub with unusual and interesting name. GBG also gives *Railway*.

MOLLINGTON 4347
Good Intent, rare name of pub in converted coach house. Open fires. (GBG).

NANTWICH 6552
Crown, timber-framed, three storeys with impressive windows on second floor. One of oldest buildings in town (*c.*1585) with added C18 Assembly Room. *Lamb*, late Georgian with Tuscan porch, former coaching house. GBG gives *Bowling Green, Oddfellows, Red Cow*.

NESTON 2877
Greenland Fishery, uniquely named country pub in former flourishing market town, port and coaching station. (GBG).

OVER PEOVER 7773
Parkgate, early C19 and after but atmosphere of beams and antiques seems older. (Letts).

PARKGATE 2778
Red Lion, Tudor according to Letts. Garden. Mostyn House School is modification of inn where Handel stayed.

PLUMLEY 7275
Smoker, pub/hotel, allegedly C16, certainly also later, recommended by Letts. GBG: unique name commemorates Napoleonic war-horse.

PRESTBURY 8978
Though becoming suburbanised there are attractive remnants of the village including long, low *Legh Arms* and *Black Boy, Admiral Rodney. Bridge* is a much altered C17 house.

PULFORD 3758
Grosvenor Arms (1880s?) built for Duke of Westminster as part of estate development (Village and neighbourhood provided names for London estates, e.g. Belgravia).

RAINOW 9575
Highwayman, possibly C17, certainly re-named, magnificent Pennine view. GBG also gives *Robin Hood*.

SANDBACH 7560
Old Hall, gabled and timber-framed, originally private house of C16, mentioned Batchelor and Richardson (together with *Bear*). GBG gives C17 *Market Tavern* and small *Iron Grey*.

SANDIWAY 6070
Blue Cap, 'traditional hunting house', built 1716. (GBG).

SCHOLAR GREEN 5569
Bleeding Wolf, uniquely named, large thatched pub with restaurant (GBG which also gives *Globe*).

SUTTON 9270
Church House, village pub, once property of parish church. (GBG).

TABLEY 7176
Windmill, unspoilt pub on A556 at Junction 19 of M6 (GBG) also listed Richardson with *Bull*, Schools Hill.

TARPORLEY 5562
On road to Dudden is *Headless Woman*, stucco with ashlar quoins, flagged roof, possibly C17 (claims ghost of that period). *Swan*, three-storeyed brick, bay windows, stately, 1769, listed Richardson who also gives *Alvanley Arms*. GBG gives *Rising Sun*.

TATTENHALL 4960
Sportsmans Arms, up-dated local in unusually rewarding village (P). GBG.

WARMINGHAM 7161
Bear's Paw, part of attractive group in brick and half-timber, production of Crewe Estate (1870?). Note also no longer operational *Church House*, timber-framed and decorated *c.*1600.

WEAVERHAM 6173
Holly Bush, preserves tradition of pub combined with working farm. Popular with steam-traction enthusiasts. Recommended Letts.

WILLASTON 6752
Nag's Head, 'genuine unspoilt village local' in Wirral. (GBG).

WILMSLOW 8480
Farmer's Arms, former village local, now catering for Manchester suburb (GBG). *George & Dragon*, former coaching house, apparently developed from three buildings, attractively grouped on two sides of courtyard.

WINCLE 9565
Ship, Georgian pub, displaying weapons from '45. Sign depicts 'Nimrod' in which local squire accompanied Shackleton to Antarctic. GBG gives *Wild Boar*.

WINDY HARBOUR 8270
Green Man, 'pleasant pub in a remote setting' (GBG).

CLEVELAND

AISLABY 8508
Blacksmiths Arms, C17 with nice, later, bow windows, attached forge converted into bar (with tools), restaurant license only. Recommended Letts. *New Inn*, Victorian tavern in attractive Eskdale village.

COATHAM 5925
Coatham, described by P as only memorable hotel of Redcar . . . 'large, imposing and very grim'. Built 1870.

EGGLESCLIFFE 4213
Pot & Glass, small C18 inn in obscure but rewarding village.

FIR TREE 1334
Duke of York, ancient sign mentioned by Batchelor.

GUISBOROUGH 6115
Buck, small C18 coaching inn with Tuscan porch between shallow bow windows. *Cross Keys*, Upsall, recommended Letts and described as medieval. *Ward Arms* listed Richardson.

HILTON YARM 4611
Falcon, late C19, built as shooting box of Hilton Manor. Much altered and developed.

LOFTUS 7118
Golden Lion, Georgian house of ashlar with rather pretentious Tuscan porch. Former coaching inn. Nearby is Grinkle Park, converted small country house (C19?).

SALTBURN 6621
Ship may be C16/17. When town was undeveloped fishing village, its landlord, John Andrews, was both Master of Roxby Hunt and leader of smuggling gang. He was twice jailed and died in prison in 1835. *Zetland*, 1861, part of a zestful development following arrival of railway. Yellow brick with central towers. Terrace overlooking valley.

SEATON CAREW 5229

Seaton Hall, early C19 former private house and most prominent building on handsome green. *Dun Cow* (GBG) is a popular out-of-the-way pub and *Seaton Lane* in neighbouring hamlet is recommended Free House. (GBG).

STOCKTON-ON-TEES 4419

Custom House, Finkle Street, originated as private house in 1730.

YARM 4112

George & Dragon ancient coaching inn which housed Promoters Meeting leading to first public railway in the world (commemorative plaque on wall). Listed Richardson. *Ketton Ox*, interesting house of *c.*1670 whose brick façade has been barbarously covered with crude cement. *Union Arms*, yellow and red brick diaper, dated 1762. Former coach house whose carriageway survives.

CORNWALL

ALTARNUN 2281

Rising Sun, C16 country pub. (GBG).

BODDINICK 1257

Old Ferry, riverside inn, formerly operating ferry over Fowey, originating in C16 but much altered and with modern annexe. (Listed Richardson).

BODMIN 0767

Hole in the Wall, originally C18 Debtors' Prison; wine and ale shop in C19, subsequently licensed. Courtyard. Free House. (Batchelor, GBG). *White Hart*, probably C17 origins, alias *Fox*. Chief coaching house in C18 and former mail house. Free House.

BOLVENTOR 1876

Jamaica Inn, lonely wind-swept house on Bodmin Moor. Sinister signboard, associations with smugglers, highwaymen, inspired Daphne du Maurier. feels older than it is (1780). (Richardson, Batchelor).

BOSCASTLE 0990

Dwelling called *Atlantic House* was formerly *Ship* inn and figures in writings of Hawker of Morwenstow. (Richardson lists *Wellington*). *Cobweb*, former warehouse with rock-hewn wine cellar (C17?), infested with spiders whose webs still 'decorate' bar. (GBG). *Napoleon*, two storey, stone and cob with slate roof, C16. Renamed early C19 when landlord recruited Home Guard. Unique sign. (GBG).

BREAGE 6128

Queens Arms, probably originated Church House, rebuilt C19. Smuggling associations, allegedly haunted. China collection.

BUDE 2006

Letts offers *Bullers Arms*. *Carriers*, two-storeyed, stone and rubble, formed from two (C16?) cottages. Oldest pub in town. Richardson lists *Falcon*. GBG gives *Summerleaze Beach Hotel*.

CALLINGTON 3669

Richardson lists *Goldings Hotel*.

CAMELFORD 1083

Masons Arms, recommended in Letts and described as Elizabethan.

CAWSAND 4350
Halfway House, C17 country inn, near sea.

CHAPEL AMBLE 9975
Malsters Arms, formed from two C17 cottages, one was smithy in C19 when landlord was blacksmith and his wife brewster. Closed in C19 through Anglican opposition. Reopened 1966. Free House.

COMFORD 6942
Fox & Hounds, formerly Hunter & Hounds, then Hare & Hounds. Two-storey cob and stone, rebuilt 1742. Tything Room upstairs, now divided. (GBG).

CRAFTHOLE 3654
Finnygook, unique name said to derive from 'Finny's ghost'. Finny allegedly was smuggler, killed here by Excise officers, who swore with his dying breath to haunt the place.

CRANTOCK 7860
Old Albion, may originate in C16; closed 1847, badly damaged by fire 1902, relicensed 1947. Secret chamber associated with smugglers. Interior well, inglenook fireplace. (Batchelor, GBG).

CREMYLL 4553
Edgecumbe Arms – L-shaped, two storeys with dormers, slate roof, built 1730 to replace *Ferry*. Housed local courtroom until C19. Associations with famous yachtspeople. Most easterly pub in Duchy. (GBG).

CRIPPLE'S EASE 5036
Engine, VIctorian pub, recommended Letts.

CURY CROSS ROADS 6721
Near Mullion, began as wheelwright's shop, which also sold ale in C18. Very much altered, added to, rebuilt.

FALMOUTH 8032
Greenbank, originally Family & Commercial and coaching terminus. Now up-market with private quay. Kenneth Grahame associations. (Batchelor).

Pandora, at nearby Restronguet Creek, was *Ship* until late C18 when it was renamed by sea-captain compulsorily retired after losing 'Pandora'. (GBG). *Royal*, listed Richardson. *Seven Stars*, private house of 1608, formerly on sea-edge, licensed later in C17. Main bar Victorian, Key-ring collection. Free House. (GBG).

FEOCK 8238
Punchbowl & Ladle, makes very dubious claim to nine centuries of life. Certainly of considerable antiquity. Huge fireplace with unusual chimney said to have been used by Excise officers for burning combustible contraband.

FOWEY 1251
Ship, formerly town house of Rashleigh family but public house by C18 at latest. C16 with upstairs fireplace dated 1570, some Tudor panelling. (Is this the same as Richardson's *Lugger*?) *King of Prussia* has interesting sign indicating smuggling associations. (GBG).

GULVAL 4831
Now a centre for the revived industry of mead brewing.

HELFORD 7526
Shipwrights, C17 rubble and cob, thatched. Once owned by shipwright of adjoining yard. (Recommended Letts.)

HELFORD PASSAGE 7626
Ferry Boat, The Passage House (1538) was ferryman's cottage, became coastguard station against smugglers in C19. Completely modernised. Free House. (GBG).

HELSTON 6527
Angel, originated in C13 as monastic hospice; developed and rebuilt after Reformation as town house of Godolphins. Later Excise house and cock-fighting centre. (Listed Richardson, mentioned Batchelor.) Bob Fitzsimmons' birthplace. *Blue Anchor*, C17 rough stone, thatched. Flagged floor, open fireplace. Own brewery produces very strong ale. (GBG).

HOLYWELL BAY 7559
Treguth, former (C16?) farmhouse, elaborate thatch, attractive wrought-iron sign. Much copper and brass. Army cap badge collection.

LAMORNA 4524
Lamorna, alias 'Wink' late C18, originally beerhouse. Simple two storey building with smuggling connections (hide in bar).

LAND'S END 3425
First & Last, listed Richardson and mentioned Batchelor but rather undistinguished apart from its site.

LANREATH 1756
Punchbowl, C16 with enclosed yard containing holy well of St Monarch (though no such name occurs in standard reference books). Originated as local Courthouse. Still serves mead. Bedrooms have not only four-posters but Cornish 'half-testers'. Imaginative wrought-iron sign said to have been designed by Augustus John. (GBG). Recommended Letts.

LAUNCESTON 3384
White Hart, principal town hotel with doorway pillaged from priory of Augustinian Canons whose ruins lie behind St Thomas's church. GBG and in Richardson's list.

LOOE 2753
Fishermans Arms, two-storeyed stone and cob, 1611? Houses fish market until C19. Claims ghost of stable-boy suicide. *Jolly Sailor*, formed of two unequal buildings. Older part said to be C15. Smuggling associations and alleged tunnel. Claims ghost of jilted girl who manifests herself as a white rabbit! GBG gives *Bullers Arms*.

LOSTWITHIEL 1059
Royal Oak makes very dubious claim to be C13, seems Georgian. Recommended Letts and GBG. Richardson lists *Royal Talbot*. There is a house of 1652 which was formerly a Malt House. GBG adds *Earl of Chatham*.

MAWNAM SMITH 7728
Red Lion, formed from three C17 cottages and was ale-house from later C17. Alleged poltergeist. Letts recommends *Budock Vean* described as 'mixed ancient and modern'.

METHERELL 4168
Carpenters Arms, C17 rubble frontage on older building, allegedly C15 and associated with Benedictine priory at Tavistock. Interior well, flagged floors. Free House. (GBG).

MEVAGISSEY 0144
Ship, three storeys, ashlar, late C18. Associated with smuggling and sea-fishing. Claims two ghosts. GBG gives *Fountain*.

MITHIAN 7450
Miners Arms. The miners are tin-miners but house is older than name. Traditionally monastic dependancy but dated beam is a generation too late. It may have recusant associations: there was a secret chamber, a chapel (now bedrooms), and a tunnel, supposedly to nearby manor house. Interesting staircase and C18 ceiling. (Mentioned in Batchelor).

MORWENSTOW 2015
Bush, two storey stone and cob about small courtyard. Said to have originated as Cistercian cell with chapel, becoming after Reformation smuggling/wreckers house. Inn from at least C17. Claims to be oldest inn in Duchy. (GBG).

MOUSEHOLE 4626
Ship, C17 stone and cob with sea-facing bay on first floor. Ground floors flagged, open fires. Richardson lists *Keigwin Arms*. *Lobster Pot* is well-sited, picturesque.

MULLION 6719
Old Inn, C17 stone and cob with thatched roof. Smuggling connections and associations with Marconi. (GBG).

NEWLYN 4628
Fishermens Arms, C17 stone and cob, slate roof. Overlooks harbour, alleged smuggling connections.

PADSTOW 9175
London, once a cottage ale-house, now up-marketed with 'lounge bar'. Mentioned Batchelor and in GBG.

PELYNT 2055
Jubilee, cunningly restored and well-furnished C16 inn with spiral staircase. (GBG).

PENDOGGETT 0288
Cornish Arms claims C15 origin. GBG gives nearby *St Kew*.

PENRYN 7834
Seven Stars, three-storeyed stone and rubble buildings with bay windows. C19 and C15 site. Interior has large and heterogeneous collection of 'by-gones'.

PERRANARWORTHAL 7738
Norway – name commemorates former trading connection. Still flies Norwegian flag and has longship on sign. C17 with later front. Once stage for 'Quicksilver' coach. (In Letts).

PENZANCE 4731
Admiral Benbow, C16 with much alteration and addition. Once smugglers' haunt with passage to harbour from well shaft. Interesting decor. *Dolphin*, small quayside inn claiming C16 origins. Present building C17 and site of local courts to C19. Posting house. Introduced billiards in 1802. Smuggling hide in roof. Base for travelling to Scillies *c.*1900. Allegedly haunted. (Batchelor). *Star*, listed by Richardson. *Turks Head*, C16 much altered and claims to be town's oldest pub. Low, stone with steeply pitched roof. A former landlord was father of founder of Holloway College, London. GBG gives *Bath, Globe, Seven Stars, Union, Yacht*.

PETERVILLE ST AGNES 8244
Peterville – C17 stone and cob with rambling additions. Smuggling associations. Allegedly haunted by C18 landlord.

PHILLACK 5539
New Inn – long low frontage may conceal medieval Church House. It is still owned by church. (GBG).

PHILLEIGH 8639
Roseland, said to originate in pilgrim hospice but present two-storeyed stone and cob seems to be from combining (C17?) cottages. Garden. (Letts, GBG).

PILLATON 3664
Weary Friar, called Royal Oak until 1963. New name results from confusion about origin: either 1250 Church House or resthouse associated with Dominican friary (at Truro?). Free House.

POLPERRO 2051
Three Pilchards, attractive old pub on quayside not far from Smugglers' Museum. (GBG).

PORTHLEVEN 6225
Ship, three-storeyed building of C18 on older site. Cellar bar hewn from rock. Smuggling associations and alleged ghost of French suicide. Connections with Henry Trengrouse and invention of life-saving apparatus.

PORT ISAAC 9980
Cornish Arms, inn 2½m away, oak-beamed, and slate flagged floor. (Batchelor). *Golden Lion*, 1715 on edge of small harbour to which it had tunnel in smuggling days. (Batchelor, GBG).

PORTLOE 9339
Lugger, tiny, squat inn with balcony, located on hard. Smuggling tradition and still possesses powerful maritime flavour, somewhat tarted up for tourists. (Letts).

ROCHE 9860
Victoria, ancient, atmospheric inn with curios.

ST AGNES 7150
Railway, C17 in spite of name, built over mineshaft associated with murder and suicide. Allegedly haunted until recently. (Batchelor, Letts).

ST AUSTELL 0152
Queen's Head, listed by Richardson. GBG gives *Seven Stars, Sun*.

ST COLUMB MAJOR 9163
New Inn, two storeys rubble and stone, coach passage and rear stabling, mounting block. Reputedly of 1660. (GBG). *Red Lion*, ashlar, two and half storeys, former coaching inn of early C19. Old skittle alley over stables. *Ring o'Bells*, allegedly dates from C13. (Batchelor).

ST ERTH 5435
Smugglers, at Praze, was originally *Calais*, then *Victoria* until 1970s. Free House on older site associated with smugglers. *Star*, stuccoed stone and cob, former carriers' inn of late C17. Usual smuggling associations. Well in garden. (GBG).

ST EWE 9745
Crown, originated as C16 farmhouse and still possesses (and occasionally uses) complex roasting spit.

ST ISSEY 9271
Ring o'Bells, originated in row of linked cottages, walls slate-hung against winds. Unspoilt and undeveloped. Delightful sign.

ST IVES 5140
Sloop, granite rubble with slate roof, mainly C17 but claims to date from 1312. Originally private house. Flagged floors. Marine Commando HQ in World War II. (Tregenna), *Castle*, listed by Richardson (together with *Golden Lion*) and recommended Letts who describes it as mixed 'ancient and modern'. GBG gives *Union*.

ST JOHN 4053
St John's Inn, probably originated as hostelry of Knights of St John (Hospitallers) whose Cross it still wears on sign.

ST JUST 3631
Star, two storeys, granite, former C18 posting house on older side. Flagged floors. Associations with John Wesley. (GBG).

SENNEN COVE 3425
First Inn in England at Sennen mentioned in Batchelor. *Old Success*, granite, two-storeyed house of late C17 formed from two cottages. Much altered and developed. Named from pilchard fishing vessels. (Letts).

STRATTON 2306
Tree, originally private house of Grattons. C16 scheduled building. Birthplace of Cornish giant in 1611, scene of minor skirmish in Civil War (1543). (Batchelor). GBG gives *King's Arms*, old coaching house.

TREEN 3923
Logan Rock, typical granite building of area, named after local rocking stone displaced and restored by Oliver Goldsmith's nephew in 1824.

TREGONY 9244
Kings Arms, stone, two-storeys with pillared porch. Said to date from 1615 and to have been visited by Charles I. Jacobean panelling. Former staging-post with archway to yard.

TRESILLIAN 8646
Wheel, low stone and rubble with sign incorporated in thatch. Probably C17 on older site. Civil War associations. Own well, period furniture, large granite fireplace. Mentioned Batchelor and GBG.

TREVANNANCE COVE 7251
Driftwood Spars, named from great ship's timbers used in its construction in C18(?). (Batchelor).

TRURO 8244
Red Lion, an important coaching house of 1671, later disfigured by Victorian alterations. Staircase survives. Mentioned Batchelor and in Richardson's list (with *King's Arms* and *Royal*). GBG gives *Coach & Horses*.

WADEBRIDGE 9872
Molesworth Arms, formerly *Fountain*. C18 front with Tuscan porch. Former tything-house and cock-fighting venue. Said to have ghost of headless horseman. Free House. Bridge is one of best medieval bridges in England.

ZENNOR 4538
Tinners Arms, two storey, rubble and cob, mainly C17 but may originate in C13 Church House. Housed local court until C19. Garden. Free House. Reminder of old industry. Marks beginning of magnificent cliff walk.

CUMBRIA

ALSTON 7146
Blue Bell, excellent old-fashioned inn of highest market town in England. *Low Byre*, hotel occupying transformed Georgian manor house. (GBG).

AMBLESIDE 3704
Prince of Wales, 1855, a response to the romantic publicity of Lakeland, described by P as 'large, dark and gabled'. *Rothay Manor*, former private house, probably early Victorian, three bays with wings. Good doorway and balcony. *Royal Oak*, small main street pub of early C19, formerly with adjoining saddlery. Associations with William Wordsworth's uncle. GBG gives *Golden Rule, Unicorn*. There are also *Waterhead*, three storeys of lakeland stone, early C19 and *White Lion*, said to be C17 and formerly a small coaching inn. Letts recommends *Three Shires* hotel, a Free House in Little Langdale.

APPLEBY 6820
Kings Head, plain ashlar-faced building of five bays. Early C19 and former coaching house. Listed Richardson, with *Tufton Arms*, a romantic 'Gothic' edivice of 1873 with gables and dormers. Mentioned Batchelor. GBG gives *Golden Ball* and *Grapes*, opposite river Eden.

ARMATHWAITE 5046
Duke's Head, modernised country inn, probably of same period as below. *Red Lion*, C17–18, former coaching house, bar with horse-racing curios.

ASKHAM 5123
Queens Head, decorated with waggon wheels from Brampton hearse. Probably began in association with butcher's premises. Much used by packmen and became coaching inn in C18. Features collection of calico printing blocks. Listed Richardson and recommended Letts.

BAMPTON 5118
Crown & Mitre, C18 country inn with riverside garden. One wonders if name is a case of 'backing both ways' or simply indicates Erastian ownership.

BARROW-IN-FURNESS 1960
Apart from Cistercian abbey on outskirts (see Furness), there is not much memorable building in pubs or elsewhere. GBG gives *Ferry*, Walney Island, *Ship* at edge of town.

BASSENTHWAITE 2328
Pheasant, Georgian hotel with coaching associations. Listed Richardson, recommended Letts.

BOOT 1700
Eden, Howard Arms – side-by-side in market-place, both of three bays and built in early C19 testifying to improved conditions and increased interest in wild scenery.

BOWNESS ON WINDERMERE 4097
Hole i' t' Wall, alias *New Hall*. Allegedly built 1612. Claims Dickens associations. (GBG). *Royal*, C19 hotel whose Jubilee Bar is decorated with old photographs of Bowness and hosts a jazz club. *Stag's Head*, possibly oldest inn in town with former coaching associations. Still has 'cocktail bar' – though it serves Theakstons. *John Peel* is mentioned by Batchelor as an interesting inn.

BRAMPTON 5361
At Talkin Tarn is *Tarn End*, a 'mixed ancient and modern' hotel according to Letts. *White Lion*, listed by Richardson.

BURTON & HOLME 5276
Station, small country pub mentioned as offering unusually good food and drink.

BUTTERMERE 1815
Fish, C18, associations with Mary Robinson, the 'Buttermere Beauty', Coleridge and Wordsworth.

CALDER BRIDGE 0405
Sella Park, originally private house of Curwents. Victorian exterior conceals medieval pele-tower and some later Jacobean work. *Stanley Arms*, former coaching house of mid C18 with gardens extending to river Calder.

CARLISLE 3955
Once had only state breweries in England, now owned by Theakstons. *Blue Bell*, Scotch Street, former coaching inn with fine Georgian façade. Richardson lists *Crown & Mitre, Red Lion*. GBG gives *Crown* in Botchergate and another in Scotland Road, Stanwix; together with *Woolpack*.

CARTMEL 3778
Kings Arms, attractive town-centre pub near priory, recommended Letts and GBG, which adds *Pig & Whistle*.

CARTMEL FELL 4188
Masons Arms, country pub recommended Letts.

CAUTLEY 6994
Cross Keys, long, low house with pentise at rear, probably *c.*1600 with C18–19 additions in magnificent and remote Pennine setting near Sedbergh with access to Cautley Snout.

COCKERMOUTH 1230
Appletree, old riverside inn, now up-marketed. *Trout*, long, low house with porch in Georgian style, recommended Letts. Richardson lists *Glebe*, unlocated. GBG gives *Swan, Tithe Barn*.

COLTON 5444
Old Sun claims origin and charter of Charles II. Evidence of building in 1654. Unpretentious white-washed exterior.

CONISTON 3097
Sun, Waterhead are in Richardson's list but no details. Former has associations with Donald Campbell's speed trials. *Ship* is a characteristic building of region with its white walls and black window frames, splendidly sited above Coniston Water. GBG gives *Crown*.

COWGILL 7586
Sportsmans Arms, delightfully situated cottage-type inn, white-washed stone (C18 or earlier) with sporting associations, in Dentdale. Mentioned Batchelor.

CROOK 4694
Wild Boar, C17 house which is said to have been renamed when last wild boar in country was killed outside. Recommended Letts: 'mixed ancient and modern'.

DALSTON 3750
Blue Bell, originally C17 coaching house with cobbled courtyard now grassed over. Part of State Combine until recently.

DALTON-IN-FURNESS 2374
Wellington, White Horse, face on to pleasant triangular market-place and are characteristic small town pubs of Victorian era. Former is in GBG together with *Black Bull* which seems of similar vintage.

EGREMONT 0110
Blue Bell, traditional town-centre pub in handsome main street. (GBG). Richardson lists *King's Arms*, also in GBG as 'smart, modern town-centre pub'.

ELTERWATER 3204
Britannia, until recently *Hare & Hounds*, roughcast stone, C17 and later, formed from group of cottages. Listed building. Fine view of Elterwater (Norse for 'Swan Lake').

ENNERDALE BRIDGE 0616
Anglers is two miles east, magnificently sited at foot of Ennerdale Water and encircled with mountains.

ESKDALE 1599
Bower House, C17 listed building with riverside garden and view of Scafell. Recommended Letts and in GBG.

FURNESS 2271
Hotel near ruins of great Cistercian abbey incorporates a good deal of the (C13) gatehouse which once gave admission to the precincts.

GRANGE-OVER-SANDS 4077
Borrowdale Green, a modernised Victorian hotel is recommended by Letts. *Commodore* and *Crown* are smaller hotels in main street and about same date. (GBG). *Grange*, an hotel built 1866, nine years after arrival of railway and consequent development as seaside resort.

GRASMERE 3307
Swan, largeish inn, possibly former coaching house, strong associations with William Wordsworth and Walter Scott. Mentioned Batchelor and listed Richardson, together with *Red Lion*, a smaller house, probably of same period. GBG gives *Traveller's Rest*, a pleasant roadside inn on A591. Dove Cottage is former pub named *Dove & Olive Branch*.

GREAT LANGDALE 3105
Dungeon Ghyll, central section three storeys of Lakeland slate and prominent bay windows, with lower additions and developments, early C19? Magnificent site. Illustrated Batchelor. *Langdales*, popular with climbers and walkers. Victorian and later. Recommended Letts.

HAVERTHWAITE 3843
Anglers Arms, pleasant house opposite Haverthwaite Lakeside railway.

HAWKSHEAD 3597
On road to Ambleside is *Drunken Duck*, formerly *Barngate*, and possibly of C17 origin. Name changed later C19 as result of ducks drinking leaking beer. Isolated. Free House. *Sun*, picturesque house (C19?) at head of Esthwaite in one of Lakeland's prettiest villages.

HEVERSHAM 4983
Blue Bell, Free House occupying former vicarage of C17. Recommended Letts.

HOLMROOK 0016
Lutwidge Arms, Victorian fishing inn whose grounds border River Irt on which it possesses a stretch of fishing.

IREBY 2338

Village inn accommodated John Keats in June 1818 and he was much impressed by a country-dancing school held on the premises.

KENDAL 5192

Fleece built 1654 as hostelry and coaching inn. Stables and 'coaching room' survive, though much altered. Allegedly haunted by servant who committed suicide in stables. *Kendal*, hotel of *c.*1840 in latest classical style with pedimented windows on first floor. *Kings Arms* on edge of town of about same time, listed Richardson. *Queens*, late Georgian hotel, once serving carriage trade and coaches. *Woolpack*, old carriers' inn, largely rebuilt *c.*1780 as coaching and waggoners house. Note enormous entrance to old yard. GBG gives *Globe, Ring o'Bells, Sawyers Arms, Shakespeare, White Hart*.

KESWICK 2723

Dog & Gun, Victorian and later, recommended Letts. Richardson lists *Pheasant*, unlocated, *George*, former coaching inn with C16(?) origins. Associations with Walpole and Wordsworth. (In Richardson's list and GBG). *King's Arms*, small C18 coaching inn with beamed ceilings. Popular with walkers. Old Peculier on draught. Recommended Letts. *Packhorse*, C18 or earlier – association with packmen. (GBG). *Royal Oak*, entirely rebuilt in C18 as packhorse centre, later (as roads improved) served carriage trade. Associations with De Quincy, Coleridge, Scott, Shelley, Southey, Stevenson, Tennyson, Wordsworth, GBG adds *Oddfellows Arms*.

KIRBY LONSDALE 6178

Red Dragon, simple country inn of C17. *Royal*, former coaching house in market square, C18 ashlar-faced, parapetted, Ionic porch. Listed Richardson. *Snooty Fox*, unusual (modern) name for trendy, former village pub (GBG and Letts who also recommends *Sun* whose front rests on three C17 pillars). *King's Arms* has a Georgian façade to match its neighbour but is older than its front and has a C17 ceiling inside.

KIRBY STEPHEN 7708

Croglin Castle, old-fashioned local named after prehistoric enclosure, ¾ mile ssw. of church (Croglam (sic) Castle). GBG. *Kings Arms*, mid C18 with Georgian façade, mid C18. Unusual powder closet survives. An important halt for mail coaches in earlier C19. Recommended Letts, mentioned Batchelor and listed Richardson with *Black Bull*.

KIRKSTONE PASS 4008

Travellers Rest, rugged stone-built with massive porch and stone-flagged roof. Licensed in mid C19. One of highest inns (1,468 ft, *c.*452m above sea-level). Remote and welcome hostelry. Listed Richardson.

LANERCOST 5563

New Bridge, former Georgian coaching house on riverside site near ruined priory and Roman wall. Recommended Letts.

LITTLE LANGDALE 3105

Three Shires. Small, picturesque with rare name. Superbly sited small Lakeland inn of local slate. Seasonal opening.

LORTON 1526

Horseshoe, village inn with some work of Georgian period, situated in picturesque Lorton Vale. (GBG). Recommended Letts.

LOWICK 2985
Farmers Arms, old timbered building (C16?), somewhat tarted-up. Magnificent views of Lakeland mountains. Originated as farmhouse selling home brew. Became a coaching inn. Retains spinning gallery and houses a good collection of paintings.

LUPTON 5581
Plough, roadside inn (C18?) on A65.

MARYPORT 0336
Crown, small town pub probably dating from commercial development of coaling port. (GBG).

MILBURN 6529
Stag, modernised traditional village pub. Free House. 'A gem in an area where standards are low' (Letts).

MILNTHORPE 4981
Cross Keys, a lively local by side of village green. (GBG).

NEWBY BRIDGE 3685
Swan, charming riverside inn at end of Windermere. Mainly C18 with featured doorway, later modern wing. Once a large coaching house. Associations with Nathaniel Hawthorne. Owns stretch of river Leven.

PATTERDALE 3915
Brotherswater, on A592 on way to Windermere. Victorian. Recommended Letts.

PENRITH 5130
Crown, façade of 1794 with five bays, good doorway, bay windows, three storeys; listed by Richardson. *George*, only left side is original where Young Pretender had his HQ in 1745. Rest is C20 work in Georgian manner. *Gloucester Arms*, former private house called Dockray Hall. Claims C15 origin but nothing earlier than C16 visible. Mentioned Batchelor. *Mitre*, dates from a least 1669. *Two Lions*, originally town house of Lowther family, built 1585. Fine plaster ceiling. Mentioned Batchelor. GBG gives *Agricultural, Salutation*.

PENTON 4476
Huntsman, tiny local with restaurant. (Recommended Letts) alias '*Annie Jones*'.

POOLEY BRIDGE 4724
Inn had a famous C19 landlord called Will Russell.

RAMPSIDE 2366
Concle, formerly *Bay Horse*, a C17 inn whose curious name is a corruption of Conkhole, a depression in Morecambe Bay which was popular for saline bathing in C19. GBG gives *Clarkes Arms*.

RAVENGLASS 0896
Ratty Arms, popular pub, Victorian and after, in market town at head of estuary. Recommended Letts.

RUTHWAITE 4242
Swan, preserves hunting horn of John Peel. Associations with Scott and Wordsworth who is said to have penned doggerel praising sign painted by landlord. Mentioned Batchelor.

RYDAL 3606
Rydal Hall, recently made into hotel, was once home of Le Fleming family with Catholic sympathies in reign of Elizabeth and later. C17 part of house said to contain a priest's hide. Two allegedly haunted areas.

ST BEES 9611
Oddfellows Arms, traditional pub at south end of township. (GBG).

SANDSIDE 2282
Ship, attractive, white-washied, two-storeyed inn. Formerly farmhouse brewing own ale, later outlet for Kendal brewery. Superb views of Kentdale and Lakeland hills.

SAWRY 3695
Tower Bank Arms, NT pub, features in Tales of Peter Rabbit, near Beatrix Potter's House. GBG adds *Sawrey Hotel*.

SCALES 3426
White Horse, unpretentious stone and flagged house serving old Keswick–Penrith route. Lease allegedly contains clause that Bible is not to be removed from inn. Interior features corn-dollies and other straw objects.

SEATHWAITE 2295
Newfields, Victorian pub in Lake District recommended by Letts.

SEDBERGH 6592
Bull, largeish small-town hotel, once coaching house, now largely catering for parents visiting school. Listed Richardson with *White Hart*. GBG gives *Red Lion*.

SHAP FELL 5410
Greyhound, curious stone sign dated 1703. Associated with Bonnie Prince Charlie and '45. Mentioned Batchelor, recommended Letts.

SILECROFT 1281
Miners Arms, much altered and developed but oldest part is said to be C16. Free House. (Letts).

SIZERGH 5188
Strickland Arms, formerly *Swayers Arms* and before that the coach house of the castle in whose grounds it is situated. Pleasant stone-built house of *c.*1810.

TALKIN TARN 5557
Tarn End, delightfully situated hotel, recommended Letts and described as 'mixed ancient and modern'.

TEMPLE SOWERBY 6127
Kings Arms, sandstone house in Eden valley on coach route between Penrith and Scotch Corner. Yard survives surrounded by (converted) stabling. Keeps besom inside entrance 'to sweep away ill-luck'.

THRELKELD 3225
Horse & Farrier, C17 possibly associated with packmen. Fine site at foot of Blencathra. (GBG).

TIRRIL 5026
Queens Head, 1715 with cellars and some rooms hewn out of solid rock. Once home of William Wordsworth. Mentioned Batchelor.

TROUTBECK 4103
Mortal Man, characteristic Lake District inn, stone with roofing flags. Original house of 1689, thoroughly rebuilt in C19. Interesting sign with doggerel. Unique name? *Queens Head*, unspoilt C17 house in superb setting. (GBG). Both have some bedrooms furnished with 'four posters'.

TORVER 2894
Church House, site perhaps C14, present building probably C18 with characteristic Long Room, also used as court room in C19.

ULVERSTON 2878
Attractive town which was linked to sea by canal in C18. *Sun*, small town hotel of this period which was probably a coaching house is listed by Richardson. GBG gives *Hope & Anchor, Old Friends, Swan*.

WASDALE HEAD 1204
Inn, popular with walkers and climbers, in one of most magnificent locations in country. Head of Wasdale and under Scafell Pike.

WETHERAL 4654
Crown, late Georgian hotel, seven bays and Ionic porch, at side of handsome village green. Salmon River.

WHITEHAVEN 9718
Jubilee, unpretentious town pub of Victorian vintage, formerly *Canteen* which served militia barracks now occupied by factory. (GBG). *Royal Standard*, early Victorian with attached Music Hall at rear, some of whose discarded fittings have furnished private theatre at Rosehill, Moresby. GBG adds *Lowther Arms*.

WIGTON 2548
Kildare, listed by Richardson. GBG gives *Throstle Nest*.

WINDERMERE 3995
Brookside, Lake Road is a pleasant, late C19 pub, away from tourists. (GBG). Letts recommends *Langdale Chase* hotel, Free House, described as 'medieval' and *Millar Howe*, 'mixed ancient and modern'. About half a mile away on A591 is *Sun*, an old posting house which once served Keswick run.

DERBYSHIRE

ALFRETON 4155
George, attractive Georgian coaching house facing down pleasant High Street.

ALVESTON 3933
Ship, ancient smuggling tradition (blocked-up passage from cellar), later stage on Bristol–Birmingham coach route. W.G. Grace learned the game on its adjoining cricket ground.

ASHBOURNE 1846
Green Man and Black's Head Royal, a mid-Georgian house of seven bays. Gallows sign and picturesque courtyard. Associations with Boswell and Johnson. (GBG). *Smith's Tavern* alias 'Wine Vaults', attractive old pub. (GBG).

ASHFORD-IN-THE-WATER 1969
Devonshire Arms, large refurbished pub. (GBG with *Bulls Head*).

ASHOVER 3463
Crispin, unusual name with Agincourt associations. Unspoilt inn, may date from 1416, in attractive village. (GBG).

BAKEWELL 2168
Rutland Arms, 1804, four bays, stone with Tuscan Doric porch. Stables. In Richardson's list, mentioned Batchelor and recommended Letts, who adds *Plough*, Flatt. GBG gives *Peacock*.

BARLBOROUGH 4777

Pebley, 2 miles north of village, maintains ancient game of 'Ring the Bull'. (GBG). *Rose & Crown* is a pleasant village pub. Letts recommends *Royal Oak*, described as 'mixed ancient and modern'.

BEELEY 2667

Devonshire Arms, claims C16 origin, possibly coaching house in C18. (GBG).

BELPER 3447

Near interesting early industrial buildings are *Grapes*, an attractive pub of some antiquity. (GBG). Two miles south on east bank of River Derwent is *Hollybush*, Makeney, with inscribed stone in wall recording first Turnpike Act for Derbys. *White Swan*, a smartened-up town centre pub. (GBG).

BIRCHOVER 2462

Red Lion, a 'classic village pub', whose ancient indoor well survives. (GBG). The name of *Druid* is a relic of C18 craze for druids.

BOLSOVER 4770

White Swan, homely town centre pub almost in shadow of C17 (sic) castle. (GBG).

BONSALL 2758

King's Head, a traditional, mullioned and gabled building (1677) in small market place.

BRASSINGTON 2354

Olde Gate, near Norman church. Pub allegedly built in 1616 and retains high-backed settles in Snug. (GBG).

BUXTON 0673

In the vicinity are stone-built *Cat & Fiddle* (0071) on exposed Axe Ridge and, at 1,707ft (*c*.525m), among competitors for highest inn. *Eagle*, a Queen Anne building of nine bays, three and half storeys. *Palace* is a substantial building of 1868. Richardson lists *George, Old Hall, Shakespeare* but with no details. GBG gives *Nineteenth Hole, Robin Hood*. On the same ridge (Axe Ridge) is *Travellers Rest* at 1,535ft (*c*.972m).

BUXWORTH 0178

Navigation on edge of canal basin made 1800.

CALOW 4071

Somerset House on A623 is enigmatically described in GBG as 'wooden casks in haunted house'.

CASTLETON 1582

Castle, named after nearby Peveril Castle, was originally C17 and has coaching associations. *Nags Head*, Georgian and former coaching house in town centre. Gritstone. Still has 13 call-bells in entrance. Free House. (Letts). GBG gives *George*.

CHAPEL EN LE FRITH 9580

Market town which grew round chapel in forest of Peak has *King's Arms*, small market-place hotel listed by Richardson. GBG gives *New Inn, Old Pack Horse*.

CHESTERFIELD 3871

Royal Oak, timber framed, C16, tidied-up but substantially original. (GBG). Letts recommends modern *Robin Hood*. GBG adds *Barley Mow* 'old coaching house of character', *Grouse, Queens Park Hotel*.

CHURCH BROUGHTON 2033
Holly Bush, pleasantly situated old pub in ancient village. (GBG).

CLOWNE 4975
De Rode Arms, Victorian, recommended Letts.

CRICH 3554
Rising Sun, low ceilinged village pub on Common near fine church, Norman and later. (GBG).

CROMFORD 1956
Greyhound, fine mid-Georgian house with five bays and a pediment, 'resembling a minor Town Hall' (P). GBG gives *Bell*.

CROWDECOTE 1162
Packhorse, stopping place at crossing of Dove for packhorsemen carrying lead ore to the hilltop smelts.

DARLEY BRIDGE 3438
Three Stags Heads, small low-ceilinged pub of some antiquity near C15 bridge. (GBG).

DERBY 3455
Bell, Sadler Street, former coaching inn whose developments have made it an attractive, rambling building. *Dolphin*, Queen Street, timber-framed and gabled, C16 with later extensions. Oldest pub in city. *Friary*, Friargate, fine detached seven bay Georgian house with contemporary panelling and stucco inside. *Green Man*, St Peter's Street, Georgian frontage masks older building. Some good panelling inside. *Greyhound*, Friargate, Georgian exterior but may be older. Former coaching house, recently modernised and extended. *Horse & Groom*, formed from two C18 cottages. Attractive exterior with windows blocked to escape tax. *Royal*, Victoria Street, 1839 with fine, well-preserved dining room on first floor. *Seven Stars*, Queen Street, small but architecturally interesting, dated 1680. *Victoria*, Midland Place, substantial house of three and half storeys, perhaps older than name. Pevsner points out that County Library, Jury Street, originated as early Georgian inn and has Royal Arms on first floor. Richardson lists *Midland* but without detail. Batchelor mentions *Copeland Arms* and *Seven Stars*, as well as *White Bear*. GBG gives *Alexandra, Blessington Carriage, Buck in the Park, Exeter Arms, Furnace, Great Northern, Liversage Arms, Sir Robert Peel, Vine*.

DRONFIELD 3578
Green Dragon, attractive and historic pub in small town which prospered in C18. (GBG). The house is T-shaped (composed from three buildings?), C18 or earlier but much restored. Letts recommends *Chantry*.

DOVEDALE 8566
Green Man listed by Richardson but no further information.

EARL STERNDALE 0967
Quiet Woman – 'superb example of village green pub' (GBG).

EDALE 1285
Church is more up-market. *Nag's Head*, gritstone house, popular with walkers. At beginning (or end) of Pennine Way. (GBG).

FENNY BENTLEY 1750
Coach & Horses is recommended by Letts.

FLAGG 1368
Duke of York, described as 'mixed ancient and modern'. Recommended Letts.

FROGGATT 2476
Chequers, recommended Letts and described as 'ancient'. Garden.

GLOSSOP 0393
Norfolk Arms, listed Richardson, no details. GBG gives *Grapes, Manor*.

HARDWICK HALL 4663
Hardwick Inn at entrance to Hall grounds is a working old pub owned by National Trust. (GBG).

HARTINGTON 1360
Charles Cotton, C17 inn whose grounds border river Dove, named in honour of Izaak Walton's friend and fishing companion. 2½ miles east on Ashbourne–Buxton road is interesting old *Newhaven* inn.

HARTSHORNE 3221
Chesterfield Arms, pleasant old pub developed from typical C18 farmhouse. Garden with peacocks. (GBG).

HAYFIELD 0386
George, possibly C17, developing coaching trade on A614. (GBG). In Little Hayfield is *Lantern Pike*, set in valley overlooked by Peak. (GBG).

HEANOR 4346
Crown, Victorian pub in substantially Victorian town. Possesses outside skittle-alley. (GBG).

HOLMESFIELD 3277
Travellers Rest, characteristic Derbyshire village pub. (GBG).

HOPE 1783
Cheshire Cheese, 'an enterprising free house' (GBG).

HORSLEY 3744
Coach & Horses, village pub, often with real cider. (GBG).

HURDLOW 1266
Royal Oak, Victorian pub, recommended Letts.

ILKESTON 4642
Rutland Cottage, unusual carved bar. Still has Billiard Room but called 'lounge'. (GBG). Is this *Rutland* listed by Richardson? GBG also gives *Durham Ox*.

INGLEBY 3427
John Thompson, rare name for rare home-brew house (GBG) also recommended Letts who describes it as 'mixed ancient'.

KNOCKERDOWN 2050
Knockerdown, small C18 pub 'in splendid isolation' (GBG).

LANE HEAD 1676
Anchor, whitewashed brick, possibly C17, once farmhouse on packhorse track. Name traditionally associated with sailor who 'swallowed anchor' as landlord. Interesting collection (banknotes).

LITTLE HUCKLOW 1678
Old Bulls Head, small, C18(?) pub with cave at the back. (GBG).

LITTON 1674
Red Lion, pleasantly situated on green in attractive village with some good C18 houses. (GBG).

MATLOCK 3060
Spa development produced *New Bath*, encloses thermal bath, and its former appendage *Temple* at beginning C19. Later in century came *Pavillion* (*c.*1886), ambitious and unimaginative. Off beaten track is *Sycamore*. (GBG). Also Victorian, but less ambitious, is *County and Station* (GBG) with possesses a pianola. Richardson lists *Crown*.

MELBOURNE 3825
Sir Francis Burdett, cosy country pub with much bric-a-brac (GBG) in attractive village possessing one of country's most ambitious parish churches. Letts recommends *Bull's Head*, Wilson (4024), Georgian with garden.

MORLEY 3941
Rose & Crown, recommended Letts and described as 'ancient and modern'. Garden.

NETHER LANGWITH 5371
Jug & Glass, pleasantly situated, stone-built pub (late C18?) in hamlet which had an early cotton mill. (GBG).

NEWHAVEN 1660
Newhaven House, built by Duke of Devonshire *c.*1800 of five bays with porch and bay windows.

NEW MILLS 0085
Bull's Head, C18 with symmetrical front and low mullioned windows. GBG gives *Crescent, Fox, Swan*.

NEWTON SOLNEY 2825
Bricklayers Arms, C18 village pub which, in spite of absorbing next door cottage still has very small bar. *Unicorn*, basically Georgian, with two extensions – one a very large bay.

NORTH WINGFIELD 4064
Chantry House, *c.*1488 as medieval chantry, dissolved by Edward VI. Some medieval masonry and windows survive.

REPTON 3026
Mount Pleasant, attractive Victorian pub, one of claimants to longest bar in country, overlooking small town with unique C10 church (crypt). GBG, Letts.

ROWORTH 0189
Little Mill, 1781, an attractive country building which has caught up with metropolitan Georgian style.

ROWSLEY 2566
Peacock, built in 1652 but very 'old fashioned' then, i.e. Jacobean style. Mullioned windows, gables and flagged roof. Later Dower House of Haddon Hall, farm and finally inn, licensed 1820. Attractive decor includes Minton peacock. Listed Richardson, mentioned Batchelor and recommended Letts.

SCARCLIFFE 4968
Horse & Groom, C17/18 country inn with agricultural 'by-gones'. (GBG).

SIMMONDLEY 0293
Hare & Hounds, 'stone-built C18, three-storey pub of character' (GBG).

SNAKE PASS 1190
Snake, a high pub at about 1,000ft (*c.*308m), on lonely pass in High Peak.

SPONDON 3935
Malt Shovel, timber-framed (C17?) building with very attractive interior. Former village pub being engulfed in suburbia. *White Swan*, old fashioned local. (GBG).

STANTON 2620
White Horse, possibly C17 and may have been coaching house on A444. (GBG).

STARKHOLMES 3058
White Lion, unspoilt country inn in neighbourhood of C18 'eye-catcher' (Riber Castle). (GBG).

STONY MIDDLETON 2275
Lover's Leap, named after suicidal young woman was saved by her crinoline acting as parachute. *Royal Oak*, typical village pub, probably C18. Free House. (GBG).

SUDBURY 1631
Vernon Arms in this pretty one-street brick village is dated 1671 but old-fashioned in a Tudorish way. Symmetrical with central carriageway, gabled.

SWADLINCOTE 3019
Angel may be one of oldest buildings in architecturally undistinguished village. (GBG). *Bear*, typical good town-centre pub.

SWARKESTONE 3728
Crew & Harpur Arms, recommended Letts and described as 'mixed ancient and modern'. The nearby bridge is a 'remarkable example of medieval public works' (P).

TAXAL 0181
Chimes of Taxal, stone-built village inn of C17 with unusual name. Free House.

TICKNALL 3524
Chequers, timber-framed (C17?), free house with garden. (GBG).
Wheel, largely unmutilated old-world pub which has maintained traditional atmosphere.

WARDLOW 1874
Bulls Head, recommended Letts and described as 'mixed ancient and modern'. Free House. GBG gives *Three Stags Heads*.

WHALEY BRIDGE 0181
Hanging Gate has an unusual sign. *Jodrell Arms* built *c.*1800 for benefit of railway travellers, with additions of about half a century later. GBG gives *Shady Oak* and difficult to find *Shepherds Arms*.

WILSON see Melbourne

WIRKSWORTH 2854
Red Lion, mid Georgian, brick with central Venetian window over archway into yard. Early C19 *Vaults*, Coldwell Street, are worth noticing. GBG gives *Blacks Head*.

YOULGREAVE 2164
George, typical village pub (GBG) in street leading to one of most impressive churches in county.

DEVON

ASHBURTON 7569
Golden Lion, C18 which still retains own farm and woodland. Listed Richardson. *Rose & Crown*, C18 or earlier when it was famous for its home-brewed 'Ashburton Pop'.

AXMINSTER 2998
George, listed Richardson, no details. *Hunters Lodge*, claims C16 origin and associations with highwaymen and smugglers. Recommended Letts together with *Cedars, Red Lion*. GBG gives *Millwey*.

AXMOUTH 2591
Harbour, Free House, recommended Letts and described as medieval. GBG gives *Ship*, recommended Letts – Georgian pub with restaurant.

BAMPTON 9522
Exeter, recommended Letts who gives date of *c*.1495. GBG gives *White Horse* described as 'C14 Post House'!

BARNSTAPLE 5533
Three Tuns claims to be 'oldest house in oldest street of oldest borough in the kingdom'. Some of its parts may antedate C16. Richardson lists *Old Ship, Royal* but with no details. GBG gives *Barnstaple, Marshalls, Rolle Quay* (Morris dancing).

BERRYNARBOR 5546
Globe, unprepossessing exterior (row of small C17 cottages) conceals interesting interior where ancient ceremony of Ashen Faggot is maintained on Christmas Eve.

BICKLEIGH 9407
Richardson lists *New Inn* (no details). Letts recommends *Trout*, described as Tudor.

BIDEFORD 4526
New Inn is an attractive C18 house overlooking river and town. Garden. *Royal* only became hotel in 1880s, adopting variety of earlier buildings: C17 merchant's house (with C. Kingsley associations), workhouse and prison. Much preliminary planning of Normandy invasion took place here. Probably corresponds with Richardson's *King's Arms*. GBG gives *Portobello*.

BIGBURY 6646
Pilchard, Free House, recommended Letts who describes it as medieval.

BLACKAWTON 8050
Normandy Arms, Free House, recommended Letts who describes it as C16.

BOVEY TRACEY 8178
Dolphin, interesting example of transferred inn. Original house on opposite side of road nearer town centre. It was subject to flooding and new house was built 1876 with traditional 'Long Room' and extensive stable round yard. In Richardson's list.

BOW BRIDGE 8049
Waterman's Arms, Free House in exceptional setting, recommended Letts who describes it as 'mixed ancient and modern'. Also mentioned by Batchelor.

BRANSCOMBE 1988
Fountain, supplies 'scrumpy', recommended Letts. GBG gives *Three Horseshoes*. One mile East is *Bovey House*, Elizabethan, now hotel. *Masons Arms*, thatched with paved forecourt, includes C15/16 elements.

BRIXHAM 9255
Smugglers Haunt, C16 inn still retaining flagstone floor and open fireplace in spite of modernising and renaming. *Quayside*, recommended Letts who describes it as 'mixed ancient and modern'. GBG gives *Burton, Globe, Golden Lion*.

BROAD CLYST 9897
Red Lion, C17 inn, formerly thatched until disastrous fire *c.*1800. Village is a Conservation Area and pub belongs to National Trust. (GBG).

BUCKLAND BREWER 4120
Coach & Horses, small post house, accommodated Court House in C17 and preserves Beadle's staff. Claims to have been involved in small Civil War skirmish.

CHAGFORD 7087
Three Crowns, mullioned windows and two-storeyed porch, C16? Formerly private house of Whiddon family. In Richardson's list and GBG.

CHUDLEIGH 8679
Clifford Arms, C17 coaching inn on A38, later updated by George III façade. In Richardson's list.

CLEARBROOK 5165
Skylark, unpretentious inn on edge of Dartmoor. Former farmhouse and still retains its bread ovens.

CLOVELLY 3124
New Inn, picturesque inn in surprisingly unspoilt show village. In Richardson's list and mentioned by Batchelor together with *Red Lion*.

CLYST ST GEORGE 9888
St George & Dragon, retention of St is rare and may be related to dedication of church which gives distinguished suffix to village. Inn is a large C17(?) structure which may replace former Church House.

COCKINGTON 8964
Drum, 1934, designed by Edwin Lutyens.

COLYTON 2493
Bear, Free House, recommended Letts who describes it as Georgian. GBG gives *Kingfisher*, also recommended Letts.

COMBE MARTIN 5846
Pack of Cards, monstrosity commemorating fortune won at cards by squire who built it. Became inn in 1716. Preserves rare 'Press Gang' table. *Royal Marine* recommended Letts.

COMBE CELLARS 9270
Inn of this tiny village was once notorious smuggling centre. Associations with S. Baring-Gould.

CREDITON 8300
Richardson lists *Ship* but no details. Letts recommends *Dartmoor Railway*, Victorian Free House, also in GBG.

DARTINGTON 7862
Cott named after C14 mine-owner and Freeman of Totnes. Free House. Mentioned Batchelor, recommended Letts who dates it 1320.

DARTMOUTH 8751
Royal Castle, claims to have been built from ship's timbers in 1587 and structure has traces of every subsequent century. Once coaching house and allegedly haunted by coach. In Richardson's list. GBG gives *Seven Stars*.

DEVONPORT 4554
Richardson lists *Royal*, casualty of World War II?

DODDISCOMBSLEIGH 8586
Nobody Inn, cottage-type pub (C17?) with good sign exploiting its whimsical name. Recommended Letts who describes it as 'mixed ancient and modern'. Also GBG.

DREWSTEIGNTON 7391
Drewsteignton (alias Drewe) *Arms*, neatly rethatched, recommended Letts who describes it as Georgian. Also GBG.

EAST BUDLEIGH 0684
Sir Walter Raleigh, recommended Letts who describes it as Elizabethan.

ERMINGTON 6353
Crooked Spire, unusually named pub, supplying 'scrumpy'. Recommended Letts.

EXETER 9292
Imperial, originally private house of Queen Anne Period. Extensive Garden. *White Hart*, medieval inn (C15) which retains its cobbled yard, mentioned Batchelor, recommended Letts. *Ship*, recommended Letts who describes it as Tudor. Also GBG. Batchelor mentions *Double Locks, Turk's Head, Valiant Soldier*. Richardson lists *Clarendon, London, Royal Clarence*. GBG gives *Crown & Sceptre, Prince Albert, Prospect, Seven Stars, Ship, Victoria*.

EXMOUTH 0080
London, Royal Beacon, Thorn are listed by Richardson – no details. GBG gives *Park, Royal Oak*.

HARBERTON 7758
Church House, originally ecclesiastical property and traditionally accommodated masons building St Andrews and subsequently clergy. Great chamber discernible, medieval woodwork and rare C13 glass. Mentioned Batchelor. Nearby and a little difficult to find is *Old Mill*, originally C17?, recommended Letts.

HATHERLEIGH 5404
Rodeo, strangely re-named former market-town inn, possibly dating from C16. *George*, recommended Letts who describes it as 'mixed ancient and modern'.

HAYTOR, Nr. Ilsington 7771
Rock, former Georgian coaching inn on edge of Dartmoor. Free House, recommended Letts.

HENNOCk 8380
Palk Arms, recommended Letts who describes it as 'medieval'.

HEXWORTHY 6572
Forest, Victorian inn, listed Richardson and recommended Letts.

HOLSWORTHY 3403
White Hart, listed Richardson but unlocated.

HONITON 1600
New Dolphin, claims C15 origin; it is certainly completely renovated. Listed in Richardson. *Angel* is C18.

HOPE COVE 6646
Hope Anchor, pleasant but sometimes busy haunt of yachtsmen. *Cottage*, small hotel recommended Letts. GBG gives *Lobster Pot*.

HORNS CROSS Nr. Bideford 3823
Hoops, thatched inn with three porches, once serving coach and post route and preserving Lorna Doone Coach (in regular use until end C19). Smuggling associations. Original ovens, four-poster bed. Mentioned Batchelor.

IVYBRIDGE 6356
London in Richardson's list, no details.

KINGSBRIDGE 7344
Church House, allegedly dates from C13 and possesses a remarkable fireplace. Traditionally rest-house for monks from neighbouring(?) abbey. *Crabshell*, country inn with several centuries' tradition of cider-making, now somewhat over-sophisticated. *King's Arms* listed Richardson. GBG gives *Hermitage* Bar.

LIFTON 3885
Arundell Arms, early C19 with old cockpit preserved in garden, described by Batchelor as 'notable inn'. Extensive private fishing.

LITTLEHEMPSTON 8162
Tally Ho, modern name for old inn, probably once Church House and accommodating courthouse on upper floor until it moved to Totnes. Fine collection of brass and copper ware. Mentioned Batchelor. Letts recommends *Pig & Whistle*, a Free House.

LYDFORD 5084
Castle, possibly C16 with neighbouring stannary prison for offenders against tin-mining laws. Local relics preserved in pub include two Saxon pennies. Free House, recommended Letts and GBG.

LYNTON 7149
Crown, Tap Room and Bar belong to original village pub which developed with C19 tourist boom. Supplied extra horse-power for ascent of hill and one of earliest telephones in Devon was installed to expedite this service. (GBG).

MARYTAVY 5078
Elephant's Nest, formerly *New Inn* formed from pair of small tin-miners' cottages. New name from C19 due to incongruity between 20 stone landlord and his small house.

MEAVY 5467
Royal Oak, probably originally Church House (C15?). Domesday Book records inn on site. Part of takings still go to parish. (GBG).

MODBURY 6551
Red Devon, according to Batchelor, an inn where Elizabeth slept on way to knight Drake. *Exeter*, recommended by Letts and described as medieval. (GBG).

MORCHARD BISHOP (Nr.) 7907
Black Dog, Free House, recommended Letts who describes it as medieval.

MORETONHAMPSTEAD 7586
White Hart, old coaching inn and rendez-vous of paroled French prisoners of Napoleonic Wars. Maintains Ashen Faggot custom. Careful observers claim that three dimensional sign represents hind not hart. In Richardson's list.

NEWTON ABBOT 8671
Globe is listed by Richardson. GBG gives *Dartmouth, Locomotive, Two Mile Oak* (C15?).

NEWTON ST CYRES 8797
Barn Owl, recommended Letts and described as Tudor. Garden.

NORTH BOVEY 7483
Ring o'Bells, delightful old inn by green in village on edge of Dartmoor. Recommended Letts who describes it as medieval. (C13). *Rugglestone*, privately owned, is near interesting logan stone.

NOSSMAYO 5447
Old Ship and *Swan* are both pleasant inns with attractive views of boatmen in estuary. Towards Kingsbridge is *Journey's End* (GBG), Ringmore: a secluded inn with smuggling associations and where R.C. Sheriff wrote his play. (It was then called *New Inn*).

OKEHAMPTON 5895
White Hart is on Richardson's list. GBG gives *Plume of Feathers*.

PETER TAVEY 5177
Peter Tavey, small hostelry with minute bar, formerly C16 farmhouse which brewed cider. Recommended Letts.

PLYMOUTH 4755
Old Chapel, built as Unitarian chapel in 1790 and converted into an inn 11 years later. Pevsner mentions *Duke of Cornwall* (*c*.1865) and *Great Western* (1898). Richardson lists *Royal* but no details. GBG includes *Abbey, Ferry House, Lugger, Seven Stars, Three Crowns*.

PRINCETOWN 5873
Richardson lists *Duchy, Plume of Feathers*. The latter (as *Three Feathers*) is recommended by Letts who describes it as 'medieval'. GBG gives *Devil's Elbow*.

RATTERY 7361
Church House, mentioned Batchelor, recommended Letts who describes it as medieval. Garden.

SAMFORD COURTENAY 6301
New Inn, part of structure probably dates from C16. Remarkable collection of 'by-gones' in and around house. (GBG and Letts).

SHEBBEAR 4309
Devil's Stone, formerly New Inn of 1678. Name recently changed to capitalise on folk custom attached to large stone in front of church.

SHEEPWASH 4806
Half Moon, cottage-type inn, once resort of shepherds now much favoured by fishermen since inn has a five-mile stretch of Torridge trout stream. (GBG).

SIDFORD 1390
Blue Ball, ancient thatched pub, said to date from C14. (GBG).

SLAPTON 8244
Richardson lists *Sands*. GBG gives *Tower* 'comfortable C14 free house' *Church House* functions as inn.

SOUTH MOLTON 7125
George, former coaching house in town centre, of Georgian brick. Mentioned in 'Lorna Doone'. In Richardson's list, together with *Unicorn*. GBG gives *Goose & Gander*.

SOUTH TAWTON 6594
Has C16 Church House, not functioning as inn.

SOUTH ZEAL 6593
Oxenham Arms, C16/17 granite, fine fireplaces, oak beams, former home of Burgoyne family. Recommended Letts.

STARCROSS 9781
Richardson lists *Courtenay Arms*.

STOKE FLEMING 8648
Green Dragon claims origins in C14. Recommended Letts.

STOKE GABRIEL 8457
Castle, former vicarage with C14 cellars. Smuggling associations. Mentioned in Batchelor. *Church House*, fine example of genre with parish hall above gained by external staircase. Originally C12?

TAVISTOCK 4774
Bedford listed by Richardson. GBG gives *Duke of York*.

TEDBURN ST MARY 8194
Kings Arms recommended Letts and described as medieval. Free House.

TEIGNMOUTH 9473
Royal listed by Richardson. GBG gives *Blue Anchor, New Quay, Talbot*.

TIPTON ST JOHN'S 0991
Bowd Inn. Name seems unexplained. Formed from pair of back-to-back cottages, cob, massive fireplace with bread oven. Free House. Garden. Recommended Letts who describes it as medieval.

TIVERTON 9512
Angel listed by Richardson. GBG gives *White Ball*.

TOPSHAM 9788
Salutation listed Richardson. GBG gives *Bridge* as 'authentic old Devon pub'. Letts recommends *Globe*, Georgian. Free House.

TORBRYAN 8266
Church House, former church property, used to provide Church Ales and dates at least from 1485. Oak screen (from church?). Skittles survive from lost skittle alley. Discussed in Batchelor.

TORQUAY 9164
Apart from churches, Torquay is C19. Batchelor singles out *Imperial* and *Palace*. Former is recommended by Letts together with *Masons Arms*. GBG gives *Banner Cross, Crown & Sceptre, Haywain, John Bull, Palk Arms*.

TOTNES 8060
Kingsbridge, originally provided for shepherds benighted when town gates were closed. Local fame for its 'Elizabethan nights' in great barn behind inn. Preserves ancient pump and trough and ancient fireplace sometimes fed with traditional 'faggots'. Mentioned Batchelor, recommended Letts. GBG gives *Albert, Pig & Whistle, Royal Seven Stars*. The latter is a fine example of early C19 inn, recommended Letts and listed by Richardson together with *Somerset Arms*.

TUCKENHAY 8156
Waterman's Arms is recommended Letts as Georgian/Victorian Free House. GBG gives *Malsters Arms*.

UGBOROUGH 6755
Anchor, genuine old (medieval?) country inn. Recommended Letts and GBG.

UMBERLEIGH 6023
Rising Sun said to have been monastic rest-house, possibly C13. Date 1010 on beam is obviously fake as arabic numerals were not introduced until end of medieval period. Has own stretch of fishing on Taw. Recommended Letts.

WARREN HOUSE 8064
Warren House, lonely inn on Dartmoor at altitude of 1,426ft (*c*.439m), claims to have a 'perpetual' peat fire. (Listed Richardson).

WELCOMBE 2218
Old Smithy, still preserves anvil of Caleb Wakeley who was local dentist as well as blacksmith. C18/19. Recommended Letts.

WEMBURY 5148
Odd (?) Wheel, recommended Letts and described as 'mixed ancient and modern'.

WIDECOMBE 7176
Old Inn, possibly C15, at least C17. T-shaped building of local materials. Allegedly haunted. Recommended Letts. C16 Church House now National Trust property.

WILLAND 0310
Verbeer Manor, recommended Letts and described as Elizabethan.

WILMINGTON 2100
Home Farm. Free House recommended Letts who describes it as Tudor.

WINKLEIGH 6308
Ring o'Bells, thatched inn which may have originated in C14 Church House *Kings Arms* recommended Letts and described as 'mixed ancient and modern'.

WOODBURY 0087
Malsters Arms recommended Letts and described as medieval.

WOODBURY SALTERTON 0189
Diggers Rest, formerly Salterton Inn originating in farmhouse which brewed cider. Attractive cob and thatched building with some fine interior panelling (C16?). Recommended Letts.

YEALMPTON 5751
Volunteer, village pub with garden. Recommended Letts.

YEAFORD 7898
Mare & Foal, recommended Letts and GBG as 'excellent village pub'.

DORSET

ABBOTSBURY 5785
Ilchester Arms, large rambling Georgian pub, recommended Letts and GBG.

BLANDFORD FORUM 8806
Crown, Georgian, built as coaching house. Gardens extend to river. Listed Richardson.

BRIDPORT 4692
Bull, alias *Knight's Bull* (unique name). Originated C16 and became notable stage on A35 in coaching era when it also provided post-chaises. (GBG). *Greyhound*, C18, popular farmers' meeting-place. In yard is notice relating to corn returns required by Customs & Excise. (GBG). Chemist's shop opposite is former *George*, visited by future Charles II in 1651. *Bull* and *Greyhound* in Richardson's list, together with *Bridport Arms*. GBG adds *Ship*, South Street, while Letts recommends *George, Travellers Rest, West Mead*.

BROADMAYNE 7286
Black Dog, recommended Letts who describes it as 'mixed ancient and modern'.

BUCKLAND NEWTON 6905
Royal Oak, Victorian pub, recommended Letts.

CERNE ABBAS 6601
Royal Oak, possibly replaces abbey guest-house and present structure may contain C16 material from destroyed Benedictine house. (GBG).

New Inn, country inn, partly thatched, possibly of C16. Garden. Recommended Letts.

CHARMOUTH 3693
George, future Charles II is said to have taken refuge here in 1651.

Queen's Arms, 'unusually complete example of small medieval house' (P), late C15 and probably manor of Cistercian abbey of Forde. Associations with Catherine of Aragon, Charles II and early Noncomformity.

CHIDEOCK 4292
George, recommended Letts and described as 'mixed ancient and modern'. Garden.

CHILD OKEFORD 8312
Saxon Inn, recommended Letts and described as Elizabethan. GBG gives *Union Arms*.

CHRISTCHURCH 1593
Kings Arms in Richardson's list but no details.

CHURCH KNOWLE 9481
New Inn, possibly converted from C16 farmhouse which may have replaced pilgrim hostel. Farmhouse theme preserved in furniture and fittings.

CORSCOMBE 5105
Fox, C17, Free House with socially distinct bars. Recommended Letts.

CRANBORNE 0513
Fleur de Lys, Hardy associations, recommended Letts: 'medieval/modernised'. *Sheaf of Arrows*, Victorian village local, (GBG), recommended Letts.

DORCHESTER 6690
Antelope, former coaching house with 'nicely composed' Georgian front of *c.*1815. (P). Listed Richardson, mentioned Batchelor. *Bridge*, also former coaching inn with C18 ashlar front. *King's Arms*, 'symmetrical composition about a generously glazed window bow above broad porch on Tuscan columns' (P). Early C19, associations with Hardy, Kitchener, Nelson, future Edward VII. Listed Richardson, mentioned Batchelor, in GBG, recommended Letts. *Old Ship*, stone-built in early C17 but fairly thoroughly reconstructed since. Upper windows are original. *Royal Oak*, recommended Letts 'mixed ancient and modern', (GBG). *White Hart* also in Richardson's list but no details.

EVERSHOT 5704
Acorn, Victorian or earlier, village pub with skittle alley. Recommended Letts.

GODMANSTONE 6697
Smiths Arms of cob, flint and thatch. Former smithy licensed by Charles II and claiming to be smallest tavern in England. (GBG).

HOLT 0203
Stocks, long, low, thatched building probably of C17. Named from stocks adjacent to prominent porch. Neighbouring Smugglers' Lane gives point to tradition of smugglers' tunnel from cellars.

HURN 1296
Avon Causeway of 1862 is recommended by Letts.

KINGSTON 7509
Scott Arms, cottage-type pub, probably C18, distinguished by traditional gypsy caravan parked outside.

LANGTON HERRING 6182
Elm Tree, probably originated from C17 farm with capacious bread oven. Some timbers are from ship. One has hook on which a man was lynched in C18. Recommended Letts. (GBG recommends *Kings Arms* in Langton Matravers, 9978).

LONG BURTON 6412
Rose & Crown, recommended Letts who describes it as Tudor.

LULWORTH 8278
Castle, recommended Letts who describes it as medieval.

LYME REGIS 3492
London, possibly C16 in origin, thatched. Former coaching inn hence (new) name? *Red Lion*, described by Batchelor as 'a pleasant inn'. He makes the same comment about *Three Cups* which is Richardson's list, together with *Royal Lion*, a Georgian inn recommended by Letts. GBG gives *Angel*, 'superb hostelry near Lepers' Well'.

LYTCHETT MINSTER 9593
St Peter's Finger, probably only C19 but on much older site and maintaining ancient name, corruption of St Peter ad Vincula, the dedication of parish church.

MANSTON 8115
Plough, Georgian pub recommended Letts.

MARSHWOOD VALE 3899
Shaven Crown, ancient inn claiming to date from C14 when it was associated with pilgrims. Free House. Recommended Letts.

MIDDLEMARSH 6607
White Horse, recommended Letts who describes it as 'mixed ancient and modern'.

NETTLECOMBE 0537
Marquis of Lorne, possesses Hammond organ, described as C16 by Letts.

OSMINGTON MILLS 7381
Smugglers, renamed coastal pub with smuggling associations. Free House. Recommended Letts who describes it as 'medieval/modernised'.

PIDDLETRENTHIDE 7099
Poachers, Free House, described as 'ancient' by Letts who also recommends *Thimble*.

PLUSH 7102
Brace of Pheasants, made from row of cob and thatched cottages with smithy at end. Interior sign of stuffed pheasants. Unusual decoration of inscribed racing plates. Free House. Recommended Letts.

POOLE 0190
Brewers Arms is said to be 400 years old. (GBG). Richardson lists *Antelope, King Charles, London* – unlocated unless last is (unlikely) *New London*, a Victorian tavern near quay. (GBG which also gives *Ansty Arms, Bull's Head, Pure Drop*).

PURBECK 9081
Greyhound, maltreated C17 building of local stone, former coaching house. Hardy associations. Sign portrays Edward, K.M. slain at Corfe Castle in 878 AD. (GBG).

SEATOWN 4291
Anchor, recommended Letts and described as 'mixed ancient and modern'.

SHAFTESBURY 8622
Crown, unremarkable inn of 1862 but it has a C15 fireplace in public bar. (GBG). *Grosvenor* in Richardson's list, contains famous 'Chevy Chace' sideboard, carved 1857–63. *Royal Chase*, described as Georgian by Letts who recommends, as does GBG which adds *Ship* 'superb C17 stone-built local'.

SHERBORNE 6316
Eastbury, md C18 façade on older house. Former coaching inn. *George*, early C16 and once abbey hostel, ceiling bosses still show abbey arms. *Julians*, now county library, is a former religious hostel dating from early C16. GBG gives *Britannia, Digby Tap* (Richardson lists *Digby*).

STOKE ABBOTT 4500
New Inn, pleasant village pub (GBG) described as medieval by Letts.

STURMINSTER NEWTON 7813
Fiddleford, Swan, both recommended by Letts. GBG gives *Bull*.

TARRANT KEYNSTON 9204
True Lovers Knot, typical village pub, Victorian or earlier with traditional games. Recommended Letts.

WAREHAM 9287
Black Bear, 'a striking inn of *c*.1800' (P), double-fronted, bow-windowed and with stone porch. On Richardson's list. *Red Lion* 'best representative of simple brick style of Wareham's rebuilding after a sweeping fire of 1762' (P). GBG gives *Lord Nelson*.

WEST LULWORTH 8280
Castle, low thatched house, possibly dating from C16, named from neighbouring ruins.

WEST STAFFORD 6778
Wise Man, dominated by magnificent thatch with rare straw birds. Rural bygones, notable sign with doggerel attributed to T. Hardy. Recommended Letts.

WEYMOUTH 6778
In archetypical Georgian seaside resort, there is *Black Dog* – has C17 work, and *Gloucester*, late C18 and originally private house of the Duke. *Royal* is late C19 and *White Hart* is most substantial relic of C17 town' (P) and formerly a private residence. *Boot* (GBG), though much restored, is of same period and said to be haunted. GBG adds *Albion, Nothe, Portland Railway*.

WHITCHURCH CANONICORUM 3995
Shave Cross, probably originated as hostel for pilgrims to St Wita's shrine which almost uniquely survives in neighbouring church. Name allegedly derived from 'penitential custom' of pilgrims shaving at presumed neighbouring (but missing) cross.

WIMBORNE 0199
Kings Head, late C18 with even more pretentious additions of *c.*1840. In Richardson's list, as is *Coach & Horses*, a delightful thatched inn just outside town strongly recommended by Batchelor. Both *George* and *White Hart* are Georgian and former coaching houses. GBG gives *Rising Sun*.

WINKTON 1695
Fishermans Haunt, comfortable roadhouse (GBG) with fishing permits. Recommended Letts.

YETMINSTER 5910
White Hart, picturesque thatched house of C16/17. (GBG).

DURHAM

BARNARD CASTLE 0516
Kings Head, ancient establishment whose yard occupies what was once Outer Ward of great episcopal castle. Later coaching house visited by Dickens. In Richardson's list and mentioned Batchelor. GBG gives *White Swan*, attractive C16 inn on outskirts. (Startforth).

BILLY ROW 1638
Dun Cow, old hostelry. Free House. (GBG).

BISHOP AUCKLAND 2029
Newton Cap, unusually named local placed high above river Wear. (GBG).

BISHOP MIDDLEHAM 3332
Dun Cow, C18 or earlier with very rare and primitively attractive stone sign.

BOWES 9913
Unicorn, once most important stage between York and Carlisle. Large yard. Said to be locale of Dickens' meeting with Shaw, original of Squeers in Nicholas Nickleby. Listed Richardson.

CHESTER-LE-STREET 2751
Lambton Worm commemorates fabulous monster eventually slain by young Lord Lambton after his return from Crusades. *Queens Head*, attractive C18 coaching house of six bays with three storeys.

COCKFIELD 1224
Queens Head, busy village local; also tiny *Welcome*. (Both GBG).

CORNSAY 1443
Fir Tree, alias 'Monkey', isolated, old-fashioned and unspoilt. (GBG).

COTHERSTONE 0119
Fox & Hounds, traditional but smartened-up pub with glorious views.

COWSHILL 8540
Cowshill, typical country pub in upper Weardale. (GBG).

CROXDALE 2636
Coach & Horses, 'friendly, isolated inn' (GBG).

DALTON-LE-DALE 4047
Times, busy village pub with unusual name. (GBG).

DARLINGTON 2914
Copper Beach has pigeon lofts used by bird-fanciers from local pigeon club. *Nags Head*, decorative red brick, gabled, mid C17 and perhaps oldest surviving house in town. (GBG). Richardson lists *Kings Head* but no details. GBG adds *Albion, Britannia, Falchion* (whose name recalls a medieval tenure of Durham cathedral).

DURHAM 2742
Dunelm (late C17 in spite of its façade) and possesses a good staircase of the earlier period. *Royal County*, seven bays with central three framed in pilasters, early C18 with later Georgian doorway. *Three Tuns* is mentioned by Batchelor and in Richardson's list together with *Rose & Crown*. GBG includes *Dun Cow, Half Moon, Old Elm Tree, Pot & Glass, Shakespeare*.

FISHBURN 3632
Beehive, interesting sign mentioned by Batchelor.

GAINFORD 1716
Cross Keys, High Row – an unpretentious house, by path leading to obscure beautiful village.

GRETA BRIDGE 0813
Morritt Arms, formerly C17 *George*. Country hotel in attractive situation on banks of Greta and on side of old Penrith Road. Developed in C19, associations with Dickens, Scott and artists: Cotman, Girtin, Turner. Mentioned Batchelor.

HEIGHINGTON 2522
George & Dragon by spacious green at unspoilt centre of village. *Bay Horse* is C17.

HOLMESIDE 1645
Wardles Bridge, delightful country pub in pleasant village. (GBG).

LANCHESTER 1647
Blue Bell is unpretentious but pleasant local. (GBG).

LANGLEY PARK 0181
Centurion, former private house, C18/19, converted into up-market country hotel. (GBG).

MIDDLETON IN TEESDALE 9425
Cleveland Arms in Richardson's list but no details.

PIERCEBRIDGE 2115
George, originated in C16, became coaching inn and staging post. Actually in Yorks. Alleged Turpin associations. Occasion of famous music-hall song 'My Grandfather's Clock' which is still there – stopped! Mentioned Batchelor. GBG which also gives *Wheatsheaf*.

PRESTON LE SKERNE 3124
Blacksmiths Arms 'popular pub off beaten track' (GBG).

ROMALDKIRK 9921
Rose & Crown, country hotel of Georgian period. (GBG and Letts).

RYTON 1564
Half Moon, pleasant pub (GBG) in 'prettiest Tyneside village in county' (P).

SEDGEFIELD 3528
Hardwick Arms, former coaching hotel in ancient township. (GBG). *Nags Head*, modernised village pub near green. (GBG).

SHERBURN HILL 3342
Lambton Arms, 'quaint, cosy village pub' (GBG) whose name commemorates great local family associated with 'Worm'.

SHOTLEY BRIDGE 0752
Manor House, Carterway Heads, former private house of Tudor period. Free House with garden. Recommended Letts.

STANHOPE 9939
Phoenix, small old-fashioned hotel in village with a number of interesting buildings. (GBG).

SUNDERLAND 3957
No pubs of particular architectural interest but Letts recommends *Wastings Hill*, Chester Road and GBG gives *Brewery Tap, Caledonia, Londonderry, Salem*.

SUNNISIDE 2159
Rose, Shamrock & Thistle, eirenical name of old ale-house which has recently been extended. GBG gives *Potters Wheel*.

TOW LAW 1139
Surtees, cosy village pub (GBG) whose rare name commemorates C19 sporting author of Jorrocks.

WASKERLEY 0545
Moorcock, like all inns of this name, an isolated moorland pub. (GBG).

WEST AUCKLAND 1826
Prince of Wales, basic village pub on green. (GBG). Behind the Hall are old brick buildings of C18(?) brewery and on Staindrop Road is *Eden Arms*, larger pub, recently 'done up'. (GBG).

WINSTON 1416
Bridgewater Arms, located in former school-house (C19) of Teeside village.

WITTON GILBERT 2345
Glendenning Arms (GBG), country inn with strong horse-racing connections in attractive village possessing a number of medieval buildings.

WOLSINGHAM 0737
Black Bull, market-place pub with coaching connections, recommended Letts. GBG gives *Black Lion*.

ESSEX

ARKESDEN 4834
Axe & Compasses, converted C17/18 barn. Free House. Recommended Letts.

ASHDON 5842
Rose & Crown, possibly C16. One ground floor room has some well preserved painted decoration. Listed Richardson. Present Guildhall (*c*.1500) probably originated as *Church House*. GBG gives *Bricklayers Arms*.

BASILDON 7189

Five Bells, pleasant C17 house on former London–Southend coach route. GBG gives *Jolly Cricketers, Treble Chance*.

BOCKING 7623

Angel, partly C17 or earlier with interesting roof line. May have originated as Church House. Allegedly haunted.

BRAINTREE 7622

White Hart, some of C16 timber-work survives and part of gallery (now walled-in) can be identified. Remains of much modified Long Room. Interesting yard and archway (blocked night-porter's door and game hooks). Listed by Richardson, together with *Horns*. Letts recommends *Red Cow*, described as Tudor. GBG gives *Kings Head*.

BRENTWOOD 5993

Swan, former coaching inn with later C19 façade. Alleged ghost. *White Hart*, also old coaching inn listed Richardson (together with *Fleece*). GBG gives *Castle, Victoria Arms*.

BURNHAM-ON-CROUCH 9496

White Hart, C18 brick building on waterside, recommended Letts. There is humbler *Anchor*, also near river. GBG gives *Victoria*.

CASTLE HEDINGHAM 7835

Near churchyard is C15 timber-framed inn which may have been former Church House. *Bell*, described as Georgian is recommended by Letts.

CHELMSFORD 7006

Saracens Head, former coaching with, according to Batchelor, Trollopian associations. Richardson lists *Lion & Lamb, White Hart* while Letts recommends *Oddfellows Arms*, a pub with garden. GBG gives *Plough, Rising Sun, Rose & Crown, Ship*.

CHIGWELL 4493

Kings Head, ornate, gabled, timber-framed, C17 coaching house, 'much vamped-up'. (P). Housed local courts to C19. Many Dickens associations. In Richardson's list and mentioned by Batchelor. GBG gives *King William IV*.

CLAVERING 4832

Cricketers recommended Letts and described as Tudor.

COGGESHALL 8522

Woolpack, licensed from C17 but some of its timber work may be C16 or earlier. Has been described as 'one of county's finest survivals of Jacobean architecture'. GBG gives *Fleece* said to be C16.

COLCHESTER 0025

Richardson lists *George, Marquis of Granby, Red Lion, Three Horseshoes, Cups* – modern façade masks nearly 400 years' history. It was formerly *Three Cups* and now is mainly Georgian with fine assembly room equipped with Musicians' Gallery. Associations with George IV and Queen Caroline. *George* is an old coaching inn which, as often in C18, was given a new front (with 'a nice cast-iron balcony'). *Marquis of Granby*, some parts may be pre-Reformation but it was heavily restored in present century. *Red Lion*, which was *White* until C17, is one of most remarkable buildings in use as an inn. It occupied a Roman site with C14 work in vaulted cellars which may have been part of a religious house. The present, richly detailed, timber-framed building was erected in two stages: *c.*1470 and *c.*1500.

Later became a coaching inn and has strong Civil War associations. Notice the inn sign in the entrance. *Bull*, at least four centuries old customs house for Italian silk in C17, involved in C18 witch trials and up to C19 was a waggoners' stage. Good panelling in bar. *Little Crown* (unique name?) basically C18 with fine collection of C19 engraved mirrors. GBG gives (New) *Cups, Hospital Arms* alias 'Ward Nine'.

CRESSING 7920
Willows, described as 'mixed ancient and modern' in Letts recommendation.

DANBURY 7805
Inn originated as C16 private house, licensed in C17. Framed from ships' timbers, central hall and wings. Some panelling is from rood screen of parish church. Associations with Sir Walter Scott.

DEDHAM 0533
Sun, claims C15 origin. Certainly a later posting house with largely unchanged courtyard. Much modernisation elsewhere. Letts recommends, together with Victorian *Dedham Vale* (nice garden). GBG gives *Lamb*, 'a C15 local'.

EASTHORPE 9121
House without a Name and worth including for that reason alone. Letts recommends and describes as Tudor. Free House. (GBG).

ELMDON 4639
Carrier, thatched inn in remote corner of county. Quaint sign.

ELMSTEAD MARKET 0624
Bowling Green, formed from two C17 cottages when village bowling green was nearby. C18 HQ of Friendly Society. Corn Dolly collection.

EPPING 4602
Mole Trap on nearby Tawney Common recommended Letts and described as Elizabethan. GBG gives *Half Moon*.

FEERING 8720
Old Anchor, originally private dwelling of 1557. Much altered and first licensed in 1968. Recommended Letts.

FINCHINGFIELD 6832
Red Lion, a traditional pub in what has been described as 'perhaps the most picturesque village in the county'.

GOLDHANGER 9009
Chequers, recommended Letts and described as Tudor.

GOSFIELD 7829
Green Man, recommended Letts and described as medieval.

GREAT DUNMOW 6221
Saracen's Head – an important C16 inn behind prosperous C18 façade. Associations with Cromwell, highwaymen and smugglers. In Richardson's list and GBG.

GREAT HORKESLEY 9731
Yew Tree, pub with garden, recommended Letts and described as Tudor.

GREAT LEIGHS 7316
St Anne's Castle, uniquely named inn which claims to be oldest in county. Traditionally originated as hermitage serving pilgrims to Walsingham and Canterbury. After Reformation associated with witchcraft trials of C16 and C17. Allegedly haunted. GBG gives *Dog & Partridge*.

GREAT SALING 7025
White Hart, possibly C16 with Georgian additions. Recommended Letts and GBG.

GREAT TOTHAM 8511
Green Man, pub with garden, recommended Letts and described as 'old'.

GREAT WAKERING 9487
White Hart, originally an old farmhouse (C16) but radically altered in 1973. GBG gives *Anchor*.

GREAT YELDHAM 7638
White Hart, C16–17 timber-framed with plaster in-filling. Tiled roof. Large yard. One cellar claimed to have been a prison. Free House. Recommended Letts.

HALSTEAD 8130
Bull, timber-framed building, possibly C16.

HARLOW 4711
Churchgate, substantially Georgian hotel (claims origin in 1560) with additions. Free House. Recommended Letts. GBG gives *Willow Beauty*.

HARWICH 2332
White Hart is in Richardson's list.

HEMPSTEAD 6338
Rose & Crown, formerly *Bell*. Claims to be Turpin's birthplace in 1705 when his father was landlord. Spy-hole from bedroom to bar. More famous landlord father was parent of William Harvey, discovery of blood circulation. Cockpit survives opposite. Mentioned Batchelor.

HIGH EASTER 6214
Punchbowl, mentioned Batchelor, now only a Restaurant.

HIGH RODING 6017
Black Lion, mentioned Batchelor. GBG.

HOLLAND-ON-SEA 2016
Oakwood, formed from two C16 cottages which, after various vicissitudes, became licensed premises in C20, restyled 1973. Attractive exterior and unusual 'double-sided' sign.

LITTLE EASTON 6023
Letts recommends two establishments: *Bull*, Georgian Hotel, Free House; *Green Man*, Tudor pub.

MALDON 8506
Blue Boar, sombre C19 front conceals C14 building with C15 and later additions. Mounting block in yard. Attested history as inn from 1632. Recommended Letts and in Richardson's list together with *King's Head*, (also recommended Letts who describes it as 'mixed ancient and modern'). GBG gives *Queens Head, Royal Oak*.

MATCHING TYE 5311
Hare & Hounds is a recommended pub (GBG) by village green. At nearby Matching is (unique?) survival of Marriage Feast Room in front of church. It is C15, timber-framed, plastered in-filling with over-sailing upper storey.

NEWPORT 5234
Coach & Horses with gallows sign in front of entrance porch. Unassuming but claims C16 origin and in C18 was used as private staging-post by George Villiers, Duke of Buckingham.

NORTH WEALD BASSETT 4704
Kings Head, one of finest timber-framed inns in Essex (C16?), formerly engulfed in Epping Forest. Rare 'Squire's Room' extending through two storeys. Restored after considerable damage in World War II. Recommended Letts.

ONGAR 5502
Two Brewers, mid C17 origin. Present building formed from two cottages. Licensed from C18 when it had livery stables (which substantially survive). Hunting meet. *Kings Head*, late C17 (William & Mary). Staging post in C18 (stabling survives). Alleged ghost of murdered serving wench. Listed Richardson. GBG gives *Bell*.

PAGLESHAM 9292
Plough & Sail is in Richardson's list.

PURFLEET 5578
Royal, pleasant C19 inn with fine views of Thames from balcony. Former sea-faring inn with later theatrical associations and with Edward VII when Prince of Wales.

RAMSDEN HEATH 7195
Letts recommends two pubs for their traditional qualities, both described as 'mixed ancient and modern': *Nag's Head, White Horse*.

RAYLEIGH 8090
Rayleigh Lodge, former hunting-lodge and private house, licensed 1963. Some timber work of C16–17, possibly earlier. GBG gives *Weir*.

ROMFORD 5188
Golden Lion, High Street, in spite of obscuring early Victorian block, there are remains of C16 building. Unfortunately *Church House* (late C15) in spacious market-place is no longer used for its original purpose.

SAFFRON WALDEN 5438
Saffron claims to be '500 years old, completely refurbished with Spanish courtyard'! *Sun* is an example of fine 'lost' inn: based on C15 hall-house with over-sailing upper floor. Good C17 pargeting. Cromwellian associations. Now National Trust property. Letts recommends *Eight Bells*, timber-framed Elizabethan with fine modern wrought-iron sign. GBG gives *Sun, Victory. Rose & Crown*, listed Richardson, was built *c.*1600 and a front (with handsome door hood) added in 1690. There was further work in 1748 and 1874. Interior retains fine C18 staircase and panelling. Some claim that 'W.H.' to whom Shakespeare dedicated his Sonnets was son of former landlord. Shakespeare visited in 1607 and there was also associations with Thomas Nash. *Cross Keys* with its corner overhang is C16. Youth Hostel in C15 timber-framed building which was once a malting.

SANDON 7404
Crown is recommended by Letts who describes it as Tudor.

SIBLE HEDINGHAM 7734
White Horse, a notable C15 house with exposed timber work and a gable on curved brackets. GBG gives *Bell*.

SOUTHEND 8885
Papillon is a plush Victorian pub on sea front. Richardson lists *Royal*. GBG gives *Cornucopia, Guildford, Liberty Bells, Spread Eagle*.

STAMBOURNE 7238
Red Lion, recommended Letts and described as 'medieval/Tudor'.

STOCK 6998

Letts recommends two houses: *Bakers Arms*, pub with garden, 'mixed ancient and modern' and *Bear*, an Elizabethan pub. GBG gives latter.

TAWNEY COMMON 4900

Mole Trap, uniquely(?) named pub is recommended by Letts who describes it as Tudor.

THAXTED 6131

Swan is listed by Richardson. GBG gives *Bull*.

THORPE LE SOKEN 1822

Bell, 'a C15 inn' (GBG), also recommended Letts.

TOLLESBURY 9510

Hope, of little architectural interest but situated at a remote dead-end and with long smuggling associations.

WEST MERSEA 0112

White Hart, indications of possible medieval origins in façade, interior entirely remodelled. Alleged smuggling associations.

WITHAM 8114

Red Lion, allegedly built in 1360, timber-framed with pargeting. Heavily restored in C20. *Spread Eagle*, Victorian façade masks much earlier (C15?) timber-framed building. Listed by Richardson together with *White Hart*. GBG gives *Morning Star, Victoria*.

WIVENHOE 0321

Possesses ancient pub, timber-framed of which some details survive. Interior decor of by-gones and corn-dollies. GBG gives *Horse & Groom*.

WOODHAM WALTER 8006

Bell, late C16/early C17 with interesting sign with Latin inscription 'I greet the living, the dead I mourn' referring to the joyful peals at baptism and the solemn tolling at funerals. Also emphasises ancient connection between church and pubs.

WRABNESS 1731

Wheatsheaf, Georgian pub with garden, recommended Letts.

WRITTLE 6706

Fox & Goose, claims C15 origin and some fragments (not always in situ) have survived massive alterations. Recommended Letts. *Chequers* is substantially C17 building. GBG gives *Wheatsheaf*.

GLOUCESTERSHIRE

AMBERLEY 8401

Black Horse, stone-built pub with garden. Free House. (GBG). Recommended Letts. *Amberley Arms* has fine site and unusual cuckoo-clock. *Bear* is a fine traditional Cotswold inn with courtyard.

AMPNEY CRUCIS 0602

Crown of Crucis, pub with garden. Recommended Letts – 'ancient', certainly much modernised. On Fossway, Nr. Wiggold is a turn-pike toll house.

ANDOVERSFORD 0219

Frogmill, recommended Letts. GBG gives *Royal Oak*.

AVENING 8797
In mid-September, on 'Pig-face Sunday', local inns serve this delicacy in commemoration of local killing of a wild boar.

BARNSLEY 0705
Village Pub. In spite of its undistinguished name, recommended Letts who describes it as Georgian.

BERKELEY 6899
Berkeley Arms, fine country inn (GBG), yellow brick C18 with arched entrance to yard. Near castle where Edward II was foully murdered.

BIBURY 1106
Largely C18 *Swan* in Richardson'slist and mentioned Batchelor. Garden with trout stream. Letts recommends *Catherine Wheel*, described as Tudor. Garden.

BIRDLIP 9214
Air Balloon, commemorating first ascent 1783, mentioned Batchelor, recommended Letts. *Royal George* is C19, stone with castellated bay windows and iron window guards. Ornamental bargeboards on porch and dormers. Recommended Letts together with *George* and *Golden Heart*. *Black Horse Ridge* (C17) was inn until 1900.

BISLEY 9005
Bear, small village inn 'with air of faded grandeur' (P), former old Courthouse. Detached columns (C17) supporting upper floor. *Bell*, built as inn *c.*1687, restored 1953 for British Legion club-house.

BLEDINGTON 2422
Kings Head, pub with garden, recommended Letts and described as medieval.

BOURTON-ON-THE-WATER 1620
White Hart, former coaching house which has preserved a local version of skittles. *Old New Inn*, paradoxically named house, built *c.*1700 and in Richardson's list. In rear garden is famous tourist attraction – model of village.

CAMBRIDGE 7403
George recommended Letts – described as Georgian.

CAMP 5893
Foston's Ash, unique name. Garden. Recommended Letts– 'Georgian'.

CHELTENHAM 9422
Royal, largely unmodified Regency house of *c.*1820 with interesting period decoration. Dining Room probably original Coffee Room. Good example of C19 luxury accommodation. Listed Richardson together with *Fleece, Queen* (Letts) and *Plough*; latter also mentioned in Batchelor. It dates from *c.*1760 and its distinguished visitors include Byron, Disraeli, Handel, Tennyson, Wellington. *Berkeley* was a less distinguished coaching inn. GBG gives, among others, *Coopers Arms, Jolly Brewmaster, Restoration, Suffolk Arms* (with skittle alley).

CHIPPING CAMDEN 1539
Cotswold House, developed from private house of Regency period with spiral staircase. Superb garden. *King's Arms*, former Georgian coaching house in Market Square, (Letts). *Red Lion*, pub with garden, also Letts recommended, described as 'medieval'. *Lygon Arms* (GBG), listed by Richardson together with *Noel Arms*, a medieval town inn with yard and bowling green. (Also in Letts).

CHIPPING SODBURY 7282
Cross Hands in Richardson's list. Cotswold stone with ancient cellars.

CIRENCESTER 0201
Black Horse claims to be oldest inn in town, dating from 1470 when it was wool-merchants' store. Inn at least by C18 when it expanded to absorb neighbouring Kings Arms. Recommended Letts. *Fleece*, much modified. Picturesque yard gives view of complex Tudor gables, left side of its entrance seems early C17 while right is early Georgian reconstruction whose assembly room survives as 'lounge'. *Plough*, recommended Letts, 'mixed ancient and modern'. GBG gives *Drillmans Arms* (unique name?), *Marlborough Arms*. Nearby *Stratton*, until recently a private house, is partly C17.

COATES 9700
Tunnel House (GBG and Letts).

COLEFORD 5711
Miners, Victorian. Free House. Recommended Letts. GBG gives *Angel*.

CRANHAM 5685
Black Horse, recommended Letts 'mixed ancient and modern'.

COLN ST ALDWYN 1405
New Inn, perfect regional example of smaller inn. Oolitic limestone, flagged roof, fronted with low stone terrace. Attractive interior with large open fireplace and appropriate decor.

DURSLEY 7597
Bell, Castle in Richardson's list, no details. GBG gives *New Inn*.

EASTLEACH 1905
Victoria, Victorian pub with garden, in Letts and GBG.

ELDERSFIELD 7931
Greyhound, Free House with garden, recommended Letts.

ELKSTONE 9612
Highway, stone-built village pub (GBG, also Letts who says 'medieval').

EWEN 0097
Wild Duck, rare name. Recommended by Letts 'Georgian hotel'. Sign painted by Peter Scott.

FAIRFORD 1501
Bull, large courty town inn with fine gardens. Own fishing. (GBG).

FORD 5155
Plough, 'splendid country pub' (GBG), described by Letts as 'medieval'.

FOREST OF DEAN 6209
Speech House, built 1676 for Foresters' Courts, still meeting-place of Verderers and occasionally of Free Miners. Many additions but C17 house substantially survives with old Court Room used for dining. Claims to preserve whipping post and punishment cell. Four-poster beds. Own farm.

FRAMPTON MANSELL 9202
Crown, recommended Letts: 'mixed ancient and modern'.

GLOUCESTER 8318
Fleece, has C12 vaults and was a pilgrims' inn owned by the abbey. Much altered: fine C18 dining-room with bay. In Richardson's list together with *Greyhound*. In Westgate: *Fountain*, much restored but with C17/18 fragments and *Lower George* of same period. *New Inn*, built *c*.1457 to accommodate pilgrims to abbey shrines. 'Few inns in England can be so old and retain so much of their original character' (P). In Richardson's list and mentioned Batchelor. C16 *Raven*, Hare Lane, once an important inn has become Old Peoples' Home. Letts recommends *Hop Pole* described as 'modernised medieval'. GBG gives *Norfolk House* which has its own brewery, *Red Lion, York House*.

GREAT BARRINGTON 2013
Inn for All Seasons, recently renamed. Free House, recommended Letts. GBG gives *Fox*.

GUITING POWER 0924
Farmers Arms, 'ivy-clad pub in Cotswold village' (GBG). Letts recommends nearby *Halfway House* at Kineton, also GBG.

KENT'S GREEN 7423
Bird in Hand, canalside pub, unaltered and unmodernised. Rare example of 'fossilised history'.

KINGSCOTE 8196
Hunters Hall, 'fine old coaching inn' (GBG). Free House, also recommended Letts who describes it as Tudor.

LECHLADE 2199
Trout. A small Augustinian hospital f.1228 was converted, due to failing finances, into a chantry in 1472 which later became inn called *St John Baptist Head*. Its name was changed to *Trout* in C18. Richardson lists *New Inn*, a C17 market-place house which accommodated early coach passengers. Free House. Recommended Letts. GBG gives *Crown*, another coaching inn, and *Red Lion*.

LITTLE WASHBOURNE 9833
Hobnails, uniquely-named, white-painted brick house with tiled roof. Claims C15 origin and has been in hands of same family for two centuries. Rare indoor skittle alley. Collection of corn-dollies and bygones. Recommended Letts.

LOWER LYDBROOK 6216
Courtfield Arms, beautifully situated on banks of Wye. Former coaching house and still gives a predominantly C18 impression.

LOWER SWELL 1725
Old Farmhouse, closed to non-residents Sunday evening and all Monday, recommended Letts who says it is C16. GBG gives *Golden Ball* which opens normal permitted hours. C17 and one of oldest houses in village.

MARSHFIELD 7773
Catherine Wheel, handsome early C18 coaching inn, unexpectedly sophisticated for village.

MICKLETON 1543
Kings Arms, recommended Letts and described as Tudor. GBG gives *Butchers Arms*, 'modernised C16 pub'.

MORETON-IN-MARSH 2032
White Hart Royal, C16 inn which earned soubriquet (only attached recently) when Charles I slept there in July 1644. His room survives together with other interesting features: cobbled entrance hall (once yard entrance) with game hook, dog-gate to

main staircase and magnificent C16 room. Listed by Richardson as '*Royal*'(?) with *Redesdale Arms*, a Georgian coaching inn recommended by Letts who adds *Manor House*, former private house in local stone and possibly C16; *Black Bear* (GBG); *Bell, Swan* and *Fox* at Broadwell. GBG adds *Wellington*.

NAILSWORTH 8499
Tipputs inn, 'an excellent pub' (GBG). Letts recommends *George*, described as 'mixed ancient and modern'.

NAUNTON 1123
Black Horse, ashlar-faced, C17 or earlier.

NEWNHAM ON SEVERN 6911
Victoria, in spite of name substantially early C18 with later wings. Former coaching inn on main route to West. (GBG). In Severn Street is former *Bear*, once a coaching house but no longer licensed.

NORTH CERNEY 0208
Bathurst Arms, recommended Letts and described as Elizabethan.

NORTHLEACH 1114
Red Lion, Cotswold stone with half-timbered above, possibly C16. Arched entrance to enclosed courtyard. Popular in coaching era. Richardson lists *Wheatsheaf*, but no details.

OVERCOTE 8019
Pike & Eel, dated 1604 and incorporates former ferry house. Modernised and extended after World War II but still harmonises with river setting.

PAINSWICK 8609
Falcon, attractive Cotswold inn which preserves a rare example of bowling green still owned by pub.

PARADISE 8611
Adam & Eve, almost inevitably named pub in Cotswold hamlet near modern abbey of Prinknash.

PRESTBURY 9624
Plough, recommended Letts and described as 'medieval'. GBG gives *Royal Oak*.

QUENINGTON 1404
Keepers Arms, unusually named pub with sign portraying very Victorian-looking gamekeeper. Also *Earl Grey*.

ST BRIAVELS 5504
George, 'old hotel just outside castle moat', (GBG) also recommended Letts who describes it as medieval. Free House.

SAPPERTON 9503
Daneway, cottage-style pub. Free House by canal. Recommended Letts.

SHIPTON CLIFF
Frogmill, recommended Letts and described as 'mixed ancient and modern'.

SLAUGHTERS 1570
Manor House, Lower Slaughter, much altered to make hotel. *Lords of the Manor*, Upper Slaughter is former Rectory and home of F.E. Witts, author of Diary of a Cotswold Parson. Georgian, much altered in Victorian period. Recommended Letts.

SNIGS END 8330
Swan on edge of former Chartist land colony (1847–1853) of which *Prince of Wales* was originally the school-house.

SOUTHROP 1903
Swan by small village green has associations with John Keble.

STANTON 0634
Mount, country house in Cotswold stone, shadowed by yews. Fine site with extensive views.

STOW-ON-THE-WOLD 1925
Talbot and *Unicorn* are former coaching inns, latter probably older of two (C17?). Both listed by Richardson. GBG gives *Queens Head*.

STROUD 8504
Letts recommends *Bear of Rodorough* and *Railway*. GBG gives *Victoria*.

TETBURY 8993
Trouble House, formerly *Waggon & Horses*. Name changed C18 after series of disaster including suicides of two landlords. In C19 it was accidently burnt down during agricultural riot. Letts gives *Talbot*, GBG gives *Crown*.

TEWKESBURY 8933
Bell, Benedictine hostel of abbey which it adjoints, largely rebuilt in 1696. Until modern times gates were shut from nightfall to dawn, isolating abbey and inn from dangers of town. Home of Abel Fletcher in 'John Halifax, Gentlemen'. Listed Richardson, mentioned by Batchelor.

Swan, C16 tavern (remains in cellar and kitchen), practically rebuilt in C18. Handsome assembly room (now dining room) with usual access to porch roof. Many contemporary bob grates survive. Principal coaching inn and Mail stop until 1864. Its bar features in J. Moore's 'Portrait of Elmbury' In Richardson's list, as is *Berkeley* Arms (GBG) which may have C16 elements.

Hop Pole, early C19 with Pickwickian associations, also in Richardson's list and GBG. Richardson additionally lists *Bear, Sun, Wheatsheaf* and GBG adds *Britannia.*

THORNBURY 6590
Swan is in Richardson's list.

WESTONBIRT 8689
Hare & Hounds, 'imposing Cotswold hotel' (GBG), recommended Letts and described as 'mixed ancient and modern'.

WINCHCOMBE 0228
George, originally pilgrims' hospice of Benedictine abbey described as 'little university' at end of C15. Doorway still incorporates initials of last legal abbot. Remains of original yard with open gallery. Mentioned Batchelor and listed by Richardson together with *Corner Cupboard*: C16 stonefaced and buttressed, mullioned windows, fine doorway with original oak door. *White Lion* is C17, stone, gabled, with mullioned windows and arched doorway. Letts recommends *Royal Oak*, described as 'mixed ancient and modern'. GBG gives *Harvest Home*. On the Bristol Road is *Bell* with more Pickwickian associations.

WITHINGTON 0315
Stream-side *Mill* in Richardson's list and recommended by Letts: 'medieval and additions'. Free House. GBG gives *Kings Head*.

WOLFORD 2534
Letts recommends *Fox & Hounds*, described as Tudor.

WOTTON-UNDER-EDGE 7593
Falcon, unspoilt C17 village inn. (GBG). *Swan*, possibly originated from Georgian coaching House. (Recommended Letts who adds *Huntingdon Mill*).

HAMPSHIRE

ALRESFORD 0621
Bell, substantially Georgian and a former coaching inn. *Swan*, former C17 coaching house. Attractive walled garden. Landlord involved in C19 case of Tichbourne claimant. In Richardson's list and both mentioned in Batchelor. Letts recommends latter.

ALTON 7139
Crown, Swan, mentioned by Batchelor. Latter which proclaims its history and hospitality in verse is in Richardson's list and recommended by Letts who adds *Sun*, described as medieval. Free House. GBG gives *Dukes Head, Kings Head*.

ANDOVER 3645
Angel, C12 original inn was destroyed by fire in C15 and replaced by Winchester which then owned it. Shortly afterwards name was changed from *College*. Associations with Henry VII, Catharine of Aragon, James II. Part was sold in C19 and entire building narrowly escaped demolition in 1960s.

George, f.1576. Cobbet spoke there in 1826 and he described the inn at length in his 'Rural Rides'. *Star & Garter* is an impressive essay in classical style (*c.*1825) replacing C16 inn on site called *White Hart*. Present inn of that name in red brick *c.*1850 replaces *Lower White Hart* of 1671. Both these are in Richardson's list. *Station*, long and low with Tuscan porch, is also mid C19. Letts recommends *Seven Stars*, described as 'mixed ancient'. GBG gives *Merrie Monk, New Railway*.

ARRETON, IoW 5386
White Lion, attractive old hostelry in village with interesting church. (GBG).

BASINGSTOKE 6351
Coach & Horses, Free House, is recommended Letts and described as Georgian. *Red Lion*, listed Richardson (no details). GBG gives *Anchor, Bounty, Queens Arms, Rising Sun*.

BEAUWORTH 5725
Fox & Hounds, cottage-type inn on castle site. Still preserves well (possibly of C12) with treadmill for hoisting water in 18 gallon barrel.

BEMBRIDGE, IoW 6488
Royal Spithead, large hotel of 1882. GBG gives *Old Village Inn, Row Barge*.

BENTLEY 7844
Hen & Chickens, former coaching house. Recommended Letts: 'Elizabethan/Georgian'.

BISHOP'S SUTTON 6031
Ship, C16, associations with Charles I, mentioned in Batchelor.

BISHOPS WALTHAM 5517
Crown, listed Richardson, no details. GBG gives *Bunch of Grapes, Mafeking Hero*.

BOLDRE 3198
Red Lion, recommended Letts, described as 'medieval/modern'.

BONCHURCH, IoW 5778
Two recommendations in Letts: *Peacock Vane*, Georgian/Regency. *Winterbourne*, Georgian. Free House.

BRANSGORE 1897
Three Tuns, Victorian pub, recommended Letts.

BROCKENHURST 2902
Green Dragon, recommended Letts who describes it as 'medieval'. *Rose & Crown*, with traditional games, also Letts: 'mixed ancient and modern'. GBG gives *Morant Arms*.

BROOK 2713
Green Dragon, alehouse enlarged to incorporate adjoining smithy. Some timbers may be ships, re-used in C17 extension. Letts gives *Bell*.

BROUGHTON 3132
Greyhound, 'first-class village pub'. GBG also Letts: 'mixed ancient and modern'.

BUCKLERS HARD 4099
Master Builders House, gracious C18 riverside house built for master shipwright who designed some of most famous vessels of period (including elements of Nelson's fleet at Trafalgar in 1805).

BURGHCLERE 4660
Queen, Victorian, Free House, recommended Letts.

BURLESDON 4809
Fox and Hounds, described by Batchelor as having 'one of the finest collections of bric-a-brac on the South Coast'. Much of this collection (mainly concerned with rural crafts) is housed in the associated 'Lone Barn' – a reconstituted tithe barn from Winchester. (Recommended Letts together with *Swan Schooner Bar*).

BURLEY 2103
Queens Head, Victorian pub with remarkable collection of souvenirs, trophies and weapons. (Letts).

CADNAM 2913
Richardson lists 'Inn', probably *Sir John Barleycorn*, long, low, thatched (one of longest in country) with three porches. It is claimed that there has been an inn on site since C12. Present building incorporates medieval material.

CHALE, IoW 4877
Clarendon Tap, characterful Free House with view towards Needles. (GBG). *Star*, Chale Green (GBG) was once a brewery.

CHALTON 0326
Red Lion, 'one of the best pre-Georgian pubs in the country' (P), timber-framed over-sailing upper storey, thatched. C16 or earlier.

COWES, IoW 4995
Fountain; small, stuccoed C18 hotel: GBG gives *Empress* with fine view of harbour, *Painters Arms, Travellers Joy* and, in East Cowes, *Prince of Wales, White Hart* (by ferry terminal).

CRAWLEY 4234
Fox & Hounds, recommended Letts, described as medieval. GBG gives *Rack & Manger*.

CRONDALL 7948
Horns, 'a remarkable collection of ancient and foreign coins' (Batchelor). *Plume of Feathers*, striking inn of obvious antiquity (basically C17?).

DOWNEND, IoW 5387
Hare & Hounds, Victorian pub recommended Letts.

DROXFORD 6018
C16 inn, Free House (GBG) also Letts.

EVERSLEY CROSS 7762
Chequers, village-green inn of C18 and earlier. Charles Kingsley associations, mentioned Batchelor. GBG gives *Golden Pot*.

FAREHAM 5806
Red Lion is listed, without details, by Richardson. GBG gives *Golden Lion*.

FARNBOROUGH 8753
Queens mentioned Batchelor, together with *Tumbledown Dick* (listed Richardson) with dubious Turpin associations. (Name probably related to Richard Cromwell). GBG gives *Imperial*, a reminder of the Empress Eugenie's son who was killed in Zulu War. (Tomb in Benedictine abbey church).

FORDINGBRIDGE 1413
George, overlooking medieval bridge over Avon and associated with Foresters of New Forest (and possibly with Augustus John). Letts recommends *Bat & Ball*.

FREEFOLK 4848
Watership Down (GBG) an example of a modern changed name, in this case to exploit a runaway best-seller.

FRESHWATER, IoW 3487
Cabin, now perhaps incorporated in *Albion* (recommended Letts & GBG) was, in C19, 'a low public-house, patronised by sailors, rustics and fishermen' (and by the painter George Morland). *Farringford*, once Tennyson's home (some relics) became hotel in 1946.

GODSHILL, IoW 5281
Griffin, pretty symmetrical building with barge-board gables in show village.

GORLEY 1810
Royal Oak, named from a majestic and ancient survivor of New Forest. Typical forest inn, originating from two cottages, converted into hunting lodge, licensed C18. Thatched.

HAMBLE 4806
Olde Whyte Harte, C16 pub recommended GBG and Letts who adds Victorian *Victory*.

HAMBLEDON 6414
Bat & Ball, Broad Halfpenny Down is a cricketer's Mecca. In 1770, landlord of inn (then called *Hut*) captained team that beat All England. Mentioned Batchelor, together with *New Inn*, HQ of Hambledon CC. Letts recommends *Horse & Jockey*, described as 'medieval'.

HARTLEY ROW 7656
Lamb, listed by Richardson and by Letts s.v. Hartley Wintney which has elegant Georgian *Whyte Lyon*.

HAZLEY HEATH 7459
Shoulder of Mutton, described as 'mixed ancient and modern' by Letts.

HINTON ADMIRAL 2195
Cat & Fiddle, low cob and thatch, formerly pilgrim hostel, supported by Christchurch to provide refuge in wild New Forest. Listed Richardson.

HOOK 7524
Raven, built 1653 and some C17 parts survive. Some notoriety in C18 as residence of 'Jack the Painter' who fired Portsmouth dockyard in 1776 in interests of USA with further attempts at Plymouth and Bristol. Mentioned in Batchelor. *White Hart*, one of many claimants to be 'oldest inn in the country'. Doubtful, but attractive inn with massive timber-work, possibly of C16. Listed Richardson, recommended Letts, GBG.

HORNDEAN 7013
Letts recommends modern *Hogs Lodge* and Georgian *Red Lion*. GBG gives *Brewers Arms*.

HULVERSTONE, IoW 4083
Sun, unspoilt roadside inn of C17. (GBG).

HURSTBOURNE TARRANT 3853
George & Dragon, C16, enlarged in Georgian period as posting house with stabling. Victorian additions included parcels office, and mail-rack survives in bar. Cobbett associations. Listed Richardson.

HYTHE 4207
Golden Hind, up-marketed by 'famous inn-keeper', Barry Neame. (Batchelor). GBG gives *Drummond Arms*.

LANGSTONE 7104
Royal Oak, C16 inn by mud-flats opposite Hayling Island (on which GBG gives *Maypole, Sinah Warren*). Stone-flagged bar with open fire. Claims a ghost (or two). Recommended Letts who adds *Ship*, 'mixed ancient and modern'.

LINWOOD 1810
High Corner, 'peculiar outside appearance hides interior charm'. (Letts who describes it as 'medieval').

LIPHOOK 8431
Royal Anchor, late C17? became famous coaching and posting house on Portsmouth road. Patronised by Prince Regent, Wellington, Blucher, Nelson and young Victoria. Cellars used to incarcerate prisoners during Napoleonic Wars. Listed by Richardson, together with *Angel*, Letts gives *Links*, described as 'medieval'.

LONGPARISH 4344
Letts recommends the Victorian *Plough*.

LONGSTOCK 3536
Peat Spade, pleasant Victorian pub (GBG), recommended Letts.

LOWER FROYLE 7544
Letts recommends *Anchor*, 'a done-up country pub'.

LYMINGTON 3295
Angel, listed Richardson, GBG and recommended Letts who describes it as 'medieval'. Richardson also lists *Old Toll House* (no details). Letts also recommends *Ship, Stanwell House* while GBG adds *Kings Arms, Old English Gentleman*.

LYNDHURST 2907
Crown, listed Richardson, together with *Stag* (GBG). Letts recommends *Waterloo Arms*, a pub with garden, described as 'medieval'. GBG adds *Swan*.

MAPLEDURWELL 6851
Letts recommends *Gamekeeper*, a Victorian pub.

MILFORD-ON-SEA 2891
Red Lion, another Letts recommendation, described as 'mixed ancient and modern'.

MINLEY 8654
Crown & Cushion, originated in pair of cottages. Pleasant topiary outside. Name claimed to derive from Colonel Blood who used it as hide-out after his theft of Crown Jewels in 1671. Mentioned Batchelor and recommended Letts.

MINSTEAD 2811
Trusty Servant (of Winchester College). Famous for its unique sign and accompanying doggerel. Pleasantly sited on village green. (GBG).

NEWCHURCH, IoW 5585
Ponters, unspoilt C18 village pub with unusual name.

NEWPORT, IoW 4989
Bugle, large Georgian hotel of six bays and three storeys. *Castle*, small, low brick building dated 1684. *Hare & Hounds*, Victorian, recommended Letts. GBG gives *Calverts, Freemasons, Rose & Crown, St Crispin*. P draws attention to 'interesting malthouse of Messrs. Maw' in Crocker Street.

NEWTOWN VALENCE 7232
Horse & Groom, recommended Letts, 'mixed ancient and modern'.

NITON, IoW 5076
Letts has two recommendations: curiously named *Buddle*, described as Tudor; *White Lion*, 'mixed ancient and modern'. GBG gives *Royal Sandrock*, a rambling old pub of character (also in Letts, s.v. Niton Undercliffe). It originated as a small C18 house to which were added wings *c.*1830. Associations with Princess Victoria and her mother.

NORTH GORLEY 1511
Royal Oak, Georgian pub with garden, recommended Letts.

NORTH WARNBOROUGH 7351
Swan, recommended Letts who describes it as Elizabethan.

ODIHAM 7350

George, C18 façade conceals older structure, some of which may be C16. Dining Room decoration removed from Basing House. Important coaching inn in Georgian period and housed court-room and cells for a long time (whipping post said to survive in a bedroom). Cellars used for French prisoners in Napoleonic Wars. Associated with C19 prize-fights. (Recommended Letts; listed Richardson, together with *Tuns*). *King's Arms*, 'a timber-framed structure dating from C14' (Batchelor).

OVINGTON 5631

Letts recommends *Bush*, a Georgian pub with restaurant. Free House.

PETERSFIELD 7423

Red Lion in Richardson's lists, no details. Letts recommends *Market*, described as 'medieval and Tudor'. GBG gives *Square Brewery*.

PILLEY 3300

Fleur de Lys, ancient inn whose attractive interior boasts a noble hearth with salt cupboard. It also possesses a rare list of landlords from late C15.

PORTSMOUTH 6501

George is in Richardson's list. Letts recommendations include *Duke of Buckingham, Still and West* in old town and *Eldon* (GBG), *Jolly Sailor, Keppels Head*. Long list in GBG includes: *Fifth Hants Volunteer, Gloucester, Mystery* and lock-side *Thatched House*.

PRIORS DEAN 7424

White Horse, a remote Free House has a strong entry in GBG and is recommended by Letts who describes it as medieval.

RINGWOOD 1405

Letts recommends *Old Beams, Red Shoot*. GBG gives *Fish*, old thatched pub on riverbank.

ROCKBOURNE 1118

Rose & Thistle, is recommended Letts and described as Tudor. Garden.

ROMSEY 3521

White Horse, Georgian front conceals much C16 work including paint and plaster. May have originated as guest-house of Romsey abbey (medieval work in cellars but substantially rebuilt in early C16). Much old furniture in good interior. (GBG). Listed Richardson, together with *Dolphin*, and recommended Letts. GBG also gives *Tudor Rose* 'excellent small C15 pub'.

ROPLEY 6431

Star, Free House with garden, recommended Letts.

ROTHERWICK 7156

Coach & Horses, C17 village pub. (GBG and Letts).

RYDE, IoW 5992

Castle is a popular Victorian pub (GBG), *Esplanade* an outstanding example of High Victorian hotel architecture, *Turks Head*, a handsome Georgian hotel as is *Crown*. *Woodlands Vale* was built 1871 as a private house for Lord Calthorpe with additions in 1880, 1894, 1912. GBG includes *Anglesea Tavern, Fleming Arms, High Park Tavern*.

ST CATHARINE'S DOWN, IoW 4975
Hermitage, former private house, now hotel/restaurant. Free House. Recommended Letts.

SANDOWN, IoW 5984
Letts offers *Broadway Park*, 'mixed ancient and modern' while GBG has *Commercial, York*.

SELBORNE 7433
Queens, recommended Letts, highly praised GBG which adds *Selborne Arms*.

SHALFLEET, IoW 4189
New Inn, genuine public bar with flagged floor, etc. (GBG recommended Letts).

SHANKLIN, IoW 5881
Daish's, mirrors town's development. Small stone cottage with large extension *c*.1870. *Crab (& Lobster)* reputedly island's most photographed pub (listed Richardson, GBG which also gives *Marine*).

SHERFIELD-UPON-LODDON 6757
White Hart, attractive brick-built inn, once coaching house on Reading–Basingstoke route. Striking polygonal window-block. Probably C17. Mail-rack from posting days is a rare survival.

SHORWELL, IoW 4582
A village 'rich in charming cottages' (P) whose local is in GBG.

SOUTHAMPTON 4212
Cowherds, somewhat engulfed by modern leisure facilities which have displaced cowherds, yet retains some 'old-world' characteristics. Developed to annex neighbouring house. Interesting exterior with dominant bay windows. *Dolphin*, ancient inn much damaged in World War II. Probably dates from C16 but drastically rebuilt in C18 (huge bow windows are said to be largest of their kind in England). Attractive Assembly Room survives as dining room. Associations with Jane Austen, Gibbon, Earl Haigh, Thackeray, Listed Richardson. *Red Lion*, said to be C16 with cellars from C12 and still retains fine former Court Room where Henry V tried Cambridge, Scrope, etc. *Star*, mostly Georgian rebuilt from time when it served as coaching terminus but there are earlier elements including medieval cellars. *Wellington*, in spite of name is largely C15 and cellars may be C12. Long list in GBG includes *Bay Tree, Joiners Arms, Junction, Old Thatched House, Osborne*.

STEEP 7525
Harrow, cottage-style, country pub (GBG) also Letts.

STOCKBRIDGE 3535
When it was smaller it had 13 inns and churchyard contains famous epitaph of John Hackett, C18 landlord of vanished *King's Head*. *Three Cups* (*c*.1560) has become a restaurant. *White Hart* receives GBG's acolade. Letts gives *Grosvenor* (*c*.1810), *Vine*, Free House, 'mixed ancient and modern'.

TANGLEY 3352
Cricketers Arms, Georgian. Free House, recommended Letts.

TWYFORD 4724
King's Arms, listed Richardson (no details). GBG gives *Bugle*.

UPHAM 5320
Brushmakers Arms, former social centre of besom makers. Preserves skittle alley. Cromwellian associations.

UPPER BURGATE 1416
Tudor Rose, half-timbered, brick-nogging or wattle and daub in-filling, magnificently thatched. Possibly C16. Private house until present century.

UPTON GREY 6948
Hoddington Arms, recommended Letts and described as 'mixed ancient and modern'.

VENTNOR, IoW 5677
Royal, former coaching inn, good garden, recommended Letts and GBG which also gives *Mill Bay, Volunteer*.

WEST LISS 7728
Spreadeagle, pub with garden, recommended Letts and described as medieval.

WEST MEON 6424
Outside village at crossing of A32 and A272 is *West Meon Hut*. It was formerly known as *George* and was a coaching stage on London–Fareham route. The 'Hut' was originally an annexe to serve Irish workers on Meon Valley railway at end of C19. Recommended Letts.

WHERWELL 3840
A picturesque village whose pub bears the anomalous name of *Twentieth Century*.

WHITSBURY 1218
Cartwheel, Free House. Recommended Letts and described as 'mixed ancient and modern'.

WHITCHURCH 4648
White Hart, said to date from 1461 but almost totally rebuilt in C18 as coaching inn at main street crossing. Stopping place for the express 'Telegraph' on London–Exeter run. Fine dining room ceiling from that period. Associations with Charles Kingsley and John Henry (later Cardinal) Newman. In Richardson's list. GBG gives *Harvest Home*, 'popular local with skittle alley and other games'.

WICKHAM 5711
Letts has two recommendations: *Bold Forester*, described as medieval/Elizabethan and *Old House*, Georgian hotel.

WINCHESTER 4829
Eclipse, C17 private house, later rectory of St Lawrence opposite. Became inn in C18 and stole trade of rival *Sun* opposite, hence name. In 1685, Dame Alicia Lisle, who had sheltered some survivors from Sedgemoor, stepped from an upper window on to a scaffold outside where she was beheaded. (She allegedly haunts the inn.) *Royal* was a C17 private house which became nunnery in late C18, housing refugees from Revolutionary France. When the nuns moved to East Bergholt in 1857, the house became an hotel. Richardson lists *George, Hostel of God Begot. Hospital of St Cross* f.1132 and originally administered by Knights Hospitaller, in spite of Reformation, still dispenses 'Travellers Dole' of bread and ale, though this is a mere shadow of medieval largesse. GBG gives *Dolphin, Exchange, Hyde Tavern, King Alfred, Queen. Hyde* is certainly a very ancient hostelry but scarcely justifies its claim to be 900 years old. The Hyde brewery has a range dating from 1821. *Royal* probably dates from C17 though frontage is C18. *Southgate* is dated 1715.

YARMOUTH, IoW 3589
George, overlooking harbour is former Governor's house of late C17 with Georgian additions. Preserves original staircase. *Pier* is adjacent to Henrician coastal fort.

HEREFORDSHIRE and WORCESTERSHIRE

ABBEY DORE 3831
Village inn represents conversion of part of domestic remains of abbey using much ancient material and with worthy attempt to bring modifications and additions more or less into keeping with original remains.

BELL END 9377
Bell, claims to date from 1577 but little evidence for this in present building. Striking interior sign in mosaic.

BEWDLEY 7875
Black Boy, white painted brick on banks of Severn. Sign represents Charles II. Claims to have been licensed for four centuries. Name probably C17. Pleasant interior whose furniture includes framed verses attributed to A.E. Housman. *George* is listed by Richardson. GBG gives *Hop Pole, Rising Sun*.

BISHOP'S FROME 6648
Green Dragon, a country inn with a rare collection, for this county, of real ale. (GBG).

BOSBURY 6943
Bell, prominent 'black and white' building opposite church.

BRETFORTON 0943
Fleece, lovely Tudor building, mentioned Batchelor, in picturesque village containing many timber-framed houses.

BROADWAY 0937
Broadway, converted C15 timber-framed building, formerly manor of Pershore abbey. *Fish*, curious small inn on Fish Hill near Cross Hands signpost which marks site of gibbet. Listed Richardson. *Lygon Arms*, formerly *White Hart* under which name it was highly commended in Torrington Diaries (Aug. 12, 1787). Possibly C16 origin, retains early C17 doorway. Associations with both Charles I and Cromwell. Attractive gardens. Listed Richardson and mentioned Batchelor. *Swan*, small Cotswold stone house, formerly C17 coaching inn.

BROMSGROVE 9750
Golden Cross, listed Richardson. *Perry Hall*, former private residence of C17. Associations with A.E. Housman. Good garden. GBG gives *Dragoon, Red Lion*.

BROMYARD 6554
Bay Horse, half-timbered inn with closely set uprights (early C17?). *Falcon*, outstanding example of medieval carpentry; timber-framed, of three storeys with closely set uprights and diagonal bracing. (C16?). In Richardson's list and mentioned by Batchelor. *Hop Pole*, former coaching house, possibly C18 or earlier with new façade added early C19. Tuscan porch and bay windows. In Richardson's lisf, recommended Letts and GBG. *Kings Arms*, C16 timber-framed with a timber bow-window added in C18. Letts adds *Live and Let Live, Royal Oak* and GBG: *Rose & Lion*.

CANON PYON 4549
Nags Head, 'appealing village free house, traditionally furnished and unspoilt, with large garden' (GBG).

CAREY 5631
Cottage of Content 'idyllic village pub' (GBG), recommended Letts who describes it as Tudor.

CHADDESLEY CORBETT 8973
Talbot, ancient (C16?), half-timbered inn in village High Street. Listed Richardson and GBG. Also *Swan*, painted black and white.

CLEEVE PRIOR 0849
Kings Head, listed Richardson.

DILWYN 4154
Crown faces on to small, triangular village green – rare features in Herefs.

DRAKES BROUGHTON 9148
Plough & Harrow, half-timbered (C16?), former village inn, recently somewhat up-marketed. Recommended Letts who describes it as Elizabethan.

DROITWICHd 9063
Eagle and Sun, ivy-covered country pub on banks of Birmingham–Worcester canal. (GBG). *Raven*, former C16 manor house which may have had ecclesiastical connections now forms part of large modernised hotel. Richardson lists *Swan*. GBG adds *Freemasons Arms, Gardeners Arms, Railway*.

EARDISLAND 4158
Cross, White Swan in 'black and white' village bisected by river Arrow.

EARDISLEY 3149
Unexpectedly named *Mountie* and *Tram* contrastingly in red brick and 'black and white'.

ELMLEY CASTLE 9841
Old Mill, recommended country pub. (GBG). *Plough*, Victorian local with garden. Brews own cider. Recommended Letts. *Queen Elizabeth* is country inn in main village street once visited by Elizabeth I. Interesting sign. (GBG). Also *Old Mill*.

EVESHAM 0344
Crown, ancient inn with original well inside. Former coaching house. Much altered and one side recently removed. Listed Richardson. *Charles II*, Vine Street (reminding that demolished abbey had vineyards as well as brewhouses) is also Georgian with carved medallion frieze. *Falcon*, four bayed, stuccoed house of C18. *Old Red House*, timber-framed with close studding is probably C16/17. *Royal Oak* is probably of same vintage though most of its 'black and white' work is modern. GBG gives *Cider Mill* and *Trumpet* in absorbed hamlet of Hampton.

EWYAS HAROLD 3828
Temple Bar, unexpectedly named pub near Norman castle mound. (GBG).

FECKENHAM 0061
Lygon Arms in High Street, *Rose & Crown* by delightful green in substantially red brick village.

FLADBURY 9946
Ferry, attractively situated inn on banks of Avon which formerly operated ferry. Listed Richardson. *Anchor* looks onto well kept village green.

FOWNHOPE 5734
New Inn, Green Man ('black and white'), *Forge & Ferry* in attractive village with beautiful and dignified church.

GOODRICH 5719
Ye Hostelrie, whimsically re-named in C19 when village pub was rebuilt in 'Gothick' style. Some parts are older, probably C17. General external impression of a cross between nonconformist chapel and C18 'Folly'.

GREAT MALVERN **see Malvern**

GREAT WITLEY 7566
Hundred House, impressive building with large bow windows which once accommodated Hundred Court. Coaching inn in C18 and later.

GRIMLEY 8360
Waggon Wheel, small thatched cottage-type inn, off beaten track.

HADLEY 6712
Bowling Green, brick, painted white. Probably formed from small farmhouse. Maintains own bowling green and claims that it is longest in continuous use (since 1572 – much longer than present building has been there.)

HANLEY CASTLE 8342
Three Kings, red brick attached to 'black and white' cottage in charming village.

HARTLEBURY 8471
White Hart, Georgian, white-painted in centre of village which contains bishop's palace, partly open to public.

HARVINGTON 0548
Coach & Horses, attractive 'black and white' house opposite village church.

HEREFORD 5040
City Arms, built 1790 as town mansion of Duke of Norfolk but by beginning of C19 it has become *The Hotel*, taking its present name shortly afterwards. A C15 house already on site was incorporated as kitchen (now Bar) and there are other remains on first floor. *Raven*, formerly *Angel* was birthplace of David Garrick in 1716 and he had a local reputation of being 'a mean, sneaking little fellow' off-stage. *Castle Pool*, listed building whose garden borders the castle moat. Richardson lists *Green Dragon, Mitre*, but no details. The former, at least, survives – a Georgian inn in city centre and recommended in GBG along with *Bowling Green, Cock of Tupseley*.

INKBERROW 0157
Bull, timber-framed, three storeyed with renewed roof. Possibly C17 and claims to have accommodated Charles II during Worcester campaign. Listed Richardson.

KIDDERMINSTER 8376
Lion, listed Richardson. GBG gives, among others, *Bay Horse, Red Man, Station*.

KINGSLAND 4461
Angel, a C16 inn in pleasant setting. (GBG and Letts). Ground of *Monument*, former private house, contain memorial to decisive battle of Mortimer's Cross (1461). On site is inn named *Mortimer Cross*. Unusually named *Corners*, 'black and white', situated at crossroads.

LEDBURY 7037
Horseshoe, Royal Oak and *Feathers* are listed in Richardson. Batchelor also mentions the latter. It began in 1560 as a heavily timbered house with five gables to which additions were made in C17. The following century saw further development for the coaching trade, including Assembly Room. *Old Talbot* is a C16 half-timbered inn which retains original panelling in dining room and became another great coaching house in C18. GBG gives *Brewery*.

LEINTWARDINE 4074
Lion, of C16 and former coaching house whose lawns run down to river Teme. Recommended Letts. Also *Sun* and *Swan*.

LEOMINSTER 4959
Royal Oak, coaching inn of C17 with developments in next century. Still retains Assembly Room with musicians' gallery. (GBG and Richardson's list). *Talbot*, town centre hotel, partly timber-framed (C17?) also in Richardson. *Chequers* is another former coaching inn. (GBG).

MALVERN 7845
Beauchamp, listed Richardson. Letts recommends Georgian *Cottage in the Wood*, Malvern Wells; *Swan*, Newland, 'mixed ancient and modern'. GBG gives *Brewers Arms, Retired Soldier, Star. Foley Arms* is a much altered former Georgian coaching house.

OMBERSLEY 8463
Kings Arms, 'a public house of great age and character in picturesque village'. Timber-framed and said to date from 1411 and to have been used by King Charles while escaping from Roundheads. GBG gives *Cross Keys* also listed Richardson with *Halfway House*. Letts recommends *Hadley Bowling Green*, described as Tudor. Also *Crown* and *Sandys*.

ORLETON 4967
Boot, recommended Letts and described as 'modernised Tudor'. Free House. Also *Maidenhead Arms*.

PEMBRIDGE 3858
New Inn: fine timber-framed house on massive stone base, in an area noted for its 'black and white' work. Originally C16 farmhouse and preserves indications of this function. Long known as *Inn without a Name* and served as local courthouse. Highly dubious legend that agreement of 1497 ending Wars of Roses was made here. In Richardson's list and mentioned Batchelor. Also *Red Lion*.

PERSHORE 9446
Angel, small town hotel in shadow of remnant of great abbey church. Originated probably in C16, front restored 1920. *Manor House*, former private residence in Victorian Tudor style (GBG) which also gives *Millers Arms*, with its headgear collection, *Plum Tree, Talbot*. Richardson lists *Royal Three Tuns*.

PIXLEY 6638
Verzons, converted farmhouse, C17. (GBG and Letts).

PONTSHILL 6521
Travelling Hen, formerly *New Inn*, re-named to commemorate 'Loosey' who hitched rides on lorry axles in 1965.

REDDITCH 0467
Unicorn is on Richardson's list. Letts recommends Victorian *Nevill Arms*, while GBG gives *Cricketer's Arms, Crown, Golden Cross*.

ROSS-ON-WYE 5924
King's Head: typical coaching house, once Head Inn of town. Much Georigan work and some possibly of earlier date. Duke of Gloucester stayed here in 1882 and was very satisfied. Listed Richardson together with *Man of Ross, Royal, Swan* (GBG with *Rosswyn*). *Royal* occupies site of episcopal manor-house (traces in rear wall). Built as luxury hotel in 1837 and is a largely unaltered example of the period. Functioned as a large coaching house with huge stable yard. Dickens stayed here before deciding to embark on his American tour. Mentioned Batchelor.

STOURBRIDGE 8984
Letts recommends *Crown*, in nearby Iverley, described as 'mixed ancient and modern', and *Whittington* described as Tudor. GBG gives, among others, *Bulls Head* (panelled lounge), *Duke William, Royal Exchange, Unicorn*.

STOURPORT 8171
Swan, listed Richardson and recommended Letts. GBG gives canalside and unusually named *Black Star* and *Old Rose & Crown*.

UPTON ON SEVERN 8540
White Lion, originally C17 but given new façade in C18 and thoroughly reconstructed interior in 1971. Features in Fielding's 'Tom Jones', associations with Sarah Siddons. Former landlord is subject of famous epitaph: 'Beneath this stone, in Hope of Zion, Doth lie the landlord of the Lion' . . . Listed Richardson with *White Hart*. Letts recommends *Swan*, described as medieval. GBG gives riverside *Plough* and *Talbot Head* (rare name) in town.

WEOBLEY 4051
Red Lion, timber-framed inn in centre of village rich in this form of construction. It has a fine cross-wing of C14 and an outbuilding at rear with exposed crucks. Mentioned Batchelor, recommended Letts. *Unicorn*, another ancient inn with excellent C14 work visible in its western part. Both these hostelries are in Richardson's list. Also *Salutation*.

WHITCHURCH 5518
Old Court, claims to be partly C12. Medieval court room largely survives in hotel and country club.

WHITNEY ON WYE 2647
Rhydspence, unusually named, 'black and white' pub which is claimed to be C14. (GBG).

WORCESTER 8555
Cardinals Hat, Friar Street, is a timbered house (C16?), in GBG. *Diglis* is a mid-Georgian house facing river. *Farriers Arms*, Fish Street, early C17, timber-framed with oversailing upper floor. *Old Pheasant*, also timber-framed, late C16 with two overhangs. Listed Richardson. *Old Talbot* is an ancient city-centre pub near some of best of Worcester's surviving 'black and white' houses. *Star*, Foregate, is large mid C19 hotel, listed Richardson. Nearby Victoria House is former *Hop Pole*. *Eagle*, Friar Street is a listed building (Victorian) in GBG which, among others, also gives *Crown & Anchor*, Hylton Road; *Five Ways*, Angel Place; *Lamb & Flag*, Tything; *Long Stop*, Broad Street.

WYRE PIDDLE 9647
Anchor, on banks of Avon, recommended Letts.

YARPOLE 4665
Bell is worthy of notice.

HERTFORDSHIRE

ALDBURY 9612
Catherine Wheel, a 'beautiful thatched pub' (GBG), C17? f.1540 vaulted cellars survive as do later stables. *Greyhound*, village pub with stocks outside. Recommended Letts who describes it as 500 years old.

ARDELEY 3127
Jolly Waggoner is recommended by Letts who describes it as Elizabethan.

ASHWELL 1639
Letts has three recommendations: *Bushel & Strike, Rose & Crown, Three Tuns*.

BALDOCK 2434
George IV, Victorian pub with garden. (GBG and Letts). *Rose & Crown* in Richardson's list, but no details. *George & Dragon* claims associations with Charles I, Pepys and Dick Turpin.

BARLEY 4038
Fox & Hounds, listed Richardson and GBG, 'unusual gantry inn sign'.

BEDMOND 0903
White Hart, early C17 and original coaching house survived later alteration and development. Its curiosities include a 'Cox's Till'.

BERKHAMSTED 9907
Bull, once belonged to a religious fraternity and much medieval (C16) work survives in spite of heavy modernisation. Graceful bow window and canalside garden. *George*, formed from two cottages. Some parts may be C16 but generally C19. *Kings Arms*, the sculptured arms which provide sign are in fact Queen Anne's in whose reign old inn was rebuilt. There are remains of earlier house: timber, cellar brickwork, saloon fireplace and there is an attractive C18 staircase. Garden occupies site of town archery 'butts'. Once a great coaching inn (twice its present size) on old Birmingham road. Associations with exiled Louis XVIII of France, Victoria and Albert. Mentioned Batchelor and listed by Richardson together with *Swan*: mainly C17 and later, but some earlier material. Became prosperous coaching house in Georgian period.

BISHOP'S STORTFORD 4821
Chequers, George are listed by Richardson without details, but there are several old inns: notably *Black Lion, Boar's Head*. GBG gives *Bakers Dozen, Foxley*, praised by Batchelor, *Three Tuns*.

BRICKET WOOD 1302
Old Fox, not fully licensed until 1960. Before that, it was a beerhouse formed from two cottages, one C18, other C17. Provides rural ambience in earshot of M1.

BROADWATER 1504
Roebuck, probably dates from *c.*1420 with remains of this period in Tap Room and one of landings. Once a coach stop, dubious associations with Dick Turpin. Allegedly haunted. Some interesting curios in collection.

BROXBOURNE 3707
Crown, in C18–19 popular inn famous for its recreational facilities which included angling, pigeon-shooting and quoits by day with cards and billiards from nightfall. Its food had a high reputation, especially the Whitsunday ordinary. Mentioned Batchelor and GBG.

BUNTINGFORD 3629
George and Dragon, listed Richardson but no details. Letts recommends *Moon & Stars*, Victorian pub with garden. GBG gives *Jolly Sailors*.

Sword in Hand, rare if not unique name. Originally C16 manor house, licensed in C18. Boasts a collection of hats. Meet for local hunt.

BURNHAM GREEN 2616
White Horse, 'traditional village pub' (GBG and Letts).

CALDECOTE 2338
George & Dragon, probably replaces C14 hostel belonging to St Alban's abbey and was built *c.*1600 with little subsequent modification though old kitchen with original fireplace is now part of 'lounge'. Became small coaching inn and for a long time housed local administrative meetings.

CHIPPERFIELD 0401

Two Brewers, originally a modest village pub, recently tripled in size by absorption of neighbouring houses. Some fame in C19 as training-quarters for famous prize-fighters who sparred in old Club Room overlooking inn yard. Idyllic setting (GBG), mentioned Batchelor, delightful sign painted by Eric Newton. Letts recommends *Boot*.

CODICOTE 2118

George & Dragon, dubiously claims to be C13, indubitably extensively restored. Fine timber-framed building, possibly C16. Recommended Letts. Batchelor mentions *Bell* with its unusual three-dimensional sign.

CROXLEY GREEN 0795

Artichoke, built 1774 and HQ of local Friendly Society in early C19. *Coach & Horses*, staging post in coaching era. Attractive exterior includes pantiled roof with dormer windows. Beer Garden. GBG gives *Sportsman*.

DIGSWELL HILL 2314

Waggon & Horses in Richardson's list but no details.

GILSTON 4413

Feathers was built in 1680.

GREAT AMWELL 3712

George IV, seems to have originated in C18 with name *Quart Pot*. Since much altered but retains considerable character.

HARLOW MILL 4711

Old Mill, near lock is a converted water mill, built 1794.

HARPENDEN 1314

Cock, mainly C18 with some remains of older work at front. Extensive stables were once used to transport villagers to parish church. The rules of the Friendly Society which used the inn as its meeting room in C19 are preserved. GBG gives *Queens Head*.

HATFIELD 2309

Eight Bells. It is claimed that there was a tavern on site in C13. Present building largely a three-storeyed Georgian house with a fascinating lower (and older) annexe. Dickens associations. Listed Richardson, together with *Red Lion, Salisbury Arms*. Latter recommended Letts.

HEMEL HEMPSTED 0506

White Hart, originally farm which developed its service side in early C17 and was granted licence in 1660. General structure, including flagged courtyard, substantially preserved from C17. GBG gives *Bell*, described as 'historic inn' and *Marchmont Arms*.

HERTFORD 3212

Blue Boy, Dimsdale Arms are in Richardson's list but no details. *Old Barge* is early C19 with later Victorian frontage. Pleasant pub near head of navigable Lea. (GBG, together with *Bell and Crown, Unicorn*).

HERTINGFORDBURY 3012

White Horse, probably originated as C16 farmhouse from which some timber survives, with developments in following centuries. Jacobean staircase. Georgian frontage. Preserves old inn sign. Recommended Letts.

HITCHIN 1829

Sun, inn dating from C16. A Parliamentary house during Civil War and therefore unpopular after Restoration. Fortunes revived in coaching area when it was a post house. New façade added early C18 and Assembly Room later. Long used as court house and later as centre for local militia. Secret chamber entered from bedroom cupboard. Large garden and unused malt and brew houses. Listed Richardson, together with *Cock, Coopers Arms, Three Tuns. Coopers Arms*, at least, survives and is an interesting house of some antiquity. GBG gives *George*, another old coaching house, and *Sailor Boy*.

HODDESDON 3709

Salisbury Arms, originally *Black Lion*, seems to have developed from an ale-house attached to the smithy. It developed into a coaching inn on the old Great North Road. Some of its structure may be C16. *Bull*, a former coaching inn with pedimented Georgian front and bow window over arch to yard whose entrance, supported on Tuscan columns, bestrides the pavement. Listed Richardson, illustrated Batchelor. GBG gives *George, Rose & Crown*.

KNEBWORTH 2320

Roebuck, listed Richardson, no details.

LEVERSTOCK GREEN 0806

Leather Bottle, formed originally from the amalgamation of three (C16) cottages. Further modifications in C18 and drastic ones in 1972.

LITTLE GADDESDON 9913

Bridgewater Arms, spacious Free House with garden. (GBG and Letts).

LONDON COLNEY 1603

Green Dragon, waterside pub with garden, recommended Letts.

MUCH HADHAM 4319

Red Lion, listed by Richardson but no details. In nearby Little Hadham is *Nag's Head* which is claimed to be C16. (GBG).

NORTHCHURCH 9708

George & Dragon with over-hanging sign at entrance to unspoilt village. Former coaching-house and now listed building.

PUCKERIDGE 3823

White Hart, village pub, C16? (GBG and Letts).

REDBOURN 1012

Bull, in Richardson's list. No details.

RICKMANSWORTH 0594

Fox & Hounds, possibly C16 elements in house which was substantially rebuilt in Georgian period. *Old Green Man*, a building of 1728, replacing medieval ale-house. Associations with Dick Turpin. GBG gives *Halfway House*, 'a busy old pub by the river'.

ROYSTON 3541

Banyers is an old coaching house, of Georgian period in white brick with three bay centre section. *Old Bull*, a comfortable former coaching house early in Victorian yellow brick (GBG) on Richardson's list together with *Crown*. Letts recommends *Cabinet*, a Georgian pub and *Hardwicke Arms*, a Victorian hotel. Free House.

ST ALBANS 1507
Fighting Cocks, unobtrusive riverside pub claimed to be oldest inhabited licensed house in England (built before flood at end of C16). Complicated history starting as monastic dove-cote, rebuilt in C16 and named *Round House*. After Reformation it became a venue for cock-fighting until prohibition in 1894 when its name was changed to *Fisherman*. Associations with Oliver Cromwell. In Richardson's list and mentioned by Batchelor. They both also list *Peahen*, a modern building on an ancient site with unique name. Richardson also lists *George, Red Lion*, but no details. *Kings Arms* is re-named survivor of a former large number of pilgrim hospices (C16 or earlier). In neighbouring township of St Michaels in *Six Bells*, a largely C16 building on a Roman site. Recommended Letts. Richardson lists *Black Lion* in St Michaels. *White Hart*, Holywell Hill makes dubious claims to be a C12 inn but it has surviving material from C16 including Minstrels' Gallery. Mentioned Batchelor and recommended Letts. *White Lion*, originated in C17 as result of conversion of two cottages. It was popular with waggoners in C18. Preserved building. Alleged C19 ghost. (GBG). GBG adds *Farriers Arms, Goat, Jolly Sailor, Rose & Crown (St Michaels)*.

ST IPPOLITTS 1927
Olive Branch, attractive timber-framed inn (C16?) and at nearby Titmore Green is *Hermit of Redcoats* whose name commemorates a local recluse.

SARRATT 0499
Boot, built 1739, using older materials from previous house. Forecourt graced by ancient lime trees. GBG gives *Cock*, 'fine old country pub'.

STANSTEAD ABBOTS 3811
Red Lion, listed Richardson but no details.

STEVENAGE 2325
Letts recommends *Roebuck* 'mixed ancient and modern', and *White Lion*. GBG gives *Crooked Billet, Red Lion, Yorkshire Grey*.

TEWIN 2714
Plume of Feathers, older pub, dated 1596. *Rose & Crown*, largely unspoilt country inn, probably C18. Though it has recently lost its skittle alley, it has preserved a rare relic in the 'Slate' in the public bar.

TRING 9211
Richardson lists *Bell, Rose & Crown* but without details. Letts describes former as Georgian and recommends along with *Cow Roast* and *Royal*. GBG gives *Rose and Crown* as 'Tudor-style Trust House'.

WALTHAM CROSS 3600
Four Swans has a picturesque gallows sign (listed Richardson) and *Queens Head* is a small town pub. (GBG). *Old English Gentleman*, small riverside tavern, popular with anglers, originally a C18(?) farmhouse.

WARE 3614
Canons, C18, yellow brick with Doric porch. *Canons Maltings* incorporates a range of two-storeyed red brick malthouses of *c.*1600 described as 'one of the most interesting buildings of Ware' (P). *Old Bulls Head*, existed in 1551 when it was helping to support a religious foundation. Timber-framed, stable yard with entrance archway. Interesting fireplace. (GBG). GBG adds *Old Rose & Crown, Spread Eagle*.

WATER END 0310
Red Lion is in Richardson's list – no details.

WATFORD 1196

One Crown dates from early C16 with alterations and additions made in C17 and C18. Coaching house on London–Oxford run. Peculiar name to distinguish it from *Three Crowns* in same road (no longer an inn). Richardson lists *Clarendon, Essex Arms, George, Rose & Crown*, but no details. GBG gives *Oddfellows Arms* and *Tantivy*, formerly *Victoria*.

WELWYN 2316

At nearby Cromer Hyde (2012) is *Crooked Chimney* which originated as a private house of C16. Later it was licensed as *Chequers* but adopted its former nickname in 1969. Large inglenook fireplaces and, of course, a crooked chimney. *Wellington* recommended Letts and described as 'mixed ancient and modern'. GBG gives *Baron of Beef* and *White Hart* described as 'interesting'.

WHEATHAMPSTEAD 1713

Bull, ancient monument but apparently unnoticed by P. Possibly C17 (dubious associations with fleeing Charles I). Attractive timbered frontage, inglenook fireplace, one with backplate dated 1754. GBG gives two pubs with interesting names: *Abbot John, Wicked Lady*.

HUMBERSIDE

BEVERLEY 0339

Beverley Arms, formerly *Blue Bell* with probably C17 origin. Turpin and Trollope associations. Attractive porch from which Parliamentary results were announced, carriage way. Head inn of town and noble kitchen survives from late C17 expansion. Usual C18 developments including porch and Long Room. Two inn yards. Recommended Letts, mentioned Batchelor, listed Richardson. *George & Dragon*, originally town house of Warton family, built 1671. Much rebuilt and now largely Georgian. *Kings Head*, Georgian inn in market place, five bays with Tuscan porch, former coaching house, much altered. (GBG gives, among others, *Durham Ox, Royal Standard, White Horse*).

BRIDLINGTON 1766

Star, Westgate, one of oldest buildings in town and may have associations with great Augustinian priory which certainly supported a hospice but present structure seems largely *c.*1700.

BRIGG 0007

Dying Gladiator has unusual name and remarkable sign. Bridge Street has inns including low-roofed *White Hart* (C17?) and *Brocklesby Ox* with high-pitched roof and massive chimney-stack (Georgian?). GBG gives *White Horse*.

BURSTWICK 2228

Hare & Hounds, traditional village local with unusual handpumps. (GBG).

BURTON UPON STATHER 8617

Sheffield Arms, dated 1697, but substantially rebuilt in 1830.

CARLTON 3610

Foresters Arms, pub with garden, nr. Goole, recommended Letts and described as 'mixed ancient and modern'.

DRIFFIELD 0799

Bell, country-town hotel on edge of Yorkshire wolds. Former coaching inn. Listed Richardson, with *Buck*.

EPWORTH 7803
Red Lion dominates market-place with its generously proportioned four bays.

GRIMSBY 2810
Barge, riverside pub of immense character, housed in old wooden dumb barge and with Old Peculier on draught. Richardson lists *Ship* and among GBG recommendations are *Freeman's Arms, Hainton, Tivoli*.

HEDON 1828
Shakespeare, 'attractive old pub' (GBG) in ancient town possessing one of finest churches in East Riding.

HESSLE 0326
George, alias 'Top House', pleasant local in small town which retains some individuality.

HOWDEN 7428
Bowmans, small hotel, 'ancient and modern', recommended Letts. GBG gives *Cross Keys* on outskirts of worthwhile small town with one of largest churches in Riding.

HULL 0929
Kingfisher, Linnaeus Street, unexpected name for characterful dockyard local. *Old White Hart*, Alfred Gelder Street claims to be oldest building in city, dating from mid C16. Very heavily restored in late C19. 'Plotting Parlour' where governor decided to resist king's entry in 1642. Secret room, containing skeleton, discovered 1930. Magnificent Victorian/Edwardian decor. Recommended Letts with modern *Darley's Hotel*, Boothferry Road. *George*, Land of Green Ginger, is a popular old pub and former coaching inn (GBG), *Old Blue Bell*, concealed down alley-way off Market Place is C18 (GBG). There is an interesting group of classically named pubs (all GBG): *Minerva*, Nelson Street, *Neptune*, Neptune Street, *Oberon*, Queen Street.

IMMINGHAM 1714
Country, 1910, one of the most prominent buildings, dating from development of former hamlet. *Bluestone* (GBG) is even more recent.

KEADBY 8311
South Yorkshire, riverside local near only bridge (completed 1916) to isle of Axholme. (GBG).

KILHAM 0564
Star, former farmhouse retaining yard as well as a village workshop.

LAXTON 7825
Bricklayers Arms, village pub with good atmosphere, popular with farmers. Recommended Letts.

LITTLE DRIFFIELD 0157
Downe Arms (Bull until 1872), also given as at Wykeham. Built 1725 as large farmhouse and converted to serve coaching trade resulting from improvements on Scarborough road. Large modern extension. (GBG).

MARKET WEIGHTON 8741
Londesborough Arms, according to P, only house in town with some 'cachet'. Red brick, five bays, two and half storeys. Former coaching house. Listed Richardson. GBG gives *Red Lion*.

NEW HOLLAND 0724
Yardborough Arms, late C19 speculative building taking account of development of Hull ferry.

NORTH DALTON 9352
Pipe & Glass, updated and up-marketed pub with restaurant. Recommended Letts.

PATRINGTON 3122
Burns Head is pleasant country house outside village with one of country's finest parish churches. (GBG). *Hildyard Arms*, seven bays, white-washed, with large colourful armorials.

PAULL 1626
Humberside village with a number of interesting buildings: *Humber Tavern, Royal Oak*. (both GBG).

POCKLINGTON 8048
Feathers, mainly C19 but some C16 remains in office and C18 in kitchen passage and still-room window. Farmers' inn with extensive accommodation for their hunters. Scene of events around Lord Brougham in 1834 when alleged inhospitality was blown up into a political squabble. Its yard once witnessed the public execution of a hangman. Allegedly haunted. (GBG). Listed Richardson.

RUDSTON 0967
Bosville Arms, interesting pub with collection of horse brasses in village containing remarkable monolith. (GBG).

SCAWBY 9605
Nags Head houses free-lance inn sign painter.

SCUNTHORPE 8910
Blue Bell is on Richardson's list. GBG gives, among others, *Talbot*.

SHIPTONTHORPE 8543
Crown, country inn which may have originated as coaching house at half way point between York and Hull.

STAMFORD BRIDGE 7155
Cornmill, a former water mill of 1723, succeeding others dating back to Domesday, imaginatively converted into pub retaining many old features and fittings. *Three Cups*, village pub near historic battle site. Recommended Letts: 'mixed ancient and modern'. GBG gives *Bay Horse*, in rustic classical style with painted sign on brick wall.

SUTTON ON DERWENT 7046
St Vincent Arms, architecturally and bibulously attractive country inn. (GBG).

SWINEFLEET 7621
Kings Head, unspoilt country inn on banks of river Ouse.

WALKINGTON 9936
Barrel, old village pub with traditional atmosphere. (GBG).

WANSFORD 0656
Trout, village pub of C18–19 with six day licence. Recommended Letts.

WELTON 9957
In 1739, Dick Turpin was arrested in surviving pub of this pretty village with stream, pond and C19 pump on green.

WEST BUTTERWICK 8205
Ferry Boat, 'all moulded brick tudoresque' (Roberts) on bank of Trent. Contrast *Three Horseshoes*, 'a brewery architect's job'.

WINTERTON 9218
Lion's Head, small refurbished pub (GBG) in pleasant Humberside village which has retained its early Victorian architectural character.

KENT

ALDINGTON 0736
Walnut Tree, (C18) exterior apart from walnut tree, unremarkable. Interesting interior with impressive fireplace and associated secret room. C19 HQ of Ransley Gang, notorious smugglers operating in Romney Marsh area. Said to be haunted and to have developed from private dwellings, allegedly C14. (Recommended Letts).

APPLEDORE 9529
Letts makes two recommendations: *Red Lion*, pub with garden near church – Georgian and modern: *Swan* – Victorian.

ASH 2958
Lion, Georgian pub recommended Letts. GBG gives *Chequer* (sic.).

ASHFORD 0142
Woodmans Arms, Victorian pub where beer is brought from cellar. Recommended Letts. GBG gives *Rose, Trumpeter*.

BEARSTED 8055
White Horse, dubious claims to be C15. Certainly much developed in 1974 (Camelot Hall). Strong cricketing associations.

BELTRING 6750
Blue Bell, dates from 1757 when there was a toll house nearby. Until recently much used by hop-pickers for whom it made the unusual provision of a trough of ale.

BOUGHTON 0348
Flying Horse, dignified brick with stone-mullioned windows. Close to old Pilgrim's Way but present building C16 at earliest and only parts at that. Nice garden. Listed Richardson, recommended Letts. GBG gives *Queens Head, Three Horseshoes*.

BOUGHTON MONCHELSEA 7749
Cock, originated in amalgamation of three C17 cottages, since much developed. Impressive fireplace and chimney. Civil War associations. Recommended Letts. GBG gives *Albion*.

BOUGHTON UNDER BLEAN 0754
White Horse, interesting tiled roof line. Possibly C16.

BRASTED 4755
Kings Arms, renovated village local, with garden. (GBG). Recommended Letts who describes it as 'ancient'.

BRENCHLEY 6741
Rose & Crown, recommended Letts who describes it as Tudor. GBG gives *Bull*.

BRIDGE 1854
Plough & Harrow, Georgian village pub. (GBG and Letts who also give *Duck*, a Free House dating from 1640 but generally Victorian.)

BROADSTAIRS 3967
Royal Albion, an early C19 inn in which Dickens lived and worked, displays autograph letter in lounge. Mentioned Batchelor. Letts gives *Wrotham Arms* and GBG *Lord Nelson, Neptune's Hall*.

BROMLEY 4628
Swan and Mitre, two smaller inns united to form Georgian coaching house, remains of great yard and stables. Edwardian interior with theatrical associations. Richardson lists *Royal Bell*. GBG gives *White Horse*.

BROOKLAND 9825
Woolpack, probably originated in C15 house once occupied by Beacon Keeper on edge of Romney Marsh. Later, like many inns in area, was resort of smugglers and preserves many reminders of their activity (including secret passage). Supposedly haunted by flute-player. (GBG).

CANTERBURY 1557
Richardson lists *Falstaff, Flying Horse, Queen Elizabeth, Rose & Crown*. *Bishops Finger*, previously *George & Dragon*, named changed to publicise trade mark of owning brewery. On Roman foundations, preserves some medieval timbering and frontage has oriel window. *County*, occupies medieval inn site above Roman forum. *City Arms*, Butchery Lane, is mentioned in Ingoldsby Legends. (GBG). *Cross Keys*, previously *Vine*, then *Dog & Trumpet*. Built 1713 and preserves much contemporary chestnut panelling. Fine open fireplace. *Falstaff*, possibly built earlier C16 to house wayfarers excluded by closure of West Gate at nightfall. Originally called *White Hart*, present name from 1783. Mentioned Batchelor, together with *Fountain* which is also in Richardson's list – a monastic hospice which in C12 was described as best inn in Europe. *House of Agnes*, St Dunstan's Street, small, gabled, three-storeys, C17? described in David Copperfield. *Royal Dragoon*, Military Road is possibly C17 (GBG) – in graveyard. *Queen's Head*, Watling Street, is a listed building, part of which dates from C15. Alleged 'priest's hole' in dining room. *Slatters* absorb part of a C16 house. *Sun*, near Christchurch gateway is C17, known to Dickens and alleged to be 'little inn' where Mr Micawber waited for 'something to turn up'. Unfortunately no longer functional but sign survives. *Three Compasses*, High Street, is Tudor and recommended Letts. GBG adds *Eight Bells, Gentyl Knight*.

CHIDDINGSTONE 5045
Castle, almost untounched C16/17 timber-framed, recommended Letts, GBG.

CHILLENDEN 2753
Griffin's Head is an example of a Wealden house, close-studded and traces of the window of the original hall can be discerned.

CHILHAM 0753
White Horse, partly C15 and may have been Church House (it abuts into churchyard) on Pilgrim's Way. Ancient inglenook fireplace. *Woolpack*, dubious claims to be C15, certainly much modernised. May have been house of C17 master-builder of C17 castle. Recommended Letts. GBG gives *Alma*.

CHISLEHURST 4469
Ramblers Rest, charming weather-boarded pub, formerly a cottage with some rooms below ground level. Features collection of autographed silk ties.

COBHAM 6768
Leather Bottle, half-timbered house (C17?) with Pickwickian associations and decor (including signboard). A leather bottle which was filled with gold sovereigns when found is preserved in dining room. Listed Richardson, mentioned Batchelor. GBG gives *Darnley Arms*.

CRANBROOK 7735

George – much reduced from its former magnificence. Its guests have varied from Queen Elizabeth I to French prisoners from Seven Years' War. It preserves a fine William & Mary oak staircase and a coaching clock in entrance hall. Dining room occupies former kitchen. Listed, with *Chequers* by Richardson and recommended by Letts with *Windmill*. GBG gives *Duke of York*.

DARTFORD 5474

Royal Victoria and Bull, originally *Bull*, dating from C15 when it housed Richard Plantagenet, father of future Richard III. Dubious legend that it was a hospice attached to Augustinian priory but it may have been a hospital under Augustinian rule. Courtyard preserves early C19 coach and gallery, glassed-in to shelter Corn Exchange in 1826. Panelled dining room with bullet holes recalling tragedy of C18. Richard Trevethick, and possibly Jane Austen, associations. Much modified in 1973. Listed Richardson. GBG gives *Malt Shovel, Victory*.

DEAL 3752

Black Horse, Georgian, formerly used as Customs House. Letts recommends *Hare & Hounds*, also described as Georgian. GBG gives *Prince Albert, Sandown Castle*.

DOVER 3141

The C14 *Maison Dieu* no longer offers free hospitality. *Dover Stage* is a striking hotel of 1957. Between these period there is *Ship*, listed by Richardson and *Britannia*, mentioned by Batchelor. *East Cliff* is typical of its period and function (GBG which also gives *New Mogul*, 'a real gem', *Old Endeavour, Royal Oak*, and *Salutation*).

DUNK'S GREEN 6512

Kentish Rifleman, village pub opposite green. Recommended Letts and described as Tudor.

DYMCHURCH 1029

Ship, brick-built structure of uncertain age (C17?), backing on to Romney Marsh. Strong associations with smugglers and many hiding places. Good sign. Mentioned Batchelor.

EDENBRIDGE 4446

Old Crown claims C15 origins and associations with Henry VIII's affair with Anne Boleyn when she was living at Hever. Later smuggling connections. Panelling from old House of Commons. Rare gallows sign. (GBG). Letts recommends *King & Queen*, described as Georgian.

FAIRBOURNE HEATH 6113

Pepper Box, popular pub with garden. Recommended Letts who describes it as Tudor.

FAVERSHAM 0161

Castle, attractive timber-framed house, probably C16 and architecturally largely unaltered. Some of structure is said to be old ship's timber. *Chimney Boy*, building may be basically medieval. Later it was a convent until C19 when nuns left and it became licensed. Reconstruction reveals ingelnook and chimney with climbing-boy steps. *Ship*, C18 façade conceals older building of C16 or earlier; some of its remains are visible from inside. Letts recommends *Shipwright's Arms*, described as Elizabethan while GBG gives *Mechanics Arms, Phoenix*, 'Faversham's show-piece'. Fremlins offices are in a medieval building, refronted in C18 and over-shadowed by their brewery, 'an eruption of C19 red-brick, multi-storeyed warehouses' (P). Opposite are Shepherd Neame's offices (1869) adorned with vertical reliefs of hops.

FOLKSTONE 2336
British Lion, c.1460 and a former dependency of priory. Renamed in patriotic fervour of Napoleonic wars. Dickens associations. Mentioned Batchelor. *True Briton*, strong sporting associations – from Channel swimming to darts, mentioned Batchelor. GBG gives *Raglan, Salisbury*.

FORDWICH 1859
George & Dragon sited at medieval port and on Pilgrims' Way. Associations with Izaak Walton though present building seems a little later than his time. Nearby is a rare example of 'ducking stool'. Recommended Letts.

GADSHILL 7166
Sir John Falstaff, an interesting early Georgian inn whose name recalls fiasco of Shakespeare's boozy knight in this area which also contains the former home of Charles Dickens. Listed Richardson and mentioned Batchelor.

GOUDHURST 7337
Star and Eagle may have been Church House or medieval hospital. Common story of tunnel from cellars to church. C18 HQ of smugglers and thieves. Heavily timbered interior and rare C17 clepsydra. *Vine* is C16 inn overlooking village pond.

GRAFTY GREEN 8748
King's Head, alias 'Hollyock'. Timber-framed and weather-boarded, dormers. Alleged ghost of smuggler who turned King's Evidence.

GRAVESEND 6473
Jolly Drayman, attractive pub that was once part of Wellington brewery' (GBG which also gives uniquely named *Markers Retreat, Prince Albert, Westcourt*).

GREAT MONGEHAM 3451
Three Horseshoes, in Richardson's list, but no details.

GOUDHURST 7238
Peacock, Free House recommended Letts.

HAWKHURST 7630
Oak & Ivy was HQ, in C18, of notorious Hawkhurst gang of smugglers. *Tudor Arms*, C16 private house which seems to have become an inn in C17. Also claims dubious honour of being Hawkhurst gang's HQ. Free House. Recommended Letts, together with *Eight Bells*, described as Tudor, 'mixed ancient and modern'. GBG gives modern *Queens Head*.

HERNE 1866
Fox & Hounds, ancient hostelry with large garden, among those distinguished by appearing by name on OS map. Allegedly haunted.

HERNE BAY 1768
Smugglers Inn, sited at 'Smugglers' Corner' and recently discovered recess in cellar contained high quality rum. Maritime decor. The white-washed and weather-boarded *Ship*, Central Parade, also has smuggling associations. GBG gives *Hampton, Prince of Wales*.

HERNE HILL 0660
Red Lion, lonely inn with very attractive exterior. May be medieval.

HOLLINGBOURNE 8455
Pilgrims Rest, recommended Letts and described as Georgian.

HORSMONDEN 7040
Gun & Spitroast, almost worth including for the name alone but also allegedly C16. Recommended Letts.

ICKHAM 2258
Duke William, attractive village pub, Georgian with garden. Free House. (GBG and Letts).

IDEN GREEN 8031
Woodcock, pub with garden, recommended Letts and described as medieval.

IGHTHAM 5956
George & Dragon, is said to be a C16 building.

KILNDOWN 7035
Globe & Rainbow, unusually named Free House, recommended Letts who describes it as 'mixed ancient and modern'.

LEWSON STREET 9661
Walnut Tree, attractive pub in Kentish style – white-painted weatherboard. Is this the same as *Plough*? Probably dates from C17 but may be earlier and ancient fireplace contains an alleged 'priest's hole'.

MAIDSTONE 7656
Fishermans' Arms, oldest pub in Maidstone, built 1430 but has not always been a licensed house. Witnessed Civil War skirmish in streets of town and baulk of wood in front of pub has a nail for each casualty. Allegedly haunted by poltergeist. GBG gives *Dog & Gun, Sun*.

MATFIELD 6541
Blue Boys, brick white-washed front with projection into roof line for name, nearby oasthouse, illustrated by Batchelor.

MINSTER 3164, 9573

(Thanet)

Bell, opposite abbey, recommended Letts and described as medieval.

(Sheppey)

GBG gives *British Queen*, a very different kind of establishment.

NORTHBOURNE 3352
Cayman Arms, Georgian pub, recommended Letts.

OTFORD 5359
Bull, in Richardson's list.

PADDLESWORTH 1939
Cat & Custard Pot, a famous name. Recommended Letts who describes pub as 'mixed ancient and modern'.

PENSHURST 5243
Leicester Arms, formerly part of estate surrounding Penshurst Place. Described as 'one of the most picturesque inns in Kent'. Recommended Letts: 'mixed ancient and modern'.

PLUCKLEY 9045
Black Horse, two and half storeys, interesting roof and fenestration. Late C17 private house which became public this century. Allegedly haunted.

RAMSGATE 3865
Belle Vue, picturesque pub with interesting frontage. Associations with Dickens, Queen Victoria and Louis Phillipe. GBG gives *Artillery Arms* and the uniquely named *Blazing Donkey*.

ROCHESTER 7467
Crown lavishly entertained Hogarth and five companions in May 1732. Still possesses medieval cellars but was rebuilt in 1863 when it had recently become *Wrights* (referred to in Pickwick Papers). *Kings Head*, unpromising exterior conceals attractive work of C18 and earlier. Inn on site recorded from C15, associations with Charles II but present building substantially Georgian with good staircase of period, obscure wall-painting on first floor (temp. Queen Anne?). Long room discernible, though now divided. Original of Winglebury Arms in Dickens' 'Sketches by Boz'. Mentioned Batchelor. *Royal Victoria and Bull*, formerly *Bull*, once a coaching house and also has Dickensian associations. Mentioned Batchelor and listed Richardson together with *George*.

SANDWICH 3358
Bell has Georgian survivals in spite of modern appearance and one of its bathrooms being occupied by an anti-tank gun in World War II. Assembly Room with musicians' gallery survives as present dining room and there is a Georgian bar. Listed by Richardson. *Fleur de Lys*, Delft Street, claims to be C16 and the stucco covering of *Kings Arms* conceals a timber-framed building of 1592. *Admiral Owen* and *Crispin* are also possibly C16. GBG gives *Red Cow* 'old market pub unspoilt by time'.

SARRE 2565
Crown alias *Halfway House* and *Cherry Brandy House*. Latter name derived from fact that licence demands availability of this liquor made from special recipe of C17 landlord. Staging post in coaching era and unpretentious exterior conceals beamed interior fitted with Adam fireplace and C18 fireback. Associations with Dickens and more recent literary and theatrical figures. Listed Richardson.

SEAL 5456
Crown Point, elegant brick and tiled building with mullioned windows, former private residence of Sir Jeffrey Amherst whose name appears on sign board. In campaign against French in Canada he captured a fort called 'Crown Point'. Part of present cellarage once used as local lock-up. Recommended Letts.

SEVENOAKS 5355
Royal Crown, Royal Oak and *White Hart* are all in Richardson's list while GBG gives *Dorset Arms*.

SHEERNESS 9274
Royal Fountain rebuilt 1727 and frontage of that date survives. Assembly Room persists as Drawing Room and there is an attractive Smoking Room off entrance hall. First floor corridor has rare survival of room identification signs. 'Royal' commemorates associations with George III and the inn has long naval connections including Nelson. GBG gives *Jolly Sailor, Ship on Shore*.

SHOREHAM 5261
George is in Richardson's list. Letts recommends *Kings Arms* as Jacobean; Free House and *Royal Oak* 'mixed ancient and modern' (also GBG).

SITTINGBOURNE 9163
Bull, Red Lion are in Richardson's list. C18 front of *George* masks a timber-framed skeleton of C17 or earlier. GBG gives *Foresters Arms* and uniquely named *Globe and Engine*.

SMARDEN 8842

Chequers, typical local structure of brick and white-painted weatherboard. Claims C16 origin, later smuggling associations and the ghost of a French prisoner from the Napoleonic Wars. Recommended Letts. GBG gives *Bell* as 'superb village local' with magnificent range of excellent beers.

SMART'S HILL

Bottle House, formerly *Monkey House*. Fireside has so-called 'polissoirs' grooves made in stone through sharpening knives, etc. Doggerel verse on inn sign. *Spotted Dog*, a rather older house in magnificent setting.

SPELDHURST 5541

George & Dragon, magnificent half-timbered building with structure particularly visible in dining room. Much C15 medieval work in present building which may replace an older C13 inn. C18 Wealdon iron fireback. In Richardson's list and recommended Letts.

STAPLEHURST 7843

Kings Head, allegedly dates from 1160 of which the foundations remain. Rebuilt C16, developed as coaching inn and later became popular haunt of hop-pickers. Allegedly haunted. (GBG).

STODMARSH 2160

Red Lion, strongly recommended by Letts who describes it as medieval.

STOKE 8275

Nag's Head figured in the peregrinations of Hogarth and his friends in May 1782.

STOKE IN OXNEY 9427

Ferry recommended Letts and *Crown* by GBG.

STONE STREET 5754

Rose & Crown (GBG) and mentioned by Batchelor.

STROOD 7369

Crispin & Crispinianus, commemorating Agincourt and may be C14. Fine painted sign. GBG gives *Cobham, Cricketers Arms*.

TENTERDEN 8833

White Lion listed Richardson and recommended Letts who adds *William Caxton*, 'mixed Tudor, Georgian and Victorian'. GBG gives *Vine*. *Woolpack* is ancient hostelry with alleged smuggling associations.

TEYNHAM 9663

Plough, ecclesiastical origins in C13, became licensed inn in 1650. A good deal of medieval fabric survives. Picturesque frontage and some interesting furniture inside.

TONBRIDGE 5845

Rose & Crown, C17 inn which became coaching house in C18. Some room labels preserved. Associations with Victoria whose parents' arms are magnificently displayed over dignified porch. Recommended Letts together with *Vauxhall*. *Old Chequers*, mainly C16, central part of two storeys, wings of three with over-sailing upper floors. Rare gibbet sign. Mentioned Batchelor together with *Bull*. GBG gives *Man of Kent*.

TUNBRIDGE WELLS 5839

Castle in Richardson's list; Batchelor mentions *Duke of York*, as does Letts together with *Bristol Arms, Hole in the Wall*. *Swan* is a former coaching inn overlooking the Pantiles, also recommended by Letts. GBG gives *Beau Nash Tavern, Rose & Crown, Sussex Arms*.

ULCOMBE 8449
Pepper Box, uniquely named pub, probably dating from C16. Attractive interior includes ancient fireplace with two inglenooks. Comparatively high site (525ft, *c.*162m) allows good views.

UPPER UPNOR 7470
Kings Arms, 'friendly pub near river and castle. Bat and Trap played during summer' (GBG).

UPSTREET 2263
Grove Ferry, formerly *Ferry House*, whose landlord formerly operated ferry before present bridge was built over Stour. In spite of staid appearance said to have smuggling associations.

WAREHORNE 9832
Woolpack, Free House. Recommended Letts: 'Tudor origins with Romney Marsh traditions'.

WESTBERE 1961
Yew Tree, in Richardson's list and GBG – 'wood-panelled C13 pub'.

WESTERHAM 4454
George & Dragon, C17, former posting-house. Associations with General Wolfe who died in the capture of Quebec from French. In Richardson's list together with *Kings Arms*. GBG gives *General Wolfe*. At nearby Moorhouse *Grasshopper*, a much restored medieval inn, is said (according to Signpost) to date back to AD 25!

WINGHAM 2457
Red Lion, timber-framed with over-sailing upper floor and projecting room over doorway. Present building probably mid C17. It had C13 origins became a private house after Reformation until *c.*1700. In C18–19 housed local court. Good Queen Anne staircase. Recommended Letts and probably identical with 'Lion' in Richardson's list. *Dog*, rebuilt *c.*1660 after a serious fire. Both houses were originally part of Wingham College founded by Archbishop Peckham in later C13.

WYE 0546
New Flying Horse, recommended Letts – 'mixed ancient and modern'.

LANCASHIRE

ACCRINGTON 7528
Richardson gives *Hargreaves Arms*: GBG – *Great Eastern, Tramway*.

AFFETSIDE 7513
Pack Horse, probably originated in C16 as stop for carriers.

AUGHTON 3804
Cockbeck Tavern, friendly village pub, characteristic of region.

BALDERSTONE 6332
Myerscough, oddly named old village pub now near airfield. (GBG).

BARDON (Nr. Carnforth) 4970
Bardon, strongly recommended Letts: 'mixed ancient and modern'.

BARNACRE (N. Lancs) 5040
Kenlis Arms, originated in 1871 as an overflow shooting lodge for the sporting guests of Earl of Bective.

BARROWFORD 8538
White Bear, gabled, mullioned window, impressive three-storeyed porch. Originally built as private house in 1607. (GBG).

BARTON 5136
Old Man & Scythe, 'charming half-timbered house built in 1636' (Batchelor). The sign is crest of Pilkington family. James Stanley, seventh earl of Derby, spent last hours at inn before being executed for his royalist activities in 1651.

BAXENDEN 7726
Alma, cosy old house now virtually in suburbs of Accrington. Built on two levels and older part is claimed to be C16. Allegedly haunted. (GBG).

BELMONT 6715
Black Dog, old village pub in shadow of Rivington Pike (and TV masts). Horse trappings decor and unusual mosaic sign. (GBG).

BICKERSTAFFE 4404
Stanley Gate, on lonely cross-roads on A570. Stanleys were Lords of Man, Earls of Derby and very influential in NW. (GBG).

BLACKBURN 6827
Old Mother Redcap commemorates Elizabethan witch whose presence was thought to bring disaster. She could be rendered powerless by being encircled in a golden ring. Richardson lists *Old Ball, White Bull*. GBG gives *Bank, Fleece, Gibraltar, Moorgate Arms, Vauxhall*.

BLACKLEY 8503
Fox, market street pub (C18?) with display of boxing photographs. *Old House at Home*, traditional North-country local.

BLACKPOOL 3035
There are notable examples of seaside hotels: *Victoria*, 1841 and substantially unaltered; climatic *Imperial* of 1868 (originally a hydropathic establishment) with additional wing of 1875 and 'wildly Edwardian' (P) addition in 1904; *Clifton* was completed by 1874; the much larger *Metropole* is about the same date and *Carlton* was also built in Victorian period. *Norbreck Hydro* seems to have begun as a private house of 1869 to which substantial additions were made in 1915 and 1934. Less pretentious are *Bispham* (GBG) and *Savoy* (GBG). Town centre pubs might include *Criterion, Kings Arms* (both GBG) *Dunes* and *Empress* are both on the foreshore. Possibly the oldest pub in vicinity is *Saddle*, Marton. In Newton Drive is a suburban pub with the unusual name of *No. 4 &Freemasons*.

BOLTON 7108
Old Man & Scythe commemorates truce by which local Royalist William Trafford outwitted looting Roundheads. (Batchelor). Among GBG pubs are *Dog & Partridge, Howcroft* with its bowling green, *Stanley Arms* alias 'Sally up t'steps'. *Swan*, Churchgate, Georgian with two bows and Tuscan porch. *Commercial*, Victoria Square, Georgian with porch and pediment.

BROOKHOUSE 5464
Black Bull, country pub with waterside beer garden, recently enlarged and up-marketed. (GBG).

BURNLEY 8332
Black Bull, typical Pennine pub, C18? *Sparrowhawk* of about same period but up-dated and up-marketed. Both are in Richardson's list, together with *Thorn*. GBG gives *Cattle Market, Lane Ends, Rifle Volunteer, Woodman*.

BURY 8010
Royal, Bank Street, a large late-Victorian hotel in a sort of French Renaissance style. GBG gives *Swan, Waterloo*.

CARK IN CARTMEL 3676
Engine, 1689 and structurally unaltered. Formerly post house (stables survive) called *Fire Engine*. C19 trade much augmented by barge-workers transhipping coal and cotton on river Lea. (GBG).

CARNFORTH 4970
Barbon, recommended Letts and described as 'mixed ancient and modern'. GBG gives *Cross Keys, West View*.

CATFORTH 4735
Running Pump, unusually named country inn in obscure village, recommended GBG in spite of irregular opening hours.

CHARNOCK RICHARD 5415
Bowling Green, 'bar exhibits many old-world effects'; GBG gives *Hinds Head*.

CHIPPING 6243
Talbot is typical village pub and *Sun* with its remarkable stone steps also has a stream running through its cellars and claims a ghost, a young woman with problems. (Both GBG).

CHURCHTOWN 3618
Bold Arms, C18 house on tree-lined green in what remains a village in spite of Southport's proximity. *Hesketh Arms*, also C18 and facing the green – its Doric entrance was added in 1932. Batchelor mentions *Horns* which is recommended by Letts and described as Victorian.

CLIFTON 4630
Windmill, pub unusually housed in a converted (C18?) windmill.

CLITHEROE 7441
Swan & Royal, 'the nicest individual building in the town' (P), *c.*1840, white with mullioned windows; in Richardson's list. GBG gives *Buck, Station*.

COLNE 8839
'Architecturally there is not much to Colne' (P) but *Hole i't'Wall* is an interesting pub, 'oldest and highest in the town, mentioned in Songs of Sunrise' (GBG which also gives *Crown, Red Lion*).

CONDER GREEN 4556
Stork with elegant wrought iron sign, early C17 former coaching house.

COPPULL 5613
Alison Arms has interesting apparatus from local mining industry in lounge. (GBG).

CROSTON 4818
Uniquely named, largely C18 village which retains six of its original ten pubs. GBG gives *Lord Nelson*.

DENTON 9295
Angel, first licensed 1597. May have originated as Church House. Later became a coaching inn and, though much altered, retains old-world atmosphere. GBG gives *Dog & Partridge, Red Lion*.

DOLPHINHOLME 5153
Fleece (GBG) and *Bay Horse* which seems to have given its name to the neighbouring hamlet.

DUNKENHAUGH 8342
Dunkenhaugh Hall between Towneley Hall and Ribble Valley, now hotel, was former home of Walmesleys, a recusant family. House is said to be haunted by 'white lady'.

FENCE 8237
Old Sparrow Hawk is an attractive house of C18 or earlier. GBG gives *Bay Horse*.

FORTON 4851
Just outside, on A6 is *Hamilton Arms*, a handsome late-Georgian hotel and possibly a former coaching house. GBG gives *Holly*.

FOULRIDGE 8942
Hole in the Wall, pub on Leeds–Liverpool canal near entrance to Pennine tunnel, locally famous anecdote about Buttercup, the swimming cow. GBG gives *New Inn*.

FULWOOD 5331
Black Bull, a pub of some considerable antiquity with modern extension.

GARSTANG 4945
Royal Oak (GBG) is in Richardson's list. GBG also gives *Crown* with attached (crown-) bowling green and *Eagle & Child*.

GISBURN 8248
Ribblesdale Arms, architecturally best house in village, 1635, once private residence of Lister family. Fine three-storeyed porch, some original windows, others of C18. Furniture includes an original four-poster bed.

GOOSNARGH 5537
Horns, roughcast and timber building of 1782, probably on older site. Served pack-men and drovers in C18. The 'horns' are deer antlers and probably represent a hunting trophy from the fells.

HASKAYNE 3507
Ship, canalside pub near top of great flight of 21 locks. Still possesses a boatyard.

HAVERTHWAITE 3485
Anglers Arms, Victorian pub recommended Letts.

HEYSHAM 4161
Middleton Arms, formerly Heysham Old Hall, a stately private house: E-shaped, gables, mullioned windows. Built probably in 1598.

HOGHTON 6125
Royal Oak, old inn of character near Hoghton Tower, spectacular historic mansion. Free House. (GBG).

HOLLINWOOD 5236
Help the Poor Struggler. Victorian pub in suburb of Oldham, once (1948–55) kept by Albert Pierrepoint, public hangman.

HOLME IN CLIVIGER 8926
Ram, long low building, probably C18. Cottage alehouse which has extended to absorb two neighbouring structures. Delightful house overlooking Cliviger Gorge. (GBG).

HORNBY 5869
Castle – unpretentious façade masks character and quality. Private fishing.

HURST GREEN 6838
Shireburn Arms, simple stone and slate building in Lancashire style, said to date from C15.

KIRKHAM 4231
Black Horse, a popular town pub and characteristic of area. GBG also recommends *Stable Bar* attached to Hillside restaurant.

LANCASTER 4761
Carpenters Arms, possibly C17 with some mullioned windows (Bridge Lane). *Kings Arms*, Market Street, large hotel of 1879 in a sort of C18 style. Listed by Richardson, together with *County*. *Ring o' Bells*, King Street, C18, replacing older house, with good doorway, frieze and pediment. Penny Street offers a pair of hotels, early C20 in Jacobean manner, *Alexandra, White Cross*. In Contrast there is *Lancastrian*, a new-style pub of 1967. GBG recommendations include *Bowling Green* which still has its own green, *Crown, Rose, Tramway, Waggon & Horses*.

LEIGH 6699
Rope & Anchor is commended by Batchelor. GBG gives *Eagle & Hawk, Railway, Ring o' Bells*.

LEYLAND 5421
Bay Horse, C17 or earlier house near village cross, given a new porch in C18. GBG gives *Eagle & Child*.

LONGRIDGE 6037
Corporation Arms, updated village pub with restaurant, recommended Letts. GBG gives *Townley Arms*.

LONGTON 4725
Dolphin, alias 'Flying Fish', on Longton Marsh. Increasingly rare example of traditional association of pub and farmhouse. (GBG).

LYDGATE 9225
White Hart, built in C18 to serve coaching trade. Cobbled frontage. Alleged scene of C19 lynching. Lonely site with magnificent views.

LYTHAM ST ANNES 3526
Clifton, Bath Street, *c*.1840, three bays, five storeys. Elegant late Georgian seaside accommodation with bay windows added later. Listed Richardson. *St Annes*, St Georges Road, *c*.1875 in Tudoresque. *Grand, Majestic* are large Edwardian hotels on the sea front. GBG gives *Hole in One, Queens*.

MAWDESLEY 4914
Black Bull, C16 inn with a notable giant poker called 'Eli Hob'. Centre of Catholic resistance after Reformation and said to be connected to nearby Hall by underground passage entered from well in kitchen. Upper floor allegedly haunted by 'white lady'.

MELLING 5970
Melling Hall, good late Georgian house of three bays and a porch. Later extended and recently converted into hotel. (GBG). The explorer should find the malthouse of 1684.

MIDDLETON 4158
Old Roof Tree, C16 building four miles south of Morecambe. (GBG).

MIDDLETON 8606
Boar's Head, fine timber-framed inn of *c*.1600. Gable decoration not contemporary. GBG gives *Dog & Partridge, Hare & Hounds, Three Arrows, White Hart*.

MORECAMBE 4364
Hardly a single building earlier than mid C19. *Midland* is of early 1930s. *Queen's*, a modest Georgian structure is one of oldest houses in town. Less elegant Victorian buildings would include *Grosvenor, Victoria* (GBG which also gives *Bull, York, Palatine, Yorkshire Brewer*).

MOSS NOOK 8488
Tatton Arms, C17 pub only a mile from Ringway airport. (GBG).

NELSON 8737
Station, 1893 and built in 'a sort of Elizajack style' (P).

OAKENCLOUGH 5248
Moorcock, remote pub 3½ miles north-east of Garstang, recommended Letts who gives date *c*.1670.

ORMSKIRK 4107
Buck i't'Vine, historic town-centre pub with unusual, if not unique name. Not far away is *Snig's Foot* (both GBG which also gives *Horshoe, Ropers Arms, Yew Tree*). *Saracen's Head*, Halsall is recommended by Letts who describes it as Tudor.

OVERTON 4357
Ship – largely unaltered Victorian pub whose name reminds us that nearby Sunderland Point was port for Lancaster in early C18. (GBG).

PADIHAM 7933
'Of the streets and houses there is nothing to report' (P), but the intrepid pub explorer might seek out *Alma*, a friendly Victorian local. (GBG). *White Horse* has large extenal sign and novel interior theme of C18 coaches.

PARBOLD 4911
Stocks Tavern is a comfortable village local (GBG) and nearby is *Ring o' Bells*, built 1738 and later flourished as canalside pub on Leeds–Liverpool where it was a stopping place for Leeds–Wigan packet.

PAYTHORNE 8251
In 1940, at least, there was behind *Buck* a Jerusalem thorn which flowers at midnight on Old Christmas Day.

PENDLETON 7539
Swan with Two Necks where a 'regular' once auctioned his wife to the highest bidder.

PENWORTHAM 5128
Black Bull, former village local being transformed as village becomes outer (and more fashionable) Preston. (GBG). *Bridge*, possibly C18 inn which developed during coaching era, still has an attached bowling green.

PLEASINGTON 6425
Railway, fine local which has retained its bowling green in village remarkable for its early C19 church. (GBG).

PREESALL 3646
Saracen's Head, attractive northern village local, so far unspoilt. (GBG).

PRESTON 5329
Stanley Arms, sedately stylish C19 hotel. County Offices inhabit former *Park* built 1882 as a railway hotel. Richardson lists *Bull & Royal* and Letts recommends *Continental*, a Georgian riverside pub with garden (GBG which among others, also gives *George, Maguire's Tavern, Maudland, Mitre, Theatre)*.

RIBCHESTER 6435
White Bull, gritstone with three-dimensional sign perched on porch whose pillars are Roman columns. More Roman masonry in cellars. Used as Court House up to C19 and one room served as temporary gaol. Mounting block outside. Listed Richardson, mentioned Batchelor together with *De Tabley Arms*, a handsome house, possibly of C17. GBG gives *Black Bull*.

RINGWAY 8184
Romper, 'small, untouched country pub' (GBG) with unusual name.

SALTERFORTH 8845
Anchor, unique pub on Leeds–Liverpool canal: one pub built on top of another due to altered levels consequent on raising road to bridge canal. At summit of trans-Pennine waterway.

SAMLESBURY 5829
Samuel Whitbread, recommended Letts and described as Tudor, GBG gives *Nag's Head*, overlooking Ribble Valley in Samlesbury Bottoms.

SCARISBRICK 3713
Heatons Bridge, Victorian canalside pub and *Kicking Donkey*, popular country pub are given by GBG.

SILVERDALE 4674
Silverdale, a comfortable Free House with squash courts and large garden (GBG) in 'most pleasant, i.e. least crowded, least urban seaside resort in this area' (P).

SLAIDBURN 7152
Hark to Bounty, ancient hostelry wich once housed courts of Forest of Bowland. Courtroom is preserved. Called *Dog* until 1875 and claims origins in C13.

SLYNE 4765
Cross Keys, much altered inn with obscure history. Originally built 1725, was beer house in later C19 and associated with butcher's shop in early C20. Rebuilt 1933 with some old panelling preserved.

SWINTON 7701
White Horse, a lively pub in building claimed to be C16.

WADDINGTON 7243
Moorcock, replacement on site of old inn, fell-side terrace overlooks Pennine moors. In village are two *Hinds* distinguished as 'Upper' and 'Lower'. The lower is more interesting and possesses vary rare servery.

WALTON-LE-DALE 5627
Bridge, former coaching inn at Ribble crossing on London route (A6). GBG. *Unicorn* (now a cafe) was an ancient hostelry (C17) said to have been Cromwell's HQ at battle of Preston. Curious features include remains of 'hides', probably connected with smugglers.

WARRINGTON 6088
Barley Mow, half-timbered, late C16 but 'has made too many efforts to look it' (P).

WATERLOO 3296
Royal, formerly *Waterloo*, 1815, large sea-front hotel of nine bays. *Alexandra*, large Edwardian pub (GBG which also gives *Marine, Volunteer Canteen*).

WEETON 3834
Eagle & Child, pub with garden, recommended Letts and described as 'mixed ancient and modern'.

WITHNELL 6322
Hoghton Arms is said to be C17, updated and upmarketed.

LEICESTERSHIRE

APPLEBY MAGNA 3110
Possesses a timber-framed inn (C17?) at corner of Mawby's Lane and Top Street.

ASHBY-DE-LA-ZOUCHE 3516
Royal, 1826, most conspicuous building in neighbourhood, façade somewhat altered, brick with porte-cochère. Handsome entrance hall. Listed Richardson, mentioned Batchelor. GBG gives *Bowling Green, Plough*.

ASHBY FOLVILLE 7012
Carrington Arms, a village pub dating from C17. (GBG also Letts).

BARROW UPON SOAR 5717
Navigation, pleasant canalside pub (C18?) with skittle alley. (GBG). For sharp contrast, compare *Lodge*.

BARWELL 4496
Blacksmiths Arms, half-timbered, C17? (GBG).

BILLESDON 7103
Queens Head, ironstone village pub, probably C18. (GBG).

BITTESWELL 5385
Man at Arms, large Victorian(?) pub, probably C18. (GBG).

BURBAGE 4492
Anchor, suburban village pub. (GBG). Letts recommends modern *Three Pots*.

CASTLE DONINGTON 4427
Cross Keys, (C18?). Free House in small town. (GBG).

CLIPSHAM 9616
Olive Branch, unusually named country pub in attractive village. (GBG).

COTTESMORE 9013
Sun, thatched C17 country inn. (GBG).

CROPSTON 5511
Bradgate Arms, 'old Free House of character' (GBG).

ELMESTHORPE 4696
Wentworth, 1895, and a rare example of a pub designed by C.F.A. Voysey. Typical of his work both outside and inside. (Letts).

EMPINGHAM 9408
White Horse. Victorian pub. (Letts).

FLECKNEY 6493
Old Crown, recommended Letts, within walking distance of canal.

GADDESBY 6813
Cheney Arms, 'a purpose-built inn of *c*.1750 and quite unaltered: brick, three storeys, and typical of county'.

GREAT CASTERTON 0009
Ancient village with nearby site of Roman town. GBG gives *Crown, Plough*.

HALLATON 7896
Berwicke Arms, 'a fine Free House' (GBG) in 'one of the most enjoyable villages in the county' (P). *Fox* is starting point of competition to find 'Bottle King'.

HINCKLEY 4294
George, listed Richardson but no details. P says 'little of architectural interest'. GBG gives *Black Horse, Weavers Arms*.

HOBY 6617
Blue Bell, 'large, lively village inn with a skittle alley' (GBG). Roof Tree Cottage by the church may have been a medieval inn.

HOSE 7329
Black Horse, village pub with skittle alley. (GBG).

HOTON 5722
Packe Arms, Free House is recommended by Letts.

KEGWORTH 4826
Cap & Stocking, 'classic village pub' (GBG) with ale served from jugs. Rare name is a reminder of domestic knitting industry and there is an old stockinger's cottage behind *Britannia*.

KIBWORTH BEAUCHAMP 6893
Coach & Horses, recommended Letts and described as Elizabethan.

KILBY 6295
Dog & Gun, recommended Letts and described as medieval.

LANGHAM 8411
Noel Arms, pub with restaurant in village with large and imposing church. Recommended Letts.

LEICESTER 5904
Grand, 1896, exemplifies both the taste and optimism behind the large hotels of the period. Richardson lists *Bell, George, Stag & Pheasant* and *Wyvern*. Batchelor also mentions *George*. Letts recommends Victorian *Bulls Head* and *Craddock Arms*, 'mixed ancient and modern'. GBG gives, among others, *Black Boy, Black Horse, Globe, Joiners Arms, Magazine*.

LIDDINGTON 8797
Marquess of Exeter, Free House, possibly C18, recently renovated (GBG and Letts) in secluded village, rich in ironstone buildings. GBG also gives *Old White Hart*.

LONG CLAWSON 7227
Crown & Plough, C18(?) village pub with rare skittle alley. (GBG).

LOUGHBOROUGH 5319
Kings Head, chief inn of the town, former coaching house, listed Richardson together with *Old Bulls Head*. *Windmill*, Sparrow Hill claims to be oldest inn in town. (GBG which, among others, recommends *Druids Arms, Old Packhorse, Peacock*).

LUTTERWORTH 5484
Denbigh Arms, 'late Georgian front with big Egyptian lettering' (P), listed Richardson together with *Hind*.

MARKET BOSWORTH 4003
Old Black Horse, recommended Letts. GBG gives unspoilt *Red Lion*.

MARKET HARBOROUGH 7387
Angel, is a former coaching house and may have C17 origins but what is visible is Georgian with widely spaced windows and a Tuscan porch. *Three Swans*, plain rendered front of three storeys, perhaps masking C17 house which issued trade tokens. Former coaching house with long stabling yard behind. Fine C18 wrought iron inn sign. Run by John Fothergill (1935–52). Recommended Letts, mentioned Batchelor and listed Richardson together with *Angel* and *Peacock*. GBG gives *Harborough Lounge, Red Cow*.

MELTON MOWBRAY 7518
Bell, former coaching inn retaining archway into its cobbled yard. *Three Tuns* has a later C18 façade with a good doorway. Richardson lists *George*. The *Maison Dieu* was a medieval inn. GBG gives *Black Swan, Noel Arms, White Hart*.

MUSTON 8237
GBG says *Wheatsheaf* is an interesting, 300 year old pub.

NORTH LUFFENHAM 9303
Horse & Panniers, alias 'Nag and Bag', village local. (GBG).

OAKHAM 8509
Crown, small High Street hotel, possibly C18 (GBG), listed Richardson, together with *George*, modernised former coaching house in attractive Market Place. *Wheatsheaf* is said to be C17 (also GBG).

PEATLING MAGNA 5992
Cock Inn, recommended Letts who says it is medieval.

ROTHLEY 5812
Rothley Court, country hotel, former private house: medieval, Elizabethan, 1893 and modern. Birthplace of historian Macauley and hosted William Wilberforce. Formerly preceptory of Knights Templar of which chapel is a rare survival. Mentioned Batchelor.

RYHALL 0311
Green Dragon, characterful village inn, formerly medieval manor house with C13 vaulted cellar, in delightful square. (GBG).

SEATON 9098
Letts recommends *George & Dragon*.

SEWSTERN 8821
Blue Dog, popular village pub (GBG) with unique name.

SOMERBY 7710
Three Crowns, described GBG as 'unspoilt C17 coaching inn'.

STRETTON 9415
Ram Jam, long, low, stone structure enclosing earlier C17 house known as *Winchelsea Arms* until early C19. Various explanations of new name: C18 cocktail named after Indian servant, confidence trick immobilising landlord's wife. Over entrance is memorial to famous prize fighter. Mentioned Batchelor.

TINWELL 0006
Crown, popular local (GBG) in village with fine church.

UPPINGHAM 8699
Crown, early C18, former coaching house, listed Richardson, recommended Letts. *Falcon*, another coaching house whose Victorian façade dominates market place and masks earlier work of C17(?), discernible round yard. Recommended Letts (GBG? which certainly gives *Exeter Arms*, 'small, old, country-town pub'). Richardson also lists *Unicorn* which seems early C18 and was once a coaching house.

WALTHAM ON THE WOLDS 8024
Royal Horseshoes – attractive thatched house with rare name.

WHISSENDINE 8214
White Lion, 'old inn with one long, rambling bar' (GBG) in attactive village with remarkably large church.

WHITWELL 9208
Noel Arms, village pub, popular with fishermen. (GBG).

WHITWICK 4316
Man within Compass – unique name.

WING 8903
Kings Arms, traditional village pub with 'cash register' handpumps (GBG) which also gives *Cuckoo*. Letts recommends '*Kings Head*'. This small village has church dating from C12 and rare maze.

LINCOLNSHIRE

ALFORD 4575
Windmil, in pleasing Market Place, Georgian façade with Doric porch. (There are two real windmills in town). GBG gives *Half Moon*.

ANCASTER 9843
Angel, six bays, two storeys in famous local stone. Georgian and one of finest houses in attractive village.

BARTON 0222
Former port with two major churches and its inns remind us of former importance as communication centre: *Coach & Horses, Sloop* (GBG which also gives *Wheatsheaf*, Holy Dike). Richardson lists *George*.

BICKER 2237
Red Lion, brick building of 1665, former posting house. Free House on edge of village with amazing village church. (GBG).

BILLINGBOROUGH 1134
George & Dragon, C17 with five bays which have lost their dormers. GBG gives *Fortescue Arms*.

BLANKNEY 0660
Some three miles west of village is *Green Man*, long mid-C18 house with Venetian window in higher wing, lighting magnificent Georgian clubroom whose fittings have been thoughtlessly destroyed.

BOSTON 3244
Barge is Georgian red brick, five bays, fanlights. *Crown & Anchor* has a notable sculptured sign dated 1803. *Lord Nelson* has attractive allegorical figures. *Magnet* is only Free House in town (GBG which gives, among others, *Britannia, Carpenters Arms, Duke of York*). *Peacock & Royal* is the 'market-place hostelry par excellence' (P), late Georgian façade masking earlier building which contains C17 panelling and magnificent chimney-piece. *Queens Head* is of *c.*1840, *Red Cow* forms part of a pretty group in Wide Bargate. *Rum Puncheon* claims to be (gutted) birthplace of John Foxe, martyrologist in 1516. *Still Pit* is early C19. *Ship* is Georgian. *White Hart*, Georgian and Victorian. Listed Richardson, along with *Red Lion*.

BOURNE 0920
Angel, two-storeyed, brick, is a market place inn, possibly with C15 origins, later a coaching house, rebuilt 1860. Retains its cobbled courtyard. Listed Richardson, together with *Bull*. GBG gives *Golden Lion*, while Letts recommends *Black Horse*.

CAISTOR 1101
George, unpretentious Georgian(?) inn in agreeable square of ancient township. Richardson gives *Red Lion*.

COLEBY 8919
Bell, traditional, unspoilt village pub. (GBG).

CONINGSBY 2258
Lea Gate, former coaching inn with big wooden ecclesiastical boss in one gable (GBG which also gives *White Bull, White Swan*).

CROWLAND 7713
George, in Richardson's list, no details.

EDENHAM 9621
Five Bells, village pub with garden (GBG), recommended Letts who describes it as Georgian.

EWERBY 1247
Finch Hatton Arms, Victorian, Free House, recommended Letts.

FOLKINGHAM 0733
Greyhound, handsome Georgian coaching inn, formed from three houses, dominating village square on main London–Lincoln road.

FOSDYKE 3133
Ship, roadside pub with nautical decor (GBG). Nearby is *Pyewipe*, uniquely named, isolated tavern on Fosdyke, the oldest navigable waterway in country.

FREISTON 3743
Kings Head, 'fine example of unspoilt village local' (GBG).

FRISKNEY 4555
Barley Mow, 'quaint old pub' (GBG) in village possessing 'one of the most rewarding of Marshland churches' (P).

GAINSBOROUGH 8189
White Hart, former coaching inn of C18 with covered yard, listed Richardson. GBG gives *Elm Cottage, Ropery*.

GRANTHAM 9135
Angel & Royal, 'one of the grandest of English pre-Reformation inns and with a remarkably rich late C15 façade' (P). Originally Templar, later Hospitaller house, where Richard III sealed Buckingham's death warrant. Former stabling replaced by C18 brick extension. GBG, listed Richardson, mentioned Batchelor, recommended Letts. *Beehive* is famous for its 'living sign' with accompanying doggerel, listed Richardson, mentioned Batchelor, recommended Letts. *Blue Lion*, fine C18 inn, five bays, two and half storeys with pedimented doorway. The odd colour of the king of beasts may be due to eccentric lord of the manor who, it is said, at the turn of the century introduced 'Blue' to inn names of town, producing a variety of blue animals as well as a blue boat and a blue inn. One assumes that he was a true-blue Tory. *George*, large and elegant High Street hotel of 1780, with fine staircase window, listed by Richardson. *Kings*, Victorian hotel, GBG and Letts, *Old Malt Shovel* is timber-framed and gabled, C17(?) GBG adds *Five Bells, Granby*.

GREAT LIMBER 1308
New Inn, built 1840 but in old-fashioned Georgian style, a modestly ambitious effort in local brick.

HALTHAM ON BAIN 2463
Marmion Arms, ancient timber-framed inn with thatched roof. Probably C16 but much restored.

HARLAXTON 8832
Gregory Arms, early C19 with centre bow unfortunately cemented over in village dominated by monstrous Hall, now outpost of American university.

HECKINGTON 1444
Nag's Head, local inn dating from at least 1684 in village possessing 'one of the grandest churches of Lincolnshire' (P). GBG gives *Royal Oak, White Horse*. Former *Railway*.

HEIGHINTON 0269
Butcher & Beast, modernised C19 village pub (GBG) probably once associated with butcher's shop.

HOLBEACH 3625
Chequers, High Street hotel (C18?) listed Richardson. Centre for wild-fowling. GBG gives *Bell, Station*.

HORNCASTLE 2669
Bull, old house but not contemporary with its 'medieval banquets', town-centre hotel listed by Richardson, together with *Red Lion*. Former in GBG with *Kings Head*.

HOUGH-ON-THE-HILL 9246
Brownlow Arms, attractive Victorian pub with garden. (GBG and Letts).

IRNHAM 0226
Griffin, mainly Georgian, later additions and alterations (including castellation). In delightfully sequestered stone village.

KIRKSTEAD 1762
Abbey Lodge, reputedly gatehouse or hospice of Cistercian abbey f.1187. It did possess extensive vaulted cellars of C12 but these have been filled in.

KIRKINGTON 1011
Marrow Bone & Cleaver, traditional country inn with unique(?) name. (GBG).

KIRTON 3038
Kings Head, 1699 but old fashioned in style, what P calls 'Fen Artisan Mannerism', in former market town with large church.

LANGRICK 2447
Ferry Boat, modernised inn of character by side of river Witham. (GBG).

LEADENHAM 9452
George, rural version of Georgian town style with good front. Free House, recommended GBG and Letts.

LINCOLN 9771
Albion, Victorian with 'Georgian' assembly room attached. *Green Dragon*, alias *Green Garrett*, possibly originated C15 in connection with St Mary's priory, an outlier of St Mary's abbey, York. Became merchant's house after Reformation, altered and increased in size. Licensed early C18 and carefully restored 1967. *Saracen's Head*, textbook example of late Georgian, fine wrought-iron balcony. *White Hart* preserves original façade of 1840s with much later addition. Both latter in Richardson's list, together with *Spread Eagle. Cardinal's Hat*, late C15 and renamed in honour of Wolsey early in C16 (rare example of name surviving but unfortunately no longer inn). *Wig & Mitre*, 'superbly restored pub close to cathedral' (GBG which, among others, gives *City Vaults, Cornhill Vaults, Crown & Anchor, Duke William*).

LONG BENNINGTON 8344
Royal Oak, former coaching house on Great North Road in street village which may be longest in country. Letts recommends *Reindeer*, Georgian.

LONG SUTTON 4322
Bull, Chislett, both probably once served coaching trade on A17. (GBG).

LOUTH 3287
Kings Arms, C17 and former coaching house in spite of Victorian Gothic additions. Richardson lists *Kings Head. Masons Arms*, Georgian vernacular 'in best town pub tradition' (P). In Westgate 'best street in Louth' is *Wheatsheaf* which may be C17. (GBG). *Woolpack*, Riverhead was once C18 wool-merchant's house. (GBG which also gives *Boars Head, Prince of Wales, Turks Head*).

MALTBY 4681
Crown, attractive ivy-covered village pub, possibly C18. (GBG).

MAREHAM-LE-FEN 2761
Royal Oak, attractive, thatched country pub which may date from C17, though the village saw a good deal of building in C19. (GBG).

MARKET DEEPING 1310
New Inn, dated 1802 though style is that of an earlier period. In Richardson's list. GBG gives *Bull*.

MARSH CHAPEL 3598
Greyhound, small, attractive village pub (GBG) in village which prospered from its salt-pans in Middle Ages, hence great church of early C15.

MORTON 8864
Kings Head, country inn, Free House, recommended Letts who gives it as Elizabethan.

MOULTON 3024
Hare & Hounds, isolated old inn (GBG) on marshes that fringe Wash. P describes Moulton as 'most satisfying village in the neighbourhood'.

NAVENBY 9857
Kings Head, small stone-built village inn. (GBG and Letts).

NETTLEHAM 0075
White Hart, apart from church, best building in village. Mid-Georgian with venetian window. Once housed local courthouse and gaol. (GBG which also gives *Plough*).

NEWTON 0436
Red Lion, picturesque, Free House, recommended Letts.

OLD SOMERBY 9633
Fox & Hounds, traditional country pub (GBG) in village with interesting church.

SALTFLEET 4593
New Inn, tall, brick, four bays, possibly early C17, a larger house than Manor House opposite indicating former prosperity of fishing village.

SAXILBY 8875
Sun, small village inn by side of Foss Dyke, two and half storeys possibly C18 with later C19 bay windows. Associated with 1805 murder when 'haunted' murder weapon vanished from this and two other local inns. GBG gives *Anglers*.

SCOPWICK 0658
Royal Oak, early C18(?) with interesting fenestration by green with stream.

SKEGNESS 5663
Lion, listed Richardson. GBG gives *Shades, Vine* (oldest in Skegness).

SKENDLEBY 4369
Blacksmiths Arms, 'picturesque country pub' (GBG).

SLEAFORD 0645
Bristol Arms, five bays, three storeys, pedimented and crenellated late Georgian coaching house. Listed Richardson but no longer functional. *White Hart*, also on Richardson's list has nearby stone inn sign dated 1691. In same street is similar sign of *Black Bull*, dated 1689. On Maltings (1892–1905) P comments 'for sheer impressiveness, little in English industrial architecture can equal the scale of this building'. GBG gives *Carre Arms, Grapes, Lion, Nags Head. Waggon & Horses*, of C18 appearance, may have originated as staging point on waggon route. Locale of mysterious 'dwile flunking' championships.

SOUTH KYME 1749
Hume Arms, traditional pub (GBG) in village which also possesses C14 tower-house and interesting church.

SOUTH LUFFENAM 9402
Boot & Shoe, Georgian pub with garden and restaurant, recommended Letts.

SOUTH RAUCEBY 0245
Bustard, (GBG), pleasantly situated pub provided in estate village of *c.*1860.

SPALDING 2422
White Hart, dignified market-place hotel of seven bays, *c.*1715 with porch added early C19, recorded C14, rebuilt C15 of which some remains may have survived fire of 1714 after which it was reconstructed in present form. Associations with Mary, Queen of Scots and one of Cromwell's Ironsides who issued trade tokens in 1666.

Scene of C18 duel (epitaph of victim in churchyard). Listed Richardson and in GBG. *White Lion* is mid-Georgian and also former coaching house. Richardson also lists *Red Lion*. *Old White Horse* is an attractively thatched pub in Churchgate which may be C16. (GBG which also gives *Bull*).

SPILSBY 4066
White Hart, market-place inn serving coaching trade, Georgian with 'genial façade' (P). Birthplace of Sir John Franklin of North West Passage fame. *George* is of about same vintage. Both listed Richardson and in GBG which also gives *Bull*.

STAMFORD 0207
Stamford Hotel, 'one of the grandest of Regency hotels' (P), 1810–1829, listed Richardson, along with *George*: incorporating part of former Augustinian priory (suppressed 1538), with later imposing façade of Georgian period. Gallows sign across main street. Mentioned Batchelor and recommended Letts. *Huntsman* has much C16 and C17 work. My own favourite is C17 *Bull & Swan* (also recommended Letts); *Wheatsheaf* is also early C17, while *Olive Branch* is dated 1666. GBG gives *Golden Fleece, Green Man, Northfields, St Marys Vaults*. There is a Brewery Museum – a genuine Victorian Steam Brewery with refreshment room and beer from the wood in All Saints Street.

STOW 8781
Cross Keys, (GBG), traditional rural Free House in village containing one of most monumental parish churches in England.

TYDD ST MARY 4418
Five Bells 'old ochre brick with a spotty orange string course and tumbled gables, all overbuilt in modern brick and slated' (D.L. Roberts). Also *Saracen's Head*.

WEST DEEPING 1009
Red Lion, dated 1795, traditional inn in 'uncommonly charming' village.

WIGTOFT 2636
Small village on former main coaching route (A17) with three inns: *Phoenix*, a Free House; *Golden Fleece*; *Swan*. First two in GBG.

WILLINGHAM 8784
Half Moon, said to be C17. (GBG which also gives *Fox & Hounds*).

WITHERN 4282
Red Lion, large family pub (GBG) in village with interesting earth works.

WOODHALL SPA 1963
Golf, Petwood, hotels in fake half-timbered style (built *c*.1900) to accommodate visitors to spa which developed in earlier C19. Letts recommends *Abbey Lodge*, described as Tudor and GBG gives *Gamecock*. *Petwood* is described as 'the hotel in a garden'.

WRAGSBY 1378
Village possesses handsome, early C19 *Turners Arms* and the older market-place pub, *Adam & Eve*. (GBG).

WRANGLE 4250
On edge of village with fine church and medieval earth works is *Coach & Horses*, 'a genuine rural pub'. (GBG).

LONDON

(see also Greater London, Essex, Middlesex and Surrey)

General arrangement is city and central, west, south-west, south-east and north.

EC1

Angel, City Road, figures in 'Pop goes the weasel'; housed Georgian theatre where Marie Lloyd first appeared in 1885 (Mentioned Batchelor). *Baptist's Head*, St John's Lane, originally medieval, associations with Knights Hospitaller; later house was frequented by Johnson and Goldsmith and visited by prisoners on way to Clerkenwell gaol. (Batchelor). *Bishop's Finger*, West Smithfield. (GBG). *Castle*, Cowcross Street, associations with George IV and alleged rights of pawnbroking. GBG gives *Crown*, Clerkenwell Green, also recommended Letts. *Hand & Shears*, Cloth Fair. Associations with famous Smithfield Fair and medieval Court of Pie Powder. *Henekey's Wine House*, first establishment of its kind (1695), present building later except cellars (used as refuge in C17 Gordon Riots). Unusual fireplace with underfloor flue replacing chimney. Claims longest bar. *Mitre*, Ely Court, formerly belonged to bishop of Ely. Alleged associations with Elizabeth I who threatened to unmake Anglican Bishop of Ely unless he gave this house and land to her courtier, Sir Richard Hatton. (GBG, Batchelor). *Old Red Lion*, Clerkenwell Road, associations with Johnson, Goldsmith, poet Thomson and Tom Paine. (Batchelor). *Raglan*, Aldersgate – ancient site occupied by C16 *Bush* which became *Mourning Bush* after execution of Charles I. Only cellars are of any antiquity and include part of Roman city wall. *St Paul's Tavern*, Chiswell Street, quiet, smart pub providing an oasis from city business but clients often bring business with them.

EC2

Bricklayer's Arms, Shoreditch. (GBG). *City Grill*, a Free House in Lawrence Lane. (GBG). *Dirty Dicks*, Bishopsgate, contains room allegedly untouched by jilted C18 bridegroom. Certainly possible to drink in very dirty environment. GBG gives *Pump*. *'199'*, formerly White Hart' on C13 site. (Batchelor). *Railway Tavern*, Liverpool Street, is recommended by Letts. *Station Buffet*, Liverpool Street underground. Unexpected late C19 decor, maintained in original building of *c*.1875.

EC3

City of London Yeoman, New London Street. (GBG). *East India Arms*, marine and mercantile associations. Part of cellars is former crypt of St Katherine's (demolished medieval church). Fish Street Hill, 'Against No. 45, inn sign of former *Peterboat & Doublet*, a very lively timber relief in a cartouche, late C17' (P). *George & Vulture*, St Michael's Alley, Cornhill. Original house claimed Chaucer and Dick Whittington among its guests. Replacement associated with Dickens and present HQ of Pickwick Club. (Batchelor). *Hand & Shears*, Middle Street, allegedly C16. (Batchelor). *Hoop & Grapes*, claims to be one of oldest pubs in London, later C17 brick house with wooden bay window. Narrow front. Early internal communication device. Sprawling cellars and underground passages. (Batchelor). *Lamb*, Leadenhall Market, built to serve Market, rebuilt 1881. (GBG). *Three Nuns*, Aldgate, 1878, brick gabled, mentioned Pevsner. *Still & Star*, Little Somerset Street. Combined name. *Tiger*, Tower Hill, successor to tavern which supplied meals to prisoners in C16. Alleged secret tunnel from cellars to Tower! (Batchelor).

EC4

Baynard Castle, Queen Victoria Street, is one of many successive buildings which have occupied site of one of the three medieval castles which once stood in the capital. *Bell*, Fleet Street, is an interesting and characterful pub. C17 replacing medieval inn. *Black Friar*, Queen Victoria Street, 'best pub in the Arts and Crafts fashion in London' (P), dominant three-dimensional 'sign' but even more interesting interior. (GBG). *Cockpit*, St Andrews Hill, occupies site of Dominican friary, suppressed 1538. Cock-fighting theme. *Harrow*, Primrose Hill, pleasant early C18 house of red brick. *Horn*, Knightrider Street, C18 house off beaten track. Dickens associations. *Old Cheshire Cheese*, Fleet Street, famous name with long literary connections: Sam. Johnson and others. Not much of present house is of great antiquity except cellars which once belonged to London house of abbots of Peterborough. In Richardson's list. GBG, Batchelor. *Old Cock*, C17 original 1887, largely rebuilt with some surviving pieces of Great Fire. Carved chimney-piece attributed to Grinling Gibbons. Many literary associations: Dickens, Garrick, Johnson, Sheridan, Tennyson. (Batchelor). *Old Watling*, Watling Street, possible associations with coach and goods traffic along this major northern artery. (GBG). Retains human scale and proclaims that it was 'rebuilt (for first time) 1666'. *Old Wine Shades*, Martin Lane, rare C17 survival. Dickensian associations, tunnel. *Popinjay*, built 1976, also occupies monastic site – London house of abbots of Cirencester. A popinjay was an imitation bird used as practice target by sporting archers. (GBG). *Printer's Devil*, Fetter Lane, printing decor and decor from presses to typography. (Batchelor). *Shades*, Cannon Street, 1663 and substantially altered. (Batchelor). *White Swan*, Tudor Street (1881). Journalists pub. Newspaper theme maintenance in decor. Pump, once supplying house's water, survives. *Williamson's Tavern*, Bow Lane, Cheapside, C17, with wrought iron gates given by William and Mary and residence of Lord Mayors until mid C18. (Batchelor).

WC1

GBG gives *Crown*, New Oxford Street, *Lamb*, Lambs Conduit Street. *Museum*, Bloomsbury (1856) associations with Karl Marx, Polish Pretender and founder of Mass Observation. *Peter's Bar*, Southampton Row is recommended Letts. GBG gives *Yorkshire Grey*, Theobalds Road.

WC2

Devereux Arms, Devereux Court, originated as C18 coffee house, remodelled 1843, provides an oasis from bustle of Strand and Fleet Street. *George*, 'large, plush, dimly-lit one bar pub down alley off Strand' (GBG). Oil painting of George III on façade trying to imitate timber-framing. *Lamb & Flag*, Rose Street, alias 'Bucket of Blood' when it was prize-fighting centre. Prize-fighters now replaced by theatricals. Dickens associations. *Marquis of Granby*, Chandos Place. (GBG). *Nag's Head*, Floral Street. Its sign is a circus horse with fine theatrical decor and upstairs there is a matchless collection of theatrical designs. (Batchelor). *Savoy*, *c.*1903, very advanced in both design and fittings. *Seven Stars*, Carey Street, claims to have been built in 1602. *Sherlock Holmes*, formerly Northumberland Arms. (Batchelor). *Ship*, Gate Street, f.1549 but only cellars are of any antiquity: provided refuge for Catholics during persecutions. *Strand Palace*, 1925–30 'all faced with soapy-looking artificial stone' (P). *Waldorf Hotel*, 1907–8, giant columns, French pavilion roofs and a real Palm Court. *White Hart*, Drury Lane (Batchelor) claims C13 origin, associations with highwayman Dick Sheppard. *White Swan*, New Row, claims to be C17, panelled. (GBG). Known to Dickens and used in several of his books. *York Minster*, renamed *French Pub* in 1981 to mark long French associations – even De Gaulle is said to have used it during World War II.

W1

Audley, Mount Street, Victorian pub recommended Letts. *Avenue Bar, Shaftesbury Avenue. (GBG). Crown*, Brewer Street. Dickensian associations. *Crown & Two Chairmen*, Dean Street. Thackeray associations. *Devonshire Arms*, Devonshire Street, off Marylebone High Street. (GBG). *Duke of Wellington*, Crawford Street. (GBG). *Henekey's*, Kingley Street. Victorian Free House, recommended Letts. *Horse & Groom*, Great Portland Street, spacious Victorian pub. (GBG). *King Charles II*, 18 Kingley Street, 'small, popular, ornate retreat' (GBG). *Newman Arms*, Rathbone Street, pleasant retreat off Oxford Street. (GBG). *Red Lion*, Waverton Street was a private house of mid C18; claims possession of a pair of Dick Turpin's pistols. Recommended Letts. *Rising Sun*, Tottenham Court Road, notable for the exuberance of its façade (1897), described as 'Belgian Gothic Renaissance with Art Nouveau influences' (P). Listed building. *Running Footman*, Mayfair, listed Richardson. *Salisbury*, St Martin's Lane, 'well-preserved, ornate, late Victorian pub' (P). Actors have replaced prize-fighters as its habitues. *Star & Garter*, 62 Poland Street, 'small, friendly, historical pub' (GBG). *Shepherds*, Curzon Street, is mid C18. *Thistle*, Vigo Street, recommended Letts. *White Horse Cellar*, Piccadilly, (Hatchetts), established 1720 and long the terminus for Westbound coach to Bath and/or Exeter.

W2
Swan, Bayswater, rare beer garden, C18. Associations with highwayman Claude Duval. (Batchelor). GBG recommends *Royal Standard*, Sale Place. *Victoria*, Strathearn Place. Victorian pub with theatrical associations. *Whites*, Lancaster Gate is recommended Letts.

W4
City Barge, Chiswick, riverside inn with Parliament clock and copper beer warmer. (Batchelor). Allegedly C16 but impression is C18 at earliest. Gallery for local artists. GBG gives *George IV, Swan. Lamb & Flag* is in Richardson's list. *Tabard* is example of Norman Shaw architecture. The pub was designed as central feature of world's first garden suburb. Notable collection of brilliant wall-tiles by William de Morgan.

W6
Doves, Hammersmith, riverside pub in which Thomson wrote 'The Seasons' (Batchelor), also *Red Lion*, associated with pre-Raphaelites and A.P. Herbert. *Rutland* and *Blue Anchor* are riverside pubs. GBG gives *Brook Green, Cross Keys, Thatched House*.

SW1
Albert Arms, Gladstone Street is recommended by Letts. Architectural Press, Queen Anne's Gate has a paradoxical basement – a pub without licence but with many interesting relics. *Antelope*, Eaton Terrace is recommended Letts. *Buckingham Arms*, Petty France. (GBG). *Cockney Pride*, Jermyn Street, famous for antique 'peek-a-boo' machines and 'puddings and mash'. *Fox & Hounds*, Passmore Street. (GBG). *Grenadier*, Wilton Row, possibly late C18; in C19 associated with nearby barracks and George IV when it was '*Guardsman*'. Allegedly haunted by officer who was flogged to death for cheating at cards. *Red Lion*, Duke of York Street, good example of 'gin palace' with mirrored walls and cast-iron staircase to latrine. There is another *Red Lion* in Crown Alley, with alleged secret passage to St James palace. *Ritz* is now a scheduled building. *Rose & Crown*, Lower Sloane Street. Victorian pub recommended Letts. *Silver Cross*, site has long and complex history but house was licensed by 1674. Has to be renewed at Buckingham Palace since it occupies palace land. Alleged ghost of Tudor maiden. *Star Tavern*, Belgrave Mews. (GBG). *Tom Cribb*, Panton Street commemorates famous C18 prize-fighter, recommended Letts and GBG. Further SW is *Cask and Glass*, Palace Street. A modern house, recommended Letts. There is the well-kown riverside *Kings Head and Eight Bells* at Chelsea, originated in C17 when they were much patronised by Navy using Chelsea pier. Former was for officers, latter for ratings. Merged mid C19. Associations with Carlisle, Whistler. Chelsea also has *Admiral Codrington*, Mossop Street which is a Georgian/Victorian pub recommended Letts which also offers, *Surprise*, Christchurch Terrace, a pub

*c.*1850, *Water Rat*, Milmans Street, another Victorian pub and *Australian*, Milner Street, Victorian/Georgian (in GBG with *Builders Arms, Queens Elm*). In Wandsworth is *Leather Bottle*, Garratt Lane, pub with garden recommended Letts and described as 'mixed ancient' – also *Old Sergeant*, Victorian pub, while Battersea has *Castle*, (C16?) fine overhanging bow window and inn sign 'unsurpassed in London, carved in the reign of the first Elizabeth' (Batchelor). *Green man*, Putney Hill. Associations with Swinburne. Beer garden. (Batchelor). GBG gives *Castle, Fox & Hounds, Jolly Gardeners*.

SE1

Southwark possesses London's last galleried inn, the C17 *George*, a shadow of what it was in 1890. See fine sign of Kings Arms taken from gatehouse of London Bridge. Alleged Dickensian associations. Mentioned Batchelor. (GBG which also gives *Rose & Crown*, Colombo Street). *Anchor*, Bankside, occupies historical site with associations of Johnson and Boswell. Its small rooms and varying levels maintain 'old-worlde' atmosphere. May be C17. Smuggling associations and fugitive's escape shaft (near Clink). Mentioned Batchelor. GBG gives *Hole in Wall*, Mepham Street, in railway arch. *Old Caledonia*, a retired paddle steamer, functioning as a floating pub moored near Waterloo Bridge. *Old Father Thames*, riverside pub on Albert Embankment. Further out are *Brockley Jack*, Brockley Road, named after highwayman, with highly dubious claims to C14 origins. (Mentioned Batchelor. GBG gives *Wickham Arms*). *King's Arms*, Peckham Rye replaces one on same site destroyed during blitz. Its cellars are allegedly haunted by some of victims who were sheltering there. *Tiger Tavern*, Thames Street. C16 cellars and tunnel. Rebuilt C20. At Greenwich is *Mayflower*, formerly *Ship*, in Richardson's list, a well restored C17 pub whose verandah overlooks the jetty from which Mayflower sailed in 1611. (GBG which also gives *Admiral Hardy, Ashburnham Arms, Richard I*). *Angel*, Rotherhithe, has C17 origins with Pepys associations. Alleged smugglers' trapdoor in kitchen. (Mentioned Batchelor). On piles over river.

EAST

Red Lion, Whitechapel High Street, E1, possibly C17. Dick Turpin murdered Tom King in its yard, 1739. (Batchelor). GBG gives *Star & Garter*, Whitechapel Road. *Lord Nelson*, Commercial Road, Stepney in GBG. *Town of Ramsgate*, Wapping High Street. (GBG). Cellars once imprisoned convicts awaiting transportation to Australia. Riverside bar occupies site of Hanging Dock. Nearby is *Prospect of Whitby*. Associations with Pepys, Judge Jeffreys, Dickens and Turner. C16 origns. Listed Richardson, mentioned Batchelor. *Dickens*, St Katherine's Dock. Part of imaginative development of Victorian site. Free House. Recommended Letts. *Grapes*, small riverside pub, overlooked by tourists, unlike 'Prospect'. Mid C17. Strong Dickensian associations – it is said that Our Mutual Friend was written here. (Listed Richardson). *Thomas Neale*, just off Commercial Road, Stepney. Modern Free House, recommended Letts. Further east, *King's Head*, Clapton, E5, on banks of Lea with views of river traffic. *Prince of Wales*, Lea Breage Road, *Ferry Boat*, Tottenham, Cook's Ferry (C18), Edmonton, are all popular with anglers. *Railway Tavern*, West India Dock Road, alias and better known as 'Charlie Browns' – world famous seamen's pub. (Batchelor). GBG gives *Queens Head. Blue Posts*, early C19 dockland tavern. Effects of window tax evident on bricked-up frontage. With other dockland pubs, it is licensed to sell drinks between 6 and 8 a.m. The traditional tipple at this early hour is rum and coffee. *Guildford Arms*, Crisp Street is recommended Letts 'probably Victorian'. *Watermans Arms*, Isle of Dogs, E14, at Greenwich reach. Interesting riverside views including Greenwich Hospital. Music Hall souvenir. Splendid Edwardian decor.

NORTH

North London seems short of interesting pubs. In Highbury there is *Canonbury*, Victorian pub recommended Letts and GBG which also gives *Compton Arms*. *Angel* merits a word in P. Hampstead has a number of famous hostelries: *Spaniards* claims to be 500 years old, some C18 remains. Associations with Turpin and more recent literary figures. Garden. In Richardson's list with *Bull & Bush*, original was of 1645 and very popular in C18 – associations with Gainsborough, Reynolds, Garrick, Sterne. Fine pleasure-gardens (now car-park used for al-fresco sing-songs in C19 – era of 'Down at . . .'). *Flask*, also recommended. Meeting place of C18 Kit-Kat clubs and named from bottles in which chalybeate water was sold. *Jack Straw's Castle*, C18 and, like *Spaniards*, once on old toll road.

GREATER LONDON

BARNES 2276

Bulls Head, riverside pub, formerly C19 coaching house of which stables have been turned into restaurant. *Sun*, rebuilt *c*.1750 on older site. Further extensive modifications in 1971. Preserves walled bowling green where Elizabeth and courtiers are said to have played. GBG gives *White Hart*.

BARNET 2496

Red Lion, former coaching inn and claims to be where Artful Dodger offered breakfast to Oliver Twist and where Esther Summerson of 'Bleak House' hired a carriage. In Richardson's list together with *Harts Horns*.

BECKENHAM 3769

George, C18 and one of oldest structures in town. Was stagecoach terminus for London in C18–19 and site of local Petty Sessions to modern times. *Jolly Woodman*, recommended Letts and described as 'mixed ancient and modern'.

BRENTFORD 1778

Beehive, Express, Pottery Arms. (GBG).

CARSHALTON 2764

Greyhound, former country retreat of Sir William Courtenay which became inn in 1773 and was rebuilt 1840. Recommended Letts.

CRANFORD 3164

Berkeley Arms, imposing house (C17?), mentioned Batchelor. GBG gives *Queens Head*, rebuilt 1936.

CROYDON 3365

Greyhound, listed Richardson. *Half Moon*, original building was C17 and posting house. Associations with William Corbett and W.G. Grace. Letts recommends *Selhurst Arms*. GBG gives, among others, C18 *Two Brewers, Ship, Tamworth Arms*.

EASTCOTE 1188

Case is Altered, originated as (C15?) farmhouse, later a shop. Claims licence from C17. Much altered.

EDGEWARE 2091

Chandos Arms is in Richardson's list.

ELTHAM 1744
Abbots Fireside, timber-framed building allegedly 1485 with ecclesiastical associations (note angel corbels and grotesques). Huge fireplace said to be from 'small monastery at Lyminge' (of which there is no record). P dates building as 1614 and draws attention to noteworthy interior chimney-piece, dated 1624. Preserves rare Parliament clock. *Rose & Crown*, largely C18 but some parts possibly earlier. Housed local Magistrate's Court for many years. Letts recommends *Kings Arms*, described as medieval.

GANNICK CORNER 2899
Duke of York, listed Richardson, no details.

GREENFORD 1382
Black Horse C18(?), pleasant canalside (Grand Union) pub. (GBG which also gives *Bridge*).

HAMPTON COURT 1370
Mitre, fine exterior of 1665 when it was built to provide extra accommodation for courtiers. Rich panelling in Cardinal Bar. GBG gives *Kings Arms* here and *Windmill*, Hampton Hill.

HARROW 1388
Kings Head claims to date from 1553.

HIGHGATE 2886
Archway has dubious associations with Dick Whittington, including mumified cat. (Batchelor). *Flask* in Richardson's list and GBG which also gives *Victoria*.

HILLINGDON 0882
Red Lion, said to have housed Charles I on his flight from Oxford. Mentioned Batchelor.

HOUNSLOW 1276
Chariot, Victorian pub recommended Letts. GBG gives *White Bear*.

ISLEWORTH 1675
Coach & Horses, C16 origins, developed C18 when it was a staging post for coaches. Dickensian associations. (GBG). *London Apprentice*, C18 scheduled building. Fine stucco ceiling in upstairs bar. Attractive riverside site. Listed Richardson.

KENTON 1788
Plough, name (and site) has a continuous history of four centuries. Associations with Dick Turpin – bricked-up 'hide' by great fireplace.

LONGFORD 0576
White Horse, 'genuine, low-beamed pub', two miles west of Heathrow' (GBG).

OSTERLEY 1576
Hare & Hounds, delightful country pub in Greater London. (GBG).

PINNER 1289
Queens Head dates from 1705. GBG gives *George IV, Victory*.

PONDERS END 3695
Falcon, 'gem of a pub' (GBG). Private zoo and vehicle collection.

RICHMOND 1874
Marlborough, formerly *Rose*, renamed to honour John Churchill's elevation. Association with Thackeray who said it was 'one of quietest, cheapest, neatest, little inns in England' and was much taken with its gardens and bowling green. Collection of key-rings. *Star & Garter* was locale of early balloon ascent in 1825. (Batchelor). *White Cross*, Georgian-style riverside inn with old fireplace in saloon bar. Name is reminder of austere Observant Franciscans who were martyred for their resistance to Henry VIII's pretensions. GBG gives *Cricketers, Orange Tree, Red Cow*.

SIDCUP 4672
Black Horse, originally C17 with later façade showing windows blocked to avoid tax. Restaurant has 'arms and armour' theme.

SIPSONS GREEN 0877
Three Magpies, successor to coaching inn on old Bath road. Mentioned Batchelor.

SOUTHALL 1280
Whitehall in Richardson's list. GBG gives *Lord Wolseley*.

SOUTHGATE 3093
Cherry Tree, recommended Letts and described as medieval.

STANMORE 1692
Vine (GBG) on site of old Vine Brewery.

STRAND ON GREEN 1878
Bulls Head, formed from two C18 cottages. *City Barge*, attractive Thameside pub with good painted sign, also *Steam Packet*.

SUTTON
GBG gives *New Inn, New Town, Lord Nelson*.

TOTTENHAM 3491
Ferry Boat, basically C18. Now popular anglers' inn with access to neighbouring reservoirs. Ferry used to cross river Lea. GBG gives *Dagmar Arms*.

TWICKENHAM 1473
Crown, originated as C17 coach house but present building basically C19 with much altered interior (1971). Exterior has unusual 'corner bay window' with heavy pediment. Imposing early C19 doorway with ponderous lamp above. GBG gives *Albany, Five Oaks, Prince Albert*.

UXBRIDGE 0583
Crown and Old Treaty House, old coaching inn with interesting architectural features of C17, C18 and C16. Civil War associations. In Richardson's list, mentioned Batchelor and GBG. *George*, once coaching inn in former market town and communications centre. GBG also gives *Crown & Sceptre, General Elliott*.

WEST WICKHAM 3866
Village pub originated as private house which became an inn in C18 and probably functioned as a small coaching house.

GREATER MANCHESTER

ALTRINCHAM 7687
Bull's Head, up-market pub at Hale Barnes is Letts recommendation. *Old Hall*, originally private house of late C18, five bays and two storeys. *Unicorn* listed Richardson. GBG gives *Faulkners Arms, Malt Shovel, Victoria*.

LOWTON 6197
Jolly Carter, first licensed in C16. Later a coaching house.

MANCHESTER 8397
Old Wellington, originally private house of *c.*1550. Many alterations and varied uses before licence in 1830. Survived bombing of World War II and even greater danger from town planners in 1951. Remarkable salvage operation involved lifting entire building 5ft. Associations with John Byron. Mentioned Batchelor along with *Grand, Midland, Old Rovers Return, Punch House, Seven Stars, Spread Eagle*. There are naturally a number of large C19 buildings: *Grosvenor*, 1879 with its columned façade; *Manchester Arms*, mid-Georgian, five bays and an attractive doorway; *Queens*, 1845, Italianate with an ornate porch; *Midland*, 1898, vast, stylistically mixed up, brick and terracotta. Among GBG's selection are *Castle & Falcon*, formerly C17 prison; *Crown & Kettle*, a listed building; *Harp & Shamrock*; *Peveril of the Peak*.

MOSSLEY 9702
Tollemache Arms, dramatically sited example of small local in former cotton town. (GBG).

MOTTRAM 9995
Roe Cross, stone-built country pub (C18?) overlooking Longdendale.

NEW HAY 9311
Moorcock, C18 inn on desolate Pennine moors. Mentioned Batchelor.

NORDEN 8614
New Inn, decor exploits theme of witchcraft, especially Pendle witches.

RAMSBOTTOM 7916
Grant Arms, a substantial late-C19 coaching house of five bays, two and half storeys and featured doorway. GBG gives *Good Samaritan, Masons Arms*.

ROCHDALE 8913
George & Dragon, Manchester Road is late C19 in picturesque Tudor style. GBG gives *Albert, Cemetery, Greengate, Healey, Wellfield*. Nearby *Healey Hotel* (1920–30) preserves service bells and centre for Morris dancing.

SADDLEWORTH 0306
Ford on A635, former coach road from Doncaster to Manchester. High Pennine hostelry deriving name from ford on packhorse route between Meltham and Holmbridge.

SALE 7900
Brooklands is listed Richardson. GBG gives canalside *Railway*.

SALFORD 7796
Bull, half-timbered, C17(?) is a rare survival from pre-industrial town. GBG gives, among others, *Crown, Duke of York, Eagle, Star, Three Legs of Man*.

UPPERMILL 9905
Cross Keys, Runninghill Gate, a C17 inn (possibly on earlier site) in wild Pennine country. (GBG).

WIGAN 5805
Brocket Arms, commended Batchelor. *Seven Stars*, C18 or later, became popular house after construction of Leeds–Liverpool canal. Pleasing tale of how it was saved from robbery and worse by a soldier guest in 1775. GBG gives, among others, *Belle Vue, Old Pear Tree, Raven, Whitesmiths Arms*.

MERSEYSIDE

BILLINGE 5300
Holts Arms, alias 'Foot o't'Causeway', possibly C18 carriers' inn. Unspoilt in spite of being in Greater Manchester. (GBG also gives *Foresters' Arms*). Explorer might be interested in Malthouse (dated 1674) in main street.

BIRKENHEAD 3188
Pevsner singles out *Angel*, Beckwith Street, mid 1840s, and *Queens*, Park Road East, large and Italianate with stucco of early 1860s. In south of city are grandiose *Grange* and *Park* in Charing Cross, both of 1840s. Rockferry has *Royal Rock* of early C19 but soon modified twice. GBG gives *Vale*, Oxton Road, *Vittoria Vaults* on corner of Vittoria Street.

EASTHAM 3580
Ferry, large early Victorian hotel (*c.*1845) for convenience of travellers by water between Liverpool and Chester. Later 'jolly verandah and balcony' (P).

LIVERPOOL 3591
Naturally preserves a number of monumental pubs, though the one adjoining Lime Street Station (*c.*1870) has been reduced to office accommodation. Survivors include nearby *Crown* (1905), *Vines* (1900), both splendid examples of their period. *Kean's*, Park Lane, is 'an architectural riot' (P), while *Adelphi* (1912) whose conception exceeded the birth is described by P as 'stodgy'. *Prince of Wales*, Edgehill represents a large essay in Victorian Gothic. *Philharmonic* (1898–1900) has an impressive exterior with sumptuous iron gates but its climax is in the splendid interior with plaster and copper work executed with the co-operation of the University's School of Applied Art. A selection from the extensive list in GBG would include: *Beaconsfield*, a cellar pub in North Street; *Carnarvon Castle*, Tarleton Street; *Eagle*, Paradise Street; *Hole in the Wall*, which transmits beer from upstairs storage to servery via iron columns supporting roof; *68 Vauxhall Road* is apparently a nameless pub; *Villiers* alias 'Ma Shepherds'; *White Star*, alias 'Quinns'.

LYDIATE 3604
Scottish Piper, formerly *Royal Oak*. Claims 1320 origin. Renamed after 1745 rising when it sheltered a wounded piper. Near Lollies Bridge on Leeds–Liverpool canal.

PORT SUNLIGHT 3483
Bridge, Bolton Road, interesting late (1900) example of philanthropic Temperance hotel in modern industrial village. Later licensed and extended.

RABY 3179
Wheatsheaf, dated 1611, some half-timbered, thatch.

SOUTHPORT 3316
Entire town is early C19 creation with *Bold*, 1832, Georgian with Doric porch; *Prince of Wales*, *c.*1880, a large brick edifice in Gothic manner. On the promenade are *Queens* (1856); defunct *Victoria* (1842); *Claremont*, *c.*1840; dominating *Royal* converted from a slightly earlier terrace in 1854. On a smaller scale are *Zetland*, a rambling suburban pub with bowling green. (GBG which also gives town centre pubs: *Coronation, Wellington* and *Rabbit*, Manchester Road).

WALLASEY 2992
Brighton, built in 1886, described by P as 'jolly Gothic pub' in centre. GBG gives *Cheshire Cheese, Egremont Ferry, Royal Oak, Wellington.*

NORFOLK

ACLE 3910
Bridge, popular water-side old-world inn.

ATTLEBOROUGH 0485
Richardson lists *Angel, Griffin*. The latter claims an origin in C15 and was probably once a coaching inn. (GBG).

BLAKENEY 024
Blakeney Hotel, modern house situated on the quay, recommended Letts and GBG which also gives *Manor*. *White Horse* deserves a mention.

BLICKLING 1728
Buckinghamshire Arms in Richardson's list and recommended Letts who describes it as medieval.

BLOFIELD 3309
Globe, unpretentious but hospitable, overlooking A47.

CASTLE RISING 6624
Black Horse, possibly former coaching house. Curiosities include former sign preserved inside, dining room with 'stalls', servery in simulated 'tun', ceiling covered with OS maps of Scotland.

COLTISHALL 2619
Red Lion – 'C16 pub' (GBG), *Anchor* – 'Flemish-style Broads hotel'.

CROMER 2142
Old Red Lion, Victorian house on sea front. In Richardson's list and GBG which also gives *Kings Head, Wellington*.

DERSINGHAM 6830
Feathers, originally Edward VII's coach house on edge of Sandringham estate.

DISS 1179
Crown in Richardson's list. Letts recommends *King's Head*, 'mixed ancient and modern' while GBG gives *Sun*.

DOWNHAM MARKET 6003
Castle, listed Richardson, recommended Letts – a Georgian hotel. *Crown*, an attractive atmospheric inn is also in Richardson and GBG which adds *Live and Let Live*.

DRAYTON 1713
Letts makes two recommendations: *Castle*, described as medieval and *Red Lion*, 'mixed ancient and modern'.

EAST DEREHAM 9913
Kings Arms on Richardson's list. GBG gives *Coachmakers Arms, Eagle, Phoenix*.

FAKENHAM 9229
Crown, Lion, listed Richardson. GBG gives *Limes*.

GISSING 1485
Crown, renovated village pub, recommended Letts and GBG.

GREAT YARMOUTH 5207
Angel, listed Richardson, no details. *Star*, three-storeyed, timber-framed, dated from 1666, overlooks river Yare. Among GBG recommendations are *Crystal, Gallon Pot, Oliver Twist, Prince Regent* alias 'Backs', *Wellington*.

HARLESTON 2483
Swan in Richardson's list. Letts recommends *Cherry Tree*, an 'ancient pub' (also GBG which adds *Duke William*).

HEIGHAM 2209
Richardson lists *Dolphin*, unlocated.

HICKLING 4124
Pleasure Boat, snug little house with long sporting tradition, mentioned Batchelor.

HILLBOROUGH 8200
Swan, Free House with garden, GBG and recommended Letts 'mixed ancient and modern'.

HILLINGTON 7225
Ffolkes Arms, attractive Victorian pub, recommended Letts and GBG.

HOLKHAM 8944
Victoria, hotel near coast (GBG) has 'Ancient House' as annexe.

HOLT 0738
Feathers, coaching inn in C18 and stage for 'Regulator' timed to reach London three times a week in three hours. In C18–19 a cock-fighting centre with 'main' on ground floor. Listed Richardson.

HORNING 3417
Ferry, waterside inn, once operating ferry and serving wherrymen and other workers, now mainly patronised by pleasure boaters. Tradition that inn occupies site of former hostel dependent on St Benet Hulme Abbey. Alleged ghost. In Richardson's list.

HUNSTANTON 6741
Globe, Golden Lion are both listed Richardson but no details.

KING'S LYNN 6220
Duke's Head, fine example of late C17 inn, replacing older one 'for the convenience of merchants resorting to the Exchange' (Customs House which survives on quay nearby). For a long time refused customers who were not travelling in their own coach but later became Head Coaching Inn of town. Associations with Edward VII when he was Prince of Wales. Listed Richardson, together with *Globe*, recommended Letts and GBG.

LITCHAM 8817
Bull, Georgian pub recommended Letts.

NORWICH 2308
Adam & Eve, pub with garden, recommended Letts and described as medieval. *Bell*, formerly Blue Bell, unprepossessing exterior conceals four centuries of continuous life: Elizabethan timbers, Georgian staircase, Victorian and later additions. Courtyard, roofed in, is now entrance hall and former gallery is discernible. Cock-fighting centre in C18 and HQ of many clubs: anti-Methodist 'Hell Fire Club', revolutionary 'Original Club' and Conservative 'Loyal and Constitutional Club' which included Wellington among its members. Listed Richardson. *Dolphin*, dubious claims to be bishop's palace of 1595. Extended 1615. Very badly damaged in World War II and recently rebuilt. L-shaped, brick and stone mullioned windows. *Maids Head*, dates from C15 but little survives subsequent rebuilding. Coaching terminus and social centre in C18. Listed Richardson, mentioned Batchelor and recommended Letts. *Red Lion*, probably C17 but much altered in 1874. Usual tale of tunnel from cellars to neighbouring

Dominican house (remains in St Andrew's Hall). Real inglenook fireplace. *White Lion*, unpretentious old house, probably once drovers' tavern. Alleged underground tunnel from cellars to Whitefriars Bridge. *Briton's Arms, Castle, Sir Garnet Wolseley* are also listed Richardson. GBG gives more than a dozen recommendations of which we select: *Gibralter Gardens, Golden Star, Micawbers Tavern, Plasterers Arms, Ten Bells, Wherry, Wild Man.*

REEDHAM 4201

Berney Arms, in shadow of windmill behind flood banks of river Yare. Unpretentious C18(?) local, illustrated in Batchelor. *Ferry*, stone-floored with glass-fronted façade overlooking wooden quay, near working ferry. (GBG). *Lord Nelson*, village inn, overlooking Yare and fleet of small boats.

RINGSTEAD 7040

Gin Trap, old-world Free House (GBG) recommended Letts who describes it as Tudor.

ROYDON 7022

Three Horseshoes, typical small Norfolk pub with 'garneted' mortar in-filling (C17?).

SALHOUSE 3114

Bell, pub with garden recommended Letts who describes it as Tudor. *Lodge*, with extensive grounds, once former rectory. (GBG).

SCOLE 1579

Scole Inn, formerly *White Hart*, splendid coaching inn built by local merchant in 1655. Its elaborate gallows sign was one of the wonders of the age. Served Ipswich–Norwich route. Mentioned as 'masterpiece' by Batchelor, listed Richardson, recommended Letts and GBG.

SNETTISHAM 6834

Rose & Crown, makes dubious claims to C14 origin, may have been Church House. (GBG).

SWAFFHAM 8109

George, listed Richardson. Georgian, former coaching house. Garden.

SWANTON MORLEY 0117

Incorporated in *Angel* are remains of house which belonged to Abraham Lincoln's ancestors.

THETFORD 8783

Anchor, listed Richardson together with *Bell*. Latter originated as medieval college or guild and still has much C15 woodwork and remains of C16 wall-painting on upper floor. Yard survives with (converted) gallery. Exterior corner post long used for posters and proclamations (still thickly studded with nails). Mentioned Batchelor, recommended Letts. GBG gives *Thomas Paine* (unique name?).

THORNHAM 7343

Kings Head, extremely picturesque country inn, possibly once C18 coaching house. GBG gives *Lifeboat*, 'authentic old coastal pub'.

TIBENHAM 1389

Greyhound, country Free House (GBG), recommended Letts who describes it as Tudor.

TILNEY ALL SAINTS 5618

Coach & Horses, country pub, recommended Letts who describes it as Elizabethan.

WATTON 9100
Hare & Barrel, rare if not unique name. 'Friendly, well-furnished house' (GBG). Letts recommends *Chequers*, a Free House, described as medieval.

WELLS-NEXT-THE-SEA 9143
Crown, listed Richardson, recommended Letts who describes it as Elizabethan.

WEYBOURNE 1143
Maltings, flint building, possibly C16, former malthouse and dairy of manor, transformed into hotel. (GBG).

WYMONDHAM 1101
Kings Head, Georgian red brick, former coaching house. *Cross Keys*, timber-framed with overhanging upper storey, (C16?). *Green Dragon*, pretty half-timbered house with mullioned windows and overhang supported by bust of bearded man, (C16?).

YARMOUTH **see Great Yarmouth**

NORTHAMPTONSHIRE

AYNHO 5133
Cartwright Arms in Richardson's list. GBG gives *Great Western Arms*.

BARNWELL 0485
Montagu Arms, pub with garden, recommended Letts who describes it as medieval.

BRACKLEY 5837
Crown, former coaching house of C16/17 origin with good early fireplace in what is now the 'foyer'. Listed Richardson, mentioned Batchelor.

BRACKLEY HATCH 6541
Green Man, Free House, mentioned Batchelor, recommended Letts and GBG. May have C17 origins (or earlier) but much altered.

BULWICK 9694
Queens Head. Free House, recommended Letts who describes it as C17/modernised.

CASTLE ASHBY 8659
Falcon, claims C16 origin. Mentioned Batchelor.

CLOPTON 9680
Red Lion, up-marketed former country pub. Recommended Letts.

COLLYWESTON 9903
Cavalier, stone-built country inn, C18(?). Recommended Letts, GBG.

CORBY 8988
Knights Lodge, C17 oasis in C20 industrial desert. (GBG).

CREATON 7071
Bricklayers Arms, mentioned Batchelor. (Instance of longevity!)

CRICK 5872
Red Lion, village pub, recommended Letts and described as Tudor.

DAVENTRY 5762
Wheatsheaf, originally farmhouse, selling ale. Became inn in 1581. Some C17 panelling. Allegedly Charles I's HQ before disastrous battle of Naseby. Listed Richardson, together with *Saracen's Head*. GBG gives *Dun Cow*, 'modernised coaching inn'.

DEENE 9492
Sea Horse, 'an excellent example of the Restoration inn' (Batchelor), listed Richardson. Rare name.

EAST HADDON 6668
Red Lion, comfortable village hotel (GBG) Georgian?, recommended Letts.

FINEDON 9272
Old Bell, claims to be one of the earliest inn foundations in England. Conversely, P says that (new) *Bell* was built in 1872 in a 'peculiar Gothic taste'. Letts makes two recommendations: *Mulso Arms*, 'mixed ancient and modern' and *Tudor Gate*, described as Tudor. GBG gives *Prince of Wales*.

FOTHERINGAY 0593
Falcon, stone-built Free House (GBG), recommended Letts who describes it as 'mixed ancient and modern'.

GRETTON 8994
White Hart is in Richardson's list, no details. GBG gives *Hatton Arms*.

HARRINGTON 7780
Tollemache Arms, recommended Letts who describes it as medieval.

HIGHAM FERRERS 9669
Green Dragon, former coaching inn with origins in C16(?).

KETTERING 8778
George, together with *Royal* in Richardson's list, no details. Letts recommends modern *Harlequin* while among GBG offerings are *Beeswing, Prince of Wales, Three Cocks*.

LAMPORT 7574
Swan, Victorian pub recommended Letts.

LITTLE ADDINGTON 9573
Bell, recommended Letts and described as 'mixed ancient and modern'.

MARSTON ST LAWRENCE 5342
Marston, 'idyllic village local' (GBG).

MARSTON TRUSSEL 6986
Sun, small country hotel, recommended Letts.

MEARS ASHBY 8366
Griffins Head, Victorian pub, recommended Letts.

NORTHAMPTON 7561
Angel, former coaching inn in Bridge Street, once Head Inn of town. Listed Richardson, together with *Cock, Peacock, Plough, Lamb*. Recommended GBG which, among others, also gives: *Garibaldi, Headland, Pig & Whistle*.

OUNDLE 0488
Talbot, built of Cotswold stone in 1626 on older site. Described by P as 'finest building in Oundle'. Fine oak staircase is said to be from Fotheringhay castle. Attractive symmetrical frontage of two and half storeys, pretty dormers, arched entrance to yard. *White Lion*, dated 1661, former posting-house with impressive bay windows of three storeys. Both in Richardson's list.

SLIPTON 9479
Samuel Pepys, Free House, recommended Letts and described as medieval.

STOKE BRUERNE 7450
Boat, ironstone, possibly C18 or earlier. Canalside inn with appropriate decor. Fire insurance plaque on exterior wall. Interior furniture includes rare swivelling oak table. Near interesting canal museum. (GBG).

TOWCESTER 6948
Pomfret Arms, late C17 house called *Saracen's Head* until 1831. Former coaching house with Pickwickian associations. GBG, mentioned Batchelor and listed Richardson together with *Folly, Talbot*.

WEEDON 8118
Cross Roads, Victorian, Free House, recommended Letts and in GBG with cryptic note 'pharmacist's bar'. GBG also gives *Globe, Narrow Boat*.

WELDON MAGNA 9289
Kings Arms, listed Richardson, no details.

WELFORD 6480
Elizabethan, pub with licensed restaurant, recommended Letts who describes it as Elizabethan. GBG gives *Swan*, quiet canalside local.

WELLINGBOROUGH 8968
Angel, Hind in Richardson's list, no details. GBG gives *Star*.

WESTON-BY-WELLAND 7791
Wheel of Compass, uniquely named pub, recommended Letts.

WHITFIELD 6039
Sun, Cotswold stone, former small village inn developed to absorb neighbouring contemporary cottages. Retains yard. (GBG).

WOOTTON 7656
Yeoman of England, recommended Letts and described as 'mixed ancient and modern'.

NORTHUMBERLAND

ALNMOUTH 2410
Red Lion, cosy and unspoilt pub in ancient township. (GBG). Letts recommends *Saddle Grill*, 'mixed ancient and modern'.

ALNWICK 1912
Old Cross, C18, named from medieval De Vescey cross built into outer wall. One of its windows displays dusty cobwebbed bottles undisturbed for two centuries, hence its alternative name: *Dirty Bottles*. Last house in Bondgate may be remains of monastic hospice associated with Alnwick priory. According to Batchelor, *White Swan* 'has claims to recognition'. It is listed in Richardson, together with *Plough* and *Star*. *Turk's Head* is early C19 with fine ashlar-faced front and unusual projecting wing with rounded corner. Letts recommends Victorian *Rat* and GBG gives *Bird & Bush, Tanners Arms, Black Bull*.

ALWINTON 9206
Rose & Thistle, until comparatively recently an unspoilt and typical North country pub. Associations with Sir Walter Scott.

BAMBURGH 1834
Lord Crewe Arms, sea-front hostelry with fine view of castle which this C18 bishop of Durham bought and whose trustees began its reconstruction.

BREADNELL 2329
Craster Arms, old house (C17?) which was given a pretty new front in C18: two bays with coat of arms.

BEDLINGTON 2581
King's Arms, dignified pre-industrial relic. Five bays, two storeys in Georgian style. GBG gives *Sun*.

BELFORD 1033
Blue Bell, fundamentally C17 with C18 façade. Developed as coaching house on Great North Road. Retains Georgian Long Room with musicians' gallery. Framed licence of 1812. Alleged smuggling associations. Ample stabling survives, now partly occupied by clock-maker. In Richardson's list. GBG gives *Salmon*.

BELLINGHAM 8383
Black Bull, busy pub in main street. Used by walkers on Pennine Way. (GBG).

BELSAY 1078
Highlander, remote country inn built in typical vernacular style. Name not original.

BENWELL 2266
Mitre, Benwell Towers, occupies former episcopal palace, including converted library and chapel.

BERWICK-ON-TWEED 9953
Kings Arms, fine North Country essay in Georgian style which provided accommodation in heyday of coaching era. Dickens stayed here in 1861 when he gave a reading in its Assembly Room. Listed Richardson, mentioned Batchelor and GBG which also gives *Hen & Chickens*, (substantial three-storeyed building of same period but lacking venetian windows of above), *Brewers Arms, Brown Bear, Free Trade, Kings Head, Rose & Thistle*. The town has a number of attractive pub exteriors including *Ravensholm, Bridge, Red Lion*. It also possesses a fine old Malt House.

BLANCHLAND 9650
Lord Crewe Arms, originated as part of Premonstratensian abbey whose site is largely occupied and materials used by present village. Grantee of monastic property made some of its domestic buildings into a grand house, bought by Lord Crewe, bishop of Durham in 1721. There is some disagreement whether medieval parts belong to former dorter or former guest house but there is no argument about the substantial medieval elements in ground floor: immense fireplace, crypt bar. This area also contains an alleged priest's hide of Reformation period. Upper floor is largely C18. Listed Richardson, mentioned Batchelor, recommended Letts.

BLENKINSOPP 6864
Castle, occupies converted stables next to C14 castle. (GBG).

BLYTH 3181
Ridley Arms, pleasant C18 house of five bays, two storeys and pedimented porch in old centre of township.

CHOLLERFORD 9272
George, substantial stone house built around mid C18 by new bridge over North Tyne. Popular coaching inn in later C18 and earlier C19. Recommended Letts.

CORBRIDGE 9964
Angel, C17 with doorway and window of that time on earlier site, Georgian and later additions and alterations. Interesting interior details. Fine courtyard with stables developed to meet demands of coaching age when it stood at junction of routes to London, Edinburgh, Carlisle, Newcastle. Mentioned Batchelor as 'outstanding Northumbrian inn'. *Black Bull*, described as Georgian, recommended Letts. *Golden Lion*, rather austere but largely C18 and constructed from stones of Dilston Hall when it was demolished in 1768. *Wheatsheaf* (GBG) is a fine stone-built house, formerly thatched, possibly of C18. Its buildings incorporate stone from Roman site at Corstopitum.

CORNHILL-ON-TWEED 8639
Collingwood Arms, mainly Georgian, developed as posting house on Newcastle–Edinburgh route. Bar decor based on caps and crests of Guards Regiments. Recommended Letts together with *Tilmouth Castle*.

ELSDON 9393
Crown, 1729 on large village green with church on island site. *Bacchus*, an ambitious two-storeyed cottage, was formerly an inn (C18?). Sign survives.

EMBLETON 2322
Dunstanburgh Castle, attractive Victorian country inn named after Lancastrian stronghold whose gaunt ruins survive nearby. Recommended Letts.

FEATHERSTONE 6662
Wallace Arms, secluded country hotel near historic stately home. (GBG).

GREYSTEAD 6591
Moorcock, remote pub near Kielder Forest, the largest of the Forestry Commission's plantations (over 7,000 acres).

HALTWHISTLE 7064
Red Lion, incorporates a medieval border tower-house. Letts recommends nearby *Mile Castle* on Military Road, described as medieval. GBG gives *Grey Bull, New Inn*.

HEXHAM 9364
Architecturally, the pubs do not compare with other splendours of this town. *Royal* is a former coaching house of C18 with a modern brick exterior, listed by Richardson, together with *Abbey*. Batchelor mentions *County Hill*. Letts recommends *Hadrian Wall, Heart of All England*, while GBG gives *Beaumont, Mill, North British*.

HOLYSTONE 9502
Salmon, popular inn in compact and pretty village with Five Kings (alignment of standing stones), recommended Letts who describes it as medieval. Behind it is a sacred well.

HORSLEY 0966
Crown & Anchor, stone-built village pub, possibly C18. (GBG). *Lion & Lamb*, fine stone house of C18 appearance (but note shield above door) with annexe forming L-shape.

LANGLEY ON TYNE 2144
Carts Bog, cosy country inn (GBG), noteworthy for its unusual name.

LOWICK 0139
Black Bull, village local (GBG), possibly C18, distinguished by its possession of antique one-armed bandit.

MARSDEN 3669
Grotto, among claimants to 'most unusual pub', set in limestone caverns at foot of 112ft cliffs, now approachable by lift. Originated in private cheap housing in 1782, became inn early C19, modernised 1938. Claims a ghost. GBG gives *White Horse*.

MITFORD 1685
Plough, near C18 bridge over Wansbeck in beautiful scattered village.

MORPETH 2085
Black Bull, fine C18 house with dominating window of three storeys. Plaster swag above second storey window. Former coaching house which preserves C18 plaster ceiling. *Queens Head*, head inn and town posting-house in 1827. Originated in C17 when it was private house (heraldic fireplace of 1656), remodelled in C18 and later. GBG gives *Wansbeck*.

NETHERTON 9907
Star, 'unspoilt gem in isolated village, unique in area' (GBG).

NEWTON-ON-THE-MOOR 1605
Cook & Barker Arms, probably unique name. In C19 it was *Moor Cock and Barker*. Curious building, probably dating from C18 in which one section abuts rear of another, with two annexes and a dominant porch.

NORHAM 9047
Masons Arms, good C18 building with two bow windows in shadow of great episcopal fortress against Scots. (GBG which also gives *Victoria*).

OTTERBURN 8893
Percy Arms, long two-storeyed house of C18 appearance. Once coaching inn on a main Scotland route. Not far from battlefield where Percy worthily bore his arms. Private grouse moors.

PONTELAND 1672
Blackbird, mainly C17 and probably once a coaching inn. Originated as C14 fortified border house and preserves tunnel-vaulted ground floor. Substantial additions and alterations in C17 when a manor house was attached.

PRUDHOE 0962
West Wylam, oddly named town pub (GBG) in shadow of border castle.

RIDING MILL 0161
Wellington, began in 1660 as private house and became inn when Hexham–Newcastle road was diverted. As a private house it was associated with Northumbrian witch trials of later C17. Allegedly haunted. GBG gives *Riding Mill* (formerly Broomhaugh House).

ROTHBURY 0601
Railway is a recommended (GBG) pub in pleasant market town. At Rothbury Thropton is uniquely(?) named *Three Wheat Heads*.

SEGHILL 2874
Blake Arms stands on remains of medieval (C14?) fortress called Seghill Tower. Large vaulted basement of this structure now cellars of inn.

STAMFORDHAM 0772
Bay Horse in township which has preserved its village quality in spite of Newcastle's proximity. There is another good inn.

TWEEDMOUTH 9952
Harrow in main street, close to Tweed with Berwick across water. GBG also recommends lively *Thatch House* in shadow of Tweed bridge, and *Queens Head*.

WALL 9168
Hadrian, apposite but modern name – older name unknown. Possibly C17 and using some cannibalised Roman stone. Roman numbered bedrooms distinguished by Imperial portraits. Interesting collection includes weapons and Chinese objects.

WARK 8238
Battlesteads, opposite Mote Hill, C18 and earlier with cosy interior. Converted farmhouse on edge of village.

WARKWORTH 2406
Warkworth House, C18 in appearance though it is said to have been reconstructed in 1830. *Sun* is given by GBG.

WELDON BRIDGE 1398
Anglers Arms, attractive small hotel on banks of river Coquet. Many fishing associations. Basically five-bayed C18 structure with C19 castellated wing. Good modern iron sign.

WHALTON 1281
Beresford Arms, pleasant stone-built house in delightful village.

WHITTINGHAM 0611
Castle, former staging inn in now by-passed and peaceful village in vale of Aln.

WOOLER 9928
Tankerville Arms, formerly *Cottage*. Developed from a cottage ale-house to become the posting house of Wooler.

NOTTINGHAMSHIRE

ARNOLD 5745
Cross Keys, traditional pub surviving suburbanisation of old village. (GBG which also gives *Friar Tuck*).

ASLOCKTON 7440
Cranmer Arms, traditional inn in village with three rare mud cottages and earthworks of C12 castle. (GBG).

BALDERTON 8151
Grove, small hotel in suburban village with fine steepled church. (GBG).

BARNBY MOOR 6684
Old Bell, fine old inn, C17, once occupying lonely spot. Contains C17 wall panelling and ceiling from other houses. Mentioned Batchelor, listed Richardson.

BLIDWORTH 5855
Black Bull, pleasant mock-Tudor alehouse in village which was traditional birthplace of Friar Tuck. (GBG).

BLYTH 6287
Angel, fine old coaching inn near junction of A1 and A634 in village with fine, but illtreated, Norman church. (GBG).

BULWELL 5345
Framesmiths Arms, genuine local with unique(?) name. (GBG).

BUNNY 5829
Rancliffe Arms, early C18 and part of model village amenities provided by Sir Thomas Parkyns (*c*.1741).

BURTON JOYCE 6443
Lord Nelson, pleasant white-washed village pub near river Trent. (GBG).

CALVERTON 6149
Gleaners, roomy pub on edge of former stocking-knitters' village. (GBG which also gives *Cherry Tree* in adjoining mining estate).

CARLTON IN LINDRICK 6141
Riddell Arms, probably former coaching inn on side of A60 in village with important Norman church. Used to sell beer 'by the pound' (GBG). In sister village of Carlton on Trent, the once well-known C18 coaching inn *Bell* has reverted to a farmhouse.

CAUNTON 7460
Plough, updated local in attractive village with church and derelict windmill. (GBG).

CAYTHORPE 6845
Pleasant hamlet with working water-mill and *Black Horse*, C18 or earlier. Alleged Turpin associations. (GBG which also gives *Old Volunteer*).

CLUMBER PARK 6574
Normanton, an OS inn, uniquely situated in Sherwood Forest.

COLSTON BASSETT 7033
Martins Arms, 'delightful village pub of great charm' (GBG).

EAST LEAKE 5526
Bulls Head, 'done-up' traditional pub in village whose church possesses rare shawm. (GBG).

EAST RETFORD **see Retford**

EASTWOOD 4646
This is D.H. Lawrence country and Lawrence père, at least, might have been acquainted with *Greasley Castle*, late Victorian with modernised interior. (GBG which also gives *Moon & Stars, Old Wine Vaults*).

EVERTON 6891
Has a nice little church, a disused windmill and *Blacksmiths Arms*, a traditional country pub. (GBG).

FARNSFIELD 6456
White Post, described by Batchelor (1963) as 'gastronomically outstanding'.

FISKERTON 7351
Bromley Arms, attractive pub which overlooks Trent along with entire village. (GBG).

GRANBY 7536
The eponymous *Marquis of Granby* is a recommended pub in attractive village of Vale of Belvoir. (GBG).

GRINGLEY-ON-THE-HILL 7390
Blue Bell, up-marketed village pub (said to be closed weekday lunchtimes!) in magnificently situated township. (GBG). *White Swan*, Drakesholes, late C18, sited where road crosses canal to catch two kinds of traveller.

HICKLING 6929
Plough, traditional inn in village whose churchyard has interesting slate headstones. (GBG).

HUCKNALL 5349
Red Lion, traditional rural pub surviving in what has become a mining village. (GBG which also gives *Green Dragon*).

KIMBERLEY 4944
Contains Hardy & Hanson's brewery with *Nelson and Railway* close by. (GBG which also gives *Lord Clyde* 'with prominent bay windows').

KIRKBY-IN-ASHFIELD 4956
Waggon & Horses, modern pub recommended Letts.

LAMBLEY 6245
Possesses magnificently proportioned village church of mid C15 and two pubs in GBG: *Nag's Head, Woodlark*.

LANEHAM 8076
Ferry Boat, once provided passage across Trent, now largely patronised by caravaners.

LANGAR 7234
Unicorn, built 1717 from Scrope family's own brickyards.

LINBY 5350
Horse & Groom, possibly former coaching inn in one of prettiest villages of North Nottinghamshire. (GBG).

LOWER BAGTHORPE 4751
Shepherd's Rest, pretty white-washed alehouse in remote hamlet, 11m. north-west of Nottingham. (GBG).

MANSFIELD 5361
Town is mainly C19 development and pubs are correspondingly of this period e.g. GBG recommendations: *Belle Vue, Crown & Anchor, Eagle*. Near latter are C16/17 cottages which may have formed part of lost inn – *Old Cock*.

NEWARK 7953
Clinton Arms, mainly C18 and most recent of many inns on site. Old yard covered in to make Edwardian conservatory. Associations with Byron, Gladstone, Wellington. Listed Richardson, together with *Ram, White Horse*. *Ram* is a designated building of historic interest. (GBG). *Old King Arms*, possibly C18, has a fine sign. (GBG). *Saracen's Head* was a large coaching inn of C18 serving traffic on Great North Road, only yard survives. *White Hart*, 'one of paramount examples of C14 timber-framed domestic architecture' (P), no longer functions as an inn. Ossington Coffee Tavern, opposite castle is 'an architectural manifesto of the Temperance movement'. *Warburton* is an impressive four bay hotel of *c.*1700 (if it has survived). The recently refurbished *Exchange* in same street has an impressive exterior. (GBG which also gives *Newcastle Arms*, 'just what a pub should be').

NOTTINGHAM 5640
Bell with neighbouring wine-merchant's shop is *c.*1830 and a good example of the period. *Dog & Bear*, *c.*1876 is an example of what P calls 'fanciful ignorance' in architecture. *Flying Horse*, some C16 work has survived considerable rebuild. Magnificent and very extensive cellars not completely investigated. Tory house in C18. Much used by actors in C19 and possesses signed portrait of comedian Paul Bedford. Listed Richardson along with *Black Boy, George. Royal Children* is said to be C17 and where children of James II played with children of inn-keeper. Whalebone over door is old sign that whale-oil was sold on the premises. *Salutation*, 'over-carefully preserved and emphasised, but still the nearest approach in external appearance to the Nottingham of C16' (P). *Saracens Head*, renamed *Milton's Head* in early C19 seems to have been scene of early demonstration of ventriloquism by James Burns. *Trip to Jerusalem* f.1189 and one of many claimants to being oldest inn in country. In spite of much alteration it has a medieval core and ancient cellars which are said to have formed part of castle prisons. Associations with Mortimer and other criminals. Possesses ancient 'Armada' chest and preserves ancient game of 'Ringing the Bull' (GBG). *Windmill* is of C16/17 work of which much survives. Short selection from GBG: *Crystal Palace, New Market, Queens* in centre and *Lord Nelson*, Sneinton.

OLLERTON 6567
Hop Pole is a largeish pedimented C18 house which once served coaching traffic. Listed Richardson. Letts recommends *Ollerton House*, a modern pub with garden and GBG gives *White Hart*.

RETFORD 7080
P calls it 'a singularly unattractive town' but it has some interesting pubs including *Crown*, Chapelgate, early C18; *Sun*, Churchgate, probably C16. Richardson lists *White Hart*, unlocated. Letts recommends *Hop Pole* (GBG with *New Sun, Ship, Turk's Head*).

ROLLESTON 7452
Crown, rural pub in village with interesting church. (GBG).

SCREVETON 7343
Royal Oak, homely pub in small attractive village. (GBG).

SELSTON 4553
Horse & Jockey, Free House of character and antiquity near interesting church. (GBG which also gives *Miners Arms* boasting a running stream in cellar).

SOUTHWELL 7053
Saracen's Head, formerly *King's Arms*, long-fronted coaching inn of C17 or earlier with adjoining (and now incorporated) assembly room of *c.*1805. Scene of Charles I's capitulation to Scots, 1647. Listed Richardson, mentioned Batchelor, recommended Letts and GBG which also gives *Bramley Apple* named in honour of local product and *Newcastle Arms*.

STAPLEFORD 4837
Old Cross, village inn which retains small room arrangement around central bar. (GBG). 'Old cross' is in nearby churchyard and one of most important Anglo-Saxon monuments in county.

STOKE BARDOLPH 6441
Ferry Boat, former riverside local operating ferry, now popular with pleasure boaters. (GBG).

STRELLEY 5141
Broad Oak, Georgian inn in unspoilt village.

SUTTON BONINGTON 5025
Village with rare possession of two churches, also two contrasting pubs: *Anchor* and *Plough*. (both GBG).

TUXFORD 7370
Newcastle Arms, seven-bayed with porch. Georgian coaching house strategically placed at main cross roads. In Richardson's list.

UPTON 7354
Cross Keys, farmhouse-type inn which has maintained unaltered its farmhouse farm, including outbuildings and dovecote – all late C17.

WATNALL 4946
Queens Head, village pub which has retained traditional woodboarded walls and ceiling in bar. (GBG).

WEST LEAKE 5226
Star, 'splendid old coaching inn' (GBG) in village with interesting church.

WIDMERPOOL 6327
Pullman, former Victorian railway station converted into pub. Bar in old ticket office. Recommended Letts.

WILFORD 5637
Ferry, white-washed inn near church. Can be approached from Nottingham side by footbridge over river Trent. (GBG).

WISETON 7189
White Swan, late C18 inn designed as eye-catching appurtenance to Hall built 1771.

WOODBOROUGH 6347
Nags Head, attractive local in former stocking-knitters' village with interesting medieval church. (GBG).

WORKSOP 5879
Old Ship is a real medieval timber-framed house surrounded by much fakery. Richardson lists *Lion, Royal* – no details. GBG gives *Cannon, Fishermans Arms, French Horn*.

OXFORDSHIRE

ABINGDON 4997
Nags Head, basically C16/17 on attractive island site in Thames. Riverside garden. Letts makes a number of recommendations: Victorian *Black Horse, Mr Warricks Arms* (almost worth including for name alone), *White Horse* and *Upper Reaches* 'mixed ancient and modern. GBG gives *Kings Head & Bell, Beehive, Old Anchor* and *Spread Eagle*. *Crown and Thistle*, Bridge Street has a pretty cobbled courtyard with arched entrance. *Lion*, High Street, timber-framed (C17?) with two slightly projecting gabled windows. *Queens*, Market Place, 1864, red and yellow brick 'and quite unbelievedly joyless' (P). *King's Head & Bell*, 'an elegant smaller inn of the early Georgian period' (Richardson).

ARDINGTON 4388
Blue Boar, Victorian pub, occasional hunt meet, recommended Letts.

ASTON ROWANT 7299

Lambert Arms, C17 timber-framed but much refurnished. Former coaching inn. Mentioned Batchelor. Now combined with motel.

ASTON UPTHORPE 5887

Boot, small village pub (C17?) with horse-racing connections. (GBG and recommended Letts).

BAMPTON 3103

Elephant & Castle, Victorian pub recommended Letts.

BANBURY 4540

Bear, originated in a group of C15(?) cottages, unified into large private dwelling in C17 and licensed C18. *Old Reindeer* (GBG) is said to be C16 and in Richardson's list with *Red Lion, White Lion. Whateley Hall* was originally C17 house with later additions. Recommended Letts. GBG adds *Wheatsheaf, Wine Vaults*.

BECKLEY 5611

Abingdon Arms, excellent small pub in quiet picturesque village, recommended Letts who describes it as Georgian.

BENSON 6191

Castle, low, stone and red brick with pedimented doorways, preserving original C18 wrought-iron frame for inn sign. *Crowns* is dated 1709 and, with *Castle*, is in Richardson's list. *White Hart* is *c*.1820 with long, plain stuccoed front. (GBG). All these were built to serve coaching trade when village was important halt on Oxford–Henley run.

BICESTER 5822

Richardson lists *Crown* – no details.

BINFIELD HEATH 7478

Bottle & Glass, picturesque pub, possibly C16. (GBG and recommended Letts).

BLADON 4414

White Horse, modernised Victorian pub recommended Letts.

BLETCHINGDON 5017

Black Head, pub with rare name, recommended Letts and described as 'mixed ancient'.

BLOXHAM 4235

Elephant & Castle, said to be former coaching house, 'beautifully restored lounge' (GBG). Letts recommends *Joiners Arms*, described as 'mixed ancient and modern'.

BOARS HILL 4801

Fox, pub with licensed restaurant, recommended Letts: 'mixed ancient and modern'.

BRITWELL SALOME 6692

Red Lion, pleasant village pub, said to be partly C16. (GBG and recommended Letts).

BROUGHTON 4238

Saye & Sele Arms, recommended Letts who describes it as Victorian/modern.

BURFORD 2512
Lamb, traditional small town inn, probably dating from C15, 'masterpiece of Cotswold stone with its garden, another masterpiece' (Batchelor). Recommended Letts and GBG which also gives *Royal Oak*. Richardson lists *Bull*, name allegedly derived from Bull of Pope Boniface IX who, in 1397, is said to have ordered the building of the original hospice. Unfortunately for this tradition, of Burford's only two medieval hostels one was f. in 1457 and the other before 1226. Letts adds *Masons Arms, Winters Tale. Bay Tree* also claims C15 origin.

CASSINGTON 4510
Letts describes both *Bell* and *Red Lion* as medieval.

CHARLBURY 3519
Bell, Georgian. Free House. Recommended Letts: 'mixed ancient and modern'.

CHIPPING NORTON 3127
White Hart, much C16 work in rear wings whose modified galleries, outside stairs and access doorway can be seen from yard. Oak panelling in drawing room may be of this period. C17 landlord issued trade tokens. Preserves rare C18 tobacco dispenser. Listed Richardson with *Crown & Anchor*. Letts recommends *Fox*, described as Elizabethan. GBG gives *Bunch of Grapes*.

CHRISTMAS COMMON 7193
Fox & Hounds, pub with garden, recommended and described by Letts as mixed.

CLANFIELD 2801
Plough, C17 coaching house at cross-roads. Three bays, gabled dormers, mullioned windows. Modern extension at rear. Recommended Letts.

CLIFTON HAMPDEN 5495
Barley mow, low timbered and thatched building, cruck construction, dating from C14. Much of 'Three Men in a Boat' written here in late C19. Listed Richardson. GBG gives *Plough*.

CROPREDY 4646
Brasenose Arms, pub with garden, recommended and described by Letts as Tudor.

CROWMARSH 6189
Bell, recommended Letts and described as Stuart.

CULHAM 5095
Waggon & Horses, another Letts recommendation: 'mixed ancient and modern'.

CUMNOR 4604
Bear & Ragged Staff, beautifully situated traditional village inn.

DEDDINGTON 4631
Unicorn, listed Richardson. GBG gives *Crown & Tuns* 'unpretentious old coaching inn'.

DORCHESTER 5794
George may have been hospice of Augustinian abbey whose church survives opposite. Parts of structure C15. Became important coaching inn on London–Oxford route. Early galleried 'lodgings'. Fine dining room said to have been abbey brewhouse. Listed Richardson, mentioned Batchelor, recommended Letts. *White Hart* is a picturesque C17 former coaching inn with courtyard, also in Richardson's list together with *Golden Cross*.

EAST HAGBOURNE 5388
Fleur de Lis, listed by Richardson, not noticed by P. alias *Feathers*.

EAST HENDRED 4588
Letts recommends two Victorian pubs: *Plough, Wheatsheaf*.

EWELME 6491
White Hart is on Richardson's list. GBG gives *Shepherds Hut*.

FILKINS 2304
Five Alls, a Georgian house, recommended Letts. *Lamb*, unassuming, cottage-type pub in Cotswold stone with Stonesfield flags. Notable collection of corn-dollies and other curiosities.

FINSTOCK 3516
Plough recommended and described by Letts as medieval.

FRILFORD HEATH 4497
Letts has two recommendations: Victorian *Dog House*, 'mixed ancient and modern', *Noah's Ark*.

FYFIELD 4298
White Hart, originally C15 chantry house. Half-timbered and tiled. After Reformation acquired by St John's College, Oxford who turned it into tavern.

GODSTOW 4908
Trout, attractive riverside inn, roofed with Stonesfield flags. Traditionally originated as guest-house of large Benedictine nunnery (f.1133). C16 fireplace, cartoons by 'Phiz', engravings by Turner. Associations with 'Fair Rosamund' and Lewis Carroll. Listed Richardson, mentioned Batchelor, recommended Letts.

GOOSEY 3591
Pound, traditional village local (GBG), recommended Letts.

GORING ON THAMES 6080
Leatherne Bottel, popular inn with riverside terrace, dating from C16. *Miller of Mansfield*, flint and brick, name derived from first landlord to whom land was granted, according to the tale, by Henry II or III (C12/13). Recommended Letts and listed Richardson together with *Swan*, Streatley. GBG gives *Catherine Wheel* which claims to be oldest pub in town and *John Barleycorn*.

GREAT TEW 3929
Falkland Arms, early C17 with C18 improvement including oval niche dated 1728. Recently rethatched.

HENLEY 7682
Angel, may have originated in C14 hermitage. Present buildings C17, cellars incorporate span of old bridge. *Red Lion*, C17 and once Head Inn in coaching era, when it was largely rebuilt. Associations with Boswell and Johnson, Blücher and Wellington, George III and Prince Regent. Both listed Richardson together with *Bull, Catherine Wheel, Little White Hart*. Among Letts recommendations are *Beehive*, ancient/modernised; *Five Horseshoes*, *c.*1600; *Little Angel*, Tudor; *White Hart*, Georgian. GBG gives *Bull, Three Tuns*.

HOOK NORTON 3533
Gate Hangs High, C18 or earlier. Highwaymen associations. (GBG).

HORTON CUM STUDLEY 5912
Studley Priory originally large Benedictine nunnery f.C12. After dissolution in 1539 buildings were converted into private house which in turn was transformed into hotel. Some C13 and more C16 remains.

KINGHAM 2523
Langstone Arms, large building of *c.*1800, possibly with earlier foundations. Cotswold stone. Tale of underground passage from cellars to Bruern Abbey. Claims ghost.

LANGFORD 2402
Bell, Free House with garden. Recommended Letts, described as Tudor.

LAWKNOR 7197
Old Letherne Bottel, pub with garden (GBG), recommended Letts: 'Tudor'.

LONG HANBOROUGH 4214
Swan, Victorian local. (GBG and Letts). Latter also recommends *George and Dragon*, described as medieval/modernised. GBG adds *Bell*.

LONG WITTENHAM 5693
Barley Mow, small, thatched Thameside village ale-house whose end wall still shows the primitive cruck construction (C15?). Associations with Jerome K. Jerome.

MARSTON 5208
Bricklayers Arms, probably mid C17 and with Civil War associations. Perhaps name should be *Brickmakers* in memory of neighbouring brick yard, now defunct.

MIDDLE BARTON 4325
Carpenters Arms, C17 house, stone with thatched roof. Garden with ancient well. Allegedly haunted by infanticide. Recommended Letts.

MIDDLETON STONEY 5323
Jersey Arms, country inn (GBG), recommended Letts – 'medieval'.

MINSTER LOVELL 3111
Swan, Cotswold stone and oak timbering. Old well under tap-room floor. Possibly C16. Associations with Richard III. Later much used by drovers. Yorkist badge 'Sun in Splendour' occurs twice in decoration. Mentioned Batchelor, recommended Letts.

MOULSFORD 5984
Beetle & Wedge, attractive brick building from which ferry was once operated. Original of Potwell Inn in H.G. Wells: *History of Mr Polly*.

MURCOTT 5815
Walnut Tree, recommended and described as medieval by Letts.

NETTLEBED 7086
Bull, early Georgian, central pediment enclosing lunette. Former coaching house. (GBG and Letts). Also *White Hart* with fine timber work which claims C15 origins before becoming coaching house(?) in C17.

NEWBRIDGE 4101
Rose Revived, Cotswold stone walls and roof, attractive interior; fireplace with inglenooks and turnspit. Ancient site first occupied by hermit who served bridge, inn named *Chequers*, later *Rose* with adjective added after Restoration. Listed Richardson, recommended Letts and mentioned Batchelor along with *Maybush*.

NORTHMOOR 4202
Dun Cow, traditional unspoilt local (GBG) with beer carried from stillage. Recommended Letts.

NUNEHAM COURTENAY 5599

Harcourt Arms, 1765 when first Earl Harcourt demolished village to create parkland and rebuilt it on present site. Inn occupies former ecclesiastical site whose chapel may have been abolished during the 'improvement'. Little alterations except loss of thatched roof and gallows sign.

OXFORD 5106

Bear. Inns on site since C13 with many changes of name – *Tabard, Ferre's, Jolly Trooper*. Some of present building may be medieval. Collection of tie-clippings. Mentioned Batchelor. *Chequers* occupies site of religious house. Some C17 elements survive as well as medieval fragments. *Golden Cross* formerly belonged to New College and some parts are C15. Has accommodated many of famous but modernisation has totally obscured character of ancient inn. *Mitre*, C18 frontage masks largely C17 building whose cellars may be medieval. Coaching inn from C17 and long favoured by academics. Atmosphere largely destroyed by modernisation. *Turf* 'has an ancient charm' (Batchelor). *White Horse*, much altered C16 building, popular with undergraduates. (GBG which also, among others, gives *Black Boy, Bulldog, Kings Arms, Royal Oak*). Letts recommendations include *Pennyfarthing*, 'very modern'.

PISHILL 7289

Crown, originated as tavern attached to farm, rebuilt C15. Large secret room under roof associated with shelter of local recussants. Connected ghost story with inconsistent details.

ROKE 6293

Home Sweet Home, Free House, recommended Letts and described as C16. GBG gives *Horse & Harrow*, Rokemarsh, 'traditional local'.

SHELLINGFORD 3193

Bridge, double gabled with dormer and long extension (C18–19?) almost surrounded by trees but with lawn sloping down to Thames.

SHIPTON-UNDER-WYCHWOOD 2717

Shaven Crown, claimed to be most beautiful village inn in country. May have originated as guest house of Cistercian abbey at Bruern (f.1147). After dissolution became hunting-lodge, then given to parish with proviso that it provided free accommodation for penniless wayfarers. This condition is allegedly still valid. GBG gives *Lamb*.

SIBFORD GOWER 3537

Wykham Arms, traditional Cotswold pub, probably C17, recommended Letts.

SOUTH LIEGH 3908

Masons Arms, small village inn, now with restaurant. Home brew. (GBG).

STADHAMPTON 6098

Bear & Ragged Staff, pub with garden, recommended Letts – 'ancient'.

STANTON HARCOURT 4105

Letts gives *Black Horse*; GBG, *Fox*.

STEEPLE ASTON 4725

Hopcrofts Holt, C16 or possibly earlier. Associations with C17 highwayman Claude Duval, scene of C18 murder. Hunting meet. Pleasant garden. Mentioned Batchelor. GBG gives *Red Lion*, possibly C17, also recommended Letts.

STEVENTON 4691
North Star, old village pub. (GBG and Letts).

SWERFORD 3731
Masons Arms, village pub with garden, possibly C18 updated, farm implements in public bar. (GBG and Letts).

SWINBROOK 2812
Swan, riverside inn, possibly C17. (GBG and Letts).

TACKLEY 4720
Gardiner Arms, C17 building of Cotswold stone, renamed C18 to commemorate bibulous aristocratic neighbour. Motoring decor. GBG gives *Kings Arms*.

TETSWORTH 6801
Swan in Richardson's list. No details.

THAME 7006
Abingdon Arms, 'Intimate old pub in town centre' (GBG). *Bird Cage*, claims to be oldest in town. Timber-framed with additions. Curious three-storeyed tower-like projection at one end. Obscure history but claims to have existed in 1430. Allegedly haunted. Listed Richardson. *Spread Eagle*, red-brick, former coaching inn with good wrought-iron sign. Up-marketed by John Fothergill who became landlord in 1922. Mentioned Batchelor, listed Richardson together with *Black Horse*.

WALLINGFORD 6089
George & Dragon, C16, two gables and over-sailing upper floor. Interesting yard with C18 brick addition, reset C16 doorway with Venetian window above. Dubious Turpin associations. Allegedly haunted. *Lamb*, early Georgian, listed by Richardson but no longer functioning. *White Hart, c.*1500 with two gables and Gothic details below.

WANTAGE 4087
Bear, large Georgian coaching house, used by racehorse trainers. Six bays with pedimental gable and name in early C19 lettering. Gates to cobbled courtyard survive.

WEST CHALLOW 3688
Leather Bottle, Free House, recommended Letts, described as Tudor.

WEST HENDRED 4488
Hare is recommended GBG while Letts gives *Lamb*, 'curious wooden building with white wooden pillars'.

WESTON-ON-THE-GREEN 5318
Weston Manor, recently converted into hotel. Some material in C15–16 when it was resthouse of Osney Abbey. Some panelling transferred in C18. Victorian frontage and castellation. Civil War associations. Allegedly haunted. There is also *Chequers*, small village pub with thatched roof.

WITNEY 3509
Angel, excellent Georgian front on older building in Market Square where No. 46 is former *Bull* (also Georgian). *Fleece* is of same period, stucco, two bay windows and nice balcony. *Marlborough Arms* is in Richardson's list. Courage's Brewery (1841) is 'best Victorian industrial building in town' (P). GBG gives *Griffin, Red Lion*.

WOODSTOCK 4416
Bear, former coaching house, three and half storeys with central archway to yard. Extended to incorporate neighbouring houses. One room allegedly haunted. Listed Richardson. Among Letts recommendations are *Duke of Marlborough*, C17; *Shepherds Hall*, medieval/modernised and *Queens Own*, renovated Victorian. (GBG).

WOOTTON 4319
Killingworth Castle, recommended Letts 'mixed ancient'; GBG gives *Kings Head*, village local.

SHROPSHIRE

ALBRIGHTON 8103
Shrewsbury Arms, opposite churchyard, timber-framed with patterned brick infillings (C16?). *Horns*, Victorian pub with garden. Recommended Letts.

ANCHOR 1785
Anchor, 'C16 inn' (GBG).

ASTON MUNSLOW 5086
Swan, timber-framed C16 with several cottages of same period.

ASTON-ON-CLUN 3981
P mentions *Kangaroo*, 'mildly Gothic' (C18?).

ATCHAM 5409
Mytton and Mermaid, finely situated coaching inn in red brick: seven bays, two and half storeys. Early C18 with large modern sculpture of mermaid in adjoining yard.

BECKBURY 7601
Seven Stars, comfortable pub in quiet village with remains of C18 cockpit concealed by holly hedge near church. (GBG).

BISHOPS CASTLE 3288
Castle, 1719, stone, seven bays and two storeys. Panelling and original staircase survive. Recommended Letts. GBG gives *Three Tuns*, 'excellent pub with its own brewery'.

BRIDGNORTH 7193
Castle, fine timber-framed hotel of mid C17 with overhang supported by four little caryatids. (GBG). *Crown*, early C19 brick façade masks older building. Three Venetian windows on second floor. Listed Richardson with *Falcon*. *Black Boy* is a typical early C18 inn. *King's Head* (Richardson's King's Arms?) is fine timber-framed inn of C16/17, recommended Letts. *Raven*, is simpler and lower, dated 1646: Carved brackets below first floor window. *Swan*, fine timber-framed inn of mid C17. Listed Richardson. GBG gives *Harp, Railwaymans Arms, Shakespeare, Vine*.

BURFORD 5768
Swan, former riverside coaching house, main road at Tenbury turning. Georgian with big bow window and later additions.

CHESWARDINE 7129
Letts recommends *Wharf*, 'Georgian/modernised'.

CHIRBURY 2598
Herbert Arms, timber-framed (C17?) with typical black and white façade of locality.

CHURCH STRETTON 4593
Church Stretton Hotel, 1865 with later additions, situated at main crossing of High Street, 'debased Gothic with unusual roof and porch' (P). *King's Arms*, timber-framed (C17?), in GBG. '*The Cottage*', of same period, is former *Talbot*. Richardson lists *Longsword* – no details.

CLAVERLEY 9993
Kings Arms and *Plough*, both brick painted white are locals in 'rare example of village which has developed without losing its essential character'. (Sir Jasper More).

CLEOBURY MORTIMER 6775
Old Lion, (C17?), GBG and Letts who also recommends *Talbot*, Georgian impression but originally timber-framed house of *c.*1600, former coaching house, 'best kind of English inn'. GBG adds *Bell*.

CLUN 3081
White Horse, C16 market-place inn much altered and added to. GBG gives *Sun*. Nearby *Anchor* on edge of Clun forest has given name to locality.

COUND 5504
Cound Lodge, late C17 brick with two gables.

CRAVEN ARMS 4382
Example of township taking name from inn lying at junction of Hereford–Shrewsbury route and road to central Wales. *Craven Arms* is dated *c.*1830, three bays, Tuscan porch and pilasters.

DITTON PRIORS 6089
Howard Arms, recommended Letts and described as Elizabethan.

EDGMOND 7119
Lamb, Victorian pub recommended Letts.

ELLESMERE 3934
Black Lion, in Richardson's list, no details. *White Hart* is 'a pretty timber-framed house with much diagonal strutting on upper floor' (P), probably oldest pub in Shropshire. (GBG which also gives *Railway*).

GRINSHILL 5223
Elephant & Castle, early Georgian, stone, five bays.

HODNET 6128
Bear, probably former coaching inn, provides focal point of village at junction of two main roads. 'black and white' opposite church.

IRONSIDE 6703
Letts mentions *Swan* whose licensee has recently opened Malthouse, licensed restaurant. GBG gives riverside *Bird in Hand*.

LEEBOTWOOD 4798
Pound, picturesque thatched house with many gables and chimneys, probably indicating development (from C17?) which has incorporated neighbouring buildings. Recommended Letts.

LITTLE STRETTON 4491
Ragleth and *Green Dragon* mark north and south limits of original village at either end of main street. Note also Malt House.

LLANYBLODWEL 2322
Horseshoe, partly C16, beautifully situated where ancient bridge crosses river Tanat.

LLANCAIR WATERDINE 2476
Red Lion, attractive country inn with fishing. Claims to be C14.

LOPPINGTON 4629
Blacksmiths Arms, 'superb country pub' (GBG) though opening hours are irregular. Rare bull-baiting ring preserved in road outside other pub.

LUDFORD 4873
Old Bell, partly timber-framed house of 1614. *Ludlow Arms* is C17 and timber-framed with remains of ancient five courts.

LUDLOW 5175
Angel, with bold bow-shaped oriels of C18, former coaching house, also in Richardson's list as is *Bull*, whose discreet early C19 front masks older building, C17 or earlier, visible from yard. (GBG). There is also *Old Bull*, one of best buildings in Bull Ring, in two sections one of two storeys, the other of three (C17?). GBG adds *Blue Boar, Church, George, Wheatsheaf. Feathers*, half-timbered, gabled, claims to be among first licensed inns. Magnificent timber façade. Good interior panelling and plaster ceilings. Dated 1603. Listed Richardson, mentioned Batchelor.

MARKET DRAYTON 6734
Corbet Arms, late Georgian, three bays and porch, listed Richardson. *Crown*, earlier coaching inn, timber-framed, C17. *Star*, timber-framed, two gables and porch, dated 1669. GBG gives *Elephant & Castle, Sandbrook Vaults*, dated 1653, *Stags Head*.

MORVILLE 6694
Acton Arms, step-gabled, dormers, brick, unusual fenestration, C18? Allegedly haunted.

MUCH WENLOCK 6199
Gaskell Arms, late C18, former coaching inn, listed Richardson. At angle of churchyard is *Church House*, timber-framed, C15/16. *Old Raven* has a remarkable wrought-iron sign bracket, mentioned Batchelor. GBG gives *Royal Oak, Talbot*.

NEWPORT 7419
Richardson lists *Barley Mow*, no details. P notices *Royal Victoria*, ashlar-faced, probably of *c.*1830, two and half storeys, five bays. GBG gives *Kings Head*.

NORTON 4581
Letts recommends interestingly-named *Hundred House*, Victorian with garden.

OSWESTRY 2829
Wynnstay, formerly *Wynnstay Arms* and earlier *Cross Foxes*, part of Wynnstay Arms are delineated on ceiling centre-piece of Assembly Room. Georgian reconstruction as coaching inn serving traffic on Holyhead road and became Head Inn. Visited 1832 by Duchess of Kent and daughter (late Queen Victoria). Preserves roasting jack and some good Georgian furniture. Bowling green at rear which gave name to inn in mid C18. Listed Richardson. *Old Vaults*, preserves good early Victorian shop front. GBG gives *Black Lion, Oak*.

REDNAL 3628
Hare & Hounds, timber-framed pub (C17?) situated by side of A38 at foot of Lickey Hills.

RUYTON OF THE ELEVEN TOWNS 3922
Bridge, country pub in delightful surroundings (GBG) in village whose name derives from fact that in C12 eleven townships were united in one manor.

SHIFNAL 7407
Nags Head, timber-framed house (C16?). GBG gives *Anvil, Union*.

SHREWSBURY 4912
Golden Cross, timber-framed with a marked overhang to first floor is probably early C16. *Kings Head*, also timber-framed and picturesquely twisted, has a sign (unusually) portraying head of Henry VIII but inn is older and may even be C15. Listed Richardson. *Lion*, partly C15 but greatly remodelled and extended in C18 when one of its landlords diverted Holyhead turnpike to bring trade. Magnificent ballroom (Adams) in which de Quincey slept when bedrooms were full (also used as ATS dormitory in World War II). Dickens associations. Mentioned Batchelor and listed Richardson with *Crown, Dun Cow, Plough, Post Office, Raven. Prince Rupert*, a rare name, is early C17 with irregular gables and original staircase. *Unicorn*, (GBG listed Richardson) is timber-framed and C16 or earlier (some of houses in this street are undoubtedly C15). Nos. 15–16, Grope Lane represent C17 Cross Keys. GBG recommendations include *Acorn, Albert, Boat House, Shrewsbury Arms* alias *Loggerheads*.

TONG 7907
Bell, pleasant inn with restaurant in attractive village. (GBG).

WELLINGTON 6411
Richardson lists *Charlton Arms, Wrekin* but no details. GBG gives *Bucks Head, Queens*.

WEM 5129
Castle, High Street hotel, C19? (GBG) listed Richardson with *White Horse*. GBG adds *Dickin Arms*.

WENTNOR 3892
Crown, Free House, recommended Letts.

WESTON 5829
Hawkestone Park, former late C18 private house, seven bay façade, pedimented, two and half storeys high.

WHITCHURCH 5441
P notices Georgian *Hughes's*, three bays, two and half storeys with single-storeyed wings. Richardson lists *Swan*, Letts recommends *Victoria* and GBG gives *Old Eagles, Old Town Hall Vaults*.

WHITTINGTON 3230
Old Boot, updated and up-marketed former country inn in village with remains of early C13 castle. Also *White Lion*.

WOORE 7242
Coopers Arms, attractive pub with unique collection of cooper's tools. *Swan*, late C19, three bays and Tuscan porch, former coaching inn. (GBG).

SOMERSET

AXBRIDGE 4254
Lamb, early C19, former coaching inn, listed Richardson.

BECKINGTON 7951
Woolpack, good pub (GBG) in village 'uncommonly rich in worthwhile stone houses' (P). '*Abbey*' was probably originally a hospice of Austin Canons f.1502.

BICKNOLLER 1039
Bicknoller, attractive pub in very pretty village, recommended Letts who describes it as medieval.

BILBROOK 8703
Dragon House, former private residence of *c*.1700, now hotel, recommended Letts.

BISHOPS HULL 2024
Old Inn, traditional village pub, recently enlarged. (GBG). Letts recommends *Cavalier*, described as Tudor/Georgian.

BLAGDON 7898
New Inn, attractive village pub with superb views over Blagdon Lake. (GBG).

BLAGDON HILL 2118
Holman Clavel, name allegedly derived from words meaning 'holly cutters recess'. Originally church property and traditionally hospice belonging to Glastonbury abbey. Now owned by local council. Preserves skittle alley. Recommended Letts. GBG gives *White Lion*.

CASTLE CARY 6332
George, thatched former coaching inn, partly built from cannibalised stones of demolished castle.

CHARD 3208
Choughs, originally C17 private house, used as lodging by Judge Jeffreys, some of materials earlier. Claims several ghosts. *George* is former coaching house, Georgian with impressive Tuscan porch, listed Richardson. Nearby Lloyds bank was built in 1849 as hotel. *Victoria* maintains Victorian theme in furniture and fittings. Letts recommends nearby *Windwhistle*, modern. P notices *Crown's* 'nice Egyptian lettering'.

COMBE FLOREY 1531
Farmers Arms, possibly C16, drink served direct from cellars. Notable collection of horse brasses and other interesting ornaments including old clock. (GBG).

CORFE 2319
Bankes Arms, possibly a former small coaching house. *Greyhound*, white-washed Purbeck stone, slate roof, dormer windows, possibly C17. Porch, straddling street, added 1733. Coach stop on Swanage route. Hardy associations. Listed Richardson, mentioned Batchelor. (GBG).

CREWKERNE 4409
George, a nice late Georgian house, built to serve coaching trade. Listed Richardson, recommended Letts along with *Red Lion*.

CRICKET ST THOMAS 3708
Windwhistle, unpretentious pub with old-world atmosphere. Adjacent to wildlife park. Façade dominated by shutters.

CROSCOMBE 5844
Bull Terrier, unusually named pub, recommended GBG and Letts who describes it as Tudor.

CROWCOMBE 1336
Church House, South-west of church. Given to parish in 1515. Early Tudor doorway, Jacobean mullioned windows. Restored, but not as ale-house! Letts recommends *Carew Arms*.

DITCHEAT 6236
Manor House, noticed by P: 'pretty three-bay Gothic Revival façade of *c.*1800'. Red brick, pointed windows.

DULVERTON 9127
Lamb, late Georgian coaching inn, five bays, three storeys, ionic porch. There is also the former Lion, C16/17 village inn. *Carnarvon Arms* is solid and spacious sporting hotel with private fishing, etc.

DUNSTER 9943
Luttrell Arms, formerly Ship. Core is C15 hall formerly belonging to abbot of Cleeve, probably summer or rest house – see Abbey Explorer. This hall is substantially intact. Lower chamber functioned for many years as kitchen when house became inn. Porch and front rooms (with magnificent plaster work) of late C16/early C17 when house may have been in private use of Luttrell family who had acquired most of monastic property. Renamed 1779. Listed Richardson, mentioned Batchelor, recommended Letts with *Castle*.

EAST COKER 5312
Helyar Arms, originally 1491, rebuilt 1834, in an attractive village associated with T.S. Eliot.

EMBOROUGH 6151
Old Down, claims C16 origin, certainly posting house C18 and accommodated franking office for mails from ports – known as *Post Town* in C19. Free House. Recommended Letts, GBG.

EVERCREECH 6438
Pecking Mill, (C16?) with 'wonderful collection of nick-nacks' (GBG). Recommended Letts. Mill is Georgian, 'treated with some dignity' (P).

EXFORD 8538
White Horse, originally C16?, situated at crossing of Exe, now stone bridge. (GBG). *Crown*, attractive small hotel with hunting, shooting and fishing.

FROME 7747
George, was Head Inn in early C19 when it belonged to Lord Cork. Mentioned disparagingly in letter to Thomas Carlyle (9 Aug. 1842). Listed Richardson, together with *Crown*, C17 with gables and mullioned windows. GBG gives, among others, *Masons Arms, Ship, Three Swans*. There is an Old Church House in Church Steps and P notices *Packhorse*, early Georgian and *Swan*, probably C19.

GLASTONBURY 4938
George & Pilgrim, built *c.*1475 as hostel for pilgrims to abbey and 'one of the most sumptuous of the small number of surviving English inns of before the Reformation' (P). Stone faced, three storeyed with stone newel staircase and some original panelling. Mentioned Batchelor and in Richardson's list with *Crown*, small market-place hotel, once a coaching house. GBG gives *Beckets*.

HATCH BEAUCHAMP 3020
Hatch, old house on side of A358. Listed building.

HENLADE 2623
Blackbrook, C17? Attractive roof-line and fenestration broken by irregularly placed deer-antlers. Formerly housed manorial court.

HENSTRIDGE 7219
Virginia, claims to be where smoking Walter Raleigh was doused with a stoup of beer by his anxious servant.

HINTON ST GEORGE 4212
Poulett Arms is a noteworthy inn.

HOLFORD 1541
Alfoxton Park, Queen Anne private house of seven bays two storeys, pedimented, recently converted to hotel. Wordsworth lived here in 1797 when Coleridge visited and they planned Lyrical Ballads.

HOLTON 6826
Old Inn, probably C18 but feels older, originally blacksmiths. (GBG).

ILMINSTER 3614
George, market-square inn of C17, later rebuilt as C18 coaching house. Said to be first hotel visited by Queen Victoria. Listed Richardson. GBG gives *Shrubbery*, *Bell* with mullioned windows (C17?) noticed by P.

KILMERSON 6952
Joliffe Arms, attractive Georgian house.

LANGPORT 4226
Langport Arms, formerly *Swan*. Began as C15 merchant's house of which a fine room survives in present lounge. Inn by C17 when it was owned by Corporation and housed visiting Puritan ministers. Later developed and refronted in C18 when it was busy posting-house on London–Devon route. Vague associations with Judge Jeffreys and aftermath of Sedgemoor. *Market House*, noticed by P – C18 inn.

LITTON 5954
Kings Arms, probably formed from two cottages, castellated porch added later. Claims to have housed fleeing Charles II. Unusual sign. Magnificent settle and rare 'Tippet' table for game similar to, but more complicated than, Shove Ha'penny. (GBG and Letts).

LONG SUTTON 4625
Devonshire Arms, pleasant pub in architecturally interesting village.

LYNG 3328
Rose & Crown, originally farmhouse made from two (C16?) cottages. Favourite shop for waggons and packhorses from C17. Fine oak panelling, Parliament clock. Beamed ceiling with unusual pattern. Stone mask inset in fireplace allegedly represents King Alfred.

MARTOCK 4619
George, attractive house of Georgian appearance, former coaching inn. Recommended Letts and described as Tudor.

MELLS 7249
Talbot, former coaching house (GBG) in attractive village replanned as model township in 1470.

MERRIDGE 2034
Letts recommends *Tavellers Rest*, described as medieval.

MILBORNE PORT 6718
Queens Head, Georgian pub with garden, recommended Letts.

MINEHEAD 9746
Plume of Feathers, (GBG), C19, listed Richardson with *Wellington*. GBG adds *Beach*. On Bridgwater Road (A39) is *Plough*, allegedly C15 and extended C17. Claims ghost of murdered guest.

MONTACUTE 4916
Philips Arms, mainly Georgian house owned by National Trust. GBG and recommended Letts with *Kings Arms*, described as Tudor/Victorian.

NORTON FITZWARREN 1925
Ring o' Bells, backing on to Taunton cider works, recommended GBG. Letts gives Victorian *Rose Cottage*.

NORTON ST PHILIP 7755
George, early C15, former hospice of Carthusian priory at Hinton. Upper floor used by wool-merchants, rebuilt *c.*1500 after fire. Original form best seen from rear. 'One of the most remarkable medieval inns in England' (P). Listed Richardson, mentioned Batchelor, recommended Letts. In GBG with *Fleur de Lys*, allegedly haunted.

PANBOROUGH 4745
Panborough Inn, 'C17 pub, carefully restored' (GBG).

PORLOCK 8846
Ship, picturesque and cosy village inn, surrounded by fine group of cottages. Near notorious Porlock Hill. (GBG) and listed Richardson.

PRIDDY 5250
Castle of Comfort, unusually named pub near many prehistoric monuments. GBG gives isolated *Hunters Lodge*.

SEAVINGTON 4015
Volunteer, pleasant pub with 'gay and arresting signboard'.

SHEPTON MALLET 6143
Hare & Hounds, listed Richardson – no details. *Crown* was built *c.*1800 as coaching inn. Letts recommends *Charlton House*, Victorian hotel with garden. GBG gives *Old Red Lion* (formerly Stage Coach) and *Field*, on edge of town.

SOMERTON 4828
Half Moon, Victorian pub with garden, recommended Letts. *Red Lion*, C18, 'the most ambitious of the inns of the town', placed in market place which is 'one of the most happily grouped urban pictures in Somerset' (P). GBG. *Unicorn* with two storeyed porch is perhaps Tudor and *White Hart* is said to incorporate some masonry and vaults of castle.

STEMBRIDGE, Nr. Martock 4619
Rusty Axe, unusually named pub with thatched roof, recommended Letts.

STOKE ST MICHAEL 6646
Knatchbull Arms, mullioned windows, gabled dormers, late C17.

STOKE SUB LAMDON 4717
Fleur de Lis, ancient inn with behind it a rare survival of old fives court.

STREET 4836
Street Inn, traditional village local which has managed, in spite of modernisation, to retain its skittle alley. *Bear* is dated 1894. .

TAUNTON 2324
Castle is said to date from C17 and has sheltered many members of Royal family. Listed Richardson, mentioned Batchelor. Letts recommends *Cottage*. GBG adds *Alma, Harp, Royal Mail, Turks Head, Westgate. County*, formerly *London* and once one of most important coaching inns in West Country. Largely rebuilt C18, with additions of 1820. Assembly Room survives as residents' lounge. Old Tap Room has recently been upmarketed to 'Gun Room' in imitation of country house. (GBG).

WALTON 4636
Pike & Musket, roadside inn with unassimilated annexe which adds to character. Name may be dim echo of Sedgemoor.

WASHFORD 0441
Dragon House, hotel with restaurant. Free House, recommended Letts and described as Tudor. GBG adds *Washford Hotel*.

WELLS 5445
Crown, C15? timber-framed building of three storeys, gabled, best seen from yard, itself interesting. William Penn associations. Coffee House in C18. *Red Lion* is a former coaching house, Georgian, listed Richardson, recommended Letts, who also gives *Kings Head*, another High Street Georgian inn in appearance but with C15 material, and *White Hart*, described as medieval. Richardson also gives *Mitre, Star* and Batchelor mentions *Cheddar Gorge*. GBG gives *Full Moon. Swan* is largely Georgian and a former coaching house, listed Richardson, mentioned Batchelor and recommended Letts.

WEST COKER 5113
Royal George, dated *c.*1584, recommended Letts, GBG.

WEST HUNTSPILL 3147
Crossways, recommended Letts and described as Tudor.

WEST PENNARD 5438
Red Lion, attractive building of local stone and slate, organised in L-shape, possibly C17. Letts recommends *Apple Tree*, 'mixed ancient and modern'.

WINCANTON 7128
Bear, 1720, former coaching house with contemporary wrought-iron bracket. *Greyhound*, early Georgian, Doric archway with canted bay window above, 'pretty wrought-iron bracket' (P). Both in Richardson's list and former recommended Letts with *Holbrook House*, 'Georgian' and *Hunters Lodge*, 'Tudor'. *Dolphin*, sophisticated C18 former coaching inn. *White Horse*, 1733, two storeys, 'especially ornate' coaching inn.

WINSFORD 9034
Royal Oak, very picturesque, white-washed, heavily thatched (even porches). Romantic idea of typical English inn, sited by village green and with open-air skittle alley. Listed Richardson, illustrated Batchelor.

WOOKEY 5145
Ring o' Bells, old house, possibly medieval, recommended Letts along with *Pheasant*, 'mixed ancient and modern'.

WRAXALL 4871
Queens Arms, C18 house in attractive village and near recently re-established vineyards. Letts recommends *Widdicombe Arms*, Free House, described as medieval.

YEOVIL 5515
Church House, across churchyard, has Georgian façade of five bays in brick. *George*, timber-framed C16 house of two storeys with two oversailing bays. *Half Moon*, seems Georgian with nice wrought-iron sign bracket. *Mermaid*, 'an entertaining Gothic version of the classical theme of an inn archway with a Venetian window above' (P). *Penn Mill*, Georgian, recommended Letts. *Three Choughs*, attractive Georgian building bearing date 1724. These last three are all in Richardson's list. *Manor*, also Georgian, give bays with recessed five bay stables. GBG gives *Fleur de Lys, Great Western, Somerset, Yellow Wagtail*.

STAFFORDSHIRE

ABBOTS BROMLEY 1170
Goats Head, probably early C17, timber-framed with typical West Midland panelling.

ALTON 0742
White Hart, makes dubious claims to be C12 but certainly old and building may have medieval elements (former Church House?). (GBG).

BISHOPS OFFLEY 7729
Old Brown Jug, traditional village pub with interesting sign. (GBG).

BLYTH BRIDGE 1345
White Cock, maintains the tradition of an associated bowling green, in this case located at rear of pub.

BURTON UPON TRENT 2423
Abbey, half-timbered, gabled and pinnacled, parts dating to C12. Memento of ecclesiastical origins of Burton's brewing fame. *Coopers*, a tavern without a bar where beer is served direct from casks on stillage. *Swan*, imposing C19 house with oriel window. Richardson lists *White Hart*, no details. Bass Museum, Horninglow Street, is in former, mid C19 joiners' shop of the brewery. A must for those interested in beer and brewing. According to A.E. Housman, brewing is the town's raison d'etre and Bass Brewery dominates High Street. Brewing seems to have originated with abbey (f.1004) of which there are some remains. GBG gives *Gladstone, Leopard, Union*.

CHURCH EATON 8417
Swan, Victorian pub recommended Letts.

CODSALL WOOD 8405
Cross Guns, modern pub recommended Letts.

COSELEY 9464
Old Bush, traditional local, now affected by subsidence. Allegedly haunted. (GBG).

ECCLESHALL 8329
Crown, Kings Arms are in Richardson's list. GBG gives *Bell, Railway. George & Dragon*, Victorian, recommended Letts. Three inns encroach on High Street to form a covered arcade.

ELLASTONE 1143

Bromley Arms, said to be original of Donnithorne Arms in George Eliot's 'Adam Bede'.

HIGH OFFLEY 7826

Anchor, rare example of unaltered waterside pub, communicating its classical past into present. (GBG).

KINGSWINFORD 8888

Crooked House (Glynne Arms) is a curious old inn distorted by subsidence. Listed Richardson, mentioned Batchelor.

KINVER 8483

Whittington, allegedly originated as manor house of grandfather of future lord mayor of London in 1310. 'C16, timber-framed, symmetrical with two gables and a gabled porch' (P). Lady Jane Grey is said to have stayed as a child and ghost is said to haunt house. There is a priest's hide, secret chapel and underground tunnel. Queen Anne was a guest here in 1711. Became inn *c.*1800. Appurtenances of bull-baiting survive. Last man to be gibbeted in England was arrested here in early C19. (GBG which also gives *Cross, Elm Tree, Vine*). *White Hart*, gabled, brick, 1660.

LEEK 9856

Richardson lists *George, Red Lion* – no details, though latter is said to be oldest inhabited building in town. (GBG). Unusually named *Jester at Leek* has some of its rooms built into the rock (GBG which also gives *Talbot*). At nearby Blackshaw Moor on A53 is *Three Horseshoes*, a half-timbered inn (C17?) with coaching associations. Mentioned Batchelor.

LICHFIELD 1209

Angel in extensive grounds near cathedral, formerly a Georgian private house. *Duke of York*, 'old beamed pub near market' (GBG). *George & Dragon* is a typical unassuming small town local; *George*, Bird Street is a former coaching inn (C17–18), associations with playwright George Farquarson. Listed Richardson. In same street is *Kings Head* with its local regimental associations and memorabilia (GBG and Richardson's list, as is *Swan*, old coaching inn, originating in C17 and with Johnsonian associations). Richardson also gives *Four Crosses*, unlocated. GBG adds *Queens Head*, Queen Street.

LONGNOR 0864

Crewe & Harpur Arms, Georgian coaching inn, brick with stone quoins in gritstone township.

LONGSDON 9554

GBG gives two: *Hollybush*, canalside, *New Inn*, country local.

LONGTON 9043

Richardson lists *Crown & Anchor* – no details. GBG gives *George & Dragon, Halfway House, Red Gate*.

MIDWAY 3020

Wheel, attractive cluster of roofs at varying levels, almost appears back to front. Former coaching house on Ashby–Burton route.

NEWCASTLE-UNDER-LYME 8445

Borough Arms in Richardson's list – no details. GBG gives, among others, *Boat & Horses, Castle Mona, Golden Lion, Syd's Bar*, Church Street.

ONECOTE 0555
Jervis Arms, smartened-up country pub with good atmosphere. (GBG).

OUTWOODS 7818
Village Tavern (GBG) – just that and among competitors for smallest pub.

PENKRIDGE 9214
Richardson lists *Littleton Arms, White Hart*, one of loveliest half-timbered inns in West (also mentioned Batchelor). GBG gives *Cross Keys*.

RAWNSLEY 0112
New Inn alias 'Rag', small country local. (GBG).

ROLLESTON ON DOVE 2327
Brookhouse, (GBG), licensed restaurant and bar in converted barn. *Spread Eagle*, basically two houses at right angles to each other, gabled and barge-boarded. Roadside section gives C17/18 impression. Picturesque setting.

RUGELEY 0418
Richardson lists *Shrewsbury Arms. Red Lion*, may be mid C17 and former coaching inn. (GBG).

SEIGHFORD 8725
Holly Bush, recommended Letts: 'mixed ancient and modern'.

SHENSTONE 1004
Bull's Head, recommended Letts: 'mixed ancient and modern'.

SMETHWICK 0288
Cock & Magpies, house formed by conversion of two (C17?) cottages. Unusual name. GBG gives *George*, near Cape Hill brewery.

STABLEFORD 7598
Cock, recommended Letts: 'mixed ancient and modern'.

STAFFORD 9223
Station was built in 1866. *Swan*, ancient hotel but much altered. Retains part of Jacobean staircase and medieval cellars. Associations with George Borrow, Charles Dickens. Listed Richardson together with *Vine*. GBG gives, among others, *Chains, Coach & Horses, Greyhound* alias 'House of Doors', *Malt & Hops*. Batchelor mentions *White Lion*, Foregate: 'once the hospital of St John Baptist'.

STAPENHILL 2521
Barley Mow, unpretentious but interesting building.

STOKE 8745
North Stafford, former station hotel, early C19, recommended Letts. GBG gives, among others, *Beehive, Jolly Potters, Victoria* of 1900 and biggest hotel of its time.

STONE 9034
Darlaston, modern pub recommended Letts. GBG gives *George & Dragon, Red Lion, Star* – 'gem of a canalside pub'. *Crown* is former coaching inn.

STONNALL 0603
Old Swan, old and traditional village pub, recently up-marketed.

STOWE BY CHARTLEY 0028
Cock, unspoilt country pub. (GBG).

STRETTON 2526
Anglesey Arms, large village pub by side of former green. GBG gives *Beech*.

SWYNNERTON 8435
Fitzherbert Arms, small inn set in heart of village and of Fitzherbert country.

TAMWORTH 2004
Castle and *Peel Arms* are both listed Richardson but unlocated. Among others, GBG gives *Bull's Head, Gate* with canalside garden, *Tam o' Shanter*.

TUNSTALL 8551
White Hart – 'a converted one room hostelry' (GBG).

TUTBURY 2129
Old Dog & Partridge – three-storeyed with dormers, stone and timber-framed, oversailing upper floor. Picturesque inn of C16/17. GBG gives *Leopard*.

UTTOXETER 0933
Black Swan, interesting old pub with largely unmodified interior. (GBG which also gives *Plough, Vaults*). *White Hart*, former coaching inn with porch across pavement, seems C18 but façade may conceal older building. Listed Richardson.

WALSALL 0198
White Hart, Caldmore Green, possibly C17 and may have originated in converted C16 manor house. Associations with 'Hand of Glory' and allegedly haunted. GBG gives, among others, canalside *Barley Mow, Duke of Wellington, Fitters Arms,* uniquely named *Hamemakers Arms, Queen Street Tavern,* Edwardian *White Lion*.

WATERHOUSES 0850
Jean Pierre, uniquely named Free House, recommended Letts: 'Georgian'.

WEST BROMWICH 0091
Manor House, mainly of C14 and C16, 'more eloquent than most' (P), due to co-operation of local council and Ansell's brewery who have adapted it to an inn and restaurant. GBG gives *Flower Pot, Leopard, Royal Oak*.

WOLSELEY BRIDGE 0220
Wolseley Arms, 'country-style' pub in central location.

WOLVERHAMPTON 9198
Mitre, one time village pub near former green (GBG which also gives, among others, *Clarendon, Combermere Arms, Posada, Swan* (with match box collection), *Wheatsheaf.*) Letts recommends *Westacres*, Finchfield Hill.

WOMBOURN 8793
Vine, village inn, modern(ised?). GBG and Letts.

YARNFIELD 8632
Labour in Vain, pleasant, hospitable pub in rural setting.

SUFFOLK

ALDEBURGH 4656
Cross Keys, recommended Letts and described as medieval. Also *Mill*, 'mixed ancient and modern' and Victorian *Wentworth*. Richardson lists *Railway*, no details. GBG gives gas-lit *White Hart* and *White Lion*, described as C16 with oak-beamed and oak-panelled dining room.

BARTON MILLS 7273
Bull, old coaching inn on A11. Retains yard. C18.

BECCLES 4290
Kings Head, C18, red brick, two and half storeys. Archway into yard. Former coaching house. *Loaves and Fishes*, converted maltings on quay with rare name. (GBG). *Waveney House*, early C18 façade of knapped flint with stone trim. Back is somewhat earlier. Undulating wall ('crinkle-crankle') is characteristic of county.

BILDESTON 9949
Crown, massive timbered structure, formerly wool-merchant's house. Handsome but much restored, Late C15. Recommended Letts. *Kings Head* impressive frontage of early C19 (?), with pediment on thickly carved brackets. GBG gives *Red Lion.*

BLYTHBURGH 4575
White Hart, said to have originated in connection with small priory of Austin Canons, cell of St Osyths but there seems no evidence. Building has indications of late medieval work. (Letts and GBG).

BROME 1376
Oaksmere, former private house, probably late C16, in magnificent grounds. Recommended Letts and GBG.

BUNGAY 3389
Fleece, ancient inn claiming to be C16 (GBG). *Kings Head*, large market-place hotel on A143, probably former coaching house, listed Richardson and GBG.

BURY ST EDMUNDS 8564
Angel, complicated history. C18 façade hides some medieval material. It is said to have been built as abbey hospice in 1452, developed as coaching house and substantially rebuilt 1779, absorbing neighbouring hotel in 1963. Dickens associations and listed by Richardson together with Half Moon. *Suffolk Hotel*, much altered C19–20 but originated as *Greyhound*, inn belonging to abbey. What little of old fabric which survives is mainly in cellars. Claims to possess two secret rooms. *Everards* is also a Georgian house and former coaching inn, recently extended. GBG gives *Dog & Patridge, Elephant & Castle.*

CAVENDISH 8046
George is in Richardson's list but no details.

CLARE 7645
Bell, beam and plaster with finely tiled roof. Possibly inn from C15, later enlarged and became posting house, apparently called *Green Dragon*. (GBG with simpler *Red Lion*). Letts recommends *Cock*, Free House, Georgian and *Nethergate Hotel* which seems Jacobean.

CODDENHAM 1354
Timber-framed building (C16?) now operating as post office was formerly an inn. *Duke's Head* of similar age or older is functional. (GBG).

COTTON 0667
Trowel & Hammer, is recommended Letts and described as medieval.

CRETINGHAM 2260
New Bell, also Letts, pub with garden, described as Tudor.

EAST BERGHOLT 0734
GBG makes two recommendations in this Constable heartland: *Royal Oak, White Horse.*

EYE 1473
White Lion, unremarkable frontage but basically unaltered C16 apart from addition of fine assembly rooms with tiny musicians' gallery in Adam style. Waggoners' inn at beginning of C19. Picturesque yard with bowling green behind former stables. GBG, listed Richardson.

FELIXSTOWE 3034
Ferry Boat, early C18 or possibly older. Nautical flavour (GBG along with *Witching Hour*, 'a lively station buffet'!)

FORNHAM ST MARTIN 8566
Woolpack, pub with restaurant, recommended Letts: 'mixed ancient and modern'.

FRAMLINGHAM 2863
Crown, parts may date from mid C16, some Jacobean panelling, but inn is substantially of coaching era: C18 staircase and Assembly Room. Housed local court in later C19, still Hunt meet. Listed Richardson, recommended Letts together with *White Horse*, described as Tudor. GBG gives *Railway*.

PRESSINGFIELD 2677
Fox & Goose, timber and plaster with brick-nogged front. Corner post carries figure of St Margaret. Formerly parish Guild House (C15?). Recommended Letts, and described as medieval.

GREAT WALDINGFIELD 9143
White Horse, recommended Letts, described as 'Tudor'.

GREAT WELNETHAM 8759
Eagle, Georgian pub, recommended Letts.

GREAT WRATTING 6848
Red Lion has a whalebone archway, a reminder of whaling expeditions from Suffolk in C18–19.

HADLEIGH 0242
Letts recommends *George* and *White Lion*, both described as Tudor. GBG gives *Falcon, Kings Head*.

HARLESTON 0160
Swan, dates from 1551 (remains at back in two wings enclosing attractive yard). Well-proportioned front added in Georgian period. Apparently first owner was implicated in Kett's rebellion and built inn after he had been pardoned. Early Georgian Assembly Room. Kitchen garden and bowling green. Window hatch survives for transfer of luggage from courtyard to bedrooms.

HAVERHILL 6745
Rose & Crown, former coaching inn on A604. Probably C17.

IPSWICH 1744
Crown & Anchor and *Golden Lion*, both in Westgate, are typical market-town hotels. Former, listed Richardson, was built in two stages: 1840s and 1897. *Great White Horse*, is famous coaching house, visited by George II in 1737 and with Dickensian associations. Remains of timber-framed yard. Listed Richardson who adds *Half Moon* and *Neptune*. The latter dates from C15 with alterations and additions in 1639. It is now no longer an inn (86 Fore Street). There is another lost inn at 7 Oak Lane where the fine timber-framed house of C15/16 is former Royal Oak. Crown Works, Crown Street is another metamorphosis – former Temperance Hall of 1840. Letts recommends the 'very modern' *Man in the Moon* and GBG gives *County, Greyhound, Mannings, Spread Eagle, Station, Woolpack*.

KERSEY 0044

Richardson lists *Bell, White Horse* – no details.

LAVENHAM 9149

Swan, one of oldest buildings in town rich in timbered edifices of C15–16. Picturesque yard, remains of gallery and of rare luggage hatch from yard to first floor. Cellars, at least, said to date from C14. Now incorporates neighbouring former Wool Hall of C15. Listed Richardson together with *Angel*, a market-place hotel, probably of C16. Both recommended Letts.

LEVINGTON 2339

Ship, old pub by creek side. Rare example surviving with little alteration. (GBG).

LITTLE STONHAM 1160

Magpie, former coaching house on Ipswich–Norwich road has rare example of surviving 'gallows' sign.

LITTLE WALDINGFIELD 8245

Swan, 'a good village pub, reputed to have a ghost' (GBG).

LONG MELFORD 8646

Bull, originated as C15 cloth-merchant's house, became inn in C16 and later a posting house. Gabled and timber-framed. Yard with remains of gallery. Allegedly haunted. Letts recommends *Crown*, pub with garden. It may appear Victorian but could be centuries older. GBG gives *Swan*. *Bull* is on Richardson's list with *Castle*.

LOWESTOFT 5493

Crown, Georgian with Victorian modifications. Associated with C18 anecdote about its landlord swallowing crown piece as cure for leprosy. Listed Richardson with *Royal*: showpiece of mid C19 development as seaside resort. Classical with Italianate roof. *Victoria* is a little later (*c.*1897) and more English in flavour. Letts recommends *Royal George*, modern hotel on Marine Parade. GBG gives *Marquis of Lorne, Spread Eagle*.

MARTLESHAM 2547

Red Lion, village inn with curious sign. Mentioned Batchelor and said to have originated as figurehead of Dutch warship. Recommended Letts who describes it as Elizabethan. This may be '*Lion*', listed by Richardson.

MELTON 2850

Melton Grange, hotel recommended by Letts and described as Tudor with the intriguing comment 'if you like pilens (buildings, that is) this is for you'.

MILDENHALL 7074

Bell, former coaching inn in C18 and earlier. Some parts of fabric are allegedly of *c.*1300. GBG gives *Queens Arms*.

NAYLAND 9734

Letts recommends *White Hart*, a Victorian hotel.

NEEDHAM MARKET 0855

Swan, High Street pub with restaurant, recommended Letts, described as Tudor.

NEWMARKET 6463

Rutland Arms, *c.*1740 designed by William Kent for Duke of Rutland. Long sporting tradition (mentioned by R. Surtees), especially with horse-racing and used by many famous jockeys. Mentioned Batchelor and listed Richardson with *Crown, White Hart*. GBG gives *Rising Sun*.

NEWTON GREEN 8741
Saracens Head, near Sudbury. C17 pub with licensed restaurant, recommended Letts.

ORFORD 4250
Crown & Castle, formerly posting house. Smuggling associations. Situated in shadow of castle with unique keep. Letts recommends *Kings Head*, given as C13! GBG offers *Jolly Sailor*.

PINMILL 2038
Butt & Oyster, attractive waterside pub, illustrated Batchelor, much used by 'messing about in boats' fraternity. Former smuggling associations in connection with neighbouring Cat House (Woolverstone Park). Listed Richardson and GBG.

PRESTON 9450
Six Bells, pub with garden, recommended Letts: 'mixed ancient and modern'.

RENDHAM 3764
White Horse, recommended Letts and described as Georgian.

SAXMUNDHAM 3865
Bell, perhaps the last purpose-built coaching inn (erected 1842). Remains of its C16 predecessor in cellars. 'Long Room' on first floor. Present reception office occupies site of original bar. George II rested in earlier house on site. Listed Richardson with *White Hart*. Letts recommends *Crown*, Georgian.

SIBTON 3770
White Horse, recommended Letts, described as medieval and having 'decor completely in keeping with its period'.

STICKLESMERE 8760
Eagle, 'friendly C16 inn' (GBG).

SNAPE 3959
Letts makes two recommendations: *Crown*, Georgian/Victorian pub and *Plough & Sail*, a Victorian Free House. GBG gives *Golden Key*.

SOUTHWOLD 5076
Red Lion, possibly C16 but much altered. Alleged smuggling connections. Still used by longshoremen when not crowded out by visitors. *Harbour*, C17/18, snug bar with panelled walls and tiled floor occasionally flooded by high tides. Letts recommends Georgian *Lord Nelson* (GBG) and *Swan*, High Street hotel with brewery next door. Former coaching house with rare example of original licence (1763) in hall. GBG adds *Kings Head* and *Sole Bay*, brewery tap under lighthouse on one of characteristic greens.

STANTON 9763
Rose & Crown, listed Richardson – no details.

STOKE ASH 1170
White Horse, pub with garden, recommended Letts and described as 'ancient'.

STOKE-BY-NAYLAND 9836
Letts makes several recommendations: *Angel*, Georgian/Victorian pub; *Crown*, Elizabethan, recently well renovated; *Rose*, medieval, Free House.

STOWMARKET 0458
Richardson lists *Fox, Kings Head*. GBG gives *Little Wellington, Royal William*.

STOWUPLAND 0659
Crown, unobtrusive inn with rare (for this county) thatch. Small courtyard, backed with trees.

STRATFORD ST MARY 0434
Black Horse, recommended Letts and described as Tudor.

SUDBURY 8741
Black Boy, timber-framed (C16?) but much restored. *Bull*, Church Street, also timber-framed and *c.*1600 with fine early C19 name-plate. Mentioned Batchelor. *Rose & Crown* is listed by Richardson. GBG gives *Horn, Waggon & Horses*.

THURSTON 9365
Black Fox, tiny Free House and example of increasingly rare ale-house i.e. tavern serving only beer. (GBG).

WALBERSWICK 4974
Bell, attractive, unspoilt, rambling C17 pub in sight of sea. (GBG and Letts who also recommends *Anchor*).

WANGFORD 4679
Plough, Georgian pub recommended Letts who also gives *Suffolk Poacher*, Free House (GBG), 'mixed ancient and modern'.

WESTLETON 4469
White Hart, pub with garden, recommended Letts: 'mixed ancient and modern'.

WICKHAMBROOK 7454
Cloak, village local with unique(?) name. (GBG).

WICKHAM MARKET 3056
White Hart, former coaching inn on A12. Claims to date from C15. Late Georgian façade of brick, nine bays and with what P calls 'a funny Ionic porch'. Listed Richardson and recommended Letts.

WOODBRIDGE 2749
Crown may date from C16 but largely constructed in C18 as coaching inn which it remained to mid C19. Then it was about twice its present size, incorporating adjoining building. Attractive panelled rooms. Assembly Room (now converted to bedrooms) discernible. Present dining room was probably C18 kitchen. Listed Richardson, together with *Bell*, strong associations with Edward Fitzgerald (best known for his translation of Omar Khayyam) and slighter ones with Alfred Tennyson. Mentioned Batchelor. *Bell & Steelyard*, may be C15 in origin. Incorporates massive steelyard which once checked weight (maximum 3 tons) of waggon loaded with grain on its way to neighbouring malster's warehouse. Sliding weight still preserved. Letts recommends *Seckford Hall*, formerly a large private house (built in 1530), now hotel. Free House. GBG gives *Kings Head, Red Lion*.

YOXFORD 3968
Griffin, village pub with garden next to church. Recommended Letts and described as Victorian. GBG gives *Blois Arms*.

SURREY

ABINGER 1145
Abinger Hatch, unpretentious but charming village inn by green with stocks. Origin of name unknown – sign portrays old-time serving wench. (GBG). Letts recommends *Royal Oak, Abinger Hammer*, described as Elizabethan.

BAGSHOT 9163
Jolly Farmer, formerly Golden Farmer, originally C17 farmhouse whose owner paid debts in sovereigns. Mentioned Batchelor. GBG gives *Foresters Arms, Three Mariners*, a C17 house built from ships timbers.

BLETCHINGLEY 3250
White Hart, C18(?), with attractive inglenook. Mentioned Batchelor, listed Richardson along with *Stag*. GBG gives *Prince Albert, William IV*.

BOOKHAM 1534
Royal Oak, small High Street pub, recommended Letts: 17/18 century.

BURFORD BRIDGE 2464
Early C19 riverside inn which has associations with Hazlitt, is where Keats worked on 'Endymion' (1813) and where Nelson kissed his Emma for the last time (1805).

CAPEL 1740
Crown, timber-framed with stone-flagged floor. May have been C16 Church House. Attractive frontage with rare Trumpet Vine.

CHARLWOOD 2441
Half Moon is in Richardson's list – no details.

CHERTSEY 0466
Crown, head inn of town in C18 and terminus for day return service to London (cost 4s. 6d.). Remains of courtyard. Internal decor exploits Crown theme. *George*, former hunting lodge, said to be C14! (GBG) which also gives *Golden Grove*, 'C15 picture postcard pub'.

CHIDDINGFOLD 9635
Crown claims origin in C13 Cistercian rest-house for pilgrims and others. Probably let as inn in 1383 but present building (tile-hung in 1940s) seems largely C15. Edward VI stayed here in C16. Fireplace dated 1584. Curiosity-telephone installed in sedan chair. Mentioned Batchelor. Letts recommends Victorian *Swan*.

CHIPSTEAD 1756
White Hart, pub with garden, recommended Letts and described as ancient.

CHOBHAM 9761
Sun, High Street village pub, C17(?), GBG recommended Letts with *Red Lion*, Victorian pub with garden. GBG also gives *White Hart*.

COBHAM 1060
Richardson lists *White Lion*, probably originating in C16 and once a famous coaching inn. Letts recommends *Plough*.

COMPTON 9547
Withies, formed from two cottages, C17(?) Coach lamps high on façade. Letts recommends *Wittner*, described as medieval.

CRANLEIGH 0638
Leathern Bottle (GBG), *Onslow Arms* is more up-market.

DORKING 1649
White Horse, ancient house with complex history. Formerly *Cross House* from badge of owners. Knights Hospitallers who had acquired it from Templars after their suppression in 1278. Tradition of underground passages; certainly cellars are ancient (C13?). Old well survives, covered and uncleared. Mentioned Batchelor, listed Richardson with *Red Lion, Star & Garter*. *Marquis of Granby* may have inspired Dickens, *Wheatsheaf* was locale of William Morris' lectures on Socialism in 1886. Letts recommends *Stephen Langton*, old inn in Friday Street, while GBG gives *Bulls Head, Cricketers, Surrey Yeoman*, 'historic pub built in 1440s'.

DORMANSLAND 4042
Old House at Home, described as medieval by Letts who adds, 'perfect example of what foreigners admire in a typically English pub'.

EAST MOLESEY 1364
Bell, alias 'Crooked House' from its roof-line. Claims C15 origins. Later provided coaching and posting service. Associations with Claude Duval. (GBG).

EGHAM 9971
Great Fosters, described as 'a very fine inn' by Batchelor. Built 1550, belonged to Anne Boleyn, favourite hunting lodge of Elizabeth I. Rare period staircase, fine fireplace, elegant Tudor garden. In the characterless village, *Red Lion* shows some C17 work.

EPSOM 2160
GBG gives *Derby Arms, Railway Guard*.

ESHER 1464
Bear, C16 building, became posting house and stage on London–Portsmouth run. Associations with Clive of India and European royalty. Listed Richardson, mentioned Batchelor. GBG gives *Albert Arms, Claremont Arms*.

FARNHAM 8446
Jolly Farmer, cottage-like dwelling and former farmhouse, was birthplace of William Cobbett in 1766. Mentioned Batchelor, listed Richardson with *Bush*, substantially rebuilt in Georgian period when it became important coaching inn, possibly C17 (also recommended Letts) and *Lion & Lamb*. GBG gives *Hop Blossom, Queens Head, William Cobbett. Hop Bag*, architecturally undistinguished C20 building in Tudorish style, claims to have a ghost from previous C18 inn on site.

FOREST GREEN 0638
Parrot, another Letts recommendation described as Tudor.

GODALMING 9743
Kings Arms & Royal, scheduled building claiming C14 origin. Became coaching inn. Associations with Peter the Great and European monarchs. Mentioned Batchelor, listed Richardson (together with *Angel*), and in GBG. Letts recommends nearby *Ram*, Catteshall Cross, dated 1550.

GODSTONE 3551
Bell, frontage is four bay structure of *c.*1700. Interior preserves Queen Anne staircase and some contemporary panelling. Rear portion is claimed to have originated in medieval hall and to be oldest structure in town. Former coaching house. *White Hart*, formerly *Clayton Arms* (listed Richardson) is a fine inn of Georgian period by attractive village green. Recommended Letts.

GUILDFORD 0049
Angel, Georgian frontage to much older inn of which C13 cellars (possibly medieval wine store) survive. Famous coaching inn and terminus of 'Times' which ran to Charing Cross via Epsom. French Prince Imperial lodged here in 1876. Alternatively this structure (and another across the road) has been described as undercroft of obscure order of friars (De Ordine Martyrum). Listed Richardson along with *Lion* and mentioned Batchelor who also names *Red Lion* at which Pepys stayed twice and *Bulls Head*, a C16 house which has been remarkably restored (GBG which also gives *Britannia, Live and Let Live, Prince Albert, Robin Hood, Sanford Arms*).

HASCOMBE 0039
White Horse, pub with garden, recommended Letts and described as medieval.

HASLEMERE 9032
Georgian, large C18 hotel with large garden and squash court. Former coaching house. Recommended Letts with *Lythe Hill*, hotel with restaurant, described as Tudor. *White Horse* is C18 and was once a posting stage. Listed Richardson. GBG gives *Crown & Cushion*.

HINDHEAD 8736
Royal Huts, modern road house with unique name and relics of nearby C18 gibbeting. GBG gives *Woodcock*.

HOLMBURY ST MARY 1144
Royal Oak, small village pub (Victorian?) with restaurant. Free House. (GBG, Letts).

HORLEY 2843
Six Bells, large L-shaped structure of brick and timber, roofed with Horsham stone, partly tile-hung. Foundations on massive timber raft to cope with spongey site. Said to have been C15 hostel dependent on Dorking monastery. (There is no evidence for any kind of religious house at Dorking.) Certainly has C15 core and may have had ecclesiastical associations. Possesses rare table for antecedant to Shove Ha'penny. Letts recommends modern Free House: *Black Horse*, GBG gives *Foresters Arms, Gatwick*.

KINGSTON 1869
Sun is in Richardson's list. GBG gives *Albert Arms, British Oak, Queens Head*. Richardson also lists *Plough*, Kingston Vale.

NEWDIGATE 2042
Six Bells, 'small, old and intimate' pub with garden. (GBG, Letts).

OCKHAM 0756
Unusually named *Hautboy*. (GBG).

OCKLEY 1640
Red Lion, listed Richardson and described as 'mixed ancient and modern' by Letts who also gives *Kings Arms*, 'Tudor with additions' and *Punchbowl*. Free House with restaurant, 'medieval'.

OXTED 3852
Bell makes dubious claim to be a C13 building but undoubtedly medieval (*c.*1500?) and close to Pilgrims Way. Upper room had communal dormitory provided by hospice. Extensively redeveloped in 1964. Listed Richardson and recommended Letts together with *Royal Oak*, Free House, described as medieval. GBG gives *George, Hoskins Arms*.

REDHILL 2749
Red Lion, Raffles Bridge, recommended Letts: 'ancient/Victorian'. GBG gives *Elmshades, Home Cottage, Lakers*.

REIGATE 2550
Richardson lists *White Hart*. GBG gives *Blue Anchor, Castle, Nutley Hall, Yew Tree*.

RIPLEY 0556
Anchor, formerly *Old George*, possibly late medieval in origin. Achieved new popularity in late C19 as objective for cyclists from London. *Talbot*, seems to have originated in C15 and was known as *Dog* until C17. Associations with Claude Duval. Important stage in C18 on London–Portsmouth run. Nelson said to have stayed here. Both *Anchor* and *Talbot* listed Richardson. Latter is in GBG with *Ship*.

SHERE 0747
White Horse, listed Richardson, mentioned Batchelor for its 'attractive inglenook', recommended Letts. GBG gives *Prince of Wales*.

SOUTH GODSTONE 3648
Fox & Hounds, timber-framed with brick in-filling and hung tiles. Pleasant, unpretentious village inn of C17(?).

THAMES DITTON 1567
Old Swan, described in C19 as 'a showpiece among country inns' when it was famous for its table, especially stewed eels. Attractive riverside site. Associations with Thomas Hood, George III.

VIRGINIA WATER 0067
Crown, Victorian pub with attractive garden. (GBG and Letts).

WARLINGHAM 3658
Olde Whyte Lion, claims to be C16. (GBG).

WEYBRIDGE 0764
Old Crown, recommended Letts who describes it as Georgian. (GBG which also gives *Mitre*, small traditional pub).

WINDLESHAM 9363
Sun, traditional village pub in centre of township, recommended Letts, GBG who both also support *Windmill*.

WISLEY 0659
Anchor is in Richardson's list.

WITLEY 9439
White Hart, originally medieval hunting lodge whose bar is said to occupy former stables. Later fireplace has facilities for smoking ham. Licensed C16 when Friday Market was located in yard. Listed Richardson. *Sun* is a timber-framed building, possibly of C16.

WONERSH 0145
Grantley Arms, originally a private house of C15 to which an annexe was added later.

WOOD STREET 9550
White Hart, recommended Letts, described as Elizabethan/Georgian. GBG gives *Royal Oak*.

WORCESTER PARK 2266
Plough, oldest material, some brickwork, is from original house of 1431. Snug with its fine medieval fireplace claims to be oldest and smallest bar in Surrey, allegedly used by Dick Turpin.

WORPLESDON 9753
Fox, busy local with garden, possibly Victorian. (GBG and Letts).

WOTTON HATCH 1348
Wotton Hatch, busy roadside pub with oak-panelled bar and dining room. (GBG and Letts).

SUSSEX

ADVERSANE 0723
Blacksmiths Arms, village inn which still has working smithy adjoining Anvil Bar, possesses fine collection of authentic horse brasses. (Letts: 'medieval').

ALFRISTON 5103
Star, probably oldest inn in county. Dates from C15 when it was pilgrim hostel of Battle Abbey. *Star* is the star of Bethlehem. Unique features include: magnificent stone roof, elaborate carved timber work (and C17 ship's figurehead). Roasting jack survives in former kitchen (lounge). GBG: listed Richardson with *Market Cross*; mentioned Batchelor with *George*, 1379; recommended Letts with *Sussex Ox* 'mixed ancient and modern with a very traditional English atmosphere'.

AMBERLEY 0313
Houghton Bridge, 'three hundred year old inn with views of the Arun' (Batchelor who also mentions nearby *George & Dragon* where future Charles II paused from his pursuers on flight to Continent). Letts recommends *Black Horse*, Georgian; and *Sportsman*, Crossgates – medieval.

ANGMERING 0704
Letts makes two recommendations: *Lamb*, described as medieval and *Spotted Cow*, Georgian.

ARDINGLY 3429
Gardeners Arms, Little London, described as medieval and *White Hart*, Georgian are further Letts' recommendations.

ARUNDEL 0107
Norfolk Arms, former Georgian coaching inn which retains its ornate contemporary staircase. Recommended Letts. *St Mary's Gate*, composite building, part C17 inn, part former toll-house. Cromwellian associations. Letts further commendations include *Black Rabbit, Golden Goose, White Swan* (also in GBG).

ASHURST 1716
Fountain, unspoilt country pub (GBG) recommended Letts, 'medieval'.

BARCOMBE 4214
Anchor, remote coastal inn with smuggling associations, C17(?). (Letts).

BARNS GREEN 1428
Queens Head, village pub near Christ's Hospital. Recommended Letts – 'Elizabethan'.

BATTLE 7416
*George, c.*1710 replacing older house. Became Head Inn of town, handling coaching and mail, accommodating public meetings, local courts and local HQ in Napoleonic Wars. Interesting staircase. Visited by Cobbett in 1882. In Richardson's list, recommended Letts with *Red Lion*, described as medieval. GBG gives *Abbey*. *Pilgrim's Rest*, former guest-house of William I's great abbey. Originally C15 hall house and retains fine timbering. Listed Richardson, mentioned Batchelor.

BILLINGSHURST 0825
Olde Six Bells, beautiful C18 inn. (GBG). Letts recommends *Kings Arms*.

BINSTED 9806
Black Horse, pub with garden and attractive view. (GBG, Letts).

BLACKBOYS 4115
Blackboys Inn, smart country inn on Lewes Road which makes claims to be C14. (GBG, Letts).

BODIAM 7826
Castle, apart from its other attractions, this pub is unique in being only pub of which Guinness is lessee. Recommended Letts with *White Dog*.

BOGNOR REGIS 9399
Royal Norfolk, grand, three-storeyed building of 1830. Associations with Victoria, Edward VII, Napoleon III. Letts recommends *Ship*, Aldwick. Free House.

BOLNEY 2622
Eight Bells, coaching inn of C18 near crossroads said to be haunted by headless highwayman. Letts recommends *Bolney Stage*, described as medieval. Free House.

BOREHAM STREET 6611
White Friars, ivy-clad Georgian country house of 1721. Gardens.

BOSHAM, OLD 8004
Letts recommends oddly named *Anchor Bleu*, pub with garden, 'mixed ancient and modern' and so near sea that high tide may lap windows.

BRIGHTON 3105
Old Ship, 1755, replacing C17 inn. Terminus for London coaches and social centre of town for century, entertained Fanny Burney, the Thrales, Prince of Wales, Mrs Fitzherbert among others. Dickens worked here on 'Barnaby Rudge' (1841) and Thatckeray wrote early parts of 'Vanity Fair' (1847–8). Listed Richardson together with *Bedford*. *Pump House*, occupies original building which housed machinery for pumping sea water into baths. Letts recommends *Queensbury Arms*. GBG gives, among others, *Albion, Eagle, Walmer Castle*.

BUCKS GREEN 0732
Fox, C17(?) country inn with attractive frontage, perhaps C17 and with unique feature of right of way through inn. Recommended Letts as 'rare pubby pub'.

BURPHAM 0408
Burpham County, early C18, tile hung and gabled. Garden. *George & Dragon*, unobtrusive cottage-type ale-house, licensed C17. Smuggling associations and possesses rare 'Spinning Jenny' for fair division of spoils. Mentioned Batchelor.

BURWASH 6724
Bell, High Street village pub, popssibly C17 (GBG with *Kicking Donkey*) and recommended Letts with *Admiral Vernon*.

BYWORTH 9921
Black Horse. Free House. Recommended Letts and described as medieval/ Georgian.

CHAILEY 3919
Five Bells, rambling C17 inn. (GBG, Letts).

CHARLTON 8812
Charlton Cat, until 1921 *Poores Arms* (which included a lion rampant). Associated with rural poet (Stephen Duck, 1705–56) in whose memory an annual feast is held. *Fox*, typical Sussex flint-built inn, C18 or earlier with remains of old well in yard. Inviting basic interior.

CHICHESTER 8605
Dolphin and Anchor, name commemorates union of rival inns, economic and political (former Whig, latter Tory) and rivalry was not always scrupulous. Probably dates from early C16 but 'feels' much later. C19 landlord was Posting Master to Queen Victoria (warrant preserved in hall). Picturesque yard whose entrance arch still has meat and game hooks. Listed Richardson, mentioned Batchelor, recommended Letts with *Castle Market, Hole in the Wall, Old Cross, White Horse* (C15–16). GBG gives *Bell, Eastgate, Fleece, New Inn, Red Lion. Ship*, built 1770 as private house for admiral. Adam spiral staircase. Ship theme extends to bedroom names.

CHILGROVE 8314
White Horse, remote and charming (C18?) house in fold of Downs.

CLAYTON 3014
Matsfield Arms, recommended Letts, described as 'mixed ancient'.

CLYMPING 0002
Birers Bailiffscourt, unique and curious hotel formed from two houses connected by underground passages. Both architecture and furnishings are in late medieval manner though building was erected for Lord Moyne in 1930s. Chapel is authentic remnant of bailiff's house belonging to Norman abbey of Séez. Many elements and details are medieval work from other sites. Architecturally a 'superb performance'. (P).

COCKING 8717
Richard Cobden, recommended Letts and described as medieval. GBG gives *Greyhound* where you may 'qualify for your HSB "B" tie'.

COOKSBRIDGE 4013
Rainbow, pub with garden is recommended Letts and described as Tudor.

COWBEECH 6114
Merry Harriers, fine old village pub with rare name and garden. (GBG, Letts).

CRAWLEY 2636
George, probably began as medieval house which became inn in 1615. Flourished in C18 when it was halfway house on London–Brighton route. Popular with afficionados of prize fights taking place on Copthorne Common. Still something of Regency atmosphere. Rare gallows sign. Listed Richardson. In New Town *White Knight* is mentioned by Batchelor because of its successful introduction of special tea and coffee bar. GBG gives *Swan, Tavern on the Green*.

CROWBOROUGH 5130
Half Moon, 'everything one would expect of a country inn' (Letts). GBG gives *Coopers Arms*.

CUCKFIELD 3024
Kings Head, listed Richardson. Letts recommends *Rose & Crown, Talbot*.

DELL QUAY 7500
Crown & Anchor, located on hard, centre of small-scale marine activity. Ancient inn site and present building may be partly C16. Interesting customs receipts from that period. Later smuggling associations. Still burns window light for benefit of sailors and preserves ancient game of 'Ringing the Bull'. Mentioned Batchelor, recommended Letts.

DUNCTON 9516
Cricketers Arms, once owned by John Wisden, compiler of famous cricket almanack. Birthplace of 'Jemmy Dean', famous county player and populariser of 'round arm' bowling.

EASTBOURNE 6199
Lamb, near church in old town, timber-framed, C16(?) but with front much retored. Cellars are medieval and rib-vaulted. New town has many late C19 hotels, some very large. Batchelor mentions *Cavendish*, Letts recommends *Grand, Marine*. GBG gives *Hurst Arms, Terminus, Victoria*.

EAST CHILTINGTON 3715
Jolly Sportsman, rural Victorian Free House. GBG and recommended Letts 'for country-lovers and down-to-earth types'.

EAST DEAN 9013
Tiger, formed from group of cottages. Described as 'among most attractive inns in county'. Wealden iron fire-back dated 1622, probably from elsewhere. Documentary evidence of modified hearth tax. Recommended Letts.

EAST GRINSTEAD 3938
Dorset Arms, former coaching house. Claims to have been built from ship's timbers in 1511. Listed Richardson, mentioned Batchelor. *Dunning Mill* is a pub in converted mill (allegedly C15), recommended GBG. Letts presents *Gallipot*, Hartfield, a Free House said to have been built *c*.1597.

EAST LAVANT 8608
Royal Oak, former staging post on A286. Simple two-storeyed house of local chalk. Allegedly haunted.

FALMER 3508
Swan, popular Free House (GBG), recommended Letts and described as medieval.

FELPHAM 9599
Fox is in Richardson's list.

FERNHURST 9028
Duke of Cumberland Arms, recommended Letts and described as Tudor.

FITTLEWORTH 0119
Swan, may have C15 origins. Later a posting house. Associations with John Constable. Preserves old inn sign in hall. Listed Richardson.

FLETCHING 4323
Griffin, possibly C17 in spite of immediate Victorian impression. Possessed a skittle alley which was sold for a groat (4d., rather less than 2p).

FOREST ROW 4235
Roebuck, possibly former hunting lodge in Ashdown Forest. Timber-framed (C16?) with added wing of C17. Extensive grounds.

FULKING 2411
Shepherd & Dog, originally served shepherds and drovers taking sheep to market from Downs. Unusual in possessing three signs – all fine.

GROOMBRIDGE 5337
Crown, attractive tile-hung pub of Georgian appearance but may be C16, on village green moated by Groombridge Place on Kent–Sussex border. Recommended Letts.

GUESTLING 8514
White Hart, pub with garden. Recommended Letts: described as Tudor.

HAILSHAM 5909
George, C16 market-town inn, later coaching house. Listed Richardson. Letts recommends *Oak*, described as C16 and *Windmill*, 'medieval'.

HAMMERPOT 0605
Woodman, brick and flint, thatched, formerly C17 cottage, licensed C18.

HARTFIELD 4735
Dorset Arms, dates from Tudor period, much oak. Ancient kitchen. Preserves much old equipment: decanters, table services, cordial bottles, etc. *Hay Waggon*, with sign depicting ancient Sussex farm conveyance of which there is a scale model in bar. Probably origin in C16 farmhouse: half-timbered, wattle and daub in-filling. Bread oven survives in open hearth. Letts recommends *Hatch*.

HAYWARDS HEATH 3324
Sergison Arms, original C16 inn which became coaching house. Remarkable survival in suburbia. GBG gives *Star*.

HEATHFIELD 6021
Star, pub with good garden, recommended Letts, described as medieval.

HENFIELD 2116
Raven, a 'thematic' pub with the emphasis on Victoriana. GBG gives *Gardeners Arms*.

Nr. HERSTMONCEUX 6410
White Friars, on A271, part of present building dates from 1720 but site may have been manor of Carmelites who had local houses at Sele and Shoreham.

HOOE 6809
Lamb, made from pair of cottages on former seaside site. Formerly belonged to Battle Abbey which granted ale-license in 1520 on condition of permanent accessibility and fire during lambing season (salt marshes were part of abbey's sheep-run). After Reformation, haunt of smugglers rather than shepherds.

HORSHAM 1730
Old Kings Head, partly timbered, two storeyed hotel at crossroads (Carfax). Claims to have been established in 1401 and to have C12 cellars. (GBG). Listed Richardson with *Anchor, Black Horse*. Recommended Letts with *Chequers, St Leonards Arms*. GBG adds *Boars Head Tavern, Horse & Groom, Rising Sun*.

HOUGHTON 0111
George & Dragon, unprepossessing exterior of flint and brick but interesting. Possibly C17 and associated with fleeing future Charles II after defeat at Worcester, 1651. (GBG, Letts).

HUNSTON 8601
Spotted Cow, C18(?) country pub with garden. (GBG, Letts).

HURSTPIERPOINT 2816
New Inn, C16 unspoilt local in High Street. (GBG, Letts).

ICKLESHAM 8816
Queens Head. Somewhat obscure village inn, formed from former village shops. Garden. Preserves remarkable collection of 'bygones'. (Letts – 'Tudor').

LEWES 4110
Lewes Arms, former C17(?) private house, licensed 1781. Preserves local game of 'Toad in the Hole'. Cellars in castle precinct with alleged subterranean passages. (GBG). *White Hart*, built 1575 as private house of Pelham family. Cellars are said to have served as prison. Associations with Tom Paine, William Cobbett. Housed Anglo-Soviet trade discussions in 1929. Listed Richardson with *Crown*. Letts recommends *Pelham Arms*, Free House, 'medieval', and *Swan*, 'medieval?'. GBG adds *Black Horse, Kings Head, Landsdown Arms*. Just outside the town, name of *Snowdrop*, records catastrophe avalanche which killed eight people in 1836. *Shelleys* claims definite connections with poet.

LINDFIELD 3425
Snowdrop (GBG), see above. Letts recommends *White Horse* in traditional setting in heart of 'village soaked in architectural history' (P).

LODSWORTH 9223
Letts recommends *Hollist Arms*. Free House stated to be C17. GBG gives *Halfway Bridge* an unusual variant on Halfway House.

LURGASHALL 9326
Noah's Ark, recommended Letts: 'ancient and modern'.

MAYFIELD 5827
Middle House, an old ironmaster's house, C17(?) with magnificent views. Listed Richardson, recommended Letts who adds *Rose & Crown*.

MIDHURST 8821
Egmont Arms, late C17. Former small coaching house of which stables survive. Some trade tokens. Garden. *Spread Eagle* is among claimants to oldest inn with C15 origin and associated with great modern inn-keeper: Captain Freemantle. Consists of two buildings: one mid C15, other mid C17. Coaching inn in C18 when Christmas travellers booked for following Christmas by reserving pudding. Custom still observed. Much admired by Belloc, mentioned Batchelor among 'glorious Sussex inns'. Listed Richardson along with *Angel*, another former coaching inn which claims origin in 1520 and recommended GBG and Letts with *Bricklayers Arms*, 'medieval' and *Half Moon*, 'modern'. GBG adds *Royal Oak*, 'quaint C17 pub', and *Wheatsheaf*.

NEWHAVEN 4401
Bridge, C17 and home of Louis Philippe and his queen after 1848 revolution. Listed Richardson, mentioned Batchelor. Letts recommends quayside *Hope*, 'first pub in England'. GBG gives *Newfield*.

NEWICK 4121
Royal Oak, 'friendly old-fashioned' (C18?) pub. (GBG, Letts).

NORTHIAM 8324
Six Bells, recommended GBG as 'comfortable old pub'. Letts recommends *Rother Valley*, a Victorian Hotel. Free House.

NUTBOURNE 7805
Barleycorn, former small coaching inn of C17. Sign reminds us that pubs until recently had their own breweries.

PETWORTH 9721
Angel, claims to be C14 and haunted. (GBG, Letts). *Swan* is in Richardson's list and mentioned Batchelor among the 'glorious Sussex inns'. Letts adds *Lickfold*, described as medieval and *Stag*, Balls Cross, also 'medieval'.

PULBOROUGH 0418

Rising Sun is medieval according to Letts who recommends it along with *Water's Edge*, modernised pub with riverside garden. Batchelor commends modern *Swan*. *Chequers* claims C16 origin, much altered and added to. Alleged 'monastery chapel' in garden – no known monastic associations.

ROBERTSBRIDGE 7323

George, former coaching house of Georgian period, five bays and tile-hung. *Seven Stars*, attractive timber-framed inn, probably C16 but much altered. May have been associated with Cistercian abbey f.1176 whose scant ruins are nearby. Listed Richardson. Letts recommends *Fullers Arms*, Free House, 'mixed ancient' and nearby *Curlew*, Victorian.

ROTHERFIELD 5529

Kings Arms, originally brewery (C17?), became inn in 1731 and Samuel Pepys allegedly stayed there! Said to be haunted. Recommended Letts: 'Tudor'.

ROTTINGDEAN 3702

Black Horse, flint structure, dated 1513, with later smithy attached. Smugglers HQ in C18 and bear-baiting centre until prohibition. (GBG *Queen* plus *Victoria*).

ROWHOOK 1234

Chequers, unpretentious inn, enlarged cottage or farmhouse (C17). Fireplace has curing loft and there is a remarkable bar formed from adapting Welsh dresser. Recommended Letts.

RUDGWICK 0934

Blue Ship, recommended Letts 'medieval/Elizabethan' – 'original true pub'.

RUSPER 2037

Plough, village pub near church, claims to be C15 (GBG and Letts) who both also recommend *Star*, ancient possibly Tudor. GBG adds *Royal Oak*, another old pub.

RYE 9220

Bell, originated in C15 and some medieval material survives. Much used by smugglers (Hawkhurst gang) in C18. *George*, C16 building which only became inn in early C18 when it moved from building of similar date (survives as 'Butchery'). Became Head Inn, chief coaching establishment and centre for municipal functions. Mid C18 improvements and firemark of period. Georgian Long Room and fine Ball Room survive. Recommended Letts. *Mermaid*, 'one of oldest and finest inns in the country', rebuilt in 1420 (earlier cellars survive) and substantially still is of that date. Smuggling connections C17–19. Setting for Russel Thorndike's 'Dr Syn' novels. Visitors have included Ford Madox Ford, Hilaire Belloc, Henry James, Ellen Terry, Rupert Brooke, Fine carpentry, secret staircase and priest's hide by fireplace. Listed Richardson, mentioned Batchelor, recommended Letts who adds *Peace & Plenty, Top of the Hill. Old Flushing* is an interesting ancient hostelry. GBG gives *Standard, Union, Ypres Castle*.

SCAYNE'S HILL 3723

Sloop, pub with garden, recommended Letts and described as ancient. (GBG).

SEAFORD 4899

Hole in the Wall. On site of old stable which used to serve travellers with drinks via hole in wall. GBG gives *Cinque Ports*.

SEDLESCOMBE 7818

Richardson lists *Queens Head*.

SHIPLEY 1422
George & Dragon, Dragons Green, pub with garden, described by Letts as medieval/Tudor and recommended as 'what a good pub should be like'. (Also *Blacksmiths Arms*).

SHOREHAM 2105
In old town is *Red Lion*, attractive, low-ceilinged inn, possibly of pre-Reformation origin. Stage-coach stop to harness additional trace-horses for ascent of neighbouring hill. There was a gibbet behind house, in use to C19. *Amsterdam*, Free House on Upper Shoreham Road is recommended Letts and described as Elizabethan. GBG gives *Burrell Arms*, Brunswick Road.

SINGLETON 8713
Horse & Groom, pub with garden, recommended Letts and described as Tudor.

SOUTH HARTING 7819
White Horse, said to be *c.*1680, recommended Letts.

STEYNING 1711
Richardson lists *Chequers*. GBG gives *White Horse*.

TICEHURST 6930
Bell is described as C16 inn in attractive village. Is this the same as GBG's 'excellent little country pub', *Bull*?

TOVINGTON 5805
Eight Bells, typical country pub with garden. Recommended Letts: 'ancient'.

TROTTON 8322
Keepers Arms, Free House. Recommended Letts and described as medieval.

UCKFIELD 4721
Maidens Head, former coaching house with good Georgian façade, three storeys, two bow windows and nice doorway. Listed Richardson. GBG gives *Ringles Cross* two miles out along London Road.

WADHURST 6431
Old Vine, Cousley Wood is recommended Letts and described as Tudor. GBG gives *Greyhound*.

WARBLETON 6018
War-bil-in-tun, with its precious rebus-like name is recommended Letts who describes it as Tudor.

WARNHAM 1633
Letts makes two recommendations: *Greets*, medieval/Georgian and *Sussex Oak*, Georgian.

WASHINGTON 1212
Washington Inn, according to Belloc: 'The swipes they take in at the Washington Inn – Is the very best beer of all'. Not in GBG. Letts recommends *Frankland Arms*, Victorian pub with garden.

WINCHELSEA 9017
New Inn, traditional pub with charming old-world garden. Recommended Letts.

WINEHAM 2320
Royal Oak, old country pub (C15?) with garden. (GBG and Letts).

WITHYHAM 4935
Dorset Arms, began in C18 as modest wayside inn in a modified C16 farmhouse. Remains of some Tudor work and a later simple C18 staircase.

WOODS CORNER 6619
Swan, recommended Letts who gives date *c.*1399 with additions.

WOODMANCOTE 2315
Wheatsheaf, pleasantly positioned Victorian pub with garden, recommended Letts. *Woodmancote Arms*, busy country Free House. (GBG).

WORTHING 1402
Letts recommends modern *Royal Oak*, Brighton Road, and *Gun* in Findon village. GBG gives *Cricketers, Selden Arms*.

YAPTON 9703
Shoulder of Mutton & Cucumbers, famous for its name. GBG gives old *Maypole*.

TYNE & WEAR

GATESHEAD 2562
Bush, Oakwellgate, one of few pre C19 buildings of note, if it still survives. Stately house of seven bays, three storeys and pedimented.

JARROW 3265
'The least likely spot for one of the most venerable churches in the kingdom' (P). The pilgrim may be grateful for *Royal Oak*, Grange Road. *Western Road* is/was a steelworkers' pub decorated with amusing murals.

LAMESLEY 2557
Ravensworth Arms, recommended Letts who describes it as Tudor.

MARSDEN 4064
Grotto, modern inn on east coast but there are many stories of smugglers and hermits connected with the caves in cliff behind it.

NEWCASTLE-UPON-TYNE 2464
Balmbra's, formerly *Wheatsheaf*, renamed when licencee started Music Hall in 1858. Associations with Blaydon races. After various vicissitudes re-opened its Music Hall in 1962 and claims to be Britain's oldest surviror of this genre. (GBG). *Old George*, probably C17. Dubious associations with Charles I. Undoubted significance as coaching and marketing inn in C18–19. Magnificent fireplace, remains of courtyard. Batchelor mentions *County, Royal Station, Royal Turk's Head* of which latter is recommended Letts. GBG gives *Duke of Wellington*, owned by CAMRA, *Percy Arms, Portland, Royal Buffet, Three Bulls Heads*, among others.

NORTH SHIELDS 3468
Northumberland Arms, monumental range with seven-bay centre piece, built 1816 as Duke of Northumberland's contribution to town development.

SOUTH SHIELDS 3677
C18/19 developments obscure continuous history of nearly 2,000 years. Seems to be no pubs of architectural merit but thirsty may appreciate Victorian *Adam & Eve*, Laygate (GBG) and popular *Stag's Head*, Fowler Street. (GBG).

WASHINGTON 3056
Sandpiper in Biddick Village is recommended by Letts.

WEST BOLDON 3561
Black Horse, attractive village pub (GBG) in township with a number of C18 buildings and C13 church.

WHICKHAM 2061
Woodmans Arms, rarely named pub (recommended Letts) in relatively unspoilt village.

WHITBURN 4061
Jolly Sailor, unexpected name for local (GBG) in attractive village with notable green.

WARWICKSHIRE

ABBOTS SALFORD 0654
Bell, listed Richardson.

ALCESTER 0857
Globe is in Richardson's list. GBG gives *Dog & Partridge*.

ARLEY 7680
Minuscule Harbour approached by pedestrian bridge over Severn. In contrast is village-centre *Valentia Arms*, 'an ambitious construction, part Victorian-Tudor, part Georgian and part Scottish Baronial'. (Sir Jasper More).

ASTON 0789
Barton Arms – a magnificent Victorian pub. (GBG).

ASTON CANTLOW 1359
Kings Head, possibly early C17 and therefore too late to be scene of Shakespeare's parents' wedding breakfast.

ATHERSTONE 3097
Old Red Lion, origins in C17, once a coaching inn but now thoroughly modernised. Nearby is milestone recording London, Lincoln and Liverpool as being equidistant at 100 miles. Listed Richardson. GBG gives *Maid of the Mill*, next door to felting mill.

BARFORD 2660
Glebe is former Georgian rectory. Former *Red Lion* has caricature of Edward VII.

BIDFORD-ON-AVON 1052
Anglo-Saxon commemorates excavation in 1923 of nearby Anglo-Saxon burial ground with some 170 inhumations. A C16 house in the village was formerly *Falcon* inn with Shakespearian associations. Listed Richardson.

CLOPTON BRIDGE 2054
Near Stratford, with possible Shakespearean associations, mentioned Batchelor.

COLESHILL 1989
Green Man, 'plain old pub in centre of town' (GBG). *Wheatsheaf* is described as 'hospitable pub with old-world atmosphere'.

DUNCHURCH 4871
Dun Cow, former coaching house opposite market cross inscribed with mileages. Early Victorian porch crossed pavement. Mentioned by Batchelor, as is former *Lion*, west of church, timber-framed with over-sailing first floor. C16 with 'Gunpowder Plot' associations.

EASENHALL 4679
Golden Lion, recommended Letts who describes it as medieval.

EDGBASTON 0684
GBG gives *Duck*.

EDGHILL 3747
Castle, interesting pub near battlefield, designed as C18 folly. (GBG).

FENNY COMPTON 4152
George & Dragon, old house, once patronised by workers on nearby Oxford canal. Garden with bird-houses.

FILLONGLEY 2787
GBG makes two recommendations: *Butchers Arms, Weavers Arms*.

FRANKTON 4270
Friendly, mentioned Batchelor for its extensive collection of horse brasses.

GAYDON 3654
Gaydon, C18 or earlier, former coaching inn and once base for infamous 'Culworth gang' of highwaymen.

GREAT ALNE 1159
Mother Huff Cap, tall, white-painted and decorated with waggon wheels. Name is said to commemorate (C17?) brewster who popularised this house through the quality of her beer. Doggerel verses to this effect.

HUNNINGHAM 3768
Red Lion, part of exterior half-timbered (C17), attractively situated on bank of river Leam.

HURLEY COMMON 2495
Anchor, 'a pleasant, comfortable old pub' (GBG).

KENILWORTH 2871
Queen & Castle, C18 inn on outskirts of town, opposite castle. Listed Richardson with *Kings Arms & Castle*. GBG gives *Clarendon Arms, Coventry Cross, Royal Oak, White Lion, Wyandotte*.

KINETON 3351
Red Lion, a typical village inn. (GBG).

KINGSBURY 2196
Two village pubs in GBG: *Royal Oak, White Swan*.

KINGS NORTON 0478
Saracens Head, two-storeyed, timber-framed building of late C15, three bays, two wings. Probably Church House originally, much altered C18–19 partly to house parish hall.

LEAMINGTON 4467
Largely mid C19 development and many hotels of period: *Manor House*, 'High Victorian Gothic, of brick, and rather grim' (P). *Crown*, planned as vicarage, becoming hotel in 1815. Three bays with Doric porch with additional six bays. Assembly Room. Listed Richardson, together with *Regent*, 1819 with Doric porch added about 30 years later. GBG gives *Black Horse, Haunch of Venison, Holly Bush, Somerville Arms, White Horse*.

LITTLE COMPTON 2530
Red Lion, pub with garden, recommended Letts: 'mixed ancient and modern'.

LOZELLS (Birmingham, 19) 0786
Village Maid 'a plain old pub' (GBG).

MARTON 4069
Black Horse recommended Letts and described as Tudor. GBG gives *Hare & Hounds*, 'extended old village pub'.

MIDDLETON 1798
Green Man, country pub of some antiquity (C17?). Pleasant interior warmed by open fires in winter.

MOSELEY 8159
GBG recommends *Regent Court* in this Brummagem suburb with, unusually an off-licence – *Mr Booze*.

NECHELLS 0791
GBG gives *Prince of Wales*, a small local. (Note Birmingham).

NUNEATON 3592
Newdegate Arms, 1915 built on site of old *Black Bull*, renamed *Newdegate Arms* in 1816. As such it was original of *Oldinport Arms* of George Eliot's novels. This tenuous connection has been enough to make C20 inn locale of annual George Eliot dinners and something of a pilgrimage centre for her admirers. Richardson lists *Gull*. GBG gives *Railway Tavern, Rose*.

OFFCHURCH 3565
Stags Head, attractive thatched pub in pleasant village. (GBG).

OXHILL 3145
Peacock, attractive old pub in village with Norman church.

PRIORS MARSTON 4857
Holly Bush, beautiful pub (GBG) said to be C15, 'in one of the most rewarding villages in this part of the county' (P).

QUINTON 9884
College Arms, Cotswold stone with small courtyard. Attractive interior with huge ingle-nooked fireplace. C16 or earlier. Arms of those of Magdalen to whom site was granted after Reformation. Recommended Letts. GBG gives *Bass House*.

RATLEY 3847
Rose & Crown in partly C16.

RUGBY 5075
Royal George, plain late Georgian, former coaching inn, five widely spaced bays. Listed Richardson with *Three Horseshoes*. GBG gives *Half Moon* in town centre; *Boat*, canalside with skittles; *Merrie Monk* on Brownsover Estate and *Stag & Pheasant*, traditional pub in absorbed village of Lower Hillmorton where Letts recommends Victorian *Hillmorton Manor*.

SHILTON 2608
Old Plough is an unspoilt local. (GBG).

SHIPSTON-ON-STOUR 2540
Bell, plain Georgian brick, five bays. *Horseshoes*, possibly originally Church House (C16 or earlier), timber-framed upper floor. Old Mill occupies a transformed water-mill (one on site at Domesday) with attractive façade and garden on riverbank. Recommended Letts: 'Georgian'.

SOUTHAM 4161
Boat: rambling roadside inn with interesting roof-line, on main road and alongside Grand Union canal. Once very popular with bargees. Richardson lists *Craven Arms* while GBG gives *Old Mint*, 'fine old C14 Free House'.

STRATFORD-UPON-AVON 2055
Butt of Malmsey has an interesting sign featuring perjured Clarence who, according to one tale, was allowed to choose the manner of his death and, according to another, was simply drowned in a convenient liquor-filled barrel. *Falcon*, three storeys, timber-framed, originally (C16?) private house, becoming inn in 1640. Listed Richardson, mentioned Batchelor. *Red Horse* absorbs earlier inn known as *Golden Lion*, listed Richardson. Associations with Washington Irving, together with *Garrick*. *Shakespeare*, originally C15 'Great House' of Sir Hugh Clopton (ob.1496). Much altered and heavily restored. May have become inn in C17 of which period a portrait sign is preserved. Rooms prettily, and often wittily, named after Shakespeare's plays. (GBG, listed Richardson, mentioned Batchelor, recommended Letts). *White Swan*, originally *Kings Head*. Medieval merchant's house which had become popular and prosperous inn by Shakespeare's time. Principal lounge is former hall with rare Tobit wall-paintings of mid C16. Gothic window probably illuminated solar of medieval house. Good woodwork includes fine Jacobean mantelpiece. Listed Richardson with *Swan's Nest*. Recommended Letts and GBG which also gives *Old Tramway*.

TANWORTH 1170
Uncommuterised village nucleus survives with small green overlooked by *Bell*.

UPPER BRAILES 3040
Gate lacks usual sign and rhyme. In Lower Brailes is *George*, probably originating late C16.

WARWICK 2865
Anchor, old house (C15?), much restored. Behind it is Old Malt House, C17, stone with mullioned windows, also restored. *Aylresford* is a former coaching inn, built 1696, 'an excellent, if a little rustic, job' (P). *Crown* is listed Richardson (with Woolpack) and recommended Letts: 'mixed ancient and modern'. *Lord Leycester*, is late C18, brick of five bays – one containing the carriageway. Recommended Letts, with *Roebuck*: 'mixed ancient and modern'. *Warwick Arms*, right wing of shortly after 1694, rest a century or so later. Interesting grape sign above door. Drawing Room is part of former Long Room and annexe incorporates two Georgian houses with attractive period features. Interesting cobbled yard with remains of accommodation for ostlers and tackle. Further yard used to contain Tap Room for socially inferior post-boys. Listed Richardson. GBG gives, among others, *Simple Simon, Wheatsheaf, Woodman, Zetland*.

WELFORD-ON-AVON 1452
Bell, recommended Letts and described as Elizabethan.

WELLESBOURNE 2755
Kings Head, possibly C17, former coaching house. Attractive and interesting protected building.

WHATCOTE 2944
Royal Oak, pub with garden, recommended Letts and described as Tudor.

WHITACRE HEATH 1990
Swan, 'charming period country inn, full of character'.

WHICHFORD 3134
Norman Knight, unusually named village pub. (GBG).

WOOTTON WAWEN 1563
Bull's Head, L-shaped, half-timbered with wattle and daub in-filling (some brick). Claims dubiously to date from C14 though there does seem to be some C16 material. Former posting house. The pursuer of antiquity should try church with early C11 work. On Stratford–Birmingham canal is *Navigation*, pub with restaurant, recommended Letts.

YARDLEY 1385
New Inn, 'excellent pre-fab behind the largest pub in Europe' (GBG).

WEST MIDLANDS

BARSTON 2078
Bulls Head, 'Mersey Bar' attempts a nautical atmosphere with decor of ancient and modern ship's fittings. GBG gives *Malt Shovel*.

BIRMINGHAM 0787
Among city centre pubs listed in GBG are *Fox, Holloway, Lamp, Old Royal, Prince of Wales, Sack of Potatoes, St Paul's Tavern*. In 1962, *Crown* was in 'select list of old inns' (AA). Same year saw building of *Albany*, Smallbrook Ringway.

COVENTRY 3379
King's Head is in Richardson's list but *Town Hall Tavern* seems to be only city centre survivor from the Blitz and even this is currently threatened by destructive developers. GBG gives, among others, *Dog & Trumpet, Elastic, Malt Shovel, Old Hall, Old Windmill* alias *Ma Browns, Rising Sun, Royal*.

HAMPTON-IN-ARDEN 2081
White Lion, unspoilt pub, old and timbered (C17?). Recommended Letts. (GBG).

HANDSWORTH 0490
Olde Gate, small friendly local. (GBG).

HARBORNE 0384
Plough, popular lively house. (GBG).

HOCKLEY
Brown Lion and *Woodman* are both in GBG.

KING'S HEATH 0781
Golden Lion, timber-framed C15 inn, surviving in conurbation. GBG gives *Horseshoe*, large canalside pub.

KNOWLE 1876
Red Lion, much restored early C17. Retains fine wrought iron sign bracket from demolished *White Swan*.

MERIDEN 2482
Queens Head, traditional English country pub in heart, and some would say at Centre, of England.

PERRY BAR 0791
Wellhead Tavern is in GBG.

SMALL HEATH 1185
GBG gives *Horse & Jockey*.

SUTTON COLDFIELD 1296
Three Tuns, recently modernised former Georgian coaching inn at town centre (GBG which also gives *Boat, Cork & Bottle, Duke, Plough & Harrow*).

WILTSHIRE

ALDERBURY 1827
Green Dragon, thought by some to be original of Dickens' inn in 'Martin Chuzzlewit', others prefer *George* at Amesbury. Listed Richardson and mentioned Batchelor.

AMESBURY 1541
Antrobus Arms, former coaching house. Impressive Georgian facade: five bays, two storeys, Tuscan porch. Free House. Recommended Letts. Smaller *George* with projecting bay over yard entrance is said to be original of 'Blue Dragon' (cf. above). Listed Richardson, mentioned Batchelor. Formerly *George & Dragon*, originally pilgrim hostel of Benedictine nuns whose church survives in Anglican use. Fairfax's HQ for a time in Civil War and, later, half-way stop for West Country 'Quicksilver Mail'.

ANSTY 9526
Possesses 'a remarkable pub, with a facade like a Victorian railway station and an interior decor which defies classification provides . . . Old Ansty Ale' (English Villages, ed. J. Hadfield).

AVEBURY 0969
Red Lion, partly half-timbered and beautifully thatched. C17 well survives in dining room. Uniquely sited at centre of prehistoric stone circle.

BECKHAMPTON 0868
Waggon & Horses, may incorporate C16 material and older cannibalised stone from prehistoric sites. Later staging post on London–Bath route and stopping place for freight waggons. Characteristic C18 room over porch. Associations with highwaymen (Gibbet on Inkpen Beacon). Listed GBG, mentioned Batchelor, recommended Letts.

BOTTLESFORD 1860
Seven Stars, recommended Letts: 'mixed ancient and modern'.

BRADFORD-ON-AVON 8260
Swan, C18 inn with many historical associations, but much altered. Listed Richardson. GBG give *Bunch of Grapes*, 'cosy little pub'.

BROUGHTON GIFFORD 8763
Bell, off beaten track, recommended Letts as 'rare specimen'. GBG gives *Fox & Hounds.*

BURCOMBE 0630
Ship, formerly *Sheep*, on old drove road. Some ships timbers incorporated in fabric have inspired 'ship theme' in bar.

CALNE 9971
Kings Arms was once a coaching inn. *Landsdown Arms*, formerly *Catherine Wheel* and originally medieval hostel. Much enlarged in coaching era, annexing adjoining house and refronted. Many relics of that period. Fine yard with remains of Brew House and bold inscription: 'Welcome ye coming, Speed ye parting Guest'. *Kings' Arms* was also once a coaching inn. GBG gives *Wheatsheaf.*

CASTLE COMBE 8477
Castle, claims C13 origins, may preserve medieval material. Certainly much restored and altered. Listed Richardson. *Manor House* is a former C17 private house in extensive grounds. *White Hart*, 'a quaint old pub' (GBG) is a Free House with garden and recommended Letts who describes it as medieval.

CHERHILL 0370

Black Horse, posting house built *c.*1766 and popular with drovers. Later associated with Cherhill gang of footpads who operated *c.*1800.

CHILMARK 9632

Black Dog, said to be of C15. Cosy bar with fine fireplace. (GBG, Letts).

CHIPPENHAM 9173

Angel, formerly *Bull*. Georgian coaching inn: three storeys. Tuscan porch with balustrade. Associations with T. Smollett and scene of 1875 election riot. Listed Richardson. Now has associated motel. GBG gives *Little George, Pheasant.*

COLERNE 8171

Vineyard, tavern with restaurant, highly praised by Batchelor.

COLLINGBOURNE DULCIS 2453

Shears, Free House of *c.*1720, recommended Letts while GBG gives *Cleaver* in twin village of Collingbourne Kingston.

CORSHAM 8669

Methuen Arms, formerly *Red Lion*. Possesses very rare example of ancient chequer tavern sign on bar doorposts. Developed from medieval house which apparently became inn in early C17. Rebuilt and name changed *c.*1805. Georgian front, C16 wing behind. Fine skittle alley in former brewhouse and malting. Attractive yard. Listed Richardson. GBG gives *Cross Keys*.

CRICKLADE 0993

White Hart is listed by Richardson, 'gabled Victorian hotel of mellow stone'.

DEVIZES 0061

(White) *Bear*, originated in C16, became flourishing town-centre coaching house and was substantially rebuilt, right wing before left, in Georgian period. In 1770s landlord used genius of his son, Thomas Lawrence (subsequently President of Royal Academy) to attract and entertain customers. Garrick visited inn several times and was impressed by boy's elocution. Listed Richardson, mentioned Batchelor, recommended Letts and GBG. *Black Swan* with picturesque C18 frontage is also a former coaching inn, serving Bristol run. Popular with farmers. GBG adds *Hare & Hounds* and Victorian *White Lion*.

DOWTON 1721

Bull, former coaching inn, probably of C17 origin. Its grounds border Avon. GBG gives *White Horse,* 'a fine old village pub'.

EDINGTON 9252

Lamb of C16 origin with some material surviving in present building. Was licensed house from beginning and some stones are alledgedly cannibalised from Roman Bath.

ENFORD 1351

Swan, unpretentious brick and thatched house whose licensee was once village constable.

EVERLEIGH 1953

Crown, associations with chief falconer to Elizabeth I and with Judge Jeffreys. Housed local court in C17 and until modern times.

HIGHWORTH 2092

King & Queen, listed building, possibly C16. Alleged ecclesiastical connections and usual tale of underground passages. Became staging post in coaching era. Local courtroom to C19. Alleged ghost. (GBG).

HINDON 9032
Lamb, C16/17. Developed as coach house: fine porch and bay window. Good copper in tap room. Home of W. H. Hudson in 1909. Recommended Letts with *Grosvenor*: Georgian. Free House.

HORNINGSHAM 8241
Bath Arms, pub with garden. Recommended Letts and described as medieval.

LACOCK 9168
Sign of the Angel, alias *Angel*. C16 or earlier with surviving medieval doorway and fireplace, stone-mullioned windows, fine timbering. Probably pilgrims' hostel belonging to abbey. Recommended Letts and mentioned Batchelor.

MALMESBURY 8787
Bell, transmogrified guest house of great Benedictine abbey, half of whose church surves in Anglican use. Listed Richardson. *Green Dragon,* probably was built to serve same function and preserves a C14 window. *Kings Arms* has a long back wing, timber-framed, probably dating from C16. Later refronted. Recommended Letts with *Suffolk Arms*: 'mixed ancient modern'. Of interest are Old Brewery and Old Brewery House both dated 1672.

MALBOROUGH 1869
Castle and Ball, puzzling name probably corruption of Castle and Bull, charges on Marlborough arms. It is said to have been *Antelope* until 1764 and another claim that it was originally *Hart* and lodged Samuel Pepys in 1688. Certainly behind present front is much C16 work. Original *Castle* now incorporated in school buildings. Involved in minor skirmish of Civil War. Associations with Elder Pitt. Mentioned Batchelor, listed Richardson with *Five Alls*. Parts of *Green Dragon* pre-date 1653. It developed in C18 as coaching inn of which stables survive. Riverside garden. *Sun*, in spite of its repellent Victorian frontage, is one of oldest inns in town with C16 elements surviving in much altered house. Attractive Tudor bar. (GBG with *Ailesbury Arms*, 'imposing Georgian hotel').

MELKSHAM 9063
Kings Arms is in Richardsons' list. GBG gives *Bear*.

MERE 8132
Ship, former private house of Sir John Coventry who lived there until 1682. Became inn in C18, serving coaches on London–Exeter run and accommodating race-goers. Interior retains some good early features. Listed Richardson, mentioned Batchelor, recommended Letts. *Talbot,* previously *George*, dates also from C17. Future Charles II is said to have dined here in disguise (1651). Sign unusually depicts dog as black instead of customary white. GBG gives *Butt of Sherry*.

MONKTON FARLEIGH 8065
Fox & Hounds, Free House with garden, recommended Letts. Victorian. GBG gives *Kings Arms*, 'large old, stone-built pub'.

NETHERHAMPTON 1029
Victoria & Albert, unpretentious thatch and whitewashed brick with curiosity: spider-infested cupboard almost filled with cob-web.

NETTLETON 8178
Codrington Arms, C15. Free House. (GBG, Letts).

NEWBURY 4666
Chequers, small posting house, drastically altered in 1833 but some older parts survive in bar (former kitchen).

PEWSEY 1659

Greyhound, listed Richardson and GBG, 'a well modernised town pub'. Letts recommends *Wheels of Pewsey,* described as Georgian. Unique name.

PITTON 2131

Silver Plough, unusually named pub with restaurant, recommended Letts and described as Elizabethan.

RAMSBURY 2771

Letts makes three recommendations: *Bell*, Georgian Free House: *Burdett Arms*, 'mixed ancient and modern'; *Crown & Anchor*.

SALISBURY 1429

Chough, formerly *Cornish Chough c.*1635. Chough was featured on arms of St. Thomas a Becket to whom nearby church is dedicated. Fine staircase. Stables converted to bar and skittle alley. 'As handsome as it is old' (Batchelor). *Haunch of Venison*, originally C14, rebuilt C18. Port and sherry delivered through pewter taps. (There was a *Round of Beef* but it has gone) GBG and listed Richardson with *Crown. Kings Arms* is C15/16, timber-framed with oversailing upper floor. Royalist stronghold in Civil War, became coaching inn in C18. *Red Lion*, claims C14 elements, became coaching inn on West Country run and was given a new Georgian frontage. Attractive yard. Listed Richardson. *Rose & Crown*, Harnham Road, claims to be C13. It is timber-framed and its lawns go down to river. Much extended and modernised. Adjoining building associated with Sayers, a prize-fighter. *White Hart*, rebuilt *c.*1800 to replace house of C16 which had associations with Henry VII, Walter Raleigh. Grandiose with imposing portico and enormous sign, erected 1827 to out-do new sign of rival Antelope. Temporary HQ of Southern Commond in WW II. Listed Richardson. *George*, probably originally pilgrim hospice of which part of C15 frontage survives. Associations with Pepys, Dickens. No longer functional. Letts recommends *Market*, 'mixed ancient and modern' and GBG adds *Railway, Salisbury Arms.* Said to be over 80 pubs in city.

SANDY LANE 9668

George in high-lying village of thatched cottages, modernised but C18 with possible coaching associations. (GBG).

SHERSTON 8585

Angel, attractive house with gables and mullioned windows, dated 1648. *Carpenters Arms*, 'a fine rustic pub' (GBG). Unusually named *Rattlebone* commemorates local Dark Age hero who fought Danes.

SUTTON BENGER 9478

Bell House, private house until *c.*1950 now hotel and restaurant. GBG gives *Wellesley Arms*.

SWINDON 1484

Goddard Arms, Kings Arms, listed Richardson. GBG gives *Bakers Arms*, Bell, Duke of Wellington, curiously named *Even Swindon, Lamb & Flag, Wheatsheaf.*

TOLLARD ROYAL 9417

King John, Victorian Free House (GBG and Letts who also gives *Compass*).

TROWBRIDGE 8557

George, listed Richardson. GBG gives *Greyhound, Lamb.*

WARMINSTER 8644

Bath Arms, large hotel of eight bays and three storeys, probably William and Mary. Former coaching house. Listed Richardson. *Masons Arms*, a rambling pub which occupies a former (early C19?) brewery. (GBG). *Old Bell*, a characteristics 'black and white' building (C17?) with distinct façade and colonnaded upper floor.

WEST DENE 2526
Red Lion, attractive pub through which the Wilts./Hants. border used to run thus producing different licensing hours between bar and dining room.

WILTON 0931
Richardson lists *Pembroke Arms*. GBG gives *Bear*.

WINGFIELD 8256
Poplars, C19 pub is recommended by Letts and GBG.

WINTERBOURNE DAUNTSEY 1734
Tything Man, originally C17 farmhouse, occupied by local rent collector or tithing man. Licensed as *New Inn* mid C19, renamed 1973.

WINTERSLOW 2232
Pheasant, previously *Hut*, ancient inn, regularly patronised by William Hazlett. Mentioned Batchelor, recommended Letts who describes it as Tudor. It appears more Georgian but it architecturally idiosyncratic with a huge bowed upper floor supported on columns and surmounted by a top-heavy gable with the inn sign painted on its end.

WYLYE 0037
Bell, listed building (C16?), stone with high pitched roof. One of neighbouring church bells was cast in its yard. 'Bell' theme in bar. Coaching connections and statue by stream commemorates hero of coaching accident. (GBG, Letts).

NORTH YORKSHIRE

AINDERBY STEEPLE 3392
Wellington Heifer, Georgian pub with rare name and good atmosphere (GBG) described by Letts as 'one of the most attractive country inns in North Riding'.

ALDBOROUGH 4065
George & Dragon, attractive C16 inn, two and half storeys, tiled roof and prominent bay on ground floor. Garden. Mentioned Batchelor. *Ship*, which is said to be C14 is in GBG.

ALLERSTON 8782
Cayley Arms, claims C17 origins and associations with Charles II. Much altered if it is really as old as this.

AMPLEFORTH 5878
White Swan, originally C17? much modernised pub (Letts) in village with largest active Benedictine abbey in country.

APPLETON LE STREET 7373
Cresswell Arms, recommended Letts and described as 'mixed ancient and modern'.

ARKENGARTHDALE 0001
C.B., one of claimants to shortest name. Much involved with shooting and fishing. Free House.

ARNCLIFFE 9371
Falcon on green, featured in TV Emmerdale Farm.

ASKHAM BRYAN 5548
Nags Head, pleasant pub on A64, possibly once carriers', a Georgian (?) nucleus extended to absorb two other cottages.

ASKWITH 1648
Black Horse, former village inn, extended and upmarketed. Recommended Letts: 'mixed ancient and modern'.

ASKRIGG 9490
King Arms, 1767, unusually designed as a unified composition with neighbouring Manor House.

BAINBRIDGE 9390
Rose & Crown, claims to originate in C15 and certainly retains some medieval features. Developed C18 and absorbed neighbouring buildings. Maintains horn-blowing custom, originally to guide travellers over desolate neighbouring countryside. Sometimes can be heard three miles away.

BEADLAM 6584
White Horse, possibly C16 or even earlier. Once popular drovers' tavern.

BEDALE 2688
Kings Head, late C17 but built in old-fashioned style (Jacobean Renaissance). Fine chimney-piece on first floor. *Oddfellows Arms*, said to be pre-Reformation in origin. Certainly name is not! In C18 developed into largest inn in town. Free House. (GBG). Richardson lists *Black Swan*.

BENTHAM 9116
Royal Oak, traditional market-town pub, modernised with active ballroom. Recommended Letts.

BILSDALE 5600
Sun, alias 'Spout House' with gravestone which parson refused to have in graveyard. Original inn was in thatched cruck cottage surviving a few yards north.

BISHOP THORNTON 2662
Drovers, originated as C16/17 inn on drovers' road through Yorkshire Dales. Free House.

BLAKEY 6799
Blakey House Inn is OS reference point. *Lyon* at *c.*1300ft (*c.*400 m) on North Yorks Moors originated to serve miners and railwaymen. Collapsed centre of nearby Blakey Howe was used as cock-fighting ring.

BOLTON ABBEY 0753
Devonshire Arms, stone built vernacular house of C18, popular with walkers. Recommended Letts. Interesting antique furniture. Recently rebuilt.

BOROUGHBRIDGE 3966
Crown, Horsefair, large white house (C18?), former posting inn on Great North Road. *Three Arrows*, modern brick, imitation manor house, named from three great monoliths nearby. Richardson lists *Three Greyhounds*. Letts recommends *Grantham Arms*.

BRADLEY 0379
Slaters Arms, former village pub used by stoneworkers, now popular with young business men. Garden. Recommended Letts.

BRIDGE HEWICK 3370
Black-a-moor, in hyphenated form, probably a unique name. Probably former coaching halt on Ripon–Boroughbridge road.

BROUGHTON 9451
Bull, 1746, recently smartened up to attract carriage trade rather than be mere village amentity. Negroni – recommended beer. (Letts).

BUCKDEN 9477
Buck, small, early Victorian, Wharfedale pub with garden. (GBG, Letts).

BURNSALL 0361
Red Lion, unspoilt country inn, formerly Bridge End, developed from C18 (or earlier) farmhouse to serve village and travellers. Mentioned Batchelor. Free House.

BURNT YATES 2461
New Inn, claims to be equidistant from Lands End and John o'Groats and from east and west coasts. On main road through Nidderdale. Characteristic stone façade (of two builds). Free House.

CATTERICK 2397
Angel, in old town is an original village inn, possibly with ecclasiastical origins. *Bay Horse*, village inn, one of few houses owned by Theakstons. *Bridge House*, former coaching inn which claims C15 origin. Gardens adjacent to river Swale. *Oak Tree*, traditional village green ale-house. (GBG).

COWTHROPE 4252
Old Oak, Georgian inn with restaurant in former barn. Free House. (Letts).

COXWOLD 5377
Fauconberg Arms, apparently originally C17 almshouse. Stone, gable and porch with three-dimensional arms on façade. Should be associations with Lawrence Sterne who was perpetual curate of this parish. Free House. Listed Richardson, *Foresters Arms*, recommended Letts: 'mixed ancient and modern' with note about landlord's commitment to horse-racing!

CRAYKE 5670
Durham Ox, traditional village pub, recently much enlarged but retains some character, particularly in Oak Room lounge. Free House.

CRIMPLE 3456
Travellers Rest, probably drovers' pub, originally f. on site in C15. Interestingly divided interior. Near Harrogate.

CROFT 2909
Spa, long, low Georgian house which groups well with church and bridge. Built to accommodate visitors to spa flourishing in C18. Ballroom with musicians gallery (now converted to 'powder room'!). Fine dining room. Free House.

DACRE BANKS 1961
Royal Oak, fine stone-built house, dated 1751.

DALTON 1108
Chequers, modern, modest village pub with restaurant. Free House.

DEIGHTON 6244
White Swan, village pub some 5 miles from York, recommended Letts: 'ancient and modern'.

EASINGWOLD 5269
George, former traditional coaching inn with appropriate public rooms. Character largely destroyed by brewery's transformation. (GBG). *York*, surviving market-place pub which retains traditional atmosphere, games and clientele.

EAST LAYTON 1609
Fox Hall, former C19 coaching inn on A66. Much refurbished. Free House.

EAST HARSLEY 4299
Village once much afflicted by Scottish raiders known as 'catarans', abbreviated to 'cats' which may explain name of inn: *Cat & Bagpipes. Cleveland Tontine* at Staddle Bridge, raised by Tontine in 1804 to provide coach house on Thirsk to Yarm run at Stokesley fork.

EAST MARTON 9050
Cross Keys, ancient hostelry (from at least C18) with its own moorings on Leeds–Liverpool canal. (GBG). Free House.

EAST WITTON 1486
Attractive Wensleydale village with *Blue Lion* and former *Holly Tree.*

EBBERSTON 8983
Grapes, small hotel, Georgian, popular with farmers. Strongly recommended by Letts.

EGTON 8006
In village is refurbished Victorian *Wheatsheaf*. Free House. At Egton Bridge, delightfully situated on island in Esk is *Horseshoe*, said to be of C16 origin, serving packhorse and, later wheeled traffic. (GBG). At Beggars Bridge is a packhorse bridge.

ESCRICK 6243
Black Bull, traditional local with dining room, recommended Letts: 'mixed ancient and modern'.

FADMOOR 6789
Plough, traditional pub, possibly retaining C16 elements in structure. Recommended Letts: 'Tudor'.

FELIXKIRK 4684
Carpenters Arms, C17, former village pub with attached smithy. Recently upmarketed and modernised to 'hark back to a more leisurely era'. Free House.

FILEY 1180
Foords, attractive early C19 seaside hotel with good doorway. (GBG).

FLIXTON 0478
Foxhound, former local in small hamlet, south of Scarborough. Now popular with new carriage trade. Recommended Letts: 'mixed ancient and modern'. *Old House*, C18 small cosy pub, easily overlooked.

FOLLIFOOT 3452
Radcliffe Arms, Georgian, possibly coaching associations. (Letts) also *Lascelles Arms*.

FYLINGDALES 9199
Flask, claims C16 origin. Later coaching inn of Whitby–Scarborough route. Free House.

GARGRAVE 9354
Anchor, former canal men's pub near loading wharf for lead and stone on Leeds–Liverpool canal. Still possesses moorings. Modernised, extended and upmarketed. Recommended Letts.

GIGGLESWICK 8163
Black Horse, 'splendid local' (GBG) in attractive Craven village.

GLAISDALE 7705
Mitre, C18, transferred building replacing former Church House. On hill-side above Eskdale. Formerly serviced ironstone mining community. Free House.

GLUSBURN 9944
Dog & Gun, 'plush, friendly, roadside inn' (GBG) in Airedale.

GOATHLAND 8301
Mallyan Spout, country hotel, Victorian and later, in fine moorland setting. Recommended Letts. GBG gives *Goathland Hotel.*

GOLDSBOROUGH 3857
Bay Horse, 1698, atractively situated in pleasant village.

GRASSINGTON 0064
Devonshire Arms more friendly and welcoming than pretentious *Wilson Arms*.

GREAT AYTON 5510
Royal Oak, former C18 coaching house, bow windows added later. Opposite green. Mentioned Batchelor.

GREAT BARUGH 7478
Golden Lion, C17 origins and associations with refugees from battle of Marston Moor, 1642. Much altered but pleasant. Free House.

GREAT BROUGHTON 5406
Jet Miners, stone pub built mid C18 to serve jet miners. Rare name. Free House. (GBG).

GREAT HABTON 7576
Grapes, developed from C17 farmhouse. Village local with strong farming and cricketing associations. Free House with restaurant. Recommended Letts.

GREAT LANGTON 2997
Wishing Well, unusually named, remote Sealedale pub worth finding. (GBG).

GREWELTHORPE 2276
Hackfall, unusually named village inn, C18(?), modernised.

GRINTON 0498
Bridge, formerly Ship. C17 hostelry with later additions. Free House.

GROSMONT 8205
Small building opposite church is former *Tunnel*, built to serve excavators of one of earliest railway tunnels (1836). *Station* next door and high above Esk is operational.

HACKNESS 9690
Everley, late C19, formed from two cottages, small cobbled yard and stables. Free House. *Grange*, originally private house – early Victorian villa in village consisting mainly of estate cottages but with Anglo-Saxon church.

HAROME 6482
Star, picturesque thatched inn of some antiquity but hardly C12 as claimed. Free House. (GBG).

HARROGATE 3055
Many large Victorian hotels built to exploit spa but *Old Swan* is more ancient: mainly mid C19 but with some earlier elements including windows. Fine three dimensional sign on post opposite accompanied, on separate plinth by coachman blowing horn. *St. George* is described by Batchelor as a 'house that has won its Yorkshire colours' and is listed in Richardson and GBG. Letts recommends *Empress, Majestic, Studley, West Park*. GBG adds *Belford, Muckles Vaults, Old Tradition.*

HARTOFT END 7397
Blacksmith Arms, originally late C16 farmhouse, with attached smithy serving draught horses from local ironworks, built partly from stones cannibalised from recently dissolved Rosedale priory of nuns. Free House. Letts.

HAWES 8789
Board, unpretentious market-place tavern, mid C19 and retaining its former designation of Board House. Hunting Meet. (GBG). *Crown*, traditional sheep-farmers pub, much modernised but retaining traditional tap-room (Theakstons house). *Fountain*, much altered and added to Free House, originally C17. *White Hart*, small, attractive, market-place hotel (C18?).

HAWNBY 5389
Hawnby, small Victorian hotel with garden. No dogs. Recommended Letts.

HELMSLEY 6183
Black Swan, 'a nice Georgian job' (P) but parts seem to be older. Always Head Inn of town and expanded in C18 to absorb neighbouring houses (C16 and C18). Large yard, stables, garden. Distinctive sign. Some details cannibalised: Jacobean panelling in porch from church, Tudor doorway of cellar from castle. Mentioned Batchelor. *Crown*, formerly *Coopers Posting House* serving Thirsk–Scarborough run in coaching period. Possibly C16 origins. Impressive high relief sign. Attractive interior dominated by oak beams. GBG. *Feathers*, 1960s, conversion of former doctor's house which allegedly absorbed C12 cottage formerly Thorpe's tavern. Much alteration and modern addition. Free House. *Feversham Arms*, 1853, replacing former *Board* inn. Free House.

HETTON 9658
Angel, up-dated traditional (Georgian?) pub with restaurant. (Letts).

HOPPERTON 4256
Mason's Arms, Nidderdale pub with draught Guinness, recommended Letts: 'mixed ancient and modern'.

HOVINGHAM 6675
Malt Shovel, pub with licensed restaurant. *Worseley Arms*, long, low and somewhat irregular house of late Georgian period facing village green. Free House. Both recommended Letts.

HUNMANBY 0977
Cottage, originally C18 cottage, recently converted into pub. Pleasant and convenient Free House. *Hunmanby*, recommended Letts: 'Victorian'. *Royal Oak*, another recent (1975) conversion of (C18?) farmhouse into licensed premises. Free House. *White Swan*, low two-storeyed house facing village green. Former coaching inn. Allegedly haunted.

HURST 0402
Green Dragon, claimant for title of remotest pub in England. Formerly served workers at now disused lead mines. Rare licence: seven day ale, but only six days games licence.

HUTTON LE HOLE 7090
Delightful village with former *Hammer & Hand*, dated 1784 with inscription relating to former lead-mine workers which it once served. *Crown* is operational, updated village inn. Recommended Letts: 'mixed ancient and modern'.

HUTTON RUDBY 4606
Station, popular pub (GBG) in Cleveland village with 'intricate green' (P).

INGLEBY ARNCLIFFE 4400
Cleveland Tontine, built to serve Yarm-Thirsk turnpike begun 1804. Five bays with pediment, Tuscan doorway. Fine stables added 1806 to service mail coaches.

INGLEBY CROSS 4400
Blue Bell, near start of Lyke-Wake walk. Attractive courtyard: hitching rail and miniature replica of sign over doorway. Cross, after which hamlet is named, was one of many dotted over moors for benefit of medieval travellers.

INGLETON 6972
Bridge, traditional stone pub of Pennine type (C18?). *Craven Heifer*, licensed from C18 and originally formed from four cottages. Developed through serving railway and quarry workers. Popular with pot-holers (GBG). GBG also gives *Masons Arms, Three Horseshoes*.

KEARBY 3447
Originally one in a row of cottages which it eventually absorbed, *Clapgate* claims to be C15! May have served several minor coach or wagon routes. Like many 'Gates', it has a verse.

KETTLESING 2256
Queens Head, C16 country inn, mentioned Batchelor. (GBG).

KETTLEWELL 9772
Blue Bell, C17 country inn on banks of Wharfe.

KILBURN 5179
Marton Arms, small hotel in attractive village. Free House, recommended Letts: 'mixed ancient and modern'.

KILNSEY 9767
Almost in shadow of Crag, painted by Turner, is *Tennants Arms*, Victorian pub, recommended Letts.

KIRBY HILL 3868
Blue Bell, country inn in what P describes as 'perfect village'. (GBG).

KIRBY HILL 1306
Shoulder of Mutton, C18 local, much refurbished and barn converted into restaurant. Free House.

KIRKBY FLEETHAM 2894
Black Horse, 1720, former coaching inn in Vale of Mowbray. Free House.

KIRKBY MALZEARD 2374
Queens Head, allegedly originated in C15. If any truth in this claim, certainly much altered and little feeling of any great antiquity. GBG gives *Henry Jenkins*, 'a tastefully modernised inn'.

KIRKBY MOORSIDE 6986
Black Swan, C16 with unusual timber-framed porch dated 1634. *George & Dragon*, makes very dubious claims to C13 origins. Gives impression of much altered C16 or later. Free House. Recommended Letts. Nearby *Kings Head* is also recommended Letts who describes it as medieval.

KNARESBOROUGH 3557
Mitre, Victorian pub. Free House, recommended Letts. *Mother Shipton*, fascinating inn with cave in rear. Once owned and ran racehorse. Owns stable said to have belonged to Guy Fawkes. Beer garden extends to river Nidd. *Town Bailiff*, has nucleus of C16 which was original town bailiff's house. General impression apart from Oak Room of C18. GBG gives *Cross Keys, Groves, Marquis of Granby, Wellington*.

KNOTTINGLEY 5023
White Swan, L-shaped house with big bay window on first floor, late C16 or early C17.

LANGTHWAITE 0002
Red Lion, well sited Free House with attractive interior. Said to be C17.

LASTINGHAM 7290
Blacksmiths Arms, long and low cottage type, local stone with tiled roof. Dated *c.*1700 and run by curate's wife in mid C18 to augment his stipend. Free House. (GBG). *Lastingham Grange*, C17 country house with C19 wing and extensive gardens has recently been converted into country hotel.

LEYBURN 1190
Black Swan, attractive country inn with most unattractive man-trap fixed to one internal wall. *Golden Lion*, frontage of 1857 masks original C17 inn at one time known as *Fothergills* and a former coaching house. Listed Richardson. *Wensleydale Heifer* claims to retain C16 elements. Free House with good atmosphere, recommended Letts.

LONG ROW 9897
Punchbowl, formerly *Miners Arms*, on magnificent Swaledale site. Said to be built in 1639, three storeys. Origin of western part said to be Roman! Free House.

MALHAM 9062
Listers Arms, updated village pub, popular with farmers. (Letts).

MALTON 7871
Black Swan, brick and stone trim, good balcony, early C19 and former coaching house. *Cross Keys*, originated *c.*1150 as hostel for poor travellers administered by Gilbertine Canons of Malton priory. Rebuilt 1539 but cellars seem to be original. Usual legend of underground passages. *Green Man* in Market Place may be medieval in origin, later coaching inn. Free House. (GBG, Letts). *Talbot*, originally private house of Strickland family (C17), became coaching house, refronted *c.*1840. Fine archway into stable yard. *Vines*, small, simple, early C19 hotel of brick. In 1850, town lock-up was converted into beer house but unlocated. GBG adds *Clarence*.

MARSKE 6322
Clarendon, old pub whose Georgian front overlooks main street of small seaside town. Attractive original interior. (GBG).

MARTON CUM GRAFTON 4162
Punchbowl, nucleus is C17 shepherd's cottage much altered and extended. 'Motoring Bar' in former byre with beer served from miniature petrol pumps. (GBG).

MASHAM 2280
Bay Horse, modernised C19 town pub. (GBG). *Kings Head*, mid C18 former coaching inn, dominating magnificent market square. (GBG). *White Bear*, next door to Theakstons brewery formed from early C19 cottages when former house was destroyed, with fatalities, by German bombs in 1941. Fascinating furniture and memorabilia, many relating to independent brewery.

MIDDLEHAM 1287
Almost in shadow of great castle is *Black Swan*, 1744, on hill-side site, producing attractive, many-levelled interior with much oak and open fires in season. Free House. (GBG which also gives *White Swan* much involved with local stables and horse-racing).

MORTON ON SWALE 3292
Non Plus, village pub (GBG), named after racehorse, in incomparable Swaledale.

MONK FRYSTON 5029
Old Hall, former private house with gable of late C13, part of front *c.*1600, much altered in C19. Recently turned into hotel.

MOULTON 2303
Black Bull, village pub, one mile south of Scotch Corner, recommended Letts: 'mixed ancient and modern'.

NABURN 5945
Blacksmiths Arms, riverside pub of character (C18). Near former ferry and lock.

NEW THORPE 4632
New Inn, formerly early C19 farmhouse of which outbuildings survive. Free House.

NEWTON ON RAWCLIFFE 7987
White Swan, attractive pub in village centre, rubble and ashlar, painted black and white. C18/19 appearance. Free House.

NORMANBY 7381
Sun, early Victorian with good atmosphere and possessed of private fishing on river Severn.

NORTHALLERTON 3793
Fleece, partly medieval with timber-framed gables, much restored and altered. Famous coaching house on Great North Road with maze of rooms isolated by thick walls. (GBG). *Golden Lion*, Georgian with impressive porch on Tuscan columns. Famous posting and coach house on London–Edinburgh turnpike. Remains of older house in cellars but mainly C18: assembly room, coaching clock. Vast stables about great yard with post-boys quarters converted to domestic accommodation. Pump, stone trough relics of town race-course.

Associations with Sydney Smith and possibly John Wesley. Listed Richardson. GBG also gives *North Riding Hotel*.

NORTH RIGTON 2849
Square & Compass, former village inn, modified upmarketwards.

NORTH STAINLEY 2876
Staveley Arms, old village inn with interesting decor. Modernised. Recommended Letts who describes it as medieval.

OLDSTEAD 5280
Black Swan, claims to be C18 and originally drovers' tavern. Somewhat cluttered façade with two bow windows and porch on narrow frontage. Free House.

OSGODBY 6433
Barn, incorporates post-Reformation building called 'Chantry' from original function and endowment. Owner was executed in 1537 and his ghost is said to haunt inn.

OSMOTHERLEY 4597
Kings Head, rough-cast stone with flagged roof, formerly *Duke William* (i.e. Butcher Cumberland). Bonnie Prince Charlie said to have stayed here on both advance and retreat of '45. Recommended Letts. *Pied Piper*, recently created by conversion of farmhouse and barn. Rescued good woodwork from local demolitions including fittings from old Northallerton court room. Free House. *Three Tuns*, 'delightful C17 local with two unspoilt rooms' (GBG).

OSWALDKIRK 6279

Malt Shovel, probably result of rebuilding of C16 house in 1725 to serve coach trade. Originally substantial and pretty private residence of five bays, two storeys, with attractive fenestration.

PANNAL ASH 3050

Squinting Cat, formerly Three Horseshoes, early C18 stone house with mullioned windows, formerly coaching inn. Name changed in 1926 because of earlier landlady who squinted at approaching customers through curtains. Mentioned Batchelor. (GBG).

PICKERING 7983

Forest & Vale, originally private house of *c.*1787, five bays, two storeys. Became hotel in 1947. GBG gives *Sun*, local in Westgate terrace. Richardson gives *Black Swan* and *White Swan* (mistake for Helmsley).

RAMSGILL 1170

Yorke Arms, creeper-covered country hotel with garden in Nidderdale. Formerly shooting lodge of Yorke family rebuilt 1843, recommended Letts: 'mixed ancient and modern'.

RAVENSCAR 9801

Raven Hall, occupies site of C4 Roman Signal Station. Hotel formed by combination of two C18 houses one of which was built as small hotel.

REETH 0499

Black Bull, C17 listed building on village green. Once had shops on ground floor. Free House. Mentioned Batchelor.

RICHMOND 1701

Bishop Blaize, slightly run down market-place hotel with unusual name (patron of woolcombers). GBG. *Fleece*, 'an extravaganza of brick and terra cotta with tourelles' (P). *Kings Head*, large C18 coaching house of brick. Eight bays, original doorway, listed Richardson. *Black Lion*, Finkle Street possibly C17 with 'attractive cocktail bar', reworked by brewers' interior decorators. On outskirts of Sleagill (2003) is *Holly Hill* where beer is brought from stillage in jugs.

RIPON 3171

Black Bull, pleasant town hotel of C18 with attractive interior (GBG, Letts) *Magdalene*, characterful street-corner local in Stonesbridge Gate (GBG). *Unicorn*, former coaching house whose C18 'Boots' possessed a curious physiognomy which allowed him to hold a coin between nose and chin. Mentioned Batchelor, listed Richardson. GBG also gives *Station*.

ROBIN HOOD'S BAY 9505

C17 *Bay* hotel has unique distinction of having a ship wrecked against its walls – the brig 'Romulus' on 18 November 1893. Smuggling associations. *Laurel*, C18 or earlier, is attractively sited in middle of picturesque village. *Raven Hall* has small chamber for signalling to smugglers.

ROECLIFFE 3675

Crown, Georgian Free House in Yoredale village, recommended Letts.

ROSEDALE ABBEY 7296

Millburn Arms, attractive small hotel in remote hamlet on N. Yorks moors. Free House recommended Letts and GBG. The exterior of *White Horse* is less welcoming but this is misleading. Attractive interior with pleasant atmosphere. Georgian?

RUSWARP 8809
Old Hall, fine early C17 (Jacobean) private house, recently converted into hotel. Retains contemporary staircase and musicians gallery.

SALTERSGATE 8594
Saltergate Inn, formerly *Waggon & Horses*, built 1759 as waggoners' halt at foot of Devil's Elbow. Also used by carriers of illegal salt. Small window survives from which warning signal could be given. Its peat fire has burnt continuously for about 180 years. Allegedly haunted.

SAND HUTTON 3881
Busby Stoop, modernised (C18?) inn with macabre legend. (GBG).

SANDSEND 8512
Hart, picturesque (C19?) pub overlooking beautiful beach in quiet seaside village. (GBG).

SCARBOROUGH 0388
Castle, three-storeyed brick, former coaching house dating from time of Queen Anne (Queen Street). *Newcastle Packet*, Sandside, with exposed framing of incorporated medieval (C13?) house. Nearby is fascinating *Three Mariners*, accessible, but no longer operational, medieval with attractive C17 front. *Pickwick*, Huntriss Row, early Victorian and exploits Dickensian theme. Centrally placed and interesting decor. Letts recommends Victorian *Holbeck Hall*, hotel. *Talbot*, Queen Street, early C18 with attractive doorway, pleasant bow windows. Extended C19. Former coaching house and terminus for 'High Flier' to York and Leeds. Among GBG list are *Cask* on South Cliffe; *Durham*, North Marine Road; *Leeds Arms*, St Mary Street; *Plough*, St Thomas Street.

SCAWTON 5483
Hare makes dubious claims to C12 origins and associations with Cistercians. Looks more like C16 and certainly was once farmhouse tavern whose byre is now lounge. Free House.

SCORTON 2400
White Heifer, small traditional village pub on edge of Dales National Park. (GBG).

SETTLE 8263
Falcon Manor, Victorian, Charles Addams building, recommended Letts. Richardson lists *Golden Lion*.

SHERBURN IN ELMET 4933
Red Bear, attractive former coaching inn in historic village with large late Norman church and former Grammar School of 1619.

SHERIFF HUTTON 6566
Highwayman, unoriginal name of attractive C17 inn in village containing ruined castle of last English king. Free House.

SHIPTON BY BEBINGBOROUGH 5558
Downay Arms, village local with pleasant atmosphere and operational beer engines.

SICKLINGHALL 3548
Scotts Arms, formed from row of C18(?) cottages with consequent variation of interior levels. Open fires. Free House.

SKIPTON 9851

Round canal basin are *New Ship*, very small, 'preserving a decent Victorian air', once part of Skipton castle which rises behind. *Rose & Crown* (GBG) and *Royal Shepherd* were once very popular with commercioal boat folk, now largely patronised by pleasure boaters. In town centre are pedimented *Devonshire Arms* which retains dignity of C18 private mansion it once was. *Black Horse* is mainly late C17, a former coaching house with mounting block and cobbled courtyard. Ground floor bays and large open fireplace in 'lounge'. Listed Richardson with *Ship*. GBG adds *Horse Close Hotel*. Unmodernised *Castle* is well spoken of.

SKIPTON ON SWALE 3679

See Sand Hutton.

SNAINTON 9182

Coachman, small country inn on edge of North Yorks. Moors, recommended Letts and described as 'mixed ancient and modern'. It originated as Georgian coaching house on York–Scarborough run. Stables survive. Garden.

SPOFFORTH 3650

Railway, pleasant stone-built wayside pub. (GBG). Letts recommends *King William*, small Georgian pub recently extended.

STAITHES 7818

Cod & Lobster, perilously placed in picturesque bay and more or less destroyed by sea on at least three occasions. Last time was Jan. 31, 1953 when kitchen scullery and two bedrooms were swept away. Walls facing sea are now well over a foot thick and reinforced with steel rods. GBG gives *Royal George*.

STOKESLEY 5208

Golden Lion, former small Georgian coaching inn with coach house converted to dining room. Free House. GBG gives *Station*.

SUTTON 4882

Whitestone Cliffe, picturesque house of late C18 on A170, named from local landmark. Free House. Recommended Letts.

TADCASTER 4843

Town dominated by breweries, founded by quarrelling C19 brothers Smith. John Smiths became absorbed in mighty Courage empire and discontinued production of real ale in 1974. Sam Smiths has preserved its independence and production of real ale. *Howden Arms* is a small one-room pub, built in 1763 (GBG). *Londesboro*, Georgian with bay windows and impressive porch, listed Richardson. *Noah's Ark*, Kirkgate, picturesque half-timbered house, C16? is a former inn.

TAN HILL 8907

Tan Hill – Beacon Hill, at summit of Arkengarthdale. Low cottage-type inn. Highest in England at 1732ft (*c*.422m) above sea level. Austere wind-swept exterior with flagged roof and deep projecting porch. Renewed interior (gutted by gas cylinder explosion in 1973).

TERRINGTON 6670

Bay Horse, C17 origin, much altered and modernised. Free House.

THIRSK 4282

Black Bull, former coaching inn (C17?). Stables survive. Market place. *Fleece*, another market place inn which once served York–Darlington run. C18 brick, three bays, pretty 'Gothic' bay added later. Adam mantelpiece, Georgian ceiling in dining room. Coaching clock. Great yard with stables. Fine sign on good wrought-iron bracket. Free House. Mentioned Batchelor, listed Richardson, recommended

Letts. *Lord Nelson*, less distinguished but also possible coaching inn (GBG). *Royal Oak*, off Market Square, much altered former coaching inn. Free House. *Three Tuns*, former Dower House of 1698 which from 1740 became coaching inn on Leeds run. Plain front of nine bays, three storeys. Good Queen Anne staircase and chimney piece in upper room. Barely escaped demolition in 1960s. (GBG). Listed Richardson, mentioned Batchelor.

THORNTON LE DALE 7545
Hall, former private house of *c.*1600 with Georgian additions, in one of Yorkshire's prettiest villages. Recommended Letts. *New Inn*, former coaching house of 1720 of which stables survive.

THORNTON IN CRAVEN 9048
Cross Keys, only canalside pub between Gargrave and Salterforth. Its towpath now forms part of Pennine Way.

THORNTON IN LONSDALE 6773
Marton Arms may have originated as Church House belonging to (largely rebuilt) Norman church. Present inn, forming attractive group with barn was built 1679 with Thomas William Marton as licensee. Carved stone shield of arms over door.

WALSHFORD 4452
Bridge, in spite of its neo-classical façade is an original C17 riverside inn with coaching associations.

WASS 5479
Wombwell Arms, much altered village inn, upmarketed. (C17?).

WATH 3227
George & Dragon, village pub, modernised with restaurant. Free House seven miles NNW of Malton. (Letts).

WEST WITTON 0688
Wensleydale Heifer, refurbished small country inn probably dating from C17.

WHITBY 8911
George, Baxtergate, Georgian with columned porch. Dormer windows added later. *Plough*, same street in GBG. *Beehive* at nearby Newholm, pub with licensed restaurant, recommended Letts and described as Elizabethan. Richardson lists *Angel*.

WHITLEY 5521
Woolpack, built 1780 to serve traders on Yorks–Lancs route. Claims to have later been coaching house. Traditional vernacular building of stone with flagged roof. Free House.

WRELTON 7686
Buck, small village inn whose modernisation (1964) includes bar partition made from witness box in old Pickering police court.

WYKEHAM 9683
Downe Arms, large farmhouse of 1725, three bays, three storeys became coaching inn called *Bull* when nearby road was improved. Name changed in 1872. Modern annexe added in 1977.

YAFFORTH 3494
Revellers Arms, named after racehorse. C18 with considerable modification. Free House.

YORK 6052
Black Swan, Peaseholme Green, twin gables, timber-framed, good staircase, *c.*1675. Listed Richardson, mentioned Batchelor. *Black Horse*, Monkgate, Victorian, 1897. (GBG). *Burton Stone*, Clifton, early C19 but with some architectural pretensions. *De Grey Rooms*, St Leonards, very attractive public bar in building which was constructed as Officers' Mess in 1841/2. *Elm Bank*, Mount Vale has a memorable C19 interior with stained glass, murals and elaborate ceiling. *Fox*, Holgate Road, is original building of 1878 and unspoilt. *Grey Mare*, noticed by P, early C20 with attractive shell-hooded door. *Kings Arms*, Kings Staithe, former *Ouse Bridge*, pleasant house whose bar indicates levels of Ouse flooding over recent years. Fine sign depicting Richard III, great benefactor of York. *Queens*, Micklegate, part of early Georgian terrace and contains splendid room with details of *c.*1730. *Roman Bath*, former *Mail Coach*, St Sampson's Square, has observation point in lounge through which can be seen unique legionary baths over which pub was built. *Youngs*, Petergate, claims to be birthplace of Guy Fawkes on April 16th, 1570. He was certainly christened in St Michael-le-Belfry opposite. GBG gives, among others, *Bootham Tavern*, Bootham; *Coach & Horses*, in historic building in Micklegate; *Grapes*, King Street; *Minster*, Marygate; *Spread Eagle*, Walmergate; *York Arms*, High Petergate. *Star* has gallows sign. Letts recommends: *Half Moon*, Blake Street; *Mount Royale*, The Mount; Victorian *Royal Station* and modern *Viking*, North Street. Batchelor recommends *Royal Station* and Richardson also lists *Windmill, White Swan* – unlocated.

WEST YORKSHIRE

APPERLEY BRIDGE 1938
George & Dragon, C16 stone-built house, gabled with stone-mullioned windows. Timber-framed interior. Wing added 1704. *Stansfield Arms*, originally C17 farmhouse, much altered.

BARDSEY 3643
Bingley Arms. Claims C10 origin! It may later have been a monastic hospice and it was known as *Priests Inn* until 1780. Present building seems mainly C18 but centre and cellars are probably medieval. Said to be priests' hide in central chimney.

BARKISLAND 0419
Fleece, updated Georgian inn above Halifax. Free House with good atmosphere. Recommended Letts. *Griffin*, C17 village pub. (GBG).

BINGLEY 1039
Brown Cow, smart pub near river (GBG), *Fishermans*, former canal pub at top of Five and Three Locks on Leeds–Liverpool canal. *Old White Horse*, attractive stone house, gabled, mullioned windows. Unlikely to be C13, as claimed but possibly C15. Later became coaching house on Skipton road.

BOSTON SPA 4245
Royal, Georgian/Victorian pub, once hotel built to accommodate visitors to Spa in attractive village now becoming dormitory.

BRADFORD 1633
Alexandra, Great Horton Road is 1877 and typical of its date. *Hare & Hounds*, Idle Road. *Midland*, C19 railway hotel at which Henry Irving died in a chair later presented to Garrick Club by Seymour Hicks. Mentioned Batchelor. Unusually named *Spotted House*, Keighley Road has typical local exterior and interior Victorian decor. *Queen* is partly C18 with additions and much alteration. *Victorian* is 1867 'a kind of round-arched Trecento with funny French domes' (P). Examples

of traditional town pubs might include *Parry Lane Tavern*, 'small, quaint and low-roofed' (GBG), *Hare & Hounds*, Idle Road. At Idle itself, *White Swan* retains some of characteristics of village pub it once was (both in GBG which also gives, among others, *Black Swan*, Frizinghall Road; *Duchess of Kent*, Saville Street; *Lancaster*, Westgate; *Moulders Arms*, Stickler Lane. *Shoulder of Mutton*, Kirkgate – substantially unaltered early Victorian, white-washed brick in city centre).

BURLEY WOODHEAD 1648
Hermit, C19 village pub with superb location, commemorating local recluse. At nearby Burley in Wharfedale is *White Horse*, 'a marvellous little pub' (GBG).

COLLINGHAM BRIDGE 3845
Old Star at junction of A58 and A659 much extended and refurbished including restaurant. Free House.

DARRINGTON 4919
Spread Eagle, pleasant village pub, just off A1. Former coach house, allegedly C15.

EAST KESWICK 3544
Travellers Rest, former village pub with added restaurant. Recommended Letts: 'mixed ancient and modern'.

EAST MORTON 1041
Busfield Arms, stone-built, traditional pub with fanciful porch, formerly 'Hare & Hounds' (mentioned in Jane Eyre).

ECCLESHILL 3285
On Hathersage Road lies much restored *Fox House*, basically C17, gabled with stone-mullioned windows.

ELDWICK 1240
Acorn, attractively sited former country pub (C18?) now much patronised by new 'carriage trade'.

ELLAND 1020
Fleece, former private house, probably C17, stone gabled with mullioned windows. Allegedly haunted by murdered traveller. *Nags Head* on A643 at Ainley Top, formed by three cottages, ivy-covered millstone grit. Became hill stop in coaching era. Continues old Yorkshire custom of free 'bread and dripping'. *Wellington*, C18 and probably coaching inn, renamed in C19 to honour 'Iron Duke'. GBG gives *Colliers Arms*, modernised canalside pub.

FAGLEY 2232
Blue Pig, architecturally undistinguished haunt of beer connoisseurs. (GBG).

FARSLEY 2135
Rodley Barge, formerly *Three Horseshoes*. Atmospheric pub on side of Leeds–Liverpool canal. Preserves boat stove and other relics from its days as bargee's tavern.

GREETLAND 0821
Branch, vernacular Pennine inn on edge of moors, C18/19 staging house on Lancs/Yorks route.

HALIFAX 0825
Calder & Hebble, uniquely named busy local (GBG): *Cat i't'Well*, another rare name at Wainstalls in secluded valley (GBG); *Old Cock*, originally town house of Saville family, fine upper room: oak-panelled, plaster ceiling and fireplace with overmantel dated 1581 (P says early C17 more likely). Modern glass

commemorates societies which have used this room. Defoe said to have written part of Robinson Crusoe while staying here. *William Deighton*, former *Wheatsheaf*, renamed to honour customs officer who smashed C18 coiners' gang whose HQ seems to hve been *Dusty Miller* at Mytholmroyd. Letts recommends whimsically named *Hobbit*, 'mixed ancient and modern'. GBG further gives, among others, *Three Pigeons, Windmill*.

HAREWOOD 3245
Harewood Arms, built 1810 as coaching house, belongs to Harewood estate along with rest of feudal village. Bird garden with penguin house. Free House.

HAWORTH 0337
Black Bull, mentioned Batchelor, frequented by Branwell Brontë. Recent 'improvements' have eviscerated pub which he would hardly now recognise from inside. *Fleece* is unspoilt local. (GBG).

HEATH 3520
'Singular village of Georgian mansions' (Nuttgens) with one group clustering round *Kings Head*.

HEBDEN BRIDGE 9927
White Lion, built 1657. Entrance and ground floor frontage survive. Situated on main Yorks–Lancs route and developed when turnpike was opened. GBG with *Albert, Hare & Hounds, Pack Horse*.

HEPTONSTALL 9827
Fascinating hill-top weavers' village with much C16/17 building including *White Lion*.

HEPWORTH 1606
Butchers Arms, attractive inn with typical Pennine exterior. Comfortable interior with open fires.

HOLMFIRTH 1408
Bareknuckles Boys, uniquely named local (GBG); *Ford*, typical low, stone-built Pennine pub on moors by A635; *Postcard* seems to be another unique name. GBG adds *Farmers Arms, Rose & Crown* alias 'Nook', a beer drinkers' Mecca.

HORBURY 2918
Shepherds Arms, in spite of much modernisation, retains several ancient features including cellar with blocked-up tunnel and massive taproom fireplace. GBG gives *Fleece*. *Quarry* was built 1800 to serve quarry workers. Stone theme maintained in modernised interior which includes table tops in variety of marbles.

HORSFORTH 2337
Queens Arms built 1620 as private house. Extended by Longfellow family in 1779 (visited by poet). Became licensed premises in early C19.

HUBBERHOLME 8869
George, converted from former rectory in mid C19. Retained in church hands until 1965. 'Poor man's pasture' auctioned on New Year's Eve.

HUDDERSFIELD 1416
Some Georgian coaching houses, erected *c.*1820, survive including *Fleece, Packhorse*. GBG gives, among others, *Albert, Commercial, White Lion* in town centre; *Black Bull*, Lindle; *Castle*, Almondbury; *Red Lion*, Lockwood Bar.

ILKLEY 1147
Large number of C19 hotels related to development as spa including *Crescent*, mentioned Batchelor, listed Richardson, and Letts recommends *Cow & Calf* on Rombald's Moor above town. *Rose & Crown* claims to be oldest pub; *Ilkley Moor Vaults*, locally known as 'Taps', is spacious and popular. (GBG). *Wharfe Gate*, originated as early C19 private house maintains attractive private atmosphere.

KEIGHLEY 0641
Fountain is probably oldest pub in town (GBG which aslo gives *Boltmakers Arms, Eastwood, Roebuck*). *Turkey*, Gooseye, at nearby Laycock is well-renovated village pub which has splendidly reactivated it own brewery. (GBG). Letts recommends *Busfield Arms* at neighbouring Morton.

KILDWICK 9845
Aireside village with *Kildwick Hall* recommended Letts: Georgian, motel/restaurant. GBG gives *White Lion*, spacious pub near canal.

KIRKBURTON 1912
White Swan, traditional Pennine pub on A629.

KIRKHEATON 1817
Beaumont Arms, served as courthouse in C18. (GBG).

KIRKSTALL 2635
Abbey, allegedly occupies site of Cistercian abbey's guest house and currently reported as disturbed by poltergeist in its ancient cellars.

LEDSHAM 4529
Chequers, ancient inn which may have been *Church House*. Certainly once owned by neighbouring church, one of oldest in country, probably dating from C8. Free House.

LEDSTON 4328
White Horse, stone-built inn in village which remains attractive in spite of industrial encroachment. C18 with Dick Turpin associations.

LEEDS 3034
Inn names and pubs themselves vary from realism of *Brick*, Armley, to romanticism of *Vesper Gate*, Kirkstall. *Whitelocks*, formerly Turks Head in passage off Briggate is C18 with much original decor from Victorian and Edwardian periods. (GBG). Mentioned Batchelor, along with *Metropole, Queens* (recommended Letts), typical city hotels. Houses with some architectural pretentions include *Black Bull*, Hunslet with pediment and impressive porch of Georgian period; *Mansion*, Roundhay Park, late Georgian (1826) with seven bays, two storeys and spectacular portico. Richardson lists *Boars Head, Golden Lion, Griffin*. Letts recommends *Oak Bank*, Shaw Lane, 'mixed ancient and modern' and Victorian *Yorkshire Crown*, City Square. *Vine*, Headrow is typical city-centre pub; *Town Hall Tavern* (GBG) is popular with legal profession at lunch-time (GBG which, among others, gives *Regent*, Regent Street and *Eagle*, North Street, one of the pubs owned by CAMRA).

LEEMING 2989
Lamb Inn, Victorian local recommended by Letts.

LINTON 3846
Windmill, up-marketed country pub which began as C16 farmhouse selling ale. Stonebuilt and retains some original features.

LINTON IN CRAVEN 9962
Fountains, 'a gem – unspoilt inn' (GBG).

LUDDENDEN 0425
Lord Nelson, obviously not original name of fine house dated 1654. Stone, mullioned windows, in picturesque situation. Associations with Branwell Brontë, employed for a time at Luddenden Foot railway station. (GBG).

MARSDEN 0411
Great Western, built 1875 and named in honour of I.K. Brunel. Entrance hall panelled with material from Cumberland castle. Some attractive furniture. Locale of art exhibitions. GBG gives *Railway*. On old Roman road above new Scammonden reservoir is *Nont Sarah's* named from C19 landlady ('Aunt Sarah') which provided welcome refuge for travellers on old Huddersfield–Oldham route over Pennines.

MIDGELEY 2714
Black Bull in Badsworth Hunt country and in sight of Emley Moor TV mast. C17 house with attractive interior.

MIRFIELD 2019
At Sherely Bridge is *Ship*, early C19(?) to serve canal workers. Very dominant marine 'theme'. *Three Nuns* recalls dissolved priory of Kirklees whose convent had legendary associations with Robin Hood and Maid Marion.

MITTON 8815
Three Fishes, over doorway is re-used stone of C15 (from earlier pub on site?).

MYTHOLMROYD 0125
Dusty Miller, HQ of notorious gang of C18 coiners who murdered pursuing excise officer (see Halifax). They were eventually arrested, tried and hanged. Inn served as Post Office in mid C19.

NEW MILL 1608
White Hart at junction of A616 and A635. Built 1773 to serve coaching routes. Display of antique pottery in bar and horse-wear in tap.

NORLAND 0622
Long, low, stone-built house with flagged room. Dates from 1610. Solitary Pennine inn formerly serving coach and waggon traffic.

OTLEY 2045
Black Horse, 1901, replacing coaching inn which was terminus for passengers and freight weekly on Tuesdays via Harewood and Tadcaster. Listed Richardson with *Royal White Horse*. *Black Bull* is basically C18 with yard, stables, outside stone stairway and water pump (probably some C16/17 elements). *Bowling Green* built 1757 as Assembly Rooms, etc., became inn in C19 and issued own tokens. Former green, now public garden, alongside. *Cross Pipes*, former ale-house, (C18?). *New Inn* is three-storeyed, C18 market place inn, once coaching house. *Red Lion*, Kirkgate, C18 with former stabling to rear. *Rose & Crown*, Bondgate, basically C17 with modifications in 1731. *Three Horseshoes*, Bridge Street, with site of smithy alongside, (C18?). *White Swan*, Boroughgate, C18 and once coaching inn; *Whitakers Arms*, Kirkgate, C18 with remains of yard and stabling in rear; *Woolpack*, basically C17 but much altered. GBG gives *Bay Horse*, market place and *Junction*, a basic pub with all the right priorities: open fire, good company and knowledgeable landlord.

OXENHOPE 0334
Bay Horse, village pub in Worth Valley and Brontë country, recommended Letts: 'mixed ancient and modern'.

PONTEFRACT 4522
Red Lion, Georgian, red brick with pediment. Former market-place coaching house, mentioned Batchelor, listed Richardson. *Flying Horse* is also of some antiquity, given in GBG along with *Beastfair Vaults* and *Blackamoor Head*.

POOL IN WHARFEDALE 2445
White Hart, originated as early Georgian farm and ale-house. Cosy lounge with open fire and oak beams.

QUEENSBURY 5554
Old Raggalds, began as farmhouse-type hostelry, developing during C18. Situated at 1200ft (*c*.369m) above sea level with panoramic views of surrounding townships. GBG gives *Mountain Eagle, Omnibus*.

RIPPONDEN 0319
Blue Ball, 'homely C17 moorland inn' (GBG).

ROBERT TOWN 1922
Star, former coaching inn having associations with Brontës and Luddites.

ROTHWELL 3428
Hare & Hounds, recommended Letts and described as C16/modernised.

SANDAL 3418
Three Houses, ancient site with hostelry in C14 at which Duke of York is said to have rested before 'Roses' battle. In later inn, Richard Nevison, highwayman was arrested. Much loss: medieval fireplace to museum, Nevison's chair to private collector.

SELBY 6132
George, listed Richardson, unlocated. *Londesbrough Arms*, small market-town hotel, C18 and former coaching house. GBG gives *New Inn*.

SHEPLEY 1909
Sovereign, traditional Pennine inn at junction of Huddersfield–Sheffield and Barnsley–Wakefield road. Former coaching house.

SHIBDEN 0624
In hidden valley, north-east of Halifax lies *Shibden Mill Inn*. C17 with two good fireplaces. Stone-built, mullioned windows interesting features and decorations.

SOUTH MILFORD 4931
Queen o't'owd Thatch, originated as farmhouse with old malt-kiln. (C18 or earlier). Modern pantiled roof belies name but walls of attractive Tadcaster limestone survive. *Cocked Hat*, occupies former stables of Milford Hall, greatly expanded to create large hotel. Extremely dubious claims to Dick Turpin connections. Free House.

SOUTH STAINLEY 3063
Red Lion, former country inn much upmarketed and highly praised by Batchelor.

SOWERBY BRIDGE 0523
Above town is *Travellers Rest* which began as farmhouse selling ale in 1623 to travellers using pack-horse trail past inn. This service became main income. Free House. Fine view from front door over 1000ft (*c*.308m) above sea-level. In town itself GBG gives *Puzzle Hall, Rams Head, William IV*.

STANBURY 0036
Old Silent, originally *Eagle*. L-shaped in local stone, white-washed. One wing appears older than other, C17 or earlier. Traditionally scene of near capture of Bonnie Prince Charlie, an incident which led to renaming of inn. Free House.

STOCKBRIDGE 3535
Marquis of Granby by Leeds–Liverpool canal and one of few waterside pubs named after this nobleman who was generally popular as a pub name.

THORNTON 1233
Ring o'Bells, old village inn now thronged by business men from Bradford of which it has become suburb. Recommended Letts. GBG gives *Hill Top*.

TODMORDEN 9324
Queen, small hotel, possibly former coaching house in small town on edge of Pennine moors. GBG gives *Weavers Arms, Woodpecker*. Richardson lists *White Hart. Shepherds Rest* was originally a private house (C18?) and first licensed in 1859. Free House.

UPPERMOOR 2232
Marsh, traditional house, attractively modernised. In Pudsey itself GBG gives *Butchers Arms, Victoria*.

UPPER POPPLETON 5554
Lord Collingwood, white-washed, double gabled inn on edge of green near church. Older than present name.

WAINSTALLS 0428
Cat i't'Wall, built *c.*1700 and name may be derived from St Catherine's Well or Wheel. Bar lined with oak penelling from Castle Carr. Associations with eccentric local preacher, John Preston, who died here in Sept. 1885. Free House.

WAKEFIELD 3320
Woolpacks, Westgate, three storeyed brick house of Georgian era whose name commemorates transport of West Riding wool to local weavers and merchants. GBG gives two pubs called *Graziers*, Doncaster Road and Market Street; *Bay Horse with possible coaching associations, Clothiers, Cock, Jacobs Well, Malt Shovel, Wheel, York Street Hotel*. Letts recommends Georgian *Kaye Arms*, Grangemoor. Richardson lists *Stafford Arms, White Horse*. *Kings Arms*, at nearby Heath, is an unaltered pub on what was once a lonely heath: gas lamps, stone floor, hand-drawn beer, landlord of character.

WENTBRIDGE 4817
Wentbridge House, C18 private residence of Leatham family until 1960. Adam fireplace in coffee lounge. Free House.

WETHERBY 4048
Angel, former coaching inn with stabling for 100 horses at half-way point between London and Edinburgh. Fine sign (St Michael). In late C19 a number of murals were discovered depicting Biblical subjects. Mentioned Batchelor and listed Richardson. *Crown* is an ancient town pub, recently renovated, dating from C17. (GBG). *Swan & Talbot* is a former coaching inn with many recent accretions.

WHITWOOD 4124
Rising Sun, built in 1805 to be an (educational) institute for Briggs colliery. It is a rare Northern example of a Voysey building and characteristic of his style.

SOUTH YORKSHIRE

BARNSLEY 3406
Queens, red-brick structure, said to be of Regency period. GBG gives, among others *Chennell's Bar, Sportsman, Wheatsheaf*.

BAWTRY 6592
Town was coaching stop on Great North Road and market place still contains number of fine former coaching inns, notably *Crown*, long low front, listed Richardson. *Old House*, two bays, pedimented with single bay attachments surmounted by urns. Both C18. GBG gives *Ship*.

BRADFIELD 2692
Strines, oddly named pub at some 1000ft (*c*.308m) on Bradfield Moor to west of Sheffield. Claims to originate in manor house of Worral family, allegedly dating from C13. Garden. Recommended Letts: 'medieval'.

BURNCROSS 3596
Crown & Cushion, mid C18; former coaching house on Sheffield route.

CAMPSALL 5313
Old Bells, local in village with fascinating large Norman church, traditionally scene of wedding of Robin of Loxley (Robin Hood?). Inn makes dubious claims to similar antiquity – may retain C15 elements.

CAWTHORNE 2807
Spencer Arms, Georgian style pub with one of few good restaurants in this area of South Yorks. Recommended Letts.

DONCASTER 5803
Corporation Brewery Taps (an unusual name) occupies site of Corporation Brewery. (GBG). *Reindeer*, Georgian/early Victorian, mentioned in Journals of Arnold Bennet (1897) when landlord always carried loaded revolver in Race Week. Listed Richardson and mentioned Batchelor along with *Turf*. *St Leger Tavern* is recommended by Letts. Among GBG list: Georgian *Salutation, White Swan* which claims highest bar in Britain and *Undergroud*, a modern cellar pub.

DORE 3081
Hare & Hounds, simple village pub in Pennine vernacular, developed to take in neighbouring houses and recently restored.

GREAT HOUGHTON 4206
Old Hall, originally Elizabethan private house, typical H-shape with staircase in angle of rear wings. Retains detached chapel (added 1650). Licensed in C20.

HATFIELD WOODHOUSE 6708
Green Tree, originally C17 farmhouse selling ale, later coaching and post house at junction of A18 and A614. Allegedly haunted by Roundhead.

MEXBOROUGH 4799
Ferry Boat, Church Street. An inn, now by side of canal, which claims C14 origins. (GBG which also gives *Highwoods*).

PENISTONE 2402
Dog & Partridge on A628 out of village is a former coaching inn and staging post on Barnsley–Manchester road. Fine oak beams give substance to its claims for C17 origin.

RINGINGLOW 2983
Norfolk Arms, *c.*1840 and showing Gothic influence. Battlemented and provided with triangular-headed windows.

ROTHERHAM 4492
Richardson lists *Crown*. GBG gives, among others, *Butchers Arms, Comedian, Cross Keys, Royal Standard, Wellington*.

SHEFFIELD 3587
Queens Head, Ponds Hill is oldest surviving house in city. C15 or early C16. Timber-framed with over-sailing first floor on fine carved brackets. Among many given by GBG are: *Beehive, Globe, Harlequin, Moseley's Arms, Old Brewery Tap, Red Deer, Red House, Roebuck, Royal Oak, Royal Standard, Three Tuns*. Out of city on road to Hathersage is *Fox House*, much restored C17 but retaining handsome gable with two superimposed stone mullioned windows. (2082).

STANNINGTON 2988
Crown and Glove, pub with restaurant and garden in village almost engulfed by Sheffield. Unique name? Recommended Letts.

WENTWORTH 3898
George & Dragon, Main Street Georgian pub, former coaching house in unspoilt village providing oasis in industrial area. Free House. Recommended Letts. GBG gives *Rockingham Arms*.

WHISTON 4490
Golden Ball, claims C16 origins and certainly seems to have served carriers and drovers on important wool route. Recommended Letts and described as Georgian. *Sitwell Arms*, former farm and ale-house on A618, developed into small coaching inn.

WORTLEY 3099
Wortley Arms, dubious claims to C16 origin. Coaching associations. Attractive interior.